Want to think smarter, feel happier, have better focus, and remember more? The neuroscience-backed strategies to make that happen are all within the pages of Dr. Amen's new book *Change Your Brain Every Day*.

UMA NAIDOO, MD, Harvard nutritional psychiatrist, chef, nutritional biologist, and national and international bestselling author of *This Is Your Brain on Food*

What makes this book so special is that it goes beyond theory and includes practices you can put into action every day. Each practice builds on the previous ones, so by the end of the year, you'll have created a whole new life.

DR. DERWIN L. GRAY, cofounder and lead pastor of Transformation Church; author of *How to Heal Our Racial Divide: What the Bible Says, and What the First Christians Knew, about Racial Reconciliation.*

Did you know you can improve your brain health in just a few minutes a day? Just one page a day of this book is all it will take to start turning your life and brain health around.

CHALENE JOHNSON, lifestyle and business expert, motivational speaker, *New York Times* bestselling author, and top-ranked podcaster

Scientific research has made it clear that our lifestyle choices affect brain health. And while some books can steer us toward a better brain outcome, the programs described are often vastly complicated and overwhelming. Dr. Amen's *Change Your Brain Every Day* lovingly gifts us the ability to alter our brain's destiny. He simply asks us to pursue one small change each day. And these changes ultimately aggregate to empower us with the attainable goal of a healthier, happier, and better functioning brain.

DAVID PERLMUTTER, MD, FACN, six-time *New York Times* bestselling author

Change Your Brain Every Day is a great addition to anyone's mental health tool kit! Dr. Amen gives you practical, easy-to-implement tips and strategies to improve your mental health and live your best life in just one year, based on his examination of more than 225,000 brain scans from 155 countries.

DR. CAROLINE LEAF, clinical neuroscientist and bestselling author of *Cleaning Up Your Mental Mess*

Every single day our brains are changing. They can be improving or declining, but they are *never* staying the same. This is why today, more than ever, having daily practices to take your brain health up a level is so valuable. *Change Your Brain Every Day* is a treasure trove of daily nuggets that will put your brain improvements on automatic.

SHAWN STEVENSON, bestselling author of *Eat Smarter* and *Sleep Smarter*

Change Your Brain Every Day is like getting a daily dose of Dr. Amen to enhance your memory, mood, and mindset.

JIM KWIK, *New York Times* bestselling author of *Limitless: Upgrade Your Brain, Learn Anything Faster, and Unlock Your Exceptional Life*

DANIEL G. AMEN, MD

CHANGE YOUR BRAIN EVERY DAY

Simple Daily Practices to Strengthen Your Mind, Memory, Moods, Focus, Energy, Habits, and Relationships

TYNDALE
REFRESH™

Think Well. Live Well. Be Well.

Visit Tyndale online at tyndale.com.

Visit Daniel G. Amen, MD, at danielamenmd.com.

Tyndale and Tyndale's quill logo are registered trademarks of Tyndale House Ministries. *Tyndale Refresh* and the Tyndale Refresh logo are trademarks of Tyndale House Ministries. Tyndale Refresh is a nonfiction imprint of Tyndale House Publishers, Carol Stream, Illinois.

Change Your Brain Every Day: Simple Daily Practices to Strengthen Your Mind, Memory, Moods, Focus, Energy, Habits, and Relationships

Designed by Libby Dykstra

Published in association with the literary agency of WordServe Literary Group, www.wordserveliterary.com.

Some material is taken from *Memory Rescue*, published in 2017 under ISBN 978-1-4964-2560-7, *Feel Better Fast and Make It Last*, published in 2018 under ISBN 978-1-4964-2565-2, *The End of Mental Illness*, published in 2020 under ISBN 978-1-4964-3815-7, *Your Brain Is Always Listening*, published in 2021 under ISBN 978-1-4964-3820-1, and *You, Happier*, published in 2022 under ISBN 978-1-4964-5452-2, all from Tyndale House Publishers.

Scripture quotations are taken from the Holy Bible, *New International Version,*® *NIV.*® Copyright © 1973, 1978, 1984, 2011 by Biblica, Inc.® Used by permission. All rights reserved worldwide.

For information about special discounts for bulk purchases, please contact Tyndale House Publishers at csresponse@tyndale.com, or call 1-855-277-9400.

Library of Congress Cataloging-in-Publication Data

A catalog record for this book is available from the Library of Congress.

ISBN 978-1-4964-5457-7

Printed in the United States of America

29	28	27	26	25	24	23
7	6	5	4	3	2	1

Contents

Introduction

You are not stuck with the brain you have. You can make it better, even if you have been bad to it, and I can prove it. You can literally change your brain, and when you do, you change your life. Over the last 30 years, I've ended most of my lectures with the above words. It's the mission that drives my work. Your brain controls everything you do and everything you are. Each day it is changing. Either it is getting better and growing younger, or it is getting worse and growing older due to your daily diet, supplements, thoughts, decisions, and habits. This daily reader is designed to help you be the master of your brain's destiny and boost your memory, mood, focus, and overall sense of happiness and peace. Learning to love and care for your brain will also decrease your stress, improve your relationships, increase your chances of success in every area of your life, help you stave off dementia, and prevent you from becoming a burden to those you love.

As an example, meet my friend—journalist and media personality Leeza Gibbons. I got to know Leeza after being on her nationally syndicated television show in 1999 when my book *Change Your Brain, Change Your Life* was first published. She's brilliant, purposeful, and has a smile that brightens any room. We became friends after I'd been on her show several times. In getting to know her, I found out her mother and grandmother both died with Alzheimer's disease, which was incredibly stressful for them and for Leeza's family. Given that I knew that Alzheimer's disease runs in families and shows negative brain changes decades before people have any symptoms, I encouraged Leeza to come see me to get her brain scanned. At Amen Clinics we do a brain imaging study called SPECT that looks at blood flow and activity patterns; it is one of the best studies to evaluate the risk for Alzheimer's disease.

Initially, Leeza was hesitant to get scanned. Many people are afraid to know if their brains may be headed for trouble. But I told her, "If you knew a train was going to hit you, wouldn't you at least want to try to get out of the way?" After going through a stressful time, Leeza came to see me, and her SPECT scan showed several areas of very low blood flow. Her brain was clearly headed for trouble. Leeza took the results seriously and did everything I asked, which is all in the daily practices of this book. Ten years later, her brain was dramatically healthier, which is not what typically happens with age. The images of her scans below tell a story—a story of hope. *You are not stuck with the brain you have. With the right guidance you can make it better, and I can prove it.*

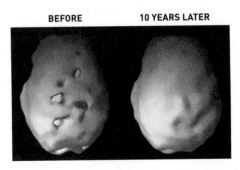

BEFORE   10 YEARS LATER

At Amen Clinics, we have thousands of stories just like Leeza's. What did she do to reverse the aging process in her brain? What did she do to have a sharper brain 10 years later? That is the story in this book. Was it hard? No. Being sick is hard. Leeza saw brain health as a daily practice.

BRAIN AND MENTAL HEALTH ARE DAILY PRACTICES

Physical health is a daily practice. You cannot be 50 pounds overweight on Monday, have a salad that day for lunch, and expect to be trim by Friday. Ridiculous, right? Physical health takes consistent effort and daily practice over a long time, including eating right, smart supplementation, exercising, managing stress, and making many, many more good decisions than bad ones. Yes, you can take pills to help manage the diabetes, hypertension, and chronic pain that result from making many bad decisions, but they won't give you the energy and vitality you want.

In the same way, brain and mental health require daily practices, which are needed now more than ever. Anxiety disorders, depression, suicide, attention deficit hyperactivity disorder (ADD/ADHD), bipolar disorder, posttraumatic stress disorder (PTSD), and cognitive decline are at epidemic levels, as are the number of prescription medications purported to help these conditions. Alzheimer's disease is expected to triple in the coming decades, and since the pandemic, anxiety disorders and depression have more than doubled in children and adults. Something needs to change.

If you want to feel happier and more relaxed; if you want to be cognitively sharper and lower your risk for Alzheimer's disease as Leeza did, it will take developing consistent brain and mental health practices over time. *Change Your Brain Every Day* will show you how. In this book I share the daily practices I've learned on the other side of the neuropsychiatrist's couch (neuropsychiatrists are psychiatrists who believe brain health is foundational to helping their patients heal and thrive). For more than 40 years, I've worked with children, teenagers, and adults seeking to overcome anxiety, depression, obsessions, compulsions, addictions, anger, past emotional trauma, past head trauma, relationship issues, and memory and learning problems. This volume condenses those 40 years of knowledge and experience into a step-by-step, daily journey of brain optimization and healing. I use these daily practices in my life and encourage those around me to do the same.

Since 1991, my team at Amen Clinics and I have built the world's largest database of brain SPECT scans related to behavior, totaling more than 225,000 scans on patients from 155 countries. We have seen patients as young as nine months and as old as 105 years. Our brain imaging work has taught us many important lessons about the daily practices and habits of brain and mental health that we teach our patients.

If you sat on my neuropsychiatrist's couch every day for a year, these are the concepts and daily practices you would learn. This book contains 366 (in case you acquired it in a leap year) short essays organized around eight major themes:

1. Major life lessons I've gleaned from looking at more than 225,000 brain SPECT scans.
2. How to understand and optimize the physical functioning of the brain—what I call the hardware of your soul.
3. Learning to manage your mind to support your happiness, inner peace, and success—the "software" that runs your life.
4. Developing a lifelong plan to deal with whatever stresses come your way.
5. Using your brain to improve your relationships—your network connections.
6. Developing an ongoing sense of meaning and purpose that informs your actions every day.
7. Brain-focused nutrition and nutraceuticals (targeted supplements) to support your brain and mind.
8. Condition-specific wisdom, such as dealing with past trauma, anxiety, depression, addictions, ADD/ADHD, and more.

Each day will also have a simple practice for you to do: a tiny habit to try, a simple exercise, a question to ask yourself or others, a meditation, or an affirmation that over time will change the trajectory of your life.

Tiny habits are the smallest things you can do that will make the biggest difference in your life. Several years ago, I partnered with Professor B. J. Fogg, director of the Persuasive Tech Lab at Stanford University, and his sister, Linda Fogg-Phillips, to develop tiny habits for our patients. You will find dozens of them in this book. B. J. and Linda teach that only three things change behavior in the long run:

1. An epiphany (seeing your brain scan can do it, like it did for Leeza)
2. A change in the environment (what and who surrounds you)
3. Taking baby steps or creating tiny habits[1]

In my book *The End of Mental Illness*, I asked myself, if I were an evil ruler and wanted to increase the incidence of mental illness, what I would do? Society has a large impact on your brain and mind. I also asked, if I were a good ruler and wanted to decrease mental illness, what strategies I would employ? You will find dozens of good ruler versus evil ruler strategies in this book so you know how to avoid the traps society lays for us.

Don't think you must do everything. Focus on a few simple ideas you can put into your life as time allows. The most important tiny habit you'll learn is this: Whenever you come to a decision point in your day, ask yourself, "Is this good for my brain or bad for it?" It will take only about three seconds, and if you can answer the question with information and love (love for yourself, your family, and your mission in life), you will quickly have a better brain. By using this habit, one of my patients told me, "I wake up at 100 percent every day because I stopped drinking alcohol, which was clearly not good for my brain."

It's up to you how fast you go through this book, but I recommend you just read a page a day. It'll only take a few minutes, but over time it'll change your life as you learn to think about and practice brain and mental health every day for a year. Just as I encourage my patients to lose weight slowly, so they develop the lifestyle habits that will help them stay trim and healthy for the rest of their lives, establishing these brain and mental health habits one at a time will help them last.

Let's get started changing your brain in a positive way every day.

Your Brain Creates Your Mind

Your brain is involved in everything you do, including how you think, feel, act, and interact with others. Your brain is the organ of intelligence, character, and every decision you make. Your brain creates your mind. It is the hardware of your soul. Your brain creates anxiety, worry, or a sense of peace. It stores traumatic events that continue to hurt you long after they've stopped, or it processes them for any important lessons to learn. Your brain focuses your attention on relevant material or on meaningless distractions; feels sadness or happiness; creates a healthy and a sick reality; and remembers what's necessary to make your life better and discards what's not.

In 2020, Justin Bieber released his docuseries *Seasons*, where he told the world I've been his doctor.[2] Fame is very hard on the brain, and it happened to Justin so early and so intensely that I'm happy he survived and is now an amazing young man. Before Justin came to see me, he had been diagnosed by another physician with bipolar disorder based on his symptoms alone, but his SPECT scan showed his brain had been hurt. I remember one day when he came into my office and said, "I think I understand what you've been trying to tell me. My brain is an organ just like my heart is an organ. If you told me I had heart disease, I would do everything you said. I am going to do what you say." By focusing on both brain and mental health together, he has continued to do well.

Your brain *is* an organ, just like your heart, lungs, and kidneys are organs. Yet most people who see cardiologists have never had a heart attack; instead, they are there to prevent them. I anticipate a day when psychiatrists will act in a similar way, when they will know the brain's risk factors (see the BRIGHT MINDS risk factors on days 7, 9, and 39–104) and address each of them in their patients as soon as possible. To have a better mind, you must first work to optimize the physical functioning of your brain.

TODAY'S PRACTICE: *List three reasons why you want or need a better brain.*

If You Are Struggling, Welcome to Normal

Normal is nothing more than a setting on a dryer or a city in Illinois. Years ago, I spoke at Illinois State University in Normal, Illinois. Imagine what it was like to make an appearance on a "Normal" radio station, stop into a "Normal" restaurant, drive by a "Normal" high school, and even encounter "Normal" people. But what I noticed is that the people who lived in Normal faced many of the same problems I'd seen in my patients.

Too many people don't get the help they need because of the shame they feel around mental health issues. They think that anxiety, depression, and problems with their focus or memory are not normal. But they're wrong. Research shows that more than 50 percent of the population will struggle with a mental health issue at some point in their lives.[3] If you are struggling with your brain or mind, welcome to normal.

If you are hurting, stop thinking you're not normal and get the help you need. It's the smart person who gets help, not the weak one. Think of an entrepreneur whose business is struggling. The smart businessperson will find the best consultant to help. Ignoring or denying the problem will lead to unnecessary stress and maybe even bankruptcy. If you are struggling, find the best doctor, psychiatrist, clinician, or therapist you can. When you realize that there are many others who struggle with the same problems you do, it'll make you feel less alone and less ashamed, and you'll be more likely to open up. As my wife, Tana, says, pain shared is pain divided.

TODAY'S PRACTICE: *Make a list of 10 of your friends. How many of them have needed help for their brain or mind in some way or another?*

When Your Brain Works Right, You Work Right

Free will is not black or white; it's gray. Our brain imaging work at Amen Clinics over the past three decades has shown us that having a healthy brain is fundamental to happiness and success. When your brain works well, it enables you to make better decisions for your life, which in turn positively affects your finances, relationships, health, and pretty much everything you do. Conversely, if your brain does not work well, you are more likely to face mental and physical health issues, have less success in relationships, and experience financial problems.

A key concept that is often overlooked in many books written about success is that optimal brain health is fundamental to achievement and prosperity. Yet the reality is, brain problems are very common and underlie a lot of failure and misfortune. They are often the missing link to failure and frustration. Undetected and/or untreated issues such as sleep apnea, concussive injuries, exposure to environmental toxins, substance abuse, and gestational trauma—to name a few—can cause a wide range of problems that interfere with a person's capacity to easily make good choices. Therefore, the idea that free will—having conscious control over one's actions—is something you either have or don't have is a misconception. Our work has shown us that free will, or the ability to intentionally choose one's behaviors, is dependent on how healthy a person's brain is; that it is not a black-or-white issue, but rather it actually falls into a gray zone.

In other words, the better overall brain function someone has, the more likely they are to exercise a high degree of free will. On the other hand, people whose brains are unhealthy often struggle with feeling ineffective in life and making good decisions for themselves. Consequently, they experience a diminished sense of free will.

TODAY'S PRACTICE: *Think of three or four people in your life whom you judge harshly. Is it possible that at least one of them has something going on with his or her brain that affects their behavior?*

Your Brain Is the Most Awe-Inspiring Creation

Do you know that the human brain has the storage capacity of six million years of The Wall Street Journal? Our galaxy, the Milky Way, is estimated to have 100 billion stars. Something so vast is hard to comprehend, but there's an organ even more complex and awe-inspiring inside your skull. The human brain has about 100 billion neurons, what we usually refer to as brain cells, and almost as many glia, which function as "helper" cells. Each neuron has multiple connections to other cells—some have just a few, while others can have more than 10,000. This adds up to having about 100 trillion connections in your brain, and all of them are important because they are constantly communicating with other cells and performing a vast range of functions.[4]

Despite the fact that your brain only weighs about three pounds and comprises just 2 percent of your full body weight, it uses a lot of energy. It needs 20 percent or more of your caloric intake. And it uses 20 percent of the blood flow in your body to supply it with a constant flow of vital nutrients and oxygen. Without these it cannot function well or for very long. This is critical to understand because anything that deprives your brain of oxygen, such as obstructive sleep apnea or carbon monoxide poisoning, can cause damage to your brain. Your very special brain makes you who you are, so it is critical to care for this most precious part of you.

TODAY'S PRACTICE: *Think of three world-changing accomplishments done by someone's brain.*

Brain Envy Is the First Step

Freud was wrong. Penis envy is not the cause of anyone's problem. I haven't seen it in 40 years of clinical practice. Brain envy is what everyone needs. Brain health basically comes down to three strategies:

1. Brain envy (you must care about your brain)
2. Avoid anything that hurts it
3. Engage in regular brain-healthy habits

Today, let's discuss brain envy. Early on when I began scanning brains, I had never thought about protecting or enhancing my own brain, even though I was the top neuroscience student in medical school, and at the time was a double board-certified psychiatrist. There was not one lecture on brain health during my five-year psychiatric residency program. In fact, the state of my own brain had never crossed my mind. That changed fast when I decided to scan my mom's brain. She was 60 years old at the time. When I looked at her scan, I saw a beautiful healthy brain. It looked much younger than she was and reflected her highly functional life as a wife, mother, grandmother, and golf phenom.

After seeing her brain, I decided to take a look at my own brain. What a contrast! My scan showed an unhealthy brain that looked much older than my 37 years. Several factors had harmed my brain, including high school football, having meningitis twice as a young soldier, and some bad health habits—fast food, poor sleep, and a lot of stress. I didn't like the fact that my mom's brain was better than mine. From then on, I developed "brain envy." I wanted a healthier brain like hers, so I spent decades working to improve it. If you look at my brain scan today, it is fuller, fatter, and healthier. Looking at the brain taught me that if I wanted to love my life, I had to start by loving my brain. I needed brain envy.

TODAY'S PRACTICE: *Write a love letter to your brain—even a short text will do.*

Doug Falls in Love with His Brain

"Seeing my brain was like seeing one of my children for the first time." Doug was referred to me by a close friend because he suffered from brain fog and fatigue. He had lived in a mold-filled home, grown up on a farm where he was exposed to a lot of pesticides, and had many concussions from martial arts. He told me that seeing his scan was like seeing one of his children for the first time. He knew he had to take care of his brain and did not want to do anything to hurt it. That is brain envy.

BEFORE   **THREE MONTHS LATER**

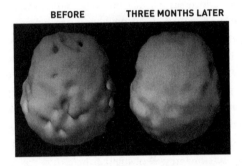

Doug did everything I asked, including improving his diet, taking targeted nutraceuticals (supplements that help support and heal your health, in his case a high-quality multiple vitamin, high-dose omega-3 fatty acids, and a brain boosting supplement), and using hyperbaric oxygen therapy. Within a few weeks, he started to feel much better. After three months, his scan had dramatically improved (see image). The brain fog lifted and his brain was better, as was his energy, endurance, mood, and memory, proving one of the most exciting lessons of brain scan work: Once you fall in love with your brain, it can get better, even if you have mistreated it.

Yet most people never care about their brains. Why? Because you can't see it. You can see your greasy hair, dry skin, or extra weight and change it if you don't like it. But not many people have a chance to peer into their brains, so why would they care about it? Brain imaging changed everything for me and Doug. If you don't yet love your brain, consider taking a look at it.

TODAY'S PRACTICE: *Meditate on this question: Do you love your brain like you love the important people in your life? If not, why not?*

Avoid Anything That Hurts Your Brain

If you want to keep your brain healthy or rescue it if it's headed for trouble, you must prevent or treat the 11 major risk factors that steal your mind. What hurts the brain? You probably know some of the obvious ones: drugs, excessive alcohol, infections, toxic chemicals, and head injuries. The lesser-known factors include being overweight; sleep apnea; high blood pressure; diabetes, prediabetes, and high blood sugar levels; drugs for anxiety; highly processed foods that have been sprayed with pesticides and include added sugar and artificial ingredients; having hormones out of whack; too much stress, negativity, and hanging out with people who have bad habits. Reflect on which of these issues are impacting your brain.

Warren Buffett has two rules of investing: Rule #1 Never lose money. Rule #2 Never forget Rule #1. In the same way, the most important rules of brain health are as follows: Rule #1 Never lose brain cells. Rule #2 Never forget rule #1. Losing brain cells is much harder to recover from than any financial loss.

At Amen Clinics we developed the mnemonic BRIGHT MINDS to help you remember the 11 major risk factors that steal brain cells and lead to cognitive impairment. You can prevent or treat almost all of these risk factors, and even the ones that you can't, such as having a family history of dementia, can be minimized with the right strategies. Here are the 11 BRIGHT MINDS risk factors (in subsequent days we'll go into much more detail).[5]

Blood flow	Mental health
Retirement/Aging	Immunity/Infections
Inflammation	Neurohormone issues
Genetics	Diabesity
Head trauma	Sleep issues
Toxins	

TODAY'S PRACTICE: *Take the Memory Rescue Quiz to see which BRIGHT MINDS risk factors you may have: memoryrescue.com/assessment.*

But How Can I Have Any Fun?

Who has more fun? The kid with the good brain or the one with the bad brain? For the past 17 years, Dr. Jesse Payne and I have taught "Brain Thrive by 25," a course that teaches teens and young adults how to love and care for their brains. Independent research by Multi-Dimensional Education, Inc., in 16 schools found it decreased drug, alcohol, and tobacco use, decreased depression, and improved self-esteem.[6] Whenever we teach the section on things to avoid, invariably a teenage boy—rarely a girl—will raise his hand and ask, "But how can I have any fun?"

Whenever we get this question, we play a game with the students called "Who has more fun? The kid with a healthy brain or the kid who has a brain that doesn't work well?"[7] Who gets into the college of his choice . . . the kid with the good brain or the one with the bad brain? Who gets the girl and gets to keep her because he doesn't act like a jerk . . . the guy with the good brain or the one with the bad brain? Who gets the best jobs and keeps them . . . the woman with a good brain or the one with the bad brain? I then tell them about superstar Miley Cyrus, who quit doing drugs and started to be serious about taking care of her brain. When I texted her a year after she was sober, I asked, "Are you having more fun with your good habits or your bad ones?" She texted me right back: "Ha! Good! By a billion!"

Whatever you want in life, it's easier to achieve when your brain works right. Make sure you have the right attitude. You are not avoiding toxic things to deprive yourself; you avoid them because it is the ultimate act of self-love. If you get this mindset right, the rest will be easy.

TODAY'S PRACTICE: *Meditate on this question: In what ways is your life harder when you engage in behaviors that hurt your brain?*

Engage in Regular Brain-Healthy Habits

Find one simple strategy to optimize each of the BRIGHT MINDS risk factors. Let me give you one simple brain-healthy habit for each of the 11 BRIGHT MINDS risk factors:

Blood flow: walk like you are late for 45 minutes at least four times a week
Retirement/Aging: engage in 15 minutes of new learning every day
Inflammation: floss your teeth regularly to avoid periodontal disease
Genetics: know your family history risk factors and start preventing them as soon as possible
Head trauma: protect your head (stop texting and driving)
Toxins: detoxify your body by taking regular saunas
Mental health: whenever you are sad, mad, nervous, or out of control, write down your negative thoughts and ask, "Is it really true?"
Immunity/Infections: know and optimize your vitamin D level
Neurohormone issues: test your hormones yearly and work with your doctor to optimize them
Diabesity: eat a brain-healthy diet
Sleep issues: aim for seven hours of sleep a night

TODAY'S PRACTICE: *Pick one of the strategies listed above to add to your daily routine.*

Boost Your Brain Reserve

Brain reserve is the extra brain tissue or function you have available to deal with whatever stress comes your way. Have you ever wondered why one person can walk away from a car accident and seem to have no negative effect, while another person's life is devastated? It has to do with the health of the brain they brought into the accident. I coined the term *brain reserve* to describe the extra brain tissue and function you have to deal with whatever stresses come your way. Even before you were conceived, your parents' habits were laying the foundation for your overall physical, mental, and brain health.[8] At its conception, your brain had amazing potential for brain reserve. However, if your mom smoked, drank too much, ate junk food, or had infections during the pregnancy, she depleted your reserve even before you were born. If, on the other hand, your mom ate nutritious foods, took prenatal vitamins, and was not overly stressed, she was contributing to a boost in your reserve.

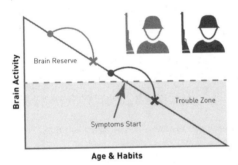

After birth and every day since, you continued to increase or decrease brain reserve by your habits, opportunities, BRIGHT MINDS risk factors, diet, and stresses.

Imagine two soldiers in the same Humvee that drives over an explosive. They both get ejected from the vehicle at the same time, same forces and angles. One walks away unharmed; the other winds up with cognitive impairment, PTSD, and anxiety. How could that be? It all depends on how much brain reserve each soldier had before the explosion. Yes, the blast hurt both of their reserves, but one soldier had more to carry him through a traumatic event than the other soldier did, who was much more at risk for serious brain health issues.

To boost your brain reserve, you need to follow three simple strategies: (1) Love your brain (you have to really care about your brain). (2) Avoid the things that hurt your brain. (3) Do the things that help your brain.

TODAY'S PRACTICE: *List three things you do that steal your brain's reserve and three things you do to build your reserve.*

Unchained from the Shackles of Failure

A balanced brain is the foundation of success. Several years ago, a very troubled teen with a history of crime was brought to Amen Clinics for help. Dale was wearing shackles when he arrived for his evaluation. My heart went out to him and his mother. I did not condemn him for his problems with the law. Like so many other young people we had treated before him, I knew he was suffering with a multitude of brain problems, which collectively led him to make one bad decision after another. Incarceration was probably the safest place for him at the time we first met. I did not judge his behavior that had impeded his life in so many ways. I knew if we could help him get his brain balanced and treat him with respect and encouragement to get well, there was hope for his future.

After being evaluated and given the right treatment strategy, this young man who had been chastised for his failure to "straighten out" was able to get a job and stay employed for a year. This motivated him to join the military and become an Army Ranger. Instead of seeing himself as a failure, he recognized his own potential and found great fulfillment in serving his country. His mother was so proud of the man Dale became.

Tragically, a few days shy of his twenty-fourth birthday, he died in combat. I received the news from his mother in a touching letter. In it she described her son's amazing progress since I had worked with him. Her closing words deeply humbled me:

I thought you might be interested in the part you played in this Hero's life. Thank you, Laura B., Proud Mother of Sgt. Dale B.[9]

Had we taken the same hard-nosed approach that so many had tried before with that once shackled 17-year-old boy, it is likely he would have never found the path to doing something he believed in and loved being a part of. Instead, we started by looking at his brain and then worked hard to optimize its health.

TODAY'S PRACTICE: *What could a healthier brain help you do better and more effectively?*

You Are in a War for the Health of Your Brain

The war for your health is won or lost between your ears. Make no mistake: You are in a war for the health of your brain and mind. Everywhere you go someone is trying to make money by shoving bad food down your throat that will kill you early. The real weapons of mass destruction are highly processed, pesticide-sprayed, high-glycemic, low-fiber, food-like substances stored in plastic containers—think of happy meals and school lunches. News corporations repeatedly pour fear and images of disaster into your brain to boost their ratings. Tech companies create addictive gadgets that hook your attention and distract you from your loved ones and your purpose.

As a society, we are clearly going the wrong way, with devastating consequences: Alzheimer's disease is expected to triple between now and 2050; depression has risen 400 percent since 1987; half of American adults are prediabetic or diabetic and 60 percent have hypertension or prehypertension; and 73 percent of American adults are overweight—all conditions that damage our brains.[10]

We can fix these problems, but it requires a new perspective. Rather than assuming each illness is distinct with its own medications, we must realize that these issues are the result of the same unhealthy choices—and the cure for all of them is the same: a brain-healthy lifestyle. To put it another way, although there are many illnesses, often the clearest path to health and vitality is simpler than you think. I call it the brain warrior's way—being armed, prepared, and aware to win the fight of your life for the health of your brain. *When my wife turns off the news, she is so much happier!*

Even my daughter Chloe has a warrior mentality. After a tough hike, when she was 7, her mother said, "Chloe, you're a tough cookie." Chloe looked up at her with an attitude, put her hands on her hips, and said, "I don't want to be a tough cookie. I want to be a tough red bell pepper." None of this is hard. It just takes the mindset of a brain warrior.

TODAY'S PRACTICE: *Look around you to see what influences are helping or hurting your brain and mind.*

Brain Warrior Marianne—Best Days Ahead

The pain was gone, and her brain fog lifted. Marianne, a 59-year-old, highly successful businesswoman, chalked up her brain fog and body aches to the consequences of
aging. She wistfully reflected on her younger days when she always felt cognitively
sharp and energetic. Despite loving her occupation, she started to think it was time
for her to resign. After a long and meaningful career, she didn't want to be seen as
the slow cog in the wheel. She shared her thoughts with one of her daughters who
had recently completed one of my weight and brain health programs. Marianne
decided to give it a try, and within a couple of months she felt remarkably better.
This encouraged her to keep going, and after about 10 more months, she had lost
more than 50 pounds. Not only were the constant body aches long gone, but her
energy level had skyrocketed, her brain was sharper, and she felt like she was in top
form, both mentally and physically. But Marianne didn't stop there. She introduced
brain-healthy foods to her colleagues at work, and they experienced the benefits of
increased focus and productivity.

Marianne and I were once together at a conference. She told me briefly how
the program had helped her reclaim her health, but what she was especially proud
of was that another one of her daughters, who had struggled with obesity and its
subsequent medical problems for many years, used Marianne's success to inspire
her own. She wanted to feel good again and be able to go for hikes and bike rides
without feeling like she might not make it home. She followed the same program
and eventually lost 140 pounds. Not to be left out, Marianne's husband decided to
get healthy too. It was wonderful to see how a single person's journey to get healthy
helped so many others along the way.

TODAY'S PRACTICE: *Name two or three people who might be inspired if you got
truly well.*

Do One Simple Thing at a Time for Massive Results

There are two major types of people seeking help: (1) Those who jump in with both feet to feel better as quickly as possible. (2) Those who take an incremental approach. They do one thing at a time, then another, and another. This is what Nancy from Oxford, England, did. She was depressed, unmotivated, anxious, obese, and had arthritis. She found one of my books in a used bookstore in Oxford and loved it. But she knew she could never do everything at once, so she decided to start with one simple strategy at a time. She began by drinking more water; her energy level went up. Then she added a multivitamin, omega-3 fatty acids, and vitamin D; she was able to focus better. Those two changes led her to add exercise to her routine—walking, dancing, and playing table tennis, which boosted her mood. The noticeable progress motivated her to overhaul her eating habits; she began to lose pounds. Her approach was to eat healthy foods first, so she would have no room for anything unhealthy. She felt so good that she tackled new learning next. She enrolled in classes to learn foreign languages and how to play the guitar. Her life totally changed. Her energy, mood, and memory were remarkably better; she lost 70 pounds and was pain-free. The last step in her journey was to advocate for her children to take brain health seriously. She knew that if she kept herself healthy as long as possible, she was also helping her children.

I met Nancy when she came to Amen Clinics for a brain scan in celebration of her eighty-third birthday. See below for typical 80–90-year-old scans. Nancy's scan looked like someone in her forties! Her brain was healthy and strong.

TYPICAL SPECT SCANS OF 80- TO 90-YEAR-OLDS   **NANCY'S SCAN**

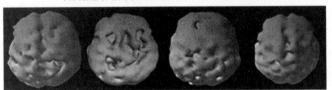

When she saw it, she cried, because she was so happy, knowing it would have looked much worse just a year earlier. Nancy changed the trajectory of the rest of her life; you can too. Just decide if the best approach for yourself is fast or slow.

TODAY'S PRACTICE: *What is one small step you can start today from Nancy's list above? Are you more likely to succeed on a fast track or at an incremental approach?*

Are You a Wolf, Sheep, or Sheepdog?

Whom do you need to protect? If you could be one of these, which would it be: a wolf, a sheepdog, or a sheep?[11] And why? I'll tell you which one I choose—a sheepdog. No, not because they are cute and fluffy canines, but because of their purpose-driven instinct to protect their flock from danger and potential predators. Sheepdogs undergo extensive training to do their job, and if necessary, they will even fight to the death defending their charges. Sheep, on the other hand, are meek creatures that are easily led. They follow the herd and do what the other sheep do, even if it means jumping to their death. Unlike the protective sheepdog, sheep try to run away rather than fight a predator; that's why they are prey animals. Wolves know this and seek them out. You see, the wolf's instinct is to look for the sheep that are sick, weak, or distracted. Despite their power, wolves are not inclined to mess with a flock guarded by a sheepdog. They don't want a fight, they just want to take advantage of a situation.

Wolves remind me of the advertising executives for major food corporations. Their efforts are targeted toward easy prey who believe their advertising lies about how sugar-filled, processed, high-fat foods will make them happier, more popular, and more fun to be with. Sadly, the majority of people unwittingly act like sheep. They do what others do, eat what others eat, even if it isn't good for their health. They don't pause to consider that what they are putting into their bodies could be hurting them.

These people need a purposeful sheepdog. They need someone to help guide them so they don't keep making bad decisions about their life and health that could otherwise lead to an earlier death. In a world where you can be almost anything you want, be a sheepdog so you can help and protect the ones you love.

TODAY'S PRACTICE: *List a few people who need you to be their sheepdog.*

Getting Started Can Feel Hard

Brain health can feel really awkward at first. Every swimmer, dancer, or guitar player remembers how strange it was to start learning new techniques. Most probably felt like they'd never get it. But with time, their bodies picked up the motions and became proficient, until eventually these new skills were second nature. The brain has a great capacity for growth, but it takes time to grow, establish new neural pathways, and adjust to new movement and new thinking.

So it's no surprise that when you set out to become a brain warrior, you may often feel awkward or overwhelmed. You may wonder, *Where's dessert? What about spaghetti and garlic bread? But I love chips and dip! I have no idea how to make a shopping list and where to find all these new ingredients. I don't have room to add one more thing to my schedule. I've been doing pizza night for 20 years; I can't quit that now.*

Months 1–3: Getting Started. Go easy on yourself. This is just the beginning. You need time to adjust. Trust what you're learning and be persistent; you will get to the place where these new habits become natural. Often it only takes 30 days if you are a go-getter, or 30 to 90 days if you prefer a slow and steady pace, for your tastes to change and your brain to make new connections. It will get easier.

- Realize you need to change.
- Learn your BRIGHT MINDS risk factors.
- Get lab work to know your baseline health numbers.
- Start taking basic supplements.
- Add a few new brain-healthy exercises and sleep habits to your routine.
- Identify your motivation for becoming healthy.
- Consider who will benefit from you becoming healthy.
- Ditch quick-fix thinking for lifestyle longevity.
- Don't worry about making mistakes. Expect them and start learning from them.

TODAY'S PRACTICE: *What one decision can you make for brain health?*

DAY 17

Develop a Healthy Rhythm

Keep going, one step at a time. After the "getting started" stage (Day 16), people who persist develop a healthy rhythm. Brain-healthy habits start to become second nature. Brain fog clears. You begin making the connections between certain foods and how high or low your energy level is. You get better at recognizing negativity and pausing to assess negative thoughts and loops in your head. Sure, it still requires that you are intentional about your choices because they are not yet habitual. It takes about one to three months for the go-getters and three to six months for slow-and-steady people to get through this phase of creating healthy rhythms.

Months 2–6: Developing a Healthy Rhythm. This is where your confidence begins to grow.

- Once you realize how much illness and poor brain health is around you, you are more committed to brain health for yourself and your loved ones. It becomes easier to ignore or respond to any criticism that comes from people with un-healthy habits.
- You have your lab values back and are working to optimize them. You attack your BRIGHT MINDS risk factors and are actively taking steps to prevent them.
- You have found multiple foods you love that love you back.
- You develop new routines, including practices such as prayer, guided imagery, walking, and standing up to automatic negative thoughts (ANTs). Your routine becomes easier and more defined. You are finding your rhythm.
- You have started to share this message with friends, coworkers, and loved ones.
- You finally feel like you can do this as your normal routine rather than for just a few weeks or months.
- By this point, mistakes will become less and less frequent. Although you will occasionally have a bad day, you quickly get right back on track.

TODAY'S PRACTICE: *Answer two questions:*
"How have I changed since starting a brain-healthy program?"
"What keeps me going?"

Brain Health Becomes Automatic and Second Nature

Being sick is hard, this is easy. The goal is for your habits to transform from hard to natural and easy. It usually takes about 4 to 6 months for the go-getters, and 6 to 12 months for those who are slow and steady to reach this phase. The goal is to remain consistent and persistent no matter what challenges arise, such as job or family changes (which we all have). If you stick with it this long, you will be a brain warrior for life.

Months 6–12: The Automatic Phase. Brain health becomes routine. You think, *No problem; I've got this.* You easily do what's best for your health.

- Mistakes rarely happen, and when they do, you simply start again. Giving up is not an option.
- You check your health numbers to see your progress.
- You love discovering new foods and recipes.
- You take vitamins and supplements as consistently as brushing your teeth.
- You immediately feel out of sorts if your health habits get interrupted; your preference is to do what's best for your body all the time.
- You want to help your friends and family get healthier.
- You may have a dessert, but you choose one that supports your health, rather than hurts it.
- You refuse bread before a meal.
- You don't even consider a glass of wine, much less a second one.
- Workouts are part of your daily routine. You don't miss them because they are just as important to you as showing up for your child's recital or a work meeting.
- You respond positively to brain-healthy choices and shut down brain-harming ones without a second thought.

TODAY'S PRACTICE: *What are three ways your life will be better if you get to the automatic phase of brain health habits?*

You Cannot Change What You Do Not Measure

The physical health of your body and brain is completely intertwined with the health of your mind. Physical ailments—such as obesity, diabetes, and chronic inflammation—are associated with an unhealthy mind and increased risk for depression, ADD/ADHD, and Alzheimer's disease. To improve your mind, you need to know and improve your important health numbers on a regular basis. Here are 12 important numbers to track on a yearly basis.

General Health

1. Body mass index (BMI): Find an online calculator and strive to be in the healthy range (18.5–25).
2. Blood pressure: Optimal range is between 90–120 systolic over 60–80 diastolic.
3. Number of hours you sleep at night: Aim for between 7–9 hours.

Blood Tests

4. Vitamin D level: Optimal is 50–100 mg/dL.
5. Thyroid-stimulating hormone (TSH): Optimal is 0.4–3.0 mIU/L.
6. C-reactive protein: Optimal is 0.0–1.0 mg/dL.
7. Hemoglobin A1c: Healthy is 4.0–5.6.
8. Total cholesterol: Optimal is 160-200 mg/dL; below 135 is associated with depression.
9. Ferritin: Optimal is 40–100 ng/mL.
10. Free and total testosterone: Age and gender dependent.
11. Omega-3 Index: Optimal is > 8 percent.

Modifiable Health Risks

12. How many of the 10 most important modifiable health risk factors do you have? Work to eliminate all of them.

____ Smoking/vaping	____ Alcohol abuse
____ High blood pressure	____ Low omega-3s
____ BMI overweight or obese	____ Low polyunsaturated fat intake
____ Physical inactivity	____ High salt intake
____ High blood sugar	____ Low intake of fruits/vegetables

TODAY'S PRACTICE: *Contact your health-care provider to schedule lab tests to measure these important health numbers.*

People Get Sick or Well in Four Circles

Always think of people as whole beings, never just as their symptoms. To help people of any age concerning any problem, I always think of them in four circles:

1. **Biological:** how your physical brain and body function.
2. **Psychological:** how you think, including any developmental issues.
3. **Social:** connections, stresses, and current life situation.
4. **Spiritual:** sense of meaning and purpose.

Think of your biology as the *hardware of your soul.* Managing this aspect of life includes preventing or treating the 11 major risk factors that damage the brain and body.

Once you optimize the hardware, you then have to *program the software*, which I think of as the psychological circle, including how you think and talk to yourself. Developing mental discipline is critical to a healthy and happy life. This will include learning to kill the ANTs (automatic negative thoughts); eliminating the little lies that keep you fat, depressed, and foggy-minded; taming the dragons from the past (the big psychological issues that steal your happiness); and breaking the bad habits that hold you back.

As you optimize the hardware and software of your life, it is time to strengthen your *network connections* or your social circle by improving the quality of your relationships, managing day-to-day stresses, and controlling the inputs that other people and society have on your brain and mind.

While the physical, mental, and relational areas of life are essential for brain health, you also have a spiritual dimension. Your mind has the capacity to think deeply about the meaning of your life. You can reflect on questions like, "What gives my life meaning? How can I make a difference for others? What supports my most important values?" Having a sense of purpose beyond yourself allows you to live a life that matters. Purpose can override trouble in the other three circles.

There will be many entries and exercises for each of these circles to help you live a balanced life.

TODAY'S PRACTICE: *Rate your health in each of the four circles. For each circle, write one strength and one vulnerability you have.*

DAY 21

Why I Collect Seahorses

 *Every day you make 700 new hippocampal stem cells.*[12] *Your behavior can protect them or murder them.* I've collected seahorses ever since I wrote *Memory Rescue* in 2017 to honor a part of the brain called the hippocampus, which is translated from the Greek as "seahorse" because of its shape. We all have two hippocampi on the inside of our left and right temporal lobes. They are critical for learning, memory, and mood. When the hippocampi are hurt, you cannot store new information or experiences. In the movie *50 First Dates*, Lucy (Drew Barrymore's character) is in a severe car accident that damages her hippocampi, and after she falls asleep, her memories of the prior day are wiped out. The hippocampi are one of the first areas damaged in Alzheimer's disease.

Hippocampi are special structures because they make 700 new stem cells (or baby seahorses) every day. Under optimal circumstances, such as a nourishing environment, good nutrition, omega-3 fatty acids, oxygen, sufficient blood flow, and stimulation, they grow. If we put them in a toxic environment, they shrink. Every day you are either nurturing and growing your seahorses or murdering them.

I often use the seahorse analogy with patients. With one of my patients, I had trouble getting her to stop using marijuana. Knowing she was an animal lover, we discussed how the marijuana was damaging her baby seahorses and not allowing them (or her) to reach their potential. She yelled at me. "Dr. Amen, that is so unfair. You know how much I love animals!" But shortly afterward, she stopped smoking pot.

TODAY'S PRACTICE: *Name three of your behaviors that nourish your hippocampi and three toxic behaviors that shrink them.*

Why I Collect Anteaters

You don't have to believe every stupid thing you think. I've collected anteaters for about 30 years. ANTs stand for automatic negative thoughts—the thoughts that come into our minds automatically and ruin our day. I was 28 years old and in my psychiatric residency at the Walter Reed Army Medical Center before I learned that I didn't have to believe every stupid thought I had. It was so liberating.

All of us have stressful days at work, some of which feel off the charts. I had a day like that once. I had seen difficult patients all day long. I could hardly wait to get home and relax. But the ants that had taken over my kitchen had a completely different idea. They were everywhere. It was gross. Although relaxation was no longer on the agenda, I had a clinical epiphany as I cleaned them up. Just as the ants had infested my kitchen, ANTs—automatic negative thoughts—were invading the minds of my patients and stealing their happiness. On the way to my office the next day, I stopped at the store to pick up another can of ant spray to illustrate the need to eliminate the ANTs that were infesting their minds.

Over time, I realized I needed a less toxic analogy than ant spray, so I went to a puppet store on Pier 39 in San Francisco and bought an anteater puppet. My patients, especially the children, loved it; and my anteater collection was born. One of my favorite stories is of an 8-year-old boy who came to see me for panic attacks. When I taught him how to eliminate the ANTs, he improved quickly. The next time I saw him, I asked him about the ANT population in his head. He said, "It's an ANT ghost town in my head."[13]

TODAY'S PRACTICE: *Ask yourself,* What is the ANT population in my head? *If it is high, start writing down your negative thoughts, and soon I will teach you how to eliminate them.*

Why I Collect Penguins

Notice what you like about others more than what you don't.
My son Antony was a strong-willed child, to say the least.
Every time I asked him to do something, he wanted to debate
me about it. It was incredibly frustrating. To help improve
our relationship, I decided we should have more father-son
bonding time, so one day we went to Sea Life Park to have
some fun together.

Before the day ended, we went to see the Fat Freddy show. Freddy was a cute,
chubby, and talented penguin that leaped through a hoop encircled with fire and
dove off the high dive. He could even count with his little flippers and bowl with
his beak. Whenever his trainer asked him to do something, he did it. I was curious
how the trainer had taught Freddy to be so compliant, especially because I had such
difficulty getting my son to do what I wanted him to do. After the show, I stopped
by to ask her how she got Freddy to respond so well to her requests. The strategy
she shared with me was remarkably simple. She said that every time Freddy does
what she asks, she gives him some type of praise, whether it's a fish, a hug, or something else he likes. She said, "I notice him when he is good, which is the opposite of
what most parents do."

I had a sudden epiphany. I rarely acknowledged Antony when he was doing the
right things, but I always paid attention to him whenever he did something wrong.
I had inadvertently been training him to do things that irritated me. He wanted me
to notice him, even if he was being bad.

Since that memorable day, I have been collecting penguins as a reminder to
notice the positive things rather than the negative things about the people in my
life. To date, I have amassed a collection of more than 2,000 penguins of every kind
imaginable. Who would have ever guessed that one of the best pieces of parenting
and relationship advice I have ever gotten came from a little penguin named Freddy?

TODAY'S PRACTICE: *Notice something you like about one or two people in your life
today, and do this as often as you can going forward.*

Why I Collect Butterflies

Butterflies are the universal symbol of change, hope, renewal, spiritual birth, and transformation. I've had the privilege to witness many transformations at Amen Clinics. People often come to us depressed, anxious, addicted, or suicidal and failing at school, work, or in their relationships. When we optimize and balance their brains and strengthen their minds, their lives often become dramatically better. "Change your brain, change your life" has been a phrase we've repeated thousands of times.

Butterflies are the perfect symbol of change and the work we do with our patients. They represent my life's work. I'm not alone in feeling this way; many cultures view butterflies the same way. They also remind us that life is short, and we need to stay focused on the present.

To be who you are truly meant to be, you must realize that you are more than a brain or body. You are also more than a job or a parent or partner; you have a spiritual side. That side of you can think deeply and consider questions, such as:

- What is the meaning of my life?
- Where do I find purpose?
- Why am I here?
- What do I value most in life?
- Where do I put my faith?
- What role does faith play in my life?
- How am I connected to people from the past and the future?
- What is my connection to Earth?

Believing that you have purpose helps you understand your connections to others and the world, allows you to realize that your life is about more than just yourself, and affirms that your life matters. Without a deeper sense of meaning and purpose, many people feel a sense of hopelessness or aimlessness. A spiritual life is essential to feel whole and connected. Research from multiple sources reports that having a sense of meaning and purpose improves your health and helps you live longer.[14]

TODAY'S PRACTICE: *Spend some time reflecting on the spiritual questions above.*

The Good Ruler vs. Evil Ruler Strategies to Create and End Mental Illness: Biological

The physical aspects of your brain and body function together. When I wrote my book *The End of Mental Illness*, I introduced the concept of the good ruler versus evil ruler. It evolved from the Brain Warrior's Way concept. The evil ruler's top priority is to create and perpetuate mental illness. How would he or she do it? The evil ruler would turn the four circles (biological, psychological, social, and spiritual) against us and create policies and promote behaviors guaranteed to increase trouble and maximize the BRIGHT MINDS risk factors. On the other hand, if a good ruler were in charge, what would he or she do to end mental illness? The good ruler would encourage people to use the four circles to enhance brain health and to advocate policies and behaviors that would help minimize the BRIGHT MINDS risk factors.

In the biological circle, the evil ruler would perpetuate the biological warfare in America to keep the majority of the population sick and tired (currently 88 percent of us).[15] The evil ruler would put fast-food restaurants everywhere and allow the media, often funded by the pharmaceutical industry, to create a narrative that natural supplements are not helpful and may in fact harm people.

The good ruler would counteract the messages and behaviors that harm physical health by creating nationwide programs for people to fall in love with their bodies and brains. It would start in schools and go into churches, businesses, and senior centers—anywhere people gather.

TODAY'S PRACTICE: *Do your behaviors in the biological circle support your health or cause harm to your brain and others' brains?*

The Good Ruler vs. Evil Ruler Strategies to Create and End Mental Illness: Psychological

Successes and failures, hope, a sense of worth, and personal power are a part of the psychological circle. In the psychological circle of health, the evil ruler would use psychological warfare to hurt his subjects. This includes ignoring past emotional trauma created by alcoholic or drug-abusing parents and not addressing current or past traumas from earthquakes, fires, floods, immigration, and criminal behaviors. He would also have politicians model undisciplined, negative thinking patterns, where they always blame the other party for the country's woes; never teach their subjects how to eliminate the ANTs that infest their minds; and allow social media outlets to create shame as they invite nonstop comparisons to other people who may or may not even be real. The evil ruler would give people free rein to spout hateful ideas anonymously without consequences.

The good ruler would help people optimize their brains; prevent social media companies from becoming monopolies so that a few people cannot control the minds of many; teach people how to deal with current or past emotional traumas; make rational thinking skills (eliminating the ANTs) part of the educational curriculum, along with ways to help people self-regulate their bodies and emotions with guided imagery and meditation; make psychotherapy readily available for those who wanted or needed it, especially if they've had past emotional trauma; require all therapists to have brain health modules as part of their education programs; and incorporate more green space into urban planning to promote better moods and reduce the incidence of mental illness.

TODAY'S PRACTICE: *How often do you feel like you are enough? How often do you think you are not enough? What factors growing up (adoption, neglect/abuse, loss, trauma, stability, praise, positive messages) influenced your psychological health?*

The Good Ruler vs. Evil Ruler Strategies to Create and End Mental Illness: Social

The quality of your relationships and current stress level indicate how healthy you are in the social circle. In the social circle of health, the evil ruler would cause polarization and strife among his or her people, subjecting them to chronic stress that separates them from each other so that the ruler can retain more power. He or she would bombard people with negative news, creating an us-versus-them mentality and pitting political and racial groups against each other. Watching just 14 consecutive minutes of negative news has been found to increase both anxious and sad moods.[16] An evil ruler would also increase the social pressure to stay connected to your phone and social media for work and relationships, not allowing enough time for sleep and self-care, and create a society where recreational marijuana dispensaries are on every corner and alcohol is promoted as a health food. In examples of evil ruler entrepreneurial genius, Girl Scouts are now selling cookies outside marijuana dispensaries. In 2014, a 13-year-old Girl Scout sold 177 boxes of Samoas, Tagalongs, and Thin Mints outside a San Francisco pot dispensary. After being there just a short time, she had to call for help to be restocked.[17]

A good ruler would make job training, health care, parent training, and financial assistance readily available to those who need it, and would advocate for stress management classes in schools and businesses. Decreasing everyday stress (relationships, work, finances, and health) lowers inflammation and improves immune system function.[18] A good ruler would provide classes on decision-making skills to help people make better life decisions and be less stressed. You make better decisions when you have clear goals, sleep more than seven hours, avoid low blood sugar states (have protein and healthy fat at every meal), and eliminate the ANTs when they attack.

TODAY'S PRACTICE: *How does stress affect your most important relationships? Which of your relationships is suffering because of stress?*

The Good Ruler vs. Evil Ruler Strategies to Create and End Mental Illness: Spiritual

We are all spiritual beings created with divine purpose. Our lives matter; each of us has a role to play and a call to fulfill. Without this spiritual connection, many people experience a sense of despair or meaninglessness.

To prevent us from connecting to meaning and purpose, an evil ruler would lead people to live frivolously, devoid of values and connection to a life beyond themselves; have leaders model amoral lives, making such behavior seem normal or even desirable; and diminish and demonize those who don't believe the way you believe.

On the other hand, a good ruler would have leaders model purposeful lives and inspire others to do the same; encourage spiritual beliefs and practices without dictating them; foster a deep connection to the past, future, and the planet; and practice tolerance, teaching people that there is no influence without a personal connection to others.

TODAY'S PRACTICE: *Ask yourself,* What is one purposeful thing I can do today? *Then add it to your to-do list.*

All Psychiatric Issues Have Multiple Causes

Giving someone the diagnosis of depression is like giving them the diagnosis of chest pain.
Why don't doctors give people the diagnosis of chest pain? Because it's a *symptom*
with many different causes. What can cause chest pain? Heart attacks, ulcers, gas,
anxiety, and grief. Depression (as well as every other psychiatric issue) is the same
way. It's a symptom cluster with many different causes. What can cause depression?
So many things: chronic stress, relationship problems, head injuries, drug abuse,
low thyroid, pancreatic cancer, many medications, genetic tendencies, and grief.

With brain imaging work, I've seen that depression has at least seven patterns.
You can have too much activity in the front part of your brain and overthink or
worry yourself sick, or you can have too little activity in this part of the brain and
have trouble thinking or controlling your impulses. Depression does not stem from
just one cause; so giving everyone the same treatment for it invites failure. Yet that
is exactly what is happening across our country every day. Many patients tell their
doctors that they are depressed and leave the office after a seven-minute appointment with samples of the latest drug, without any sense of the type of depression
they have. This can cause problems.

Before my wife, Tana, and I met, she had become depressed after being treated
for thyroid cancer in her twenties. A psychiatrist prescribed her Prozac, which
lowered her anxiety so much that she started making risky decisions—something
completely out of character for her. When I scanned Tana's brain, we found she had
low activity in her prefrontal cortex, which made Prozac a poor choice for her. Prozac calms brain activity and tends to work for people who have overactive brains.
But for people with low activity, it can disinhibit them and lead them to make bad
decisions. Knowing the type of depression, ADD/ADHD, or addiction you have is
critical to getting the right help. At Amen Clinics we use SPECT imaging to help
us understand and treat patients, but a long time ago I realized not everyone is able
to get a scan. So based on thousands of scans, we developed a questionnaire to help
people predict what their scan might look like if they could get one.

TODAY'S PRACTICE: *Take the Brain Health Assessment at brainhealthassessment.com.*

Why I Hate the Term *Mental Illness* and You Should Too

The term mental illness *shames people, perpetuates stigma, and prevents people from getting help.* I've always hated this term, and you should too. It places the emphasis on the wrong domain—on your psyche or mind—which is vague and hard to define, when brain-imaging work clearly teaches that brain health issues are what steal your mind. When someone is diagnosed with a "mental illness," it often stigmatizes them or makes them feel ashamed, thus leaving them less likely to want to seek help.

Early in my career I learned that few people want to see a psychiatrist because they're afraid of being labeled as defective or abnormal, but everyone wants a better brain. We must relabel mental health as brain health! Changing the discussion from mental health to brain health changes everything. People begin to see their problems as *medical* and not *moral*, lowering their shame and guilt and eliciting understanding and compassion from their families. Brain health is also more accurate. It raises hope and the desire to get help, and it sparks motivation to make the necessary lifestyle changes to improve their brain. Once people understand that the brain controls everything they do and everything they are, they want a better brain so they can have a better life.

TODAY'S PRACTICE: *Whom do you know who could benefit from this message? Who needs a better brain? Send them a short text about today's lesson, such as: "With a better brain always comes a better life. Let's get our brains better together."*

How Brain Imaging Changes Everything: Steve and Schizophrenia

I never expected a kiss of gratitude. A number of years ago, I met a leader of the National Alliance on Mental Illness (NAMI). She made an appointment for me to see her son, Steve. He had paranoid schizophrenia. He had been living on the streets because he was violent and resisted any help. When I met Steve, there was no doubt that he was psychotic. He would not go on any medication and made sure I knew that no one could force him. But I kept talking to him and asked if he would be open to having a brain scan. He had seen the scans posted in my office, and they sparked his curiosity, so he agreed. There was so much damage on his scan. When I compared his scan to a healthy brain, he went silent and stared at them. Surprisingly, then he asked me whether I could help him. Seeing the scans helped changed his perspective from anger and resistance to openness and curiosity. I've seen this kind of transformation so many times.

BEFORE   **ONE MONTH LATER**

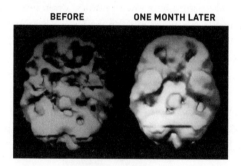

This allowed me to tell Steve about the treatments we had that were better than anything he had tried. First, I asked him to take a newer antipsychotic and then come back to see me in three weeks. A week later, I saw Steven's mother sitting in the waiting room. She did not have an appointment. When she saw me, she stood up and kissed me. She excitedly told me that Steve was already so much better. Because he was now calmer, she had invited him back home. She was so grateful.

At Steve's next appointment, I could see how much better he was. When I did another brain scan, I let him compare his original scan to his new one. Then I asked, "Which brain do you want?"

"The healthy one!" he replied.

"Then you have to take your medication and be good to your brain," I told him.

Seeing the state of his own brain was the turning point for Steve and those who loved him.

TODAY'S PRACTICE: *Ask yourself if there is an alternative reason why the difficult people in your life do what they do.*

It's Easy to Call Someone Bad; It's Harder to Ask Why

Calling someone insane or bad or crazy is just another way to say their brain may be troubled. I began my book *The End of Mental Illness* with a story about a homeless man I saw on the corner of Hollywood and Vine while driving to record a podcast. The man was stumbling as he ranted to no one in particular. Most people would immediately think he had a severe psychiatric problem, such as schizophrenia, and wonder why he wouldn't just take his medication.

In cases like this man, I want a deeper explanation as to *why* people act certain ways, what has happened to them to make them behave so erratically. After more than 40 years of practice, I've learned that many things can harm your brain and steal your mind due to no fault of your own. Having a head injury or brain cyst, being infected with Lyme disease or COVID-19, suffering from gut health problems, or being exposed to environmental toxins like mold—these can all ravage the brain and cause people to act erratically.

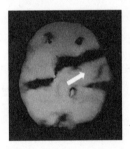

This concept was anchored in my brain after I assessed my 9-year-old nephew, Andrew, who had attacked a little girl on a baseball field for no particular reason. It would have been easy to call Andrew a bad boy, and 999 out of 1,000 child psychiatrists would have put him in psychotherapy or given him psychiatric medications. I needed to know why. When I scanned him, it turned out he had a cyst the size of a golf ball occupying the space of his left temporal lobe, a part of the brain involved in violence. Once the cyst was drained, Andrew's behavior completely went back to normal. It was easy to call Andrew bad but so much more effective to ask why.

TODAY'S PRACTICE: *If somebody does something you think is bad, don't make a snap judgment. Pause and ask yourself what might be behind their behavior.*

The Structure of Scientific Revolution

Learn to cope with criticism. My career has been dedicated to trying to end mental illness by creating a revolution in brain health, but I have met with more than a fair share of rejection. One thing that has helped me power past the naysayers is something philosopher Thomas Kuhn wrote in 1962 about how scientific revolutions typically occur in five stages. These same stages can apply to groundbreaking ideas in other fields as well and may help you stay focused in the face of criticism.

Stage I: The Discrepancies Show. *In the first stage, the revolution is started when the standard paradigm begins to fail.* For example, when I would diagnose patients based on DSM (*Diagnostic and Statistical Manual of Mental Disorders*) criteria with major depression or ADD/ADHD, put them on standard treatments, such as Prozac or Ritalin, and then see them become suicidal or aggressive. This paradigm-based failure occurred too often and was emotionally traumatic for patients and myself.

Stage II: The Disagreements Start. Once the paradigm begins to fail, experts begin to look for ways to fix their theories, but they resist discarding their old models entirely and instead look for small fixes, so they can preserve their power and influence. This makes me think of the six versions of the DSM, which have been tweaked but not substantially overhauled since 1980.

Stage III: The Revolution. Over time a new paradigm emerges that resolves many of the problems in the field. A new paradigm—such as "Get your brain right and your mind will follow"—reinterprets existing knowledge, retaining the best of the old thinking and integrating the latest knowledge into a fresh model.

Stage IV: The Rejection. The new paradigm is then rejected and ridiculed by the leaders in the field. This stage may last for decades. Nobel Prize–winning physicist Max Planck wrote, "A new scientific truth does not triumph by convincing its opponents and making them see the light, but rather because its opponents eventually die, and a new generation grows up that is familiar with it."[19] Science advances through funerals.

Stage V: The Acceptance. The new theory is adopted gradually as younger, more open-minded scientists accept it early in their careers and later become the leaders of the field. Kuhn also noted that new paradigms are often championed by professionals who are outsiders and not wed to the status quo.[20] Currently, thousands of medical and mental health professionals have been trained in our work and have referred over 10,000 patients to our clinics.

TODAY'S PRACTICE: *Think of a big idea you have had that was shot down by others. Before giving up due to the rejection, identify which stage you are in as it may help you stay motivated to keep trying.*

DAY 34

Your Brain Can Be Better Tomorrow

Every day your actions are either helping or hurting your brain. Nick, 25, was an MMA fighter who was brought to the clinic by his mother because he had been arrested after a drunken bar fight and started to express suicidal thoughts. I met him when I gave a lecture at the clinic. Afterward, I reviewed Nick's scan with him. It showed damage with low prefrontal cortex (PFC) and temporal lobe activity. I asked him if he wanted to do an experiment the next day. At the time, I was doing a large study on active and retired NFL players. We saw high levels of damage on their SPECT scans, especially to the PFC and temporal lobes. This was not a surprise. The exciting news from our study was that 80 percent of our players showed improvement when we worked to rehabilitate their brains, especially in blood flow, memory, mood, motivation, and sleep. Our rehabilitation program included a combination of nutritional supplements (a high-level multivitamin, high-dose omega-3 fatty acids, and other nutrients to support brain function, including ginkgo biloba and phosphatidylserine).

I told Nick I knew the supplements worked, but I didn't know how quickly they took effect. I asked him to come to the office at eight the next morning and I would give him the supplements. We would then scan him two-and-a-half hours later. Nick was excited to see if the supplements could help (see the before and after scans). After just a couple of hours, he had marked increased blood flow to his whole brain, especially the PFC and temporal lobes. This does not mean he was cured after one dose of supplements; it meant that his brain had the potential to respond if he consistently put it in a healing environment and gave it the nutritional support it needed.

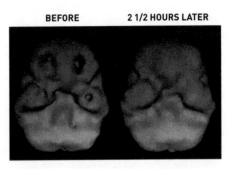

BEFORE   **2 1/2 HOURS LATER**

TODAY'S PRACTICE: *List one thing you typically do that hurts your brain. Stop doing it for a week to see how you feel. List one thing you typically do that helps your brain (and make sure you do it today).*

The Brain Is a Sneaky Organ

Please do not say every stupid thing you think. We all have weird, crazy, stupid, sexual, or violent thoughts that no one should ever hear. How many of us have seen someone in a grocery store with an armload of boxes and wondered what it would be like to trip him or her just to see the boxes fly everywhere? Am I the only person? Now, of course we don't act on that thought. It is our prefrontal cortex (PFC), in the front third of the brain, that protects us from these compulsions. The PFC is the most human, thoughtful part of the brain. It acts as the brain's brake that prevents us from saying or doing stupid things. Comedian Dudley Moore once said that the best car safety device is a rearview mirror with a cop in it. Your PFC acts like the cop in your head.

But what happens if this part of the brain is hurt? I remember sitting with a friend who had a brain injury that damaged her PFC. We were sitting near two overweight women who were discussing their weight. When my friend overheard one woman say, "I don't know why I am so fat; I just eat like a bird," my friend blurted out, "Yeah, like a condor!" I was mortified. Once she realized everyone around us had heard her, she slapped her hand over her mouth and uttered, "Oh no, did that get out?"[21]

Now, it would have been easy for me to judge my friend as a bad person, but when you look at her behavior with the benefit of brain imaging, you begin to understand why she exhibited poor judgment. Her PFC was hurt.

TODAY'S PRACTICE: *Notice the crazy or weird thoughts that go through your head and how many of them you do not act on or share with anyone.*

How Do You Know Unless You Look?

We must look at the brain if we want to fix it. Why are psychiatrists the only medical doctors who virtually never look at the organ they treat? Cardiologists, gastroenterologists, orthopedists—in fact, all other medical specialists—look at the organs they treat, while psychiatrists only guess at what's wrong with a patient based on their symptoms. Unfortunately, this often leads to missed diagnoses and failed treatments. Here's an example.

CYST

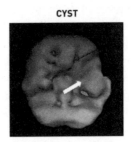

When I first met 17-year-old Coti, he told me he wanted to cut his mother up into little pieces. His dark, evil thoughts were out of control. He had failed treatment with six psychiatrists and been in a 15-month residential treatment program, along with a 30-day drug treatment program. He had the largest brain cyst I'd ever seen. It was the size of a tennis ball, occupying the space of his left frontal and temporal lobes. His behavior improved when the cyst was removed, although he still had leftover issues because of the lasting damage the cyst had caused. Over the years, I have heard many people complain about the cost of scans, yet for people like Coti, untreated brain problems are dramatically more expensive in terms of money, family stress, and lack of freedom.

Most people who struggle with "mental health" issues see a professional who'll ask them to describe their symptoms. Based on what patients tell them, they'll give a diagnosis and prescribe a treatment plan, all without any biological information. For example, a patient may say, "I'm depressed," and it's likely they'll get a diagnosis with the same name—depression—and then be prescribed an antidepressant, which according to a number of large studies works no better than a placebo except for the most severely depressed. If they say they're anxious, unfocused, or have mood swings, they'll likely end up with the diagnostic labels of an anxiety disorder, attention deficit hyperactivity disorder, or bipolar disorder, and be prescribed anti-anxiety medication, such as Xanax (which has been found to be associated with causing dementia[22]); stimulant medications, such as Adderall; or lithium to stabilize their moods. All without any information about how their brain works. And they call me crazy?

TODAY'S PRACTICE: *Watch my TEDx talk titled "The Most Important Lesson from 83,000 Scans," which can be found at youtube.com/watch?v=esPRsT-lmw8.*

Is It Depression or Dementia?

Stop flying blind. I remember one of my first brain scan patients, Matilda. She was an older woman who had absentmindedly left her stove on, almost causing her house to catch fire. She had also been in a few car crashes, resulting in her losing her license. Her family brought her to the hospital because they didn't know what to do. She had been diagnosed with Alzheimer's disease, and it was clearly getting worse. Her adult children wanted to put her in a care facility to keep her safe. But one of her daughters had heard about Amen Clinics and made an appointment. They decided this would be their last try to get her help. She told me we were their last hope.

My first thought when I met Matilda was that she did indeed have Alzheimer's disease, but her SPECT scan showed something else. In the regions that usually show Alzheimer's damage, her scan looked healthy. What I saw instead were signs of depression. The two often present similar symptoms. So I prescribed an antidepressant for Matilda, which can be exactly what someone needs for their brain health.

TYPICAL ALZHEIMER'S   **MATILIDA PSEUDO DEMENTIA**

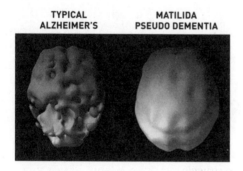

The great news was that it didn't take long for Matilda's memory to improve. Once it did, she was more talkative and began assisting other patients in the same wing of the hospital. Within four weeks, she was ready to go back to her own home. That's when she asked me for a favor. Would I send a letter to the DMV so she could get her driver's license back? So we made a deal. If she continued to take her medication and do everything I prescribed and she was still better in six months with a scan to prove it, I would do what I could to help her get her license again. Guess who was able to drive again just six months later? Her follow-up SPECT scan showed so much improvement that she was able to get back behind the wheel safely.

TODAY'S PRACTICE: *Think of the times when you were nearly out of hope for yourself or a loved one. Could brain health have been involved?*

Keeping Memories Alive

Memory makes us who we are. It is the fabric of our soul. It allows us to keep our loved ones close, even when they are far away. Memory houses our joys, our hurts, and all of life's lessons. Memory helps keep us centered and growing. It's also what provides us with a sense of purpose that gives our life meaning. When our memory is diminished, it can rob us of our ability to make good decisions. Memory problems limit our success at work, steal our independence, and ultimately make us vulnerable to the wolves in society who are out to take advantage of us.

Alzheimer's disease (AD), the most common cause of dementia, robs memories, making a person's life unrecognizable. Over six million Americans are living with AD, and that number is expected to more than double by 2060. And the really bad news is that if you are blessed to live to 85 or beyond, you have more than a 33 percent chance of being diagnosed with it.[23] You have a one in three chance of losing your mind. That should motivate all of us to be on an AD prevention program our whole lives.

Most doctors and scientists think that AD is genetic. It partially is, but my colleagues and I have come to believe that AD is, in large part, a lifestyle illness, and if you get your habits right, you significantly lower your risk for AD and other forms of dementia. Getting your brain healthy also decreases your risk for anxiety, depression, attention deficit hyperactivity disorder, or addictions.

If you want to keep your brain healthy or rescue it if it is headed for trouble, you must prevent or treat the 11 BRIGHT MINDS risk factors that steal your brain, memory, and mind. In the next few weeks, we will explore all of these risk factors in detail.

TODAY'S PRACTICE: *If you have not taken the Memory Rescue Quiz to see which BRIGHT MINDS risk factors you may have at memoryrescue.com/assessment, do it now.*

B Is for Blood Flow

Brain cells do not age; it's your blood vessels that age. Blood flow is critical to life. Blood carries nutrients to every cell in the body and removes toxins. Low blood flow is the number one brain imaging predictor of Alzheimer's disease. Anything that damages your blood vessels starves your brain of the nutrients it needs.

So how do you improve blood flow today? Limit caffeine and nicotine. Both constrict blood flow to the brain. A cup of coffee a day is not a problem, but more caffeine than that can be trouble. Be serious about treating high blood pressure—as blood pressure goes up, blood flow to the brain goes down. If you have any heart issues, be serious about treating them—anything that damages your heart also damages your brain. Avoid being a couch potato. Eating chili peppers and beets can help increase blood flow, as can taking the supplement ginkgo (the prettiest brains I've ever seen take ginkgo). Exercise, particularly activities that involve coordination, such as tennis or table tennis, and walk briskly. Did you know that people who are 80 who can walk three miles an hour have a 90 percent chance of living to 90, but those who can only walk one mile an hour have a 90 percent chance they won't live to 90?[24] I also like a treatment called hyperbaric oxygen therapy because I've seen it increase blood flow to the brain. More on hyperbaric oxygen therapy soon.

TODAY'S PRACTICE: *Walk like you are late everywhere you go today.*

The World's Best Brain Sport

In table tennis, you have to get your eyes, hands, and feet all working together while you think about the spin on the ball. My favorite brain game is table tennis. Some people laugh when I say this at lectures, but I'm serious. If you think it is only a basement recreational game, you haven't met my mother (the same mother with the perfect brain). When I was a child, she beat everyone who played on our backyard table. Table tennis is like aerobic chess. It is great for hand-eye coordination and reflexes and requires you to use many different areas of the brain at once while you track the ball, plan shots, and figure out spins. It works the cerebellum at the back bottom part of the brain, which is critical for coordination but also thought coordination, or how quickly you can integrate new information. Plus, unlike many other sports, table tennis causes very few head injuries.

In the United States there are many table tennis clubs and, increasingly, many great players. Pickleball has many of the same benefits. It's played on a smaller version of a tennis court and is exploding in popularity. The best way to start playing either sport is to get the equipment and learn the basics of the game. I often recommend getting a USATT (United States of America Table Tennis) coach to ramp up skill quickly. It will be more fun if you can play well. You can learn more about table tennis—including its rules, equipment, coaches, and places to play—at usatt.org or pickleball at usapickleball.org.

TODAY'S PRACTICE: *Find a place to play at least one game of table tennis or pickleball.*

Brain Health Can Improve Your Sex Life

Whatever is good for your heart is good for your brain—and your genitals. This is one of my favorite sayings to help people realize they are often missing an important element when it comes to a healthy and satisfying sex life. It's all about blood flow, and anything that decreases blood flow damages both your brain and your ability to make love.

One of the reasons that Viagra-like medicines are so popular is that so many people have blood flow problems. If a man has erectile dysfunction, it also means he likely has brain dysfunction. If you have blood flow problems anywhere, they are typically everywhere, including in the brain. So if you want to improve your sex life, you must improve your blood flow. Here are four simple ways to improve your blood flow:

1. Spend 10–20 minutes a day in prayer or meditation—both improve blood flow to the prefrontal cortex, reduce anxiety, and boost mood.
2. Get hyperbaric oxygen therapy (HBOT). Before-and-after SPECT scans from a 2011 study showed remarkable overall improvement in blood flow following 40 sessions of HBOT.[25] Learn more about HBOT on Day 43.
3. Drink more water and limit your salt intake.
4. Get enough sleep. A lack of sleep can cause testosterone, estrogen, and progesterone (all essential sex hormones) to drop.

I don't know about you, but this makes me want to take better care of myself. To be a great lover you have to protect your blood flow. You do this by eliminating anything that decreases blood flow, such as smoking or ingesting too much caffeine, and fully treating illnesses that negatively affect blood flow, such as high blood pressure, heart disease, and diabetes. Improved sexual function is one of the biggest benefits of a brain health program.

TODAY'S PRACTICE: *List any blood flow risk factors you have and start tackling one of them.*

Caffeine and the Brain

Caffeine constricts blood flow to the brain. Dwayne, 45, came to the clinic because his energy had been waning and his mind felt older than his age. He had trouble concentrating, was starting to mix up names, was increasingly forgetful, and was struggling with mental fatigue throughout the day, especially midafternoon and evening. He was working two jobs, an Air Force pilot during the day and a psychotherapist in the evening. His SPECT scan showed decreased blood flow. Dwayne had a slew of bad brain habits. He rarely got more than five hours of sleep, drank eight to ten cups of coffee a day, did not exercise, and mostly had a fast-food diet on the run. Dwayne had sent me plenty of patients for scans, so when he saw his own brain, he knew something had to change. "But I can't stop the caffeine," he said. "I will not be able to work at night. I will be a mess."

"That is only your distorted thought giving a justification for the caffeine," I said. Because of our relationship and the fact that Dwayne was a psychotherapist who understood my work, I could be candid with him. "You do not want to go through the pain of withdrawal, so you rationalize that it is easier to continue to poison yourself."

"No, seriously, I will fall apart without the caffeine," he replied.

"Is that true?" I asked. "Can you absolutely know that is true?"

Dwayne thought for a moment, then said, "I guess I really don't know, but something has got to change." Dwayne realized that his thoughts were only setting him up to fail, and he agreed to cut back on his caffeine use, get better sleep, and get on a brain-healthy diet. (See days 234–258.) A month later, I got an excited call from Dwayne. He told me he had completely cut out the caffeine and that he was sleeping and eating better. "I feel 10 years younger," he said.

TODAY'S PRACTICE: *How much caffeine do you consume each day? Cut it down by 25 percent and see how you feel.*

Consider Hyperbaric Oxygen Therapy

The chamber of healing. In Justin Bieber's docuseries *Seasons*, he showed the world how he slept in his hyperbaric oxygen chamber.[26] I don't think you need to sleep in it, but it does have many healing benefits. Hyperbaric oxygen therapy (HBOT) uses the power of oxygen to create a healing environment for the body, speeding up the healing process and reducing inflammation. During HBOT, a person lies down or sits in a chamber with increased air pressure, which allows the lungs to gather more oxygen. That means more oxygen gets into blood vessels and tissues, which can increase production of growth factors and stem cells, promoting healing.

Normally, oxygen is carried throughout the body by red blood cells alone. With HBOT, oxygen dissolves into other bodily fluids, such as plasma, cerebral spinal fluid, and lymph, and can be carried to regions where circulation is low or damaged. In vascular problems—strokes and non-healing wounds, for example—adequate oxygen cannot reach damaged areas, diminishing the body's natural ability to heal. When extra oxygen reaches these troubled areas, it speeds the healing process. Researchers have found that increased oxygen strengthens the ability of white blood cells to kill bacteria, reduces swelling, and allows new blood vessels to grow into damaged areas.[27] It is a simple, noninvasive, and painless treatment with minimal side effects.

BEFORE   AFTER HBOT

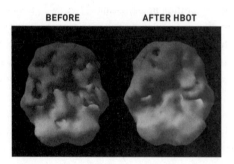

Research suggests HBOT can be helpful for head injuries, low blood flow to the brain, strokes, fibromyalgia, Lyme disease, burns, diabetic skin ulcers, wound healing, and more.[28] Dr. Paul Harch and I, along with other colleagues, published a study on soldiers who had experienced blast-induced traumatic brain injuries. We showed with SPECT that HBOT improved blood flow, as well as increasing IQ, memory, mood, and quality of life scores.[29] The scan on this page is of one of my NFL players before and after HBOT.

TODAY'S PRACTICE: *Try HBOT or another method to boost your oxygen intake. HBOT is available at Amen Clinics, or find an HBOT chamber near you by checking the International Hyperbarics Association website (ihausa.org).*

The Good Ruler vs. Evil Ruler Strategies to Create and End Mental Illness: Blood Flow

The number one strategy to support your brain and mental health is to protect, nurture, and optimize your heart and blood vessels. To keep us from having good blood flow, an evil ruler would pass out video game consoles and online streaming services to all her subjects, stealing their time and attention so they can't find the time to exercise; encourage schools to cut physical education programs from the curriculum; make coffee shops plentiful (caffeine constricts blood flow to the brain); encourage a higher incidence of hypertension, heart disease, heart attacks, and hardening of the arteries by making cigarettes and marijuana widely available for a low price (both decrease blood flow); put fast-food restaurants on every street corner; allow subjects to supersize meals for just a few pennies; withhold calorie counts on menus so people have no idea how much they are consuming; and give away free desserts with every meal—because the population deserves it!

A good ruler would encourage exercise in schools, churches, and the workplace; limit video games and screen time so children and adults spend more time outdoors exercising; advocate annual screening for any vascular issues and enthusiastically treat them early when signs of trouble arise; and make brain health education mandatory at schools and businesses so people understand the blood flow effects of caffeine, energy drinks, nicotine, and marijuana.

TODAY'S PRACTICE: *Get help for any issues that damage your blood flow, such as coronary artery disease, heart arrhythmias, prediabetes, diabetes, high blood pressure, insomnia, sleep apnea, or erectile dysfunction.*

R Is for Retirement and Aging

One of the most exciting lessons I've learned from looking at all our scans is that your brain does not have to deteriorate. You can slow or even reverse the aging process. Increasing age is a major risk factor for memory loss and other brain issues. The older you get, the more serious you need to be about doing the right things. From our imaging work, it's clear that your brain typically becomes less and less active with age. I hate that! Here is a SPECT scan of a healthy 35-year-old compared to a 55-year-old man with mild memory problems and a typical 82-year-old woman who suffers from memory problems and depression. Now, compare these to my grandmother's scan at 92. She lived to 98 with a completely clear mind.

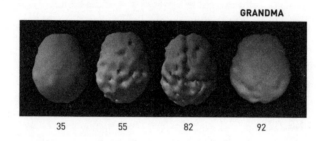

GRANDMA

35   55   82   92

To decrease the risks that come with retirement and aging, avoid loneliness (a big issue during the pandemic), being in a job that does not require new learning, or being retired and not challenging your brain. When you stop learning, your brain starts dying. Avoid having short telomeres if you can help it. Telomeres are the end caps of chromosomes that protect your genes. Shorter telomeres are associated with aging and memory problems, but it's not inevitable. Several years ago, I had my own telomeres tested. I was 63 at the time, but my telomere age was 43.

To slow the effects of retirement and aging, research shows that lifelong learning and memory training programs help.[30] Whenever you learn something new, your brain makes a new connection. You need to vary mental workouts (see tomorrow's essay). You can increase telomere length by being socially connected and volunteering, taking a multivitamin, meditating, and eating foods that contain vitamin C, such as strawberries and red bell peppers. One of my grandmother's secrets was that she kept her mind active and spent thousands of hours knitting blankets for those she loved. Knitting is a coordination exercise that activates a part of the brain called the cerebellum, involved with processing speed and memory.

TODAY'S PRACTICE: *Spend 15 minutes today learning something new.*

Best Mental Exercises for Your Brain

Just doing crossword puzzles is like going to the gym, doing right bicep curls, and then leaving. You have to work out your whole brain. The best mental exercise is acquiring new knowledge and doing things you've not done before. Even if your routine activities are fairly complicated, such as teaching a college course, reading brain scans, or fixing a crashed computer network, they won't necessarily boost your brain because they aren't new. Whenever the brain does something over and over, it learns how to do it using less and less energy. Continuous new learning, such as learning a new medical technique, a new hobby, or a new game, helps establish new connections, thus maintaining and improving the function of other less-used brain areas.

Here are some ideas for exercising various parts of the brain:

- Prefrontal cortex: language games, such as Scrabble, Boggle, Wordle, and crossword puzzles; strategy games, such as chess; meditation
- Temporal lobes: memory games, learning to play new instruments
- Parietal lobes: math games like Sudoku, juggling, map reading
- Cerebellum: coordination games, such as table tennis, dancing, yoga, tai chi

NEW LEARNING TIPS

- Spend 15 minutes a day learning something new. Einstein said that if you spend 15 minutes a day studying something, you'll be an expert in a year. In five years you'll be a national expert.
- Take an online course (we offer courses at amenuniversity.com).
- Gain new skills. At work, train for another job or level up with advanced courses in your field. Why not swap roles with one of your coworkers for a few days? This could benefit not only your brain, but also your team as you both develop the ability to back each other up in an emergency.
- Step out of your routines to arouse other parts of your brain. Switch it up by doing some tasks with a different hand or going in the opposite direction; that will activate the other brain hemisphere. Brush your teeth, operate your computer mouse pad, or throw a ball with your less dominant hand; take a different route to work; or walk backwards for a few minutes (as long as you have a guardrail or friend to help you). The goal is to make your brain uncomfortable so it grows.

TODAY'S PRACTICE: *Spend another 15 minutes today learning something new.*

The Good Ruler vs. Evil Ruler Strategies to Create and End Mental Illness: Retirement/Aging

As the brain deteriorates with age, it leads to mood problems, anxiety, irritability, temper flare-ups, and irrational behavior. You don't have to age that way. An evil ruler would promote aging and tell you there's nothing you can do about it. An evil ruler would recommend everyone retire early, stop learning new things, and watch all the television they want, especially the news that focuses on violence, natural disasters, and partisan politics that breeds anger and stress. He would let people watch as many scary movies as they want or play video games for hours on end, both of which wear out the pleasure centers in the brain; encourage people to spend their days in meaningless activities in isolation; demand that people spend hours on social media every day, which increases the risk of depression and obesity; and start children in school too young. Research shows that younger children in school are more likely to be diagnosed with attention deficit hyperactivity disorder (ADD/ADHD), which has been associated with symptoms of mild cognitive impairment in people over age 50.[31] And he would promote lockdowns as a pandemic management strategy, further isolating the elderly, which is associated with cognitive decline and depression.

A good ruler would encourage lifelong learning, purpose, and knitting; discourage children from starting school too young, which can lead to ADD/ADHD; promote cross-training at work; limit television, social media, and scary movies to keep the pleasure centers healthy; encourage regular blood donation for those who have high iron levels; educate people about the benefits of intermittent fasting; provide treatment for ADD/ADHD and learning disabilities so people would enjoy learning; mandate brain health education at schools and businesses, which would highlight the positive effects of lifelong learning.

TODAY'S PRACTICE: *When you don't feel like working out or eating well, ask yourself,* Do I want an old brain or a young one? *Then make sure to include potent antioxidants in your diet, such as berries and green tea.*

/ Is for Inflammation

Inflammation comes from the Latin word "to set a fire." When you have chronic inflammation in your body, it's like you have a low-level fire destroying your organs, which increases your risk of depression and dementia. Three common tests for inflammation include C-Reactive Protein (CRP), Erythrocyte Sedimentation Rate (ESR), and the Omega-3 Index. Rosacea, joint pain, fatigue, and frequent infections are signs of chronic inflammation.

The best way to decrease inflammation is to eliminate anything that causes it, such as an unhealthy gut, low omega-3 levels, high iron levels, a diet filled with processed foods and sugar, and gum disease. I was always too busy to floss until I saw the research showing that gum disease is a major cause of inflammation and memory loss.[32] Now I floss every day. I was recently at the dentist, and he told me that my mouth looks better than ever. I was like a 7-year-old kid, so happy that I wanted to put a sticker on the refrigerator. I even called my wife, Tana, to tell her, and she said, "Seriously? That's what makes you happy?"

To reduce inflammation, floss every day, cook with the yellow spice turmeric or take the supplement curcumins (made from turmeric), and boost your omega-3 fatty acids by eating more fish or taking omega-3 supplements. In a study we published in the *Journal of Alzheimer's Disease*, the hippocampus was healthiest in people who had the highest omega-3 levels.[33] Also take care of your gut health, consider probiotics, and check your ferritin level (a measure of iron storage). Donate blood if your ferritin level is high.

TODAY'S PRACTICE: *Floss today and start making it a daily habit.*

Boost Omega-3s to Calm Inflammation

Omega-3 fatty acids are essential. Insufficient levels of two of the most important omega-3s—eicosapentaenoic acid (EPA) and docosahexaenoic acid (DHA)—have been linked to depression and bipolar disorder, suicidal behavior, inflammation, heart disease, ADD/ADHD, cognitive impairment and dementia, and obesity.[34] Ninety-five percent of Americans do not get enough dietary omega-3 fatty acids.[35] The human body doesn't produce omega-3s on its own, so you have to get it from outside sources, such as fatty fish. If you aren't getting enough of this essential nutrient from your diet, it's bad news for your brain. That's because omega-3s contribute to about 8 percent of your brain's weight. At Amen Clinics, we tested omega-3 levels of 50 consecutive patients who were not taking fish oil supplements. A shocking 49 out of 50—that's 98 percent!—had suboptimal levels. In a subsequent study, we analyzed the scans of 130 patients with their omega-3 levels. Patients with the lowest levels had lower blood flow in the areas of the brain associated with depression and dementia.

Now for happier news. Increasing your intake of omega-3s promotes a more positive mood. For example, studies show that eating fish with high levels of omega-3 fatty acids is correlated to decreased risk of depression and suicide.[36] Even better, having higher levels of EPA are associated with happiness. That's according to exciting research out of Japan, where researchers enlisted 140 female nurses and nursing care workers to assess happiness (measured by the Subjective Happiness Scale), a sense of fulfillment, and omega-3 levels. The research team found that subjective happiness significantly correlated with a sense of fulfillment—being purposeful equated with being happy—as well as the levels of EPA and DHA. The correlation was particularly strong with the levels of EPA.[37] Other studies have also suggested that EPA is more effective in treating depression and other disorders.[38] Most adults should take between 1,000–2,000 mg of omega-3 fatty acids, with a ratio of 60 percent EPA to 40 percent DHA.

TODAY'S PRACTICE: *Make sure to take an omega-3 supplement daily, or focus on eating fatty fish such as salmon or mackerel twice a week.*

The Gut-Brain Connection

Your gut is often called the second brain. Pop quiz: Where are three-quarters of neurotransmitters made? What organ contains two-thirds of immune tissue? What organ contains 10 times more cells than the rest of your body? Your gut. It's lined with about 100 million neurons that are in direct communication with your actual brain, which is why you get butterflies when you are excited or feel queasy when you're upset. Emotional and psychological pain are often also expressed with gut distress. I had chronic diarrhea when I went through a period of grief. You have about 30 feet of tubing that goes from your mouth to the other end. It is lined with a single layer of cells connected to each other with tight junctions that protect your insides from foreign invaders. When the cell junctions widen or become leaky, known as leaky gut, big trouble happens. This condition is associated with chronic inflammation, autoimmune diseases, digestive issues, and brain problems, including mood and anxiety disorders.

Your GI tract is host to an estimated 100 trillion bugs or microorganisms (bacteria, yeast, and others) known as the microbiome. Some of these bugs are beneficial to your health, while others are harmful. Keeping your gut microbiome in proper balance is essential, as it plays a vital role in protecting your gut lining, digestion, and the synthesis of vitamins (K, B12) and neurotransmitters (brain chemicals, such as serotonin). What decreases good bugs? Medications, such as antibiotics, oral contraceptives, and NSAIDS; low levels of omega-3 fatty acids; stress; sugar and artificial sweeteners; gluten; insomnia; toxins such as pesticides; and more.

To increase the health of your microbiome, eat prebiotic foods filled with fiber, such as apples, beans, onions, and root vegetables; as well as consuming probiotics in food or supplement forms. Probiotic foods include kombucha, kimchi, pickled fruits and vegetables, and sauerkraut. Probiotic supplements can also help. Prebiotic and probiotic foods feed the good bacteria in your GI tract.

TODAY'S PRACTICE: *Add more fiber to each meal by adding seeds, nuts, legumes, avocados, berries, or veggies. Which foods will you add today?*

The Good Ruler vs. Evil Ruler Strategies to Create and End Mental Illness: Inflammation

If you have been treated for a brain health issue without success, look at inflammation as a possible root cause. Just as inflammation can ravage your body, it can also damage your brain. An evil ruler would love to promote inflammation by limiting availability of sustainable fatty fish; increasing the availability of processed foods loaded with corn and soy products (high in omega-6 fatty acids that promote inflammation) and sugar (pro-inflammatory); banning flossing; increasing the use of pesticides and spraying crops with potentially dangerous glyphosates; promoting alcohol as a health food and dictating that everyone must drink two glasses of wine a day; encouraging the use of antibiotics, which can kill beneficial gut bacteria, at the first sign of a cough or sniffles; and demanding that food manufacturers add hidden sugars to their products to wipe out good bugs in the gut.

A good ruler would lower inflammation by regularly testing subjects for CRP (C-Reactive Protein), ESR (Erythrocyte Sedimentation Rate), and Omega-3 Index; encouraging healthy gut linings and microbiome by limiting unnecessary antibiotic therapy, pesticides, processed foods, and sugar and by promoting diets loaded with organic colorful vegetables and prebiotic and probiotic foods; making prebiotic and probiotic nutraceuticals available to everyone; encouraging healthy fish consumption (see seafoodwatch.org) and passing out high-quality omega-3 nutraceuticals; teaching about inflammation in schools, especially how important flossing and gum health are to the brain.

TODAY'S PRACTICE: *Ask yourself:* Am I modeling evil ruler or good ruler inflammation strategies?

G Is for Genetics

When I turned 50, my doctor wanted me to have a colonoscopy. I asked him why he didn't want to look at my brain. Wasn't the other end just as important? Brain health issues, such as depression, addiction, attention deficit hyperactivity disorder (ADD/ADHD), and Alzheimer's disease, run in families. Having family members with brain health issues increases your risk, but having the genetic risk is not a death sentence. It should rather be a wakeup call. Here are five strategies to help.

1. **Know your vulnerability and work on prevention as soon as possible.** Obesity and heart disease run in my family, but I am not overweight and do not have heart disease. I know my risks and work hard to avoid them.
2. **Avoid any risk factors that accelerate disease for your genetics.** Any child who wants to play a contact sport with a high likelihood of concussions (football, soccer, hockey, horseback riding, etc.) should be screened for the Apo E4 gene. Its presence increases the risk of cognitive decline and dementia later in life tenfold if there is also a head injury involved. If they have an Apo E4 gene, they should consider non-contact sports, such as golf, tennis, table tennis, cross-country running, track, and dance.
3. **Engage in regular healthy habits to decrease the expression of problem-promoting genes.** Research has shown that vitamin D, blueberries, turmeric, and green tea can decrease the plaques that contribute to Alzheimer's disease.[39]
4. **Early screening.** If you think you're at risk for brain health issues, early screening is essential. As a society we screen our hearts, bones, breasts, and prostate glands, but very few people ever look at their brains. That needs to change.
5. **Stop making excuses, like it's too hard, too expensive, or you don't want to feel deprived.** Trust me, losing your memory and independence is hard and expensive, and you and your family will feel deprived!

TODAY'S PRACTICE: *Evaluate your family history, and list which illnesses tend to run in your family. What can you do to help prevent them? Also, have a cup of green tea or a cup of organic blueberries in honor of your genes.*

Brain Warrior Chalene Transforms Her Life

She was finally able to get out of the basement. Chalene Johnson is a bestselling author, motivational speaker, podcaster, and mother of two. She and I had been friends for a number of years before I was on her podcast. At the end of the show, she said, "You think I have ADD, don't you?" The thought had crossed my mind. Despite all her success, she struggled with memory, focus, distractibility, procrastination, and always being late to appointments. To give you an idea of how bad it was, she had to shut herself in the basement closet just to get work done because any noise seemed to distract and irritate her. To make things worse, Chalene had a family history of Alzheimer's disease, and after listening to me, she hoped to get a plan to avoid it.

Her initial SPECT scan looked terrible. It showed evidence of ADD/ADHD, with low activity in her frontal lobes and low activity in areas vulnerable to Alzheimer's (parietal and temporal lobes). The scan really got her attention. Over the next two years, she did everything we asked, including hyperbaric oxygen therapy and supplementation, and her follow-up scan showed dramatic improvement, decreasing her risk of future problems. More important, she told me that her performance at work, at home, and in her relationships all improved. Plus, she was finally able to get out of the basement!

BEFORE TREATMENT	TWO YEARS LATER
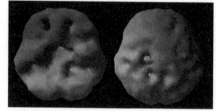	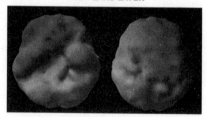

TODAY'S PRACTICE: *How might poor brain function be holding you back? List three ways.*

The Lincoln Legacy

Lincoln's depression gave him the tools to save a nation. Abraham Lincoln's family tree is loaded with brain health issues. His mother, Nancy Lincoln, was described as sad, and his father often got the "blues," with strange spells where he wanted to be alone. His paternal great uncle told a court he had a "deranged mind." His uncle Mordecai Lincoln had severe mood swings, which got worse with heavy drinking. Mordecai's three sons struggled with depression, and one of them swung between depression and mania. One of Abraham Lincoln's first cousins had a daughter, Mary Jane Lincoln, who was committed to the Illinois State Hospital for the Insane. During her trial, the jury concluded that "the disease with her is hereditary," meaning that "mental illness" ran in her family.[40]

According to biographer Joshua Wolf Shenk, Lincoln fought clinical depression all his life, even voicing suicidal thoughts. Yet, at the same time, in many ways he was the epitome of mental health, and he was able to keep the United States together during its darkest days. His genes were not his destiny. Being a politician, "if Lincoln was alive today, his condition would be treated as a 'character issue'—that is, as a political liability. His condition was indeed a character issue: it gave him the tools to save the nation."[41] Shenk argues that because of his depression, Lincoln knew how to suffer and how to rise above his bad feelings in difficult times. Of note, Lincoln had a serious head injury at age 10, when he was kicked in the head by a horse and was unconscious all night. Head injuries, which damage the brain, are a common and often overlooked cause of emotional and behavioral problems.

TODAY'S PRACTICE: *How have your struggles made you a better, stronger person?*

Turn Off the Genes That Make You Vulnerable

Very few of us are free from a family history of trouble. At Amen Clinics, we always take a detailed family history because psychiatric issues tend to run in families. Here are five reasons we do that: (1) Many people who struggle have genetic vulnerabilities. (2) They are more likely to experience lasting stress if they have psychiatric challenges in their family. For example, children who grow up with stress or abuse from a parent or relative are significantly more likely to experience lasting anxiety or depression. (3) The stress of illnesses in prior generations changes genes to become more vulnerable to trouble. Stress, poor diets, environmental toxins, and prenatal nutrition in earlier generations actually change future genes (epigenetics) to be more likely to express trouble. (4) If your family members self-medicate with bad habits, you are likely to pick up those same behaviors, which increases your risk of brain health issues. (5) If your family doesn't care enough about their own health or about your well-being to change their behavior, it can be harder for you to learn to love yourself enough to adopt a healthier lifestyle.

The more of these factors you have, the higher your risk. Think of it this way: When my daughters Breanne, Kaitlyn, and Chloe and granddaughters Emmy and Haven were born, they were born with all of the eggs in their ovaries they will ever have. They were all influenced by their mother's habits and my habits; in turn, their habits will turn on or off certain genes that will make illness more or less likely in them and subsequently in their babies and grandbabies. Similarly, my nieces Alizé and Amelie were born with genes that were influenced by the habits of their parents and grandparents. To end mental illness, we need to focus on brain health in an attempt to turn off any of those genes that increase future generations' vulnerability to psychiatric issues.

TODAY'S PRACTICE: *Go through each of the five reasons above to see which ones might be affecting you or your children.*

The Good Ruler vs. Evil Ruler Strategies to Create and End Mental Illness: Genetics

Your behavior is not just about you. It is about generations of you. But an evil ruler would strive to convince you otherwise. An evil ruler would tell people who have a family history of brain health/mental health illnesses not to worry about taking care of their health because there is nothing they can do about it. An evil ruler would also adopt "Live It Up While You Can" as the nation's public health slogan and tell subjects that they do not have to deal with their emotional baggage because once you are dead you are finished. Yet, the truth is, your behavior is not just about you.

A good ruler would remind you that your behavior impacts the genetics of your children and grandchildren. A good ruler would inform the population that genes are not everything and learn from the misguided eugenics movement of the nineteenth and twentieth centuries; educate the population to know their genetic risks and vulnerabilities by having families tell accurate stories of their ancestors and be serious about prevention as soon as possible; encourage people to be serious about healthy BRIGHT MINDS lifestyle habits; and develop public service programs to let people know about epigenetics and inform them that their behavior is not just about them but also about future generations.

TODAY'S PRACTICE: *What part of your family history or genetic issues do you need to address for the sake of your brain?*

DAY 57

H Is for Head Trauma

Brain injuries are a major cause of psychiatric problems that few people know about because most mental health practitioners never look at the brain. Most people don't know that the brain is the consistency of soft butter, tofu, or somewhere between egg whites and Jell-O. It is also housed in a very hard skull that has many sharp bony ridges. Jarring motions and head injuries can cause the brain to slam into the hard interior of the skull, making brain cells susceptible to tears, bruises, micro-bleeding, and inflammation. Brain injuries can ruin lives, even without a loss of consciousness.

INSIDE THE SKULL

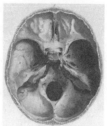

Traumatic brain injuries (TBIs) are often behind issues such as addiction; abuse; anxiety; panic attacks; depression; problems at home, work, or school; suicide; and so much more.[42] While some people develop symptoms immediately after a TBI, others find that symptoms emerge over a period of weeks or months. Because of this delay, the underlying cause of the symptoms is often forgotten and never uncovered. Many times, doctors don't ask about possible brain injuries and don't actually look at the brain with imaging. Instead, the problems are frequently attributed to a psychiatric condition and the person is treated with medication. The impact of head trauma is often overlooked in psychiatry. Even minor head injuries to vulnerable parts of the brain can cause problems for years to come.

There are millions of emergency room visits because of TBIs in the US each year. Imagine how many more unreported incidents of head trauma and undi-agnosed concussions occur. Let's do a better job of preventing head injuries and healing the brain if they do occur. In 2018, several former NFL players called for an end to tackle football for children.[43] In 2021, Brett Favre (who played 20 seasons in the NFL) warned parents about the risks of children playing tackle football.[44] That's a start, but we need this principle to become part of our cultural fabric.

TODAY'S PRACTICE: *To avoid possible head injuries, stop checking your texts while driving or walking today—and all days going forward—to prevent falls or accidents in which you might bump your head.*

Identify Head Injuries of Any Kind

We have to ask people 10 times whether or not they had a head injury. Many people forget they've had a significant head injury. At Amen Clinics, we routinely ask patients several times before they see our physicians. If they say no, I'll ask again, and if I get another no, I'll say, "Are you sure? Have you ever fallen out of a tree, fallen off a fence, or dived into a shallow pool? Did you play contact sports? Have you ever been in a car accident?" I'm constantly amazed at how many people forget they have had significant head injuries. When asked the question for the fifth time, one patient put his hand on his forehead and said, "Oh yeah! When I was 7 years old, I fell out of a second-story window." Likewise, I have had other patients forget they went through car windshields, fell out of moving vehicles, or were knocked unconscious when they fell off their bicycles.

Consider YouTube superstar Logan Paul. The controversial internet personality, who is known for his risk-taking pranks and dangerous stunts, has gained more than 40 million social media followers. But he has also amassed some harsh critics. Logan came to see me to find out why he makes bad decisions, why he lacks empathy, and why he is incapable of maintaining a committed relationship. "I want to figure out why I think and act the way I do," he said. "I'm a bit of a hooligan, a troublemaker."

I asked him if he had ever had a head trauma. He initially said no several times before telling me about a trampoline accident that had fractured his skull when he was in seventh grade. He was also a linebacker and running back in high school. Logan's scan showed low blood flow in his prefrontal cortex, which is associated with bad decisions, lack of empathy, and trouble with relationships.

LOGAN'S SCAN

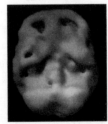

TODAY'S PRACTICE: *Think back through your childhood, teen years, and adulthood for any accident, fall, or sports played that may have impacted your brain. How many head injuries have you had?*

Reversing Brain Damage Is Possible: Amen Clinics NFL Brain Rehabilitation Study

Most thoughtful 10-year-olds could guess that football is a brain-damaging sport. In July 2007, former professional football player Anthony Davis came to see me because he was experiencing problems with memory, periods of confusion, and irritability. A professor at University of Southern California told him about our work, and he thought we could help him. At 54, Anthony's brain looked like he was 85. It showed clear evidence of brain trauma to the prefrontal cortex and left temporal lobe. He was also concerned about the cognitive problems he saw in other retired football players. AD, as he is called by most who know him, is a College Football Hall of Fame running back from the University of Southern California. I put AD on the same brain rehabilitation steps discussed in this book, and within several months he told me that he felt better, was more focused, and had more energy and a better memory.

Meeting AD was the impetus for our large-scale study of brain injury and brain rehabilitation in professional football players. At the time, the NFL was saying they did not know if playing football caused long-term brain damage, but they had never done any brain imaging studies on players to find out. My colleagues and I decided to tackle it. To date, we have scanned and treated more than 300 active and retired players. Clear evidence of brain damage was seen in almost all of them. The most exciting part of our study was that 80 percent of our players showed significant improvement on their SPECT scans and their neuropsychological testing while on our program,[45] proving once again that you are not stuck with the brain you have. Ten years later, AD's brain was significantly better.

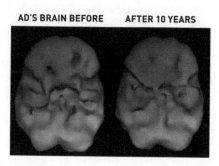

AD'S BRAIN BEFORE   AFTER 10 YEARS

TODAY'S PRACTICE: *Avoid contact sports. Ask yourself if you can continue to watch football the same way now that you know about head trauma.*

Amen Clinics' Position on Chronic Traumatic Encephalopathy (CTE)

I am interested in the living and doing everything I can to delay their journey to the autopsy table. Chronic traumatic encephalopathy (CTE) was brought into the public's awareness largely through the movie *Concussion*, starring Will Smith, based on the work of neuropathologist Bennet Omalu. When he did the autopsy on Pittsburgh Steeler Hall of Fame center Mike Webster, he noticed something very different in his brain that had not been reported: There were excessive deposits of an abnormal protein called tau in his brain.[46] He subsequently noticed this pattern in other NFL players who struggled with severe cognitive and emotional issues. Tau protein is essential, as it provides the lattice-like structure of brain cells. However, when the brain is damaged from repeated concussions, as is common in football and soccer players, tau breaks down and pierces through cell membranes, causing an inflammatory response that damages the brain.

Since CTE can only be diagnosed with certainty on autopsied slices of brain tissue, it can only be diagnosed after death. I am friends with Dr. Omalu, and we have published scientific papers together. I tell him that while his patients are the dead, I am interested in the living. The lore in medical circles is that CTE is permanent, progressive, and untreatable. I think that is nonsense, and there is virtually no scientific evidence to support the lack of hope. Yet because many people believe it, former football players and other professional athletes avoid getting help. Some in the media have accused me of giving people with CTE false hope. Let me be clear: The scans we do at Amen Clinics do not diagnose CTE (you need a pathology slide for that). But what SPECT scans can do is diagnose the current impact of past concussions, and with proper help, the brain can improve. To not do anything to ameliorate the chronic effects of concussions is unconscionable. Let's not wait until people are dead to uncover that something is wrong.

TODAY'S PRACTICE: *Have hope. Even if you have been bad to your brain, it can be better if you put your brain in a healing environment.*

You Must Know about Irlen Syndrome

Certain colors of the light spectrum can change your brain. Irlen syndrome, also called scotopic sensitivity syndrome, is a visual processing problem in which certain colors of the light spectrum irritate the brain. This condition, discovered by therapist Helen Irlen, runs in families and is common after traumatic brain injuries. Anyone experiencing symptoms of anxiety, depression, irritability, decreased concentration, learning issues, or light sensitivity should be screened for it. Common symptoms include headaches, fatigue, problems staying focused in the presence of bright or fluorescent lights, and trouble reading words on white, glossy paper. When reading, words or letters tend to shift, shake, blur, or disappear. Also, there are often problems with depth perception and judging distance and difficulty with such things as escalators, stairs, ball sports, or driving.

Heather, 42, had been in ten car accidents when she came to see us for symptoms of ADD/ADHD, anxiety, and depression. During her history, she told us that she had trouble reading and fluorescent lights gave her headaches. Suspecting Irlen syndrome, we sent her for an evaluation. When we saw her a few weeks later, she was beaming. With Irlen lenses (colored glasses), her focus was better, her anxiety was reduced, and her mood had improved. With Irlen lenses, her follow-up scan was much calmer.

IRLEN SYNDROME: BEFORE AND AFTER IRLEN LENSES

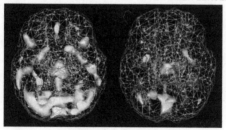

Overactive white areas   Calmer

Despite her improvement, Heather began struggling with depression again. When Heather was young, she was a prodigy guitar player, but she could never learn to read music because the notes would dance on the page. At 12, she smashed her guitar and never played again. Now, 30 years later, she was mourning the loss of what could have been. Heather did not need Prozac to deal with the depression. She needed grief therapy, which we gave her. Within a few weeks, she was back to feeling great and bought herself a new guitar.

TODAY'S PRACTICE: *If any of this sounds familiar, take the self-tests at irlen.com.*

Brain Warrior Captain Patrick Caffrey

When your personality changes, think about the brain. While on mission in the Middle East in the early 2000s, combat engineer officer Captain Patrick Caffrey was part of a team that cleared improvised explosive devices (IEDs). He and his team were bringing in new armored vehicles. At the time, the military believed these armored vehicles were so strong that they could endure a major blast while letting the people inside make it out alive and relatively unharmed. Of course, like most people, Patrick had no clue about traumatic brain injuries, even though he had had several concussions before. He didn't think anything of them, or anything of being in an armored truck that could get blown up. Which it did—three times. Each time he wound up with another concussion. He chalked it up to being a Marine—brave and strong.

When he was done with his tour and headed back to the States, he thought he felt fine, but his personality started to change. He would lash out in anger, which he had never done before.[47] He also noticed that he got irritated easily, often had bad headaches, and couldn't focus or concentrate when trying to listen to other people. His memory was also slipping, and he wasn't sleeping well. Some of the changes he noticed; others he didn't, especially how rude he could be to people. He happened to read one of my books and thought it would be a good idea to come to Amen Clinics for a scan. It turned out that his prefrontal cortex and temporal lobes had both been noticeably damaged, which correlated with his symptoms. We put him on several simple supplements, and in no time he was able to focus, monitor his behavior better, and improve his memory. Patrick became Patrick again and never again underestimated the value of protecting his brain.

PATRICK'S SCAN

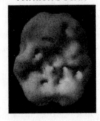

Having served in the US Army for 10 years, first as an enlisted soldier, then as a military physician, I have a heart for war fighters. We've been able to help many through the Change Your Brain, Change Your Life Foundation.

TODAY'S PRACTICE: *If you've experienced a head injury, consider neurofeedback, a noninvasive technique that helps retrain the brain to optimize emotional and behavioral health. Neurofeedback is offered at Amen Clinics. Other providers can be found at isnr.org/find-a-member.*

Distinguishing PTSD from Traumatic Brain Injuries

Discover *magazine listed Amen Clinics' research as one of the top 100 stories in science for 2015.* One of the highlights of my life came in January 2016, when *Discover* magazine listed our research as number 19 of the top 100 stories in all of science for 2015. Our research was sandwiched between Tesla's new entry into renewable energy at number 18 and the discovery of a new dinosaur species at number 20. The research team at Amen Clinics, in collaboration with scientists from UCLA, Thomas Jefferson University, and the University of British Columbia, published one of the world's largest functional brain imaging studies on about 21,000 patients that demonstrated we can distinguish between posttraumatic stress disorder (PTSD) and traumatic brain injury (TBI) using brain SPECT imaging with high accuracy. Our study was published in the prestigious journal *PLOS ONE.*[48] We then replicated the results on a group of veterans, published in the journal *Brain Imaging and Behavior.*[49]

Why were these studies important? These two conditions have many overlapping symptoms, including irritability and/or anger, insomnia or other sleep problems, depression, anxiety, social isolation, impulse control problems, and difficulty with concentration. However, even though some of the symptoms are the same, PTSD and a TBI present with very different patterns on SPECT. Most commonly, PTSD reveals areas of overactivity, while a TBI has areas of decreased activity in the brain. Our study found that with brain SPECT imaging, we were able to distinguish PTSD from TBI with 80 percent to 100 percent accuracy.

The ability to differentiate these disorders from each other is critical for determining the most effective treatment for an individual. Without knowing the underlying biological issue, it is easy to mistake one condition for the other—and the treatments for each are very different. Typically, treatment for PTSD and emotional trauma is to calm the brain, while treatment for a TBI often focuses on increasing activity in the injured areas of the brain. So, for example, if a doctor diagnoses someone with PTSD (but it's really a TBI), a sedating medication might be prescribed. Unfortunately, this is not what someone with a TBI needs because the activity in the brain is already suppressed as a result of the injury, and thus this type of treatment will not likely be of any help and may actually cause further harm.

TODAY'S PRACTICE: *Consider brain SPECT imaging to find out if you have PTSD or a TBI. If you know people who suffer from PTSD or a TBI, send them today's entry.*

The Good Ruler vs. Evil Ruler Strategies to Create and End Mental Illness: Head Trauma

The brain is vulnerable. It is soft and floats in cerebrospinal fluid inside a very hard skull. Whiplash, jarring motions, and blows to the head can slam the brain into the sharp ridges of the skull. An evil ruler would promote anything that puts you at risk for head injuries. An evil ruler would allow children to hit soccer balls with their heads, play tackle football, ski, ride bicycles without helmets, ride large horses, play hockey, and engage in other high-risk behaviors; encourage players on a team (especially the better ones) to go back into the game as quickly as possible after suffering a concussion; put fluorescent lights in all classrooms and workspaces to increase symptoms of anxiety, irritability, depression, or decreased concentration related to Irlen Syndrome (see day 61); create movies where head butting is a common fight tactic.

A good ruler would protect people against head trauma. A good ruler would encourage the population to love their brains and the brains of their children and protect them at all costs; ban children and teenagers from hitting soccer balls with their heads or engaging in high-risk activities. They would make sure the parents of children and teens sign informed consent admitting they know and accept the risks of head injuries. Often parents approve of behaviors because they are unaware of the risks. A good ruler would also consider delaying teens getting their driver's licenses by a year to help cut down on motor vehicle accidents and head injuries.

TODAY'S PRACTICE: *How often do you engage in activities that put you at risk for a head injury? Protect your head by reducing your risk for accidents: Always fasten your seatbelt, wear a helmet when you ride a bike or go skiing, and hold on to railings when walking up or down stairs.*

T Is for Toxins

Many things are toxic for your brain. Know and limit them. Toxic exposure is one of the most common causes of depression, memory loss, and aging.[50] When I first started performing scans, I noticed a toxic pattern on the brains of substance abusers—whether alcoholics, cocaine addicts, or marijuana users. The scans taught me another important lesson: There are many other things that are toxic to your brain, such as smoking, secondhand smoke, mold exposure from water damage, carbon monoxide, cancer chemotherapy and radiation, and heavy metals, including mercury, aluminum, and lead. Did you know that when the government took lead out of gasoline, they left it in small airplane fuel? At Amen Clinics, we scanned 100 pilots and found that 70 percent had toxic-looking brains. Lead is also found in 60 percent of lipstick sold in the US.[51] Be careful whom you kiss; it could be the kiss of death. If you have any toxic exposures, including chemotherapy or mold exposure, similar to having a genetic risk or head trauma, you need to be even more serious about taking care of your brain.

To decrease your toxic risk, limit exposure whenever you can, buy organic to decrease pesticides, and read the labels. If a product lists ingredients such as phthalates, parabens, or aluminum, don't buy it. What goes on your body goes in your body and affects your brain. In addition, support the four organs of detoxification. For your kidneys, drink more water; for your gut, make sure to eat plenty of fiber; for your liver, eat brassicas, which are detoxifying vegetables such as broccoli, cauliflower, cabbage, and brussels sprouts; for your skin, sweat with exercise and take saunas. A recent study showed that people who took the most saunas had the lowest risk of memory problems.[52]

TODAY'S PRACTICE: *Drink more water to help flush out your toxic load. Engage in regular cardio exercise that makes you sweat.*

15 Toxins That Damage Your Brain and Steal Your Mind

Every day we are exposed to a host of chemicals, pesticides, fumes, and products that poison the human brain. Common toxins in the air we breathe, the foods we eat, and the products we rub on our skin are absorbed into our bodies via our lungs, digestive systems, and pores and can eventually impact the brain. The more exposure you have to these everyday toxins, the more you're putting your brain at risk and increasing your chances of mental health issues.

Take the following quiz to get a better idea of your brain's toxic load. The more questions you answer *yes* to, the more toxic your brain is likely to be.

1. Do you smoke or are you around secondhand smoke?
2. Do you use marijuana?
3. Have you been exposed to carbon monoxide?
4. Do you pump your own gas or breathe automobile exhaust?
5. Do you live in an area with moderate to high air pollution, or are you being exposed to wildfires?
6. Have you lived or worked in a building that had water damage and mold in it?
7. Do you come in contact with clothing, carpet, or furnishings sprayed with chemicals to prevent stains?
8. Do you spray your garden, farm, or orchard with pesticides or live near an area with pesticides?
9. Do you have more than two glasses of alcohol a week?
10. Do you regularly eat conventionally raised produce, meat, dairy, or farm-raised fish?
11. Do you eat nonorganic fruits and vegetables on a regular basis?
12. Do you consume foods with artificial colors or sweeteners, such as diet sodas, or use artificial sweeteners, such as aspartame (NutraSweet), sucralose (Splenda), or saccharin (Sweet'N Low)?
13. Do you use more than two health and/or beauty products per day? (Most people never read the labels and don't realize how many chemicals are included. See day 70.)
14. Do you have mercury amalgam fillings?
15. Do you use plastic containers to store food and drink?

TODAY'S PRACTICE: *Write down the number of potential toxins you have and make a plan to eliminate at least one of them.*

I Told You So: Why the American Cancer Society Says to Stop Drinking

When I was dating my wife, she said, "I will never tell you 'I told you so.'" She lied. It is one of her favorite things to say. Now it's my turn to say it. For more than 30 years, I've been telling my patients that alcohol is not a health food. Many of them respond by asking, "But what about all the studies saying moderate drinking is good for your heart?" It's true that some studies point to benefits for heart health with moderate drinking, but others show a different result. Recently, the American Cancer Society (ACS) took a major position in the debate by revising its cancer prevention guidelines, stating, "It is best not to drink alcohol." I told you so! Any alcohol use is associated with an increase in seven types of cancers (mouth, pharynx, larynx, colorectal, esophageal cancers, liver, and breast). The ACS website says, "Alcohol use is one of the most important preventable risk factors for cancer, along with tobacco use and excess body weight."[53]

Our brain imaging work on thousands of patients shows that "moderate" drinkers often have a toxic-looking brain, which can increase cognitive and emotional dysfunction. Furthermore, research has shown that people who drink every day have smaller brains, especially in the hippocampus.[54] Alcohol lowers activity in the prefrontal cortex, which decreases judgment and decision-making skills and increases cravings. Excessive alcohol use is a major cause of divorce, domestic violence, and motor vehicle accidents and deaths. Alcohol is also a disinfectant, which means it can negatively impact the microbiome or health of your gut. About three-quarters of your neurotransmitters are produced in your gut, and they are in direct communication with your brain. Trouble in the gut has been linked to depression, anxiety, ADD/ADHD, and Alzheimer's disease.

When you see all the negative effects of alcohol, it becomes apparent that it is not a health food. If you want a better brain, a better mind, better physical health, and a better life, it's best to avoid or severely limit alcoholic beverages.

TODAY'S PRACTICE: *Begin a weeklong (or permanent) break from any alcohol.*

Is Marijuana Innocuous?

People ask me about all sorts of things on social media, but I've noticed that one of the most common questions I get is about the use and safety of marijuana. In scanning thousands of marijuana users over the years, it is clear that this plant powerfully impacts the brain. Over time, it gives the brain a toxic appearance in many users. Marijuana significantly lowers brain activity, and I've seen it decrease memory, motivation, learning, focus, and coordination. In young people it also increases the risk of psychosis. According to the National Institutes of Drug Abuse, marijuana can lead to a drop in IQ by eight points and is linked to lower educational outcomes, with users less likely to graduate from high school or college. Users also have a lower overall satisfaction with life and are more likely to earn a lower income or be unemployed.[55]

HEALTHY   **AGE 18, DAILY USER**

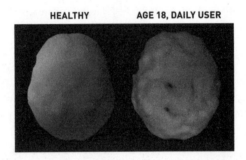

People who come to our clinics report that using marijuana makes them feel less socially anxious and sometimes less depressed, which is why they use it, but chronic recreational use clearly takes its toll and outweighs any benefit in the moment. In one study on veterans with posttraumatic stress disorder (PTSD), researchers tested marijuana as a treatment. Results showed that marijuana use was significantly associated with higher PTSD symptom severity, as well as higher levels of violent behavior and alcohol and drug use.[56] In another study of 322 children, those whose mothers' placenta tested positive for marijuana had an increased risk of severe anxiety, aggression, and hyperactivity.[57]

Is marijuana worse than alcohol or some legal prescription drugs, such as Xanax or Valium? Not really, in my experience. None of them are good for your brain over the long term. I posted the image above to social media, and it has over a million views and thousands of shares.

TODAY'S PRACTICE: *Quit marijuana use, even if it's only occasional. The damage outweighs the potential benefits.*

Can General Anesthesia Damage the Brain?

There's a risk anesthesiologists don't warn you about. I first became aware of the potentially toxic risk of general anesthesia when a patient of mine called me in tears after knee surgery. She felt like she had brain fog and was afraid she was getting Alzheimer's disease. I had already done a SPECT scan on her, so I rescanned her to see if her brain had changed. On the new scan, her brain looked toxic and was significantly worse in her frontal and temporal lobes, which are both involved in memory and attention. It was clear that something had negatively affected her brain after that first scan.

With the approach in this book, she was able to clear the brain fog and regain her memory. Current research on general anesthesia is mixed, with some studies showing no lasting negative effects and some showing toxic effects, but two recent studies stand out. In one, children who had undergone general anesthesia before the age of 4 had lowered IQs, diminished language comprehension, and decreased gray matter in the back of their brains.[58] That is very concerning. Also a before-and-after SPECT study of patients who underwent coronary artery bypass surgery showed that 68 percent had diminished blood flow, which was linked to decreased verbal and visual memory six months later.[59] Often surgery and general anesthesia are unavoidable, so make sure to do everything you can to optimize your brain before and after going under the knife.

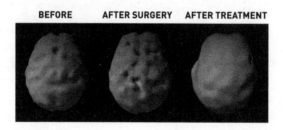

BEFORE   AFTER SURGERY   AFTER TREATMENT

My assistant Karen, whom my patients love, discovered she had an aortic aneurysm and had an eight-hour procedure to repair it. But she was not the same person when she returned. We had a prior SPECT scan, one shortly after the procedure, and then one after she worked hard to rehabilitate her brain. The surgery had a very negative impact on her brain and mind that was recoverable with the right BRIGHT MINDS program.

TODAY'S PRACTICE: *If you must have surgery, opt for local or spinal anesthesia if possible and do everything you can before your procedure to optimize your brain health.*

Personal Care Products:
The Ugly Side of Health and Beauty Aids

What goes on your body goes in your body and affects your body. How many personal care and cosmetic products do you use each day? If you're like the average American woman, that would be about 12 products, and for the average man, about six.[60] According to Statista, the cosmetics, perfume, and personal care industry spent close to 4 billion dollars on advertising in 2020[61] to encourage us to use more of these everyday items. But the chemicals in these products are easily absorbed through your skin and can be transported to every organ in your body, including your brain. This means that while trying to look better on the outside, you could be poisoning yourself on the inside and increasing your risk for brain health or mental health issues. The risk from these items is real. In 2016, Johnson & Johnson was ordered to pay 72 million dollars to the family of a woman whose death from ovarian cancer was associated with the daily use of Johnson's Baby Powder among other company products.[62]

Chemicals in health and beauty products to nix include acrylates (artificial nails), aluminum (deodorants), parabens (cosmetics, conditioners, lotions), phthalates (nail polish, cosmetics, soaps, shampoos, packaging), formaldehyde (shampoos, body wash, nail color), fragrance (shampoos, color cosmetics), oxybenzone (sunscreen), polyethylene glycols (PEGs) (soaps, bubble baths), and triclosan (toothpaste).

If you have symptoms associated with brain health issues, I highly recommend that you ditch personal care products with harmful ingredients to lighten your toxic load. The Environmental Working Group's Skin Deep database (ewg.org/skindeep/) can help, as can the app Think Dirty. They contain information on many products with toxic ingredients and suggest healthier options. The book *The Toxin Solution,* by Joseph Pizzorno, ND, a founder of Bastyr University, is an excellent resource.

TODAY'S PRACTICE: *Download the Think Dirty app and scan the products in your bathroom. For the products you use every day, get rid of two that score high in toxins and replace them with nontoxic alternatives.*

Brain Warrior Dave Asprey and Mold

It's not me; it's my biology. After reading *Change Your Brain, Change Your Life*, Dave Asprey had a SPECT scan done in 2003. An exceptionally bright computer engineer, he'd been employed by a tech start-up that had been acquired for over half a billion dollars while working on his MBA at Wharton. But something was off with his mental sharpness. On exams, he could get through the first few questions, but then serious brain fog would cloud his thinking, and he could barely recall his own name. He felt like he must just be lazy or wasn't trying hard enough. He admits that it was so debilitating he almost didn't graduate.

The results of his SPECT scan weren't good. "Total chaos" is how his psychiatrist described his abnormal brain activity. Rather than being demoralized by the sight of his unhealthy brain, Dave felt a sense of relief as he thought, *It's not me; it's my biology.* Gone were the negative feelings of shame, and in their place was a new resolve to take action to change his biology and heal his broken brain. The biohacker was born.

DAVE'S SCAN BEFORE   13 YEARS LATER

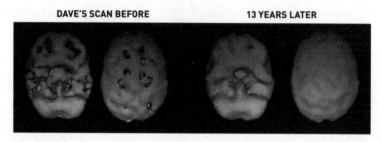

Further investigation revealed why Dave's brain looked so bad—his home was filled with toxic mold. Following a brain rehabilitation program helped him regain his mental clarity. Seeing his scan was the key that unlocked his ability to take control of his health and turned him into a brain warrior. More than a dozen years later, his follow-up SPECT scan was significantly improved. Passionate about sharing his story of how toxic mold can negatively impact health and psychological well-being, he produced a landmark documentary called *Moldy: The Toxic Mold Movie*. Common symptoms of mold exposure include fatigue, tremors, brain fog, trouble focusing, headaches, numbness and tingling, memory problems, mood swings, and anxiety.

TODAY'S PRACTICE: *Watch the documentary* Moldy: The Toxic Mold Movie *(https:// www.youtube.com/watch?v=VI0_azQv6N8).*

The Vulnerability of First Responders

Our heroes need protection. Steven, 32, was a firefighter who suffered from depression, brain fog, and symptoms of posttraumatic stress disorder (PTSD) when he first came to see me. I had already seen his brother for learning issues at school, his father for job-related anxiety, and his stepmother for depression. All of them had mentioned to me their concern for Steven, especially after learning about the connection between brain health and mental health. Firefighters are exposed to environmental toxins, head trauma, and emotional trauma.

BEFORE   AFTER

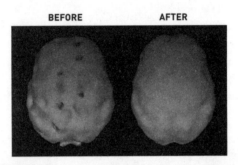

    Steven initially asked me, "How can I deal with the trauma? I wish I could forget what my eyes have seen, from children being burned to losing whole families in car crashes and fires." His scan showed signs of PTSD, with his emotional brain working way too hard, plus he also had evidence of toxic exposure, likely from breathing carbon monoxide and the poisonous chemicals often released by burning furniture. This toxic look is very common among the many firefighters we've seen. Seeing his scan caused Steven to get serious about brain health. Within six months he felt much better and his brain was healthier.

    Steven isn't alone. Firefighters, police, and first responders—the everyday heroes in our society—are involved in dangerous professions that pose many health risks and can have a long-lasting, negative impact on their brain function. They are exposed to environmental toxins such as carbon monoxide, benzene, asbestos, and diesel exhaust; head injuries; and emotional trauma. Studies show an elevated risk of PTSD, depression, heavy drinking, and suicide in first responders.[63] Unfortunately, they are less likely to seek help because of the stigma associated with having a mental illness. They fear they will be labeled as weak or unfit for duty.[64] Their professions have convinced them that they are superheroes and that nothing can hurt them, which is false.

TODAY'S PRACTICE: *Whether or not you are a first responder, identify any traumatic events in your life that may have led to PTSD, anxiety, depression, drug use, or alcohol abuse. Schedule therapy to address them.*

The Key to Marriage Therapy

"I used to paint cars in a closed garage." I've given many lectures to large groups over the years. Often people then come to visit Amen Clinics for a brain checkup. When I show up to a conference or church for a second time, I often encounter quite a few people who want to show their SPECT scans to me. One time, a young man in his midthirties approached me in a lecture hall and asked me to look at his scan (below). It looked like Swiss cheese, which means he had very low activity all over—a pattern we usually see in people who abuse drugs or alcohol.

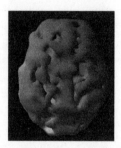

He asked me if I thought he was a drug addict. That was my first thought! But he told me he had never used drugs and didn't consume alcohol. The problem came from one of his hobbies: He used to paint cars in his garage, and he had never ensured there was good ventilation. After getting his brain scanned, he stopped exposing himself to those toxic fumes.

"That is the sign of intelligent life," I told him. "New information causes you to change your behavior."

His change in behavior not only helped his brain; it also helped his marriage. For years, he and his wife had been meeting with a counselor without making progress. That all changed after his brain scan. He started taking a multivitamin, fish oil, and the other brain-healthy supplements we recommended, along with eating better and exercising. As his brain got better, he was able to be a better husband.

I wonder how many marriages are suffering because one partner has a brain problem that no one is aware of. How do you do marital therapy with this brain? It will never work until you heal your brain.

TODAY'S PRACTICE: *Think about your typical day. Are you exposed to toxic fumes on a regular basis from construction work, carpentry, home remodeling, airport/gas station work, or nail/hair salons?*

Your House May Be Harming Your Brain

The human body is designed to detox itself, but it needs your help. Every day we're exposed to chemicals, pesticides, fumes, and products—even if we never leave the house. Environmental toxins occupy the air we breathe (pollution, vehicle exhaust, cleaning fumes, mold), make up the substances we ingest (pesticides, artificial dyes and preservatives, medications), and fill the products we put on our skin or hair (beauty and personal care products).

Our lungs, digestive system, and pores absorb these chemicals, which inevitably make it to the brain. And that's where these toxins can poison the brain; they inhibit blood flow, interrupt hormone production, and mess with the gut microbiome. On top of physical issues—such as autoimmune diseases, diabetes, and cancer—toxins are often a culprit of many mental health symptoms. Conventional psychiatrists frequently overlook toxic exposure as a potential root cause of symptoms, which can lead to a misdiagnosis. And getting the wrong diagnosis means you get the wrong treatment, which doesn't help you get better and can actually make you worse!

The greater your level of exposure to common toxins, the greater your risk of damage to your brain. Although you can't eliminate all your exposure, you can reduce your risk. Considering how much time you spend at home, a thorough detox of where you live is the best place to start.

1. Use apps such as Healthy Living from the Environmental Working Group or Think Dirty to help you identify household and beauty products you should toss. Both apps rate products based on how many toxic ingredients they include (parabens, phthalates, lead, aluminum, PEGS). They also offer "approved" products to help you find suitable replacements.
2. Don't eat or drink out of plastic containers. Don't warm up food in plastic containers.
3. Don't forget to look at what's in your garage (such as paint, solvents, antifreeze) and what you're using on your lawn (such as weed killers and pesticides).

Rid your home of any cigarettes, alcohol, or drugs (including legal substances like marijuana) that contribute to brain toxicity.

TODAY'S PRACTICE: *Find five products in your home (outside of the bathroom, which you scanned on day 70) that are toxic. Replace them with a clean alternative.*

Vaping and the Brain

The smaller the particle you inhale, the greater its ability to cause inflammatory reactions and damage your brain. Vaping nicotine or THC causes you to inhale a host of fine and ultrafine toxins that can penetrate your lungs and brain. Does size matter? Yes! Smaller particles cause greater inflammatory reactions and damage your brain. There's no question that vaping is addictive, and teens and adults are getting hooked. E-cigarettes contain nicotine, a highly addictive substance that is quickly absorbed into the blood vessels that line the lungs. With vaping, it takes only about 10 seconds for nicotine to reach the brain. That's where it hijacks the brain's reward system. Nicotine binds to receptors in the brain, causing it to pump out large doses of the feel-good neurotransmitter dopamine. This dopamine surge can be 2 to 10 times what your brain releases for natural rewards—such as hearing your favorite song on the radio, hitting a home run in baseball, or eating a delicious peach. Over time, large dopamine surges diminish dopamine's effectiveness, and this makes people need more and more of it to get the same effect. Nicotine causes other problems too. It constricts blood vessels, lowering blood flow to the brain. This deprives the brain of the nutrients it needs and eventually causes lower overall activity.

E-cigarettes raise the risk of mental health problems. A 2019 study found that university students who used e-cigarettes were significantly more likely to have mental health disorders, such as ADD/ADHD, anxiety, PTSD, gambling issues, and drug use.[65] The problem with vaping is getting worse. In 2018, the U.S. Surgeon General called e-cigarette vaping among youth an "epidemic." In one report, more than 20 percent of high school students nationwide said they had vaped nicotine in the previous month. That's twice the number who had reported vaping in 2017.[66] Younger kids are also jumping on the trend, with 11 percent of eighth graders saying they had smoked e-cigarettes in the past year.[67]

TODAY'S PRACTICE: *Discourage your kids from vaping, and stop vaping yourself if it's a habit you've picked up.*

The Good Ruler vs. Evil Ruler Strategies to Create and End Mental Illness: Toxins

The more exposure you have to everyday toxins, the more you are putting your brain at risk. An evil ruler would never tell you to protect yourself. Instead, he would repeal laws that ensure clean air, water, and safe buildings; ignore companies that dump toxic waste; promote chemically laden foods; highlight research that touts the health benefits of alcohol and marijuana; and encourage teens to start smoking cannabis because it has been found to increase the risk of depression and suicide. One study found that using the drug as an adolescent contributes to depression in more than 400,000 people.[68] He would also disallow the labeling of the ingredients in personal care products so you wouldn't have to worry about the chemicals you are putting on your body.

A good ruler would do all he could to protect you from toxic exposure. He would strengthen laws that ensure clean air, water, and safe buildings; penalize companies that dump toxic waste; expose the dangers of chemically laden foods; highlight research that reveals how alcohol and marijuana affect brain health; discourage tweens and teens from smoking cannabis; and require truthful labeling of all ingredients in personal care products so you can make an informed decision about what you are putting on your body.

TODAY'S PRACTICE: *How many changes have you made to protect your brain from toxic exposure?*

M Is for Mental Health Issues

Mental health and physical health go hand in hand. Most people equate chronic illnesses with the elderly, but a recent Harris Poll study reveals that 44 percent of millennials born between 1981–1988 have been diagnosed with at least one chronic health condition,[69] such as high cholesterol, high blood pressure, and Crohn's disease. What's really alarming is that the top chronic health conditions among millennials fall into the mental or behavioral health category—depression, hyperactivity, substance use disorder—according to a study from Blue Cross Blue Shield.[70] The rates for these conditions are rising dramatically, and not just among millennials. Our physical and mental health are suffering—and you can't separate one from the other.

Inside your brain, there is a constant dance between your prefrontal cortex (forethought, judgment, and control), your amygdala (emotional area that responds to threats), and your basal ganglia (which forms habits). When your PFC is healthy and strong, it can help direct and supervise the addition of healthy habits. When it is weak, you more easily make bad decisions and let impulses guide your choices. That's when bad habits form. The rampant stress and uncertainty of the pandemic weakened people's PFCs and led to an increase in bad habits. This helps explain the rise in substance use and abuse during COVID-19.

Here's the problem: Anyone who has mental health symptoms is at greater risk of having chronic physical health conditions. Your physical health greatly impacts your mental well-being. Problems with blood flow, inflammation, head injuries, toxic exposure, infections (such as Lyme disease or COVID-19), autoimmune diseases, hormonal imbalances, obesity, and diabetes all contribute to psychiatric problems. Improving these areas of your life can enhance your mental health. Take care of your brain, and you'll take care of your body. It goes both ways.

TODAY'S PRACTICE: *Find the connections between your physical health and mental health. When you feel anxious, depressed, or stressed, how have you been caring for or ignoring your body? When your physical health is good, how does it affect your mental state?*

Natural Ways to Help ADD/ADHD

I am not opposed to medication, but it should never be the first or only thing you do to help someone. Here are nine things to consider before medication if you struggle with ADD/ADHD (short attention span, distractibility, disorganization, procrastination, impulsivity, restlessness).

1. Try an elimination diet for three weeks—eliminate sugar, gluten, dairy, corn, soy, and artificial dyes and sweeteners. Then add these back one at a time (except artificial dyes and sweeteners) and see how you feel. If there's a culprit, avoid it.
2. Try a higher protein, lower carbohydrate diet, such as ketogenic or paleo, for a month to see if it helps your focus.
3. Boost exercise—walk like you are late for 45 minutes four times a week.
4. Increase sleep and maintain good sleep habits.
5. Decrease screen time.
6. Work closely with an integrative physician to check ferritin, vitamin D, magnesium, zinc, and thyroid levels, and balance any that are not optimal.
7. Take 1,000 mg of EPA+DHA omega-3 fatty acids per day.
8. Take 200–300 mg of phosphatidylserine per day.
9. Take 100–500 mg of magnesium glycinate, citrate, or malate per day.

If someone truly has ADD/ADHD, they will still have it a few months after I first see them, so it is worth the investment and time to get their brain health optimized before starting a medication that they may be on for years or even decades. I often recommend nutraceuticals or medications targeted to their specific type of ADD/ADHD (see my book *Healing ADD*). There is negative bias against medication for ADD/ADHD, and it is not always warranted. Miracle and horror stories about stimulants abound. One of my own children went from being a mediocre student to getting straight A's for 10 years while using a stimulant medication. I was never more proud than the day she was accepted to one of the world's best veterinary schools. On the other hand, I've had patients referred to me because they became suicidal on stimulants. Their brains were already overactive to start, so stimulating it further made them more anxious and upset. The problem is, physicians assume everyone with ADD/ADHD is the same, which invites failure and frustration.

TODAY'S PRACTICE: *If you struggle with ADD/ADHD, choose one of the tips to start today. Stick with it for at least 30 days and keep track of how you feel.*

Natural Ways to Help Anxiety

Don't start something you may not be able to stop. After the pandemic, anxiety disorders more than doubled in children and teenagers.[71] Prescriptions for antianxiety medications, such as benzodiazepines like alprazolam (Xanax) and clonazepam (Klonopin) dramatically increased. The problem is that they are addictive, and once you start them they are often very hard to stop. Here are 11 strategies to consider before going on antianxiety medications.

1. Check for hypoglycemia, anemia, and hyperthyroidism.
2. Try an elimination diet for three weeks. (See day 257 for more detail.)
3. Practice meditation and hypnosis daily (research shows they can both calm stress and anxiety).
4. Try heart rate variability (HRV) training (anxiety is linked to low levels of HRV, but you can hack your way to a healthier HRV with biofeedback apps such as Welltory). See day 202 for more information.
5. Practice diaphragmatic breathing—deep breathing from your belly—when you feel anxious.
6. Eliminate the ANTs (automatic negative thoughts). See days 22, 116–117.
7. Incorporate a calming exercise, such as yoga or qi gong, into your week.
8. Take 200–400 mg of L-Theanine per day.
9. Take 500–1,500 mg of GABA per day.
10. Take 100–500 mg of magnesium glycinate, citrate, or malate with 30 mg of vitamin B6 per day.
11. Schedule neurofeedback to help retrain your brain.

Anxiety disorders are very painful, but too often people reach for marijuana, alcohol, or prescribed benzodiazepines, which can be of short-term benefit but cause long-term problems with addiction and memory issues. If the above interventions are ineffective or only partly effective with my patients, I'll try other nutraceuticals or medications targeted to a specific type of anxiety (take the test at brainhealthassessment.com).

TODAY'S PRACTICE: *Put together a playlist of seven of your favorite songs that calm your brain and mind and listen to it whenever you are anxious. There is scientific evidence that "Weightless" by Marconi Union calms anxiety by 65 percent.*[72]

Natural Ways to Help Depression

Depression is not one illness. Like anxiety, the pandemic spawned a whole new level of people being diagnosed with depression and placed on antidepressant medication, without ever getting a proper evaluation or trying simple fixes. Here are nine common things I do for patients before prescribing antidepressant medication.

1. Check for and (if necessary) correct thyroid hormone abnormalities.
2. Work with a nutritionally informed physician to optimize your folate, vitamin B12, vitamin D, homocysteine, and omega-3 fatty acids. I'm convinced that without doing these nutritional fixes, patients are less likely to respond to the medications.
3. Try an elimination diet for three weeks.
4. Add colorful fruits and vegetables into your diet.
5. Eliminate the ANTs (automatic negative thoughts). See days 22, 116–117.
6. Exercise—walk like you are late for 45 minutes four times a week. This has been found to be as effective as antidepressant medication.[73]
7. Add one of the following supplements to your daily routine: Saffron 30 mg/day; curcumin, not as turmeric root but as Longvida, which is much more efficiently absorbed; zinc as citrate or glycinate 30 mg (tolerable upper level is 40 mg/day for adults, 34 mg/day for adolescents, less for younger kids); or magnesium glycinate, citrate, or malate, 100–500 mg with 30 mg of vitamin B6.
8. Consume probiotics daily.
9. Try morning bright light therapy with a therapeutic lamp of 10,000 lux for 20–30 minutes.

If someone comes to me with depression, I order screening labs, teach them not to believe every negative thought they have, give them basic supplements (saffron, zinc, curcumins, and omega-3s), and encourage them to exercise. Many people never need medication if they follow through with the program. If the above interventions are ineffective, I'll try other nutraceuticals or medications targeted to their specific type of depression (take the test at brainhealthassessment.com).

TODAY'S PRACTICE: *Get treated for any depressive symptoms. Early treatment can be key in preventing long-term health issues for your brain.*

Is Bipolar Disorder the New "Fad" Diagnosis?

Can you really diagnose a lifelong condition in a 10-minute office visit? In the last two decades, an increasing number of people have been diagnosed with bipolar disorder. Until 2000, bipolar disorder (formerly known as manic-depressive disorder) was diagnosed in about one percent of the population.[74] Now that number has jumped to between 5 and 7 percent. Here's the problem: Many of those diagnosed don't actually have bipolar disorder, which is associated with dramatic swings in moods, energy levels, and impulsivity that repeat in a cyclical pattern. A 2010 study found that 57 percent of a group of people identified as having bipolar disorder between 2001 and 2005 had been misdiagnosed.[75]

That's what happened to Jessica, who'd been dealing with severe moodiness, periods of depression, and irritability. After a 10-minute visit with her primary care physician, she was diagnosed with bipolar disorder and given a prescription for a mood stabilizer that she was told she should take for the rest of her life. But the medication didn't work. A scan showed that Jessica was suffering from multiple concussions. She didn't have bipolar disorder; she had multiple traumatic brain injuries (TBIs) that needed healing. With the right treatment plan, her mood improved, and she started feeling like her old self again.

Here are four conditions commonly misdiagnosed as bipolar disorder: (1) Traumatic brain injuries, which can cause mood instability and irritability, are the most common misdiagnosis. (2) ADD/ADHD has many of the same symptoms, including impulsivity, racing thoughts, restlessness, trouble concentrating, and irritability. (3) Posttraumatic stress disorder leads to feelings of hypervigilance, irritability, and sleep issues and can mimic the symptoms of mania. (4) Infections, such as Lyme disease or the post-effects of COVID-19, can activate or inflame the limbic or emotional structures in the brain, causing symptoms of mood instability and irritability.

Being misdiagnosed with bipolar disorder is very problematic because the treatments won't work and often make the symptoms worse. Some people who've been misdiagnosed spend years going from one mood-stabilizing medication to another without relief. This can increase the risk of alcohol and drug abuse as they try to self-medicate. It also raises the risk of suicidal thoughts and behavior.

TODAY'S PRACTICE: *If you have been diagnosed with bipolar disorder but treatment isn't working, investigate if you may have been misdiagnosed.*

The Good Ruler vs. Evil Ruler Strategies to Create and End Mental Illness: Mental Health

Brain health is mental health. If we do not erase—or at least lower—the stigma for these brain health issues, many people will unnecessarily suffer and die without getting the help they need. The more people who get better, the more future generations will know about and protect their mental health. Don't let anyone persuade you to ignore mental health concerns; they signal that your brain is in need of help. The tactics of an evil ruler to harm your brain health are simple. She would cause rampant stress among the population; encourage lockdowns; make drugs and alcohol widely available; promote a diet high in sugar, red dye, MSG, and other food additives; encourage video game playing for hours on end; and limit exercise opportunities.

A good ruler, however, would make mental health her top priority. She would model stress management techniques; encourage seven to eight hours of sleep each night; educate people on negative effects of drugs and limit access to them; promote a brain-healthy diet; limit video games; encourage exercise; and teach people how to kill the ANTs.

TODAY'S PRACTICE: *List any mental health concerns you have for yourself or for loved ones. What keeps you from getting help?*

DAY 83

I Is for Immunity and Infections

Mom was unwilling to accept the diagnosis, for good reason. The second I in BRIGHT MINDS does double duty and stands for Immunity and Infection. Autoimmune disorders and infections, like Lyme disease or COVID-19, can steal your mind.

Adrianna, 16, was healthy and smart when her family went on a trip to the mountains. As soon as they got to their cabin, six deer showed up. The family thought the deer were so cool. The strange thing is that 10 days later Adrianna became incredibly irritable and started hallucinating. Her parents took her to a hospital, where doctors prescribed antipsychotic pills, but the medication didn't change anything. For about 90 days, they tried several doctors and other prescriptions, spending nearly $100,000. The worst part was that a psychiatrist told Adrianna's mother, Deb, that her daughter had schizophrenia and would need to be on medication for the rest of her life, and as her mother she just needed to accept it. But Deb was unwilling to accept that and brought her to us.

Adrianna's SPECT scan showed areas of unusually high activity, which caused us to look for other causes for her symptoms, such as an infection. It turned out she had Lyme disease, a bacterial infection transmitted by deer ticks. Once she was on antibiotics, she got her life back, and she recently got her master's degree from the University of London. Every day at about noon for the last 10 years, I get a text from Deb, asking how she can pray for me.

If you are struggling with your mood or memory and standard treatments do not work, autoimmunity and infectious diseases need to be explored by your health-care professional. To strengthen your immune system, make sure your vitamin D level is optimal; take probiotics, because gut health is critical to your immunity; and eat foods such as garlic, onions, and mushrooms.

TODAY'S PRACTICE: *Cook a meal that includes garlic, onions, and mushrooms—such as an omelet or stir-fry—to enhance immune system function.*

Vitamin D: The Sunshine Vitamin

Vitamin D is actually a hormone. Often referred to as the "sunshine vitamin," vitamin D is a hormone that should be called the "immunity vitamin" thanks to its positive effects on the immune system.[76] It also plays an essential role in overall brain health, mood, memory, weight, and other important bodily processes. Low levels of vitamin D have been associated with approximately 200 conditions, including brain health issues (depression, autism, and psychosis), autoimmune diseases (MS, rheumatoid arthritis, and diabetes), as well as heart disease, cancer, and obesity.[77] The link between vitamin D and mental health is strong, and more than half of psychiatric inpatients have a deficiency in vitamin D.[78] Low vitamin D has also been associated with memory problems and dementia.[79] People with the lowest levels of vitamin D have as much as a 25-fold higher risk of having mild cognitive impairment, the predecessor to Alzheimer's, when compared to those with the highest vitamin D levels.[80]

At Amen Clinics, we test the vitamin D levels of all of our patients, and a staggering number of them have low levels. A report that looked at vitamin D levels for American adults in 1988–1994 compared with 2001–2004 showed that our levels are dropping.[81] The percentage of people with levels of 30 ng/mL or more fell from 45 percent to 23 percent. This means that three out of four Americans have low levels of this important vitamin. In part, this is due to the fact that we are spending more time indoors and using more sunscreen when we're outdoors. The following groups are more likely to experience vitamin D deficiency:

- Older adults
- People with darker skin (reduced ability to make vitamin D from sunlight)
- People with limited sun exposure (i.e., northern latitudes, colder climates)
- People taking certain medications, such as antihypertensives, antidiabetics, or benzodiazepines[82]
- People with fat malabsorption syndrome, such as liver disease, cystic fibrosis, and Crohn's disease
- People who are obese or have undergone gastric bypass surgery

---

TODAY'S PRACTICE: *Get your vitamin D level tested and work to optimize it. Most of my patients take between 2,000 and 5,000 IUs a day.*

The Impact of COVID-19 on the Brain

COVID-19 is not innocuous. Two months after beating COVID-19, a 60-year-old woman was experiencing fatigue and depression so severe she was contemplating suicide. The patient's doctor said she experienced ongoing confusion. The woman told her doctor, "COVID has killed me." It hadn't physically taken her life, but it had stolen her mind and left her with no will to live. While most people are worried about the threat of respiratory failure, there is another invisible COVID-19 risk that could have more lasting consequences. Some are calling it long-haul COVID; we call it COVID brain. Among the symptoms are confusion, headaches, loss of smell and taste, tingling sensations, strokes, aphasia, and seizures. In a study of 69 million health records, one in five COVID-19 patients with no previous history of psychiatric illness developed brain health issues within the first 90 days, especially anxiety disorders, insomnia, and dementia.[83]

BEFORE   AFTER COVID

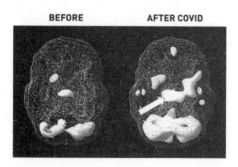

Research suggests that COVID-19 can cross the blood-brain barrier, a lining that typically protects the brain from viruses and other foreign invaders.[84] Once inside the brain, it can cause damage in a variety of ways, especially inflammation, which I have seen again and again on SPECT scans of people affected. In the images on this page you can see a dramatic activation of the patient's limbic or emotional brain (more white areas), just a few months after she contracted COVID. This disease is leaving a lasting legacy of brain dysfunction, but it doesn't have to. Working to get and keep the brain healthy by boosting the immune system and calming inflammation are the first steps in healing COVID brain. My colleagues and I have been using corticosteroids, fluvoxamine (if there are mood symptoms), curcumins, omega-3 fatty acids, vitamin C, and vitamin D. Anyone who has had COVID should be aware of any new or worsened symptoms of depression, anxiety, obsessive-compulsive disorder (OCD), or PTSD and be screened by a brain-informed mental health professional. Considering that COVID-19 attacks the brain, it is critical to look at the brain as part of the screening process.

TODAY'S PRACTICE: *If you or anyone in your family had COVID-19, start taking one of the supplements listed above.*

The Good Ruler vs. Evil Ruler Strategies to Create and End Mental Illness: Immunity and Infections

Infectious illnesses are a major cause of psychiatric and cognitive problems.[85] *Your vulnerability to illness depends on many factors: the strength of your immune system, the level of exposure, stress, and daily habits.* To harm immunity and promote illness, an evil ruler would disallow throat cultures for strep or testing for COVID in people with sore throats and fever; never allow health-care professionals to test vitamin D levels; encourage the consumption of common allergic foods—such as gluten, dairy, corn, and soy—that can trigger autoimmune responses; promote hiking on trails where deer ticks are plentiful without people wearing protective clothing; and promote unprotected sex.

A good ruler would warn people about the risk of infections and help boost immunity. A good ruler would encourage people with sore throats and fever to get a throat culture for strep and a COVID test; encourage physicians to routinely test vitamin D levels; discourage people from consuming potential allergens—gluten, soy, corn, dairy—that can trigger autoimmune responses; encourage food manufacturers to reduce their use of these substances in packaged foods; inform hikers to wear protective clothing on trails where deer ticks can be found; and inform the public about the risks of unprotected sex.

TODAY'S PRACTICE: *How often do you get sick, even just a case of the sniffles? This is a sign that your immunity is low. Work to lower your stress so your body has a chance to rest and recover.*

N Is for Neurohormone Issues

Neurohormones are like Miracle-Gro for your brain. Without healthy hormones, you feel tired and foggy, and your hippocampus (one of the mood and memory centers of the brain) will become smaller and weaker.

- Testosterone helps you feel happy, motivated, sexual, and strong.
- Your thyroid gives you energy and mental clarity. My friend Dr. Richard Shames says, "Low thyroid doesn't kill you. It just makes you wish you were dead."[86]
- DHEA helps to fight aging.
- In women, estrogen and progesterone help boost blood flow and keep the brain young.

To keep your hormones healthy, test them every year after the age of 40, avoid hormone disruptors, such as pesticides, phthalates, and parabens in personal products, and work with your doctor.

Mercedes Maidana is a famous big-wave surfer, motivational speaker, and life coach from Argentina. She suffered a serious concussion surfing a 30-foot wave off the coast of Oregon. Subsequently, she suffered from anxiety, depression, and memory problems. Her scan showed low activity in her right hippocampus. Mercedes also had low thyroid, which is common in people who've had head injuries. This is new information but commonly found after traumatic brain injuries. Optimizing her thyroid, changing her diet, taking targeted supplements, and doing hyperbaric oxygen therapy, she is happier, thriving, and leading health retreats for women.

TODAY'S PRACTICE: *Set up an appointment to test all your hormone levels. Boost healthy hormones naturally through exercise, strength training, adequate sleep, healthy diet, and stress management.*

The Pill's Surprising (and Scary) Side Effects

Bouts of depression were reported in 16 to 56 percent of women taking birth control pills.[87] Millions of women take synthetic hormones in the form of oral contraceptive pills *(OCP)*. If you or a loved one is taking them, you should be aware of what they do to your hormonal system and the side effects that come with them. OCPs hijack your cyclical hormonal processes, replacing them with a steady supply of low levels of synthetic estrogen and progesterone. You may already know that OCPs have been shown to cause problems with blood pressure and blood clots and increase the incidence of strokes, especially in people who smoke or have a history of migraine headaches. But did you know that OCPs also affect your brain?

Research shows that taking the pill causes structural changes in the brain, alters neurotransmitter function, and messes with mood regulation. Scientists from Denmark found that women ages 15–34 taking OCPs were 23 percent more likely to start taking antidepressants for the first time than non-OCP users.[88] Oral contraceptives also put you at greater risk for autoimmune diseases, elevate cortisol levels, and lower levels of testosterone—yes, women produce and need testosterone—which can decrease your sex drive. And low-testosterone problems can remain even after stopping OCPs, putting you at increased risk for long-term sexual and brain health/mental health problems. Synthetic birth control can also disrupt the gut microbiome and interfere with the absorption of essential vitamins and minerals, which can lead to deficiencies. If you are taking birth control pills, be sure to supplement your diet with B vitamins (folate, B6, and B12), vitamin E, and magnesium. If you are experiencing psychiatric symptoms, you may want to ask, is it a mental health issue or is it the pill?

Stopping OCPs isn't necessarily a quick-fix solution. Some women experience a rash of symptoms—including mood swings, anxiety, and depression—in the months following cessation of hormonal birth control. Some hormonal experts have started calling this effect "post-birth control syndrome."

TODAY'S PRACTICE: *If you are on an OCP, consider switching to an alternative birth control method that does not use hormones.*

Change Your Hormones, Change Your Dog

Hormones decide how affectionate you may be. When I met my wife, Tana, she was a nurse in a neurosurgical intensive care unit. Neurosurgeons are their own breed, so she had learned how to be assertive and bold. She liked to poke fun at them by saying, "What is the difference between a neurosurgeon and God? At least God knows he is not a neurosurgeon." Tana also worked hard to earn black belts in Tae Kwon Do and Kenpo Karate. So when it came to romance, she acted more like a man. She could only cuddle for a little while, then when she'd had enough, she'd get up and tell me she had to go work out. Initially, she also had issues committing and would come and go for about the first 18 months of our relationship. She also loved masculine dogs. Our first disagreement was on the type of dog we would have together. I wanted a sweet King Charles Cavalier, and she wanted a mastiff.

Then one day Tana was diagnosed with polycystic ovarian syndrome (PCOS), which is associated with excessive testosterone and can cause anxiety and more masculine tendencies in a relationship. On a medicine for PCOS that helped to balance her testosterone levels, she became much more relaxed, affectionate, and committed. After about six months, she called me up at work and said she just had to have a pocket poodle. Thinking she must be playing a joke on me, I said, "Who stole my wife?" That is when a three-pound poodle named Tinkerbell came into our lives.

How many of you ever had the idea that your hormones could completely interfere with your relationships? Changing your hormones can change your brain and even the kind of dog you have. Low testosterone can be the culprit of anxiety, depression, lack of motivation, low libido, trouble sleeping, fatigue, trouble concentrating, low bone density, hot flashes, and hair loss. High testosterone can reduce your empathy and lead to an excessively high sex drive, which are also problematic.

TODAY'S PRACTICE: *If you have any of the symptoms of imbalanced testosterone, get your hormones checked. In the meantime, steer clear of endocrine disruptors (pesticides, plastics, etc.) Refer back to days 70 and 74 for information about personal care and household products that can interfere with hormones.*

The Good Ruler vs. Evil Ruler Strategies to Create and End Mental Illness: Neurohormones

Hormones are the chemical messengers that control and regulate the activity of certain cells or organs. When hormones are healthy, you tend to feel young and energetic. When they are out of balance, you may feel older, experience mental health issues, and become more susceptible to anxiety, depression, and even psychosis.

An evil ruler would damage neurohormones by subjecting people to chronic stress and having them live in overcrowded cities, feeding us processed foods with a high sugar content, and encouraging high-risk behaviors that easily damage the pituitary gland. He would flood our environment and homes with pesticides, plastics, and other products that act as endocrine disruptors; discourage health-care providers from testing thyroid, cortisol, DHEA, estrogen, progesterone, testosterone, human growth hormone, and insulin levels; and make policies allowing insurance companies to avoid reimbursing patients for these tests and deny claims for hormone treatment.

A good ruler would protect neurohormone production by reducing chronic stress, encouraging schools and work cafeterias to serve brain-healthy foods, and discouraging high-risk behaviors. He would limit the use of pesticides on crops and outlaw the most toxic pesticides, reduce the use of plastics, and limit products that are endocrine disruptors. He would encourage the medical community to include testing for thyroid, cortisol, DHEA, estrogen, progesterone, testosterone, human growth hormone, and insulin levels during checkups and require insurance companies to provide reimbursements for these tests as well.

TODAY'S PRACTICE: *When you take your vitamins, include ashwagandha, a cortisol-reducing supplement that also supports thyroid function.*

D Is for Diabesity

As your weight goes up, the size of your brain goes down. Diabesity is a double-barreled threat to your brain. It involves being prediabetic or diabetic, overweight or obese, or both. I've published three scientific studies that show that as your weight goes up, the actual physical size and function of your brain decreases. With 50 percent of Americans prediabetic or diabetic and over 73 percent overweight and over 42 percent obese,[89] we are facing the biggest brain drain in the history of the United States. The excessive fat on your body is not innocuous. In fact, it increases five other BRIGHT MINDS risk factors. Being overweight or obese lowers blood flow to the brain, speeds up aging, increases inflammation, stores toxins, and disrupts your hormones. When being overweight or obese is combined with being diabetic or prediabetic, the risk is worse. High blood sugar levels damage your blood vessels and delay healing.

I was once speaking at a conference in Nashville. Later that night I met a friend for dinner. He looked like he had gained weight since I had last seen him. When I saw him pull out a small syringe and give himself an insulin injection at the dinner table, I knew he had diabetes. I was shocked when he placed his dinner order—all fried foods and starches. I was concerned for my friend's health, so I asked him his height and weight, then quickly determined his BMI. When I not-so-subtly told him he was in the obese category, he got offended. I warned him that he was sending himself to an early grave. The message sank in. He started dropping weight, and over the next couple years, he lost more than 50 pounds and reduced his insulin by 50 percent. Life was good, he told me. And compared to having diabetes, following a healthy lifestyle was easy. An added bonus was a better sex life, he said with a wink. He even thanked me for caring enough about him to be honest with him about his weight.

TODAY'S PRACTICE: *Calculate your BMI (go to any online BMI calculator).*

What We Learned from the Weights of 20,000 Patients

Diet is as important to psychiatry as it is to cardiology, endocrinology, and gastroenterology. Everybody knows that maintaining a healthy weight can be beneficial for physical health, but what does the weight of your body have to do with your brain function and mental health? We analyzed the SPECT scans of 20,000 of our patients to see how body mass index (BMI) impacts brain activity. The results were mind-blowing. In our analysis, it was clear that as a person's weight went up, *all* the regions of the brain went down in activity and blood flow, in a linear correlation. Here is just one graph showing how blood flow and activity went down in the prefrontal cortex. 1 = underweight; 2 = normal weight; 3 = overweight; 4 = obese; 5 = morbidly obese.

Take note that although this chart shows that activity was highest in people who

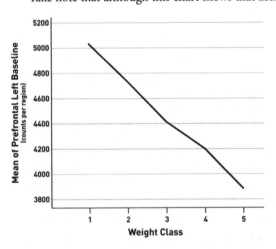

are underweight, this doesn't mean that being underweight is healthy. Being underweight is associated with a number of health risks, including nutritional deficiencies, reduced immune function, fertility issues, and a lack of protein reserves you would need if you got into an accident. Low weight isn't healthy, but it doesn't seem to shrink your brain.

Having low blood flow and activity across the entire brain is terrible for psychological well-being, mental clarity, and cognitive function. A "low activity" brain is associated with increased risk-taking, poor judgment, impulsiveness, low motivation, slowed thought processes, trouble problem-solving, and memory problems. It becomes a self-perpetuating cycle. The excess weight can cause more issues with judgment, making getting well harder to accomplish.

Adopting brain-healthy eating habits can help you reach and maintain a healthy weight and boost your brain function. Count your calories, eat colorful fruits and vegetables, and help your body, brain, and mind get healthy.

TODAY'S PRACTICE: *If you need to lose weight, get started by cutting out one unhealthy food habit.*

A Half Dozen Ways Doughnuts Can Ruin Your Life

No one had ever explained to Tami in such graphic detail what the sugar-laden dough-nuts were doing to her body. Tami had diabetes and was addicted to doughnuts when she first started a nutrition class my wife, Tana, taught. She admitted she was struggling with the idea of giving up these sweet treats. Starting your day with pastries, sugary cereal, pancakes, waffles, or muffins spikes insulin levels and triggers inflammation. Tana sensed that Tami needed a more emotional push where the doughnuts were concerned and prepared a slide show for her with graphic images on "A Half Dozen Ways Doughnuts Can Change Your Life." She showed how doughnuts are associated with:

1. Chronically high blood sugar, which leads to type 2 diabetes
2. High blood sugar, which can also lead to skin ulcerations and eventually amputation
3. Diabetes, which can lead to blindness
4. Alzheimer's disease, which is now referred to as type 3 diabetes and is significantly increased by obesity[90]
5. Strokes and heart damage, due to the sugar and trans fats in doughnuts
6. High insulin levels, which are associated with many forms of cancer[91]—sugar feeds cancer

The slide show horrified Tami. No one had ever explained to her in such graphic detail what the sugar-laden doughnuts were doing to her body. Just hearing that she needed to get her blood sugar under control had no impact on her. Two weeks later, Tami reported that she hadn't eaten a single doughnut since she watched the slide show, and she didn't think she'd ever be able to look at food the same way. She beamed as she told Tana that since being diagnosed with diabetes six years ago, her blood sugar was usually between 150 to 160, but that for more than a week her blood sugar had been averaging between 89 and 95. That was a huge drop into the normal range!

TODAY'S PRACTICE: *List foods that are a struggle for you to give up. How many of them are sugary?*

Love Food That Loves You Back

You are in a relationship with food. Your brain eats up 20 to 30 percent of your daily calories, even though it only accounts for 2 percent of your total weight. What you eat and drink makes a big difference in how you feel physically, emotionally, and cognitively. You are in a relationship with food. Have you ever been in a bad relationship? I have, and it was very stressful. I'm not going to do it again. I'm married to my best friend, who adds to my happiness. Being in love with foods that hurt you is like being in love with someone who always mistreats you. Too many people tell me they love ice cream, doughnuts, cookies, fries, pizza, pasta, and alcohol. I call them weapons of mass destruction because they are all addictive, expand your waistline, and shrink your brain. Your brain is one of the few organs where size really does matter. Most of the foods in the Standard American Diet (SAD) are the culprits behind too much inflammation, weight gain, heart problems, depression, and Alzheimer's.

Here's a starter list of foods that enhance the function of your brain: organic colorful fruits and vegetables, especially avocados and blueberries; dark chocolate (without the sugar and dairy); beets (which increase blood flow to the brain); healthy fats (including healthy oils, fatty fish—such as sardines and salmon—nuts, and seeds); and herbs and spices, especially saffron, turmeric, and cinnamon. Also eat foods loaded with fiber, such as asparagus, leeks, and garlic, and immunity-boosting foods, such as onions, mushrooms, and garlic.

Now compare those to the SAD foods that make people unhappy, including most baked foods, fried foods, highly processed foods, high-glycemic foods (which raise your blood sugar), and low-fiber foods that quickly turn to sugar, such as sugar, bread, pasta, potatoes, and white rice. People who have these foods as the primary staple of their diets have nearly 400 percent increased risk of getting Alzheimer's disease.[92]

I love what Drew Carey said when he got healthy: "Eating crappy food isn't a reward. It's a punishment."[93] That is the mindset you must have to get and stay healthy and happy.

TODAY'S PRACTICE: *Start asking yourself, "Is this a food or drink I love that loves me back?" every time you eat or drink something.*

Brain Warrior Carlos Influenced Everyone He Loved

266 lbs.

"It's not hard," he said. "I have the program dialed in." I met Carlos when he was 48 years old. He was a worrier, fixated on negative thinking. He was depressed and angry, and he couldn't focus. No one had recognized his dyslexia when he was young, and he had been a heavy drinker for a while. He was overweight and his brain was a mess, so it was no wonder he was having all those other issues. Below is Carlos's initial brain SPECT scan.

I told Carlos what he needed to do and laid out a program for him. To him, it all made sense, and he said he would follow it. In just over two months, he lost 24 pounds. By the end, he lost a total of 50 pounds. What was even better was that he felt better and his focus and memory improved. He looked and felt like he was 38! The plan we gave him helped him learn how to stop overeating when he felt sad or angry. Instead, brain-healthy meals throughout the day helped him avoid energy crashes and being susceptible to stress. The changes showed up on the outside, but we also saw the same dramatic changes on the inside. His follow-up SPECT scan showed overall increased activity. By loving and caring for his brain, Carlos changed his brain and his life!

243 lbs.

What I love about Carlos's story is that the transformation didn't stop with him. His wife was impressed with what she saw in Carlos, so she started the same brain-healthy plan. Although she wasn't overweight, she lost 10 pounds. Then their teenage daughter got on the bandwagon. Carlos's improvements affected his family for the better. When I saw him two years later, I asked him how he was able to stay on track. "It's not hard," he said. "I have the program dialed in."

216 lbs.

BEFORE   AFTER

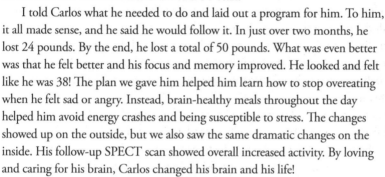

TODAY'S PRACTICE: *List two people who will benefit if you work hard to get truly healthy.*

The Good Ruler vs. Evil Ruler Strategies to Create and End Mental Illness: Diabesity

Excess body fat is not your friend. Diabesity is destroying brains, minds, and bodies, and it's robbing our children and grandchildren of their future. An evil ruler would relish an epidemic of diabesity, demanding that high-sugar desserts be served with all school lunches as a way to boost inattention among children and encouraging companies to put doughnuts in the break room and candy in bowls to raise the risk of diabesity. This ruler would also fool people into viewing sweet desserts that spike blood sugar and contribute to anxiety and other psychiatric symptoms as a "reward" for good behavior or a job well done and allow unhealthy, artificially flavor-enhanced foods and drinks to be aggressively marketed as desirable (think Coke's "Open Happiness" slogan). In fact, the evil ruler would encourage professional athletes and coaches to visibly drink Coke, Pepsi, or Gatorade (all filled with sugar, artificial colors, and preservatives) on the sidelines of games as a way of marketing these products to children and teens; tell people that diabetes isn't that bad; and discourage making any lifestyle changes because there are drugs you can take for it. At the same time, an evil ruler would blame genetics for the obesity epidemic, saying there's nothing you can do about it.

A good ruler would limit sugar-laden snacks and desserts in school lunches to promote stable blood sugar levels and healthy weight; encourage corporations to serve brain-healthy snacks to employees to prevent diabesity; tell the truth that drinking and eating foods that make you fat and diabetic is not a smart way to celebrate; prevent food and beverage manufacturers from easily marketing products that increase the risk for diabesity; educate people about the consequences of diabetes and encourage lifestyle changes—exercise and diet—to regulate blood sugar levels; and inform people that your DNA is not your destiny. Your daily habits can influence your genes, and it is within your power to control your weight.

TODAY'S PRACTICE: *How seriously do you take your physical health? What needs to change?*

S Is for Sleep

When you sleep, your brain cleans or washes itself. It is estimated that 50–70 million Americans have sleep-related issues.[94] Chronic insomnia, sleeping pills, and sleep apnea significantly increase the risk of memory problems. Below is a scan of someone with sleep apnea. In these scans we often see low activity in areas that die early in Alzheimer's. If you snore and stop breathing at night or someone tells you that you do, get assessed. When you sleep, your brain cleans or washes itself. If sleep is disrupted, trash builds up in your brain, which damages your memory. Getting fewer than seven hours of sleep at night is associated with weight issues, hypertension, accidents, and trouble in your marriage (because you are more likely to say something you wish you hadn't). In one study, soldiers who got seven hours of sleep at night were 98 percent accurate on the range. Those who got six hours of sleep were only 50 percent accurate, five hours 28 percent accurate, and four hours only 15 percent accurate. In fact, they were dangerous.

SLEEP APNEA

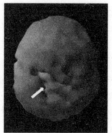

You can improve your mind tomorrow by improving your sleep tonight. In the evening, do this by avoiding caffeine, a warm room, light and noise, especially from your gadgets, and alcohol. Yes, alcohol will put you to sleep, but when it wears off, your brain will rebound and wake you up a few hours later.

To sleep better, make your room cooler, darker, and quieter. Turn off your gadgets so they don't disturb you. Listening to music with a specific rhythm can help, as can some supplements. Magnesium and melatonin are often very effective, as is 5-HTP if you're a worrier. If you have bad thoughts that keep you awake, journaling helps to get them out of your head.

TODAY'S PRACTICE: *Go to bed 20 minutes earlier tonight and don't look at any screen within an hour of going to bed. Then see how you feel tomorrow.*

Natural Ways to Improve Sleep

If you want to improve your memory tomorrow, get better sleep tonight. Sleep is a miracle worker. It revitalizes every cell in your body, allows your brain to heal and repair, flushes out toxins that you took in while you were awake, and stimulates neurons to prevent inactivity and deterioration. A good night's rest is also a necessity for healthy skin, rebuilding your energy, feeling happier, and maintaining your weight. The bad news is that 50–70 million people in the US don't get good sleep, and gadgets and bad habits are making it worse. Don't become one of those statistics; improve your sleep with these strategies:

1. Care about your sleep. Make it a priority.
2. Avoid anything that hurts sleep, such as caffeine, blue light from gadgets, light, warm rooms, noise, alcohol, evening exercise, unchallenged negative thoughts, and worries.
3. Treat any issues that steal your sleep—restless leg syndrome, sleep apnea, hyperthyroidism, low progesterone, or chronic pain.
4. Engage in positive sleep habits, such as blue light blockers, turning off gadgets, hypnosis, meditation, soothing music, warm baths, a cool room and pillow, a regular sleep schedule, and aromatherapy with lavender.
5. Add one of the following supplements before bedtime: Melatonin 0.3 mg–2 mg, gradually increasing it until it works for you; magnesium glycinate, citrate, or malate 100–500 mg; zinc 15–30 mg; 5-HTP 100–200 mg, if you are a worrier; GABA 250–1,000 mg.

Too often people are prescribed addictive sleeping pills that can affect memory without searching for the underlying cause or doing the simple strategies first. If the above interventions are ineffective, try nonaddictive, sleep-promoting medications, such as low-dose trazodone, gabapentin, or amitriptyline.

TODAY'S PRACTICE: *Do you have any issues that steal your sleep? See a doctor to test for hormone issues or sleep apnea. Add one positive sleep habit to your bedtime routine tonight.*

Understanding Dreams and Nightmares

Our past can haunt us in the present through our dreams and nightmares. Whenever assessing any dream, I look for: (1) a wish or a fear, (2) a current event, and (3) something from the past. Understanding these three components helps you interpret your dreams. Early on when I saw a patient named Jimmy, he sent me this note: "I had nightmares all night. One was losing my niece at a plaza and another was being stabbed in prison." When we examined the first dream, it turned out he feared losing the connection with his niece, which was triggered by a news story he saw before bed about a kidnapping. In the past his sister had lost his niece in a mall for an hour, which made her panic. The second dream came from a fear when he was a young adult and visited his father in prison. His father would make him visit other gang member inmates, and he worried he would be stabbed. This dream was triggered by talking to his father in prison a few days before.

The nightmare about being stabbed in prison was a repetitive one. Repetitive nightmares are common in people who have been traumatized. Whenever a nightmare has occurred more than three times, write it out in as much detail as you can, then give it a better ending. For example, Jimmy wrote out the "being stabbed in prison" dream in detail. He then wrote a different ending for it. Rather than being stabbed and lying in a pool of his own blood, he wore a bulletproof vest with a blaring alarm that would go off if it was ever punctured. In the new version, the prison guards were more watchful and would rescue him if the prisoner got aggressive. He only had the dream twice more, then it stopped. By writing out your nightmares and giving them a different ending, you are no longer held hostage by your unconscious mind.

TODAY'S PRACTICE: *Write down your last dream in detail, analyze it for the three components mentioned above, and write a new ending for it.*

Hypnosis for Sleep

Hypnosis is not magic; it's a natural way to direct your mind for health. Curious, I took a monthlong elective in hypnosis as a medical student. I got the opportunity to put hypnosis into practice when I was an intern at a busy military hospital in our nation's capital. With all the noise and commotion, it was hard for patients to get good rest, and they often requested sleep medication. I started asking if we could try hypnosis first. If they still couldn't sleep, I would prescribe the sleeping pills. The vast majority of them agreed to try it, and it helped in most cases.

One of the most impactful experiences I have had with medical hypnosis was with a World War II veteran who had helped Jews escape from Germany. Decades later, he was diagnosed with Parkinson's disease. Most people associate tremors with Parkinson's, but sleep problems are also very common in the illness. While I was on call at the hospital, he requested a sleeping pill. As I did with so many other patients, I asked if I could first try hypnosis. To my surprise, once he was in a hypnotic state, the tremors subsided. With Parkinson's, the shaking typically stops while a person sleeps, but this war hero's tremors went away before he nodded off. I was so excited that I shared what had happened with our attending physician. The neurologist didn't share my enthusiasm and looked at me as if I was stupid. Determined to show him it was true, I put the World War II veteran in a trance again. Once again, the tremors stopped even though he wasn't asleep. Our attending physician was so impressed, we repeated the process using an EEG on the patient and filmed the whole thing. Together we wrote a research study—my first one ever—which led me to publish over 80 more scientific papers.

TODAY'S PRACTICE: *If you are having trouble sleeping, try my hypnosis audio with a free trial of our app, available for download in the App Store.*

The Good Ruler vs. Evil Ruler Strategies to Create and End Mental Illness: Sleep

Having too few hours of good quality sleep can have catastrophic consequences, which would make an evil ruler happy. An evil ruler would mess with your sleep by making you so addicted to TV and social media that you tune into stressful news before bed, read your emails late into the evening, respond to texts in the middle of the night, and tweet outrageous messages and post to Facebook or Instagram at all hours. She would also encourage you to regularly cross several time zones for work, giving you jet lag; refuse to give up the outdated practice of losing sleep with the time change; advocate caffeine consumption morning, noon, and night to disrupt sleep and create an unhealthy cycle that primes you for symptoms of mental illness; and encourage starting school early to diminish sleep time, which increases many forms of brain health/mental health issues.

A good ruler, however, would know the importance of sleep. She would limit social media and TV time so you can go to sleep early and get the rest you need; limit excess travel to reduce the incidence of jet lag; do away with the twice-a-year time change that messes with your sleep; encourage people to adopt a brain-healthy sleep regimen that promotes more restorative sleep; start school later to allow children good sleep; start days with exercise; and have walking meetings at work.

TODAY'S PRACTICE: *What would change for you if you had better sleep strategies?*

Tiny Habits for BRIGHT MINDS

Make BRIGHT MINDS as easy as possible. Here is a list of 11 tiny habits for each of the BRIGHT MINDS risk factors.

1. After I have used the bathroom, I will drink a glass of water. (Blood flow)
2. After I hang up my car keys, I will learn a new chord on my instrument. (Retirement/new learning)
3. When I finish brushing my teeth before bed, I will floss. (Inflammation)
4. After I open the refrigerator, I will grab a handful of organic berries. (Genetics)
5. When I go downstairs, I will hold the handrail. (Head trauma)
6. When I pump gas, I will stand away from the nozzle so I don't inhale fumes. (Toxins)
7. When I am feeling sad, I will take a walk in nature. (Mental health)
8. When I prepare vegetables for dinner, I will add garlic and onions to the mix. (Immunity)
9. When I go to the salad bar, I will get a half cup of beans or peas. (Neurohormones)
10. When I eat dinner, I will add one colorful vegetable to my plate. (Diabesity)
11. After I get into my bed, I will focus on what went well today. (Sleep)

TODAY'S PRACTICE: *Adopt one tiny habit from the list above. (It's okay to adopt more than one.) Remember to celebrate whenever you do a tiny habit.*

Digital Obsessions

Technology connects us to a world of distraction. Have you ever noticed how many people in an airport are on their phones or tablets? Have you ever had a romantic dinner ruined by a date who kept answering text messages rather than focusing on a live conversation with you? I know I don't have to ask how many times you see people driving and looking at their phones.

While technology has brought a lot of advantages to our world, it also brings challenges. And we are becoming more and more dependent on it. In fact, neuroscientists have identified new brain disorders linked to technology, such as separation anxiety (from one's phone!) and hearing phantom rings.[95] The compulsive need to stay connected at all times has become a type of addiction. How can we prevent it from becoming an obsession or an addiction? Try one of these five practices on a regular basis.

1. **Take a time-out.** Schedule a time when you will turn off all your devices for the remainder of the evening. You might find that you spend more quality time with friends and family or finish those home projects you've been working on for months.
2. **Fast from the internet.** Reserve one day of the week (for maximum effect, choose a day you have off from work) when you will shut down your internet connection.
3. **Ban screens from your bedroom.** Remove TVs, computers, phones, and tablets from your bedroom. This will allow you to create a relaxing environment for better sleep and reduce the amount of electromagnetic frequencies (EMF) your body absorbs (which are known to damage healthy cells).
4. **Use your brain.** It's great at remembering facts and solving problems if you let it. Instead of asking Google or Siri for answers, try to figure it out for yourself.
5. **Never talk and text.** When you're having a live conversation with someone, shut off your phone notifications. Stay engaged with the person next to you. In general, aim to keep phone and text conversations to a minimum when you are with other people.

Live in harmony with technology rather than being controlled by it.

TODAY'S PRACTICE: *How much do you let technology control your attention? How often do you turn off notifications? Pick one of the habits above to start doing today.*

When Getting Healthy Starts with Love

Sometimes motivation is about love. Ray was a retired NFL player who was overweight and had trouble focusing. But when he came to us, it wasn't to address his own issues. He was hoping we could help his 56-year-old wife, Nancy, who had been diagnosed with early-onset dementia. Her prognosis wasn't good, and her doctor recommended placing her in a memory care facility. He told Ray that in a year's time, she likely wouldn't recognize him anymore. Ray was devastated and desperate to help her.

Nancy's scan showed severely decreased activity in the front part of her brain, consistent with a dementia process. I had to give Ray the truth. "We have no proven cure for this," I said. I quickly added that if she were my wife, I would encourage her to do all of the BRIGHT MINDS strategies, including exercise, a complete dietary change, no alcohol, hyperbaric oxygen therapy, targeted supplements, new learning, and more.

BEFORE　　　　**10 WEEKS LATER**

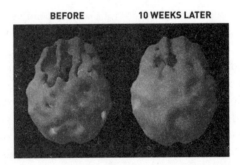

Ten weeks later, Nancy and her brain were remarkably better. I was under no illusion that we had won the war for the health of her brain, but there is so much hope, even if you've been diagnosed with memory problems, that you can be better if you do all of the right things.

During the same period, Ray shed more than 25 pounds and said he was more focused than ever. Amazed, I asked him how he did it. He told me his secret to getting Nancy to follow a brain-healthy lifestyle was to act as a role model for her. He knew that if he did it, she would follow his lead. Sometimes motivation to get healthy is about love, and Nancy was deeply loved by Ray.

TODAY'S PRACTICE: *Are you modeling health or illness for those you love? Whom could you influence if you got healthy?*

Introduction to Brain Types

Everyone's brain is different. Knowing your brain type can help you understand what makes you uniquely happy or unhappy. More than 30 years ago, the brain SPECT scans we were doing at Amen Clinics led us to the concept of brain types. We had been using scans to look for brain activity patterns for a number of brain health/mental health issues. What we learned was that things such as depression and ADD/ADHD had more than one pattern. Different patterns needed different treatments. There was no one-size-fits-all scenario. I had suspected as much because I knew not all depressed people are the same, and neither are people with ADD/ADHD. The symptoms and feelings can vary drastically. Brain scans brought biological understanding to the nuances of so many mental health concerns, allowing us to find the best solutions for each patient's brain, rather than just assessing a cluster of symptoms. This dramatically improved our ability to help people.

We also realized that we could see personality traits in scans and discovered five primary brain types:

1. **Balanced:** overall healthy activity in people who tend to be emotionally balanced.
2. **Spontaneous:** low activity in the front part of the brain in those who tend to be creative, but also easily distracted and impulsive.
3. **Persistent:** with high activity in the front, people with this type tend to be tenacious, rigid, and can hold grudges.
4. **Sensitive:** with increased activity in the limbic or emotional centers, these people tend to be deeply empathic, but also vulnerable to depression.
5. **Cautious:** with increased activity in the fear centers, often due to childhood trauma, these people tend to be prepared, but also anxious and can startle easily.

Brain typing explains so much. It helps us understand why you do what you do, why others do what they do, and what makes people happy or unhappy.

It is common to have more than one brain type, and when we look at all of the potential combinations of types, it adds up to 16. The interventions for these brain types are a combination of Brain Types 2–5. At brainhealthassessment.com you can find out which of the 16 types you are likely to have and get a detailed report for each. If you have symptoms of brain health issues, these reports can give you a head start in finding strategies that can minimize your symptoms while boosting your brain reserve.

TODAY'S PRACTICE: *If you have not done so before, take my Brain Health Assessment to learn about your brain type at brainhealthassessment.com.*

Balanced Brain Type

The Balanced brain type is the most common brain type I see in our studies through Amen Clinics. These people are focused, conscientious, flexible, positive, resilient, and emotionally stable, and they have good impulse control.

They tend to score low on the following traits: short attention span, impulsivity, unreliability, worry, negativity, and anxiety. People with a balanced brain type often live longer than others because of their level of conscientiousness. They do what they say they're going to do. They show up on time and follow through on tasks they promise to get done. Typically, they do not like taking big risks, are not first adopters, and tended to play in the sandbox when they were children. They are not likely to be entrepreneurs or industry disruptors. They like rules and are inclined to play by them.

Our brain imaging work shows that people who have the Balanced brain type tend to show full, even, symmetrical activity throughout the brain, with the most activity in the cerebellum, which is one of the brain's major processing centers.

The Balanced brain type does best by using general strategies to keep the brain healthy, including taking a multivitamin, omega-3 fatty acids, probiotics, and optimizing vitamin D levels to support brain health.

TODAY'S PRACTICE: *Make sure to include a multivitamin, omega-3s, and probiotic supplements in your daily routine.*

Spontaneous Brain Type

The Spontaneous brain type is very common among entrepreneurs, entertainers, politicians, and Realtors. People with this type tend to be spontaneous, risk-taking, creative, out-of-the-box thinkers, curious, interested in a wide range of things, restless, and easily distracted. They need to be highly interested in something in order to focus, struggle with organization, like surprises, run late or rush to meetings, and tend to be diagnosed with ADD/ADHD.

They tend to score low on the following traits: hatred of surprises, risk aversion, desire for routine and sameness, playing by the rules, practicality, and attention to detail. Our brain imaging work has shown that this type typically has lower activity in the front part of the brain in an area called the prefrontal cortex (PFC), which can be either positive or troublesome.

Our research team has published several studies showing that when people with this brain type try to concentrate, they actually have less activity in the PFC, which causes them to need excitement or stimulation in order to focus (think of firefighters and race car drivers). Smokers and heavy coffee drinkers also tend to fit this type, as they use these substances to activate their brains.

The Spontaneous brain type is best optimized by boosting dopamine levels to strengthen the PFC. Higher protein, lower carbohydrate diets tend to help, as do physical exercise and certain stimulating supplements, such as green tea, rhodiola, and ginseng.

TODAY'S PRACTICE: *If you have the Spontaneous brain type, eat a high-protein, lower-carbohydrate diet to help increase dopamine in your brain.*

Persistent Brain Type

The Persistent brain type is common among chief operating officers, project managers, and web engineers. They get things done. People with this type tend to be persistent and strong-willed. They like routine, can get "stuck" on thoughts, hold on to hurts, tend to see what is wrong, are oppositional/argumentative, and tend toward OCD. They score low on the following traits: affinity for change, timidity, spontaneity, trust, positivity, forgiveness, and cooperation.

People with this type often take charge and won't take no for an answer. They tend to be tenacious and stubborn. In addition, they may worry, have trouble sleeping, be argumentative and oppositional, and hold grudges from the past. Our brain imaging work shows that the Persistent brain type often has increased activity in the front part of the brain, in an area called the anterior cingulate gyrus.

The best strategy to balance the Persistent brain type is to find natural ways to boost serotonin, because it calms the brain. Physical exercise boosts serotonin, as does using certain supplements, such as 5-HTP and saffron. High-glycemic carbohydrates turn to sugar quickly and increase serotonin, which is why many people become addicted to simple carbohydrates like bread, pasta, and sweets. These are "mood foods" and are often used to self-medicate an underlying mood issue. Avoid the quick fix of bad food because it can cause long-term problems.

TODAY'S PRACTICE: *If you have the Persistent brain type, make an effort to compare yourself to others in a positive way, and add more seafood to your diet, which includes tryptophan and omega-3 fats to boost serotonin production.*

Sensitive Brain Type

The Sensitive brain type is common among therapists, health-care professionals, social workers, and creatives. People with this type tend to be sensitive, deeply feeling, and empathic. They struggle with moods and pessimism, have lots of ANTs (automatic negative thoughts), and may lean toward depression. They have an innate ability to understand others' experiences and feelings outside of their own.

They tend to score low on the following traits: emotional detachment, superficiality, consistent happiness, apathy, and positive thoughts. Our brain imaging work shows that the Sensitive brain type often has increased activity in the limbic or emotional areas of the brain. They are happiest when they can chill out and spend time in silence or with just one friend or loved one.

Exercise and certain supplements, such as saffron, s-adenosylmethionine (SAMe), vitamin D, and omega-3 fatty acids can help the Sensitive brain type. If someone with this type is also a Persistent brain type, the supplements or medications that boost serotonin may help.

TODAY'S PRACTICE: *If you have the Sensitive brain type, give or get a massage to boost your oxytocin, and add yoga to your weekly workout routines.*

Cautious Brain Type

The Cautious brain type is common among accountants, researchers, and data analysts. People with this type tend to be prepared, cautious, risk averse, motivated, early to appointments, reserved, and temperamental. They have a busy mind, have difficulty relaxing, and tend toward anxiety.

They often score low on the following traits: risk-taking, calmness, relaxation, even-tempered, secure, and indifferent toward preparation. They have high standards (for themselves and others), analyze issues in great detail before taking action, and are thorough and reliable. They're the type who gets things done and does them well. Someone who's on the extreme end of the Spontaneous type and has ADD could never accomplish what a Cautious person can do in the same amount of time.

On SPECT images, we often see heightened activity in the anxiety centers of the brain, such as the basal ganglia, insular cortex, or amygdala. Often due to low levels of the neurotransmitter GABA, people with this type tend to struggle more with anxiety, which causes them to be more cautious and reserved, but on the flip side, also more prepared. Soothing this type with meditation and hypnosis can help, as can a combination of vitamin B6, magnesium, and GABA.

TODAY'S PRACTICE: *If you have the Cautious brain type, try hypnosis or tapping, also known as Emotional Freedom Technique (visit medicalnewstoday.com/articles /326434 to learn more), to balance your cortisol levels and stay calm in the face of stress.*

Natural Treatments Whenever Possible

When making treatment recommendations, I first think about whether I would prescribe it to my parents, my spouse, or my kids. I do not object to prescription medications when they are necessary, but I do recommend taking advantage of other options as well, particularly if they can produce results, are more affordable, and don't come with as many side effects. A case involving one of my younger relatives spurred my interest in natural supplements. The second grader was having issues with anger outbursts and mood swings. When standard prescription medications didn't work, I decided to try her on some well-researched natural supplements. When I got a call from the girl's mother a couple months later, I was pleased to learn that the young girl was being more agreeable, feeling calmer, and doing better academically. The nutraceuticals were beneficial, and there were no side effects. In my practice, I eventually decided to start with natural supplements first, and if they didn't work, then I would try prescription medications. Here is a quick look at the upsides and downsides of nutraceuticals.

On the positive side, well-studied nutraceuticals can be beneficial, may be more affordable, and don't come with a litany of side effects like so many medications do. Maintaining your privacy is another plus, as having a history of psychiatric medications on your medical chart may impact your ability to obtain insurance or may raise your rates.

There are some negatives, however. Considering that health insurance companies do not cover nutritional supplements, your out-of-pocket costs may be higher than what you would pay for some medications that are covered. Natural supplements may produce some side effects, so you need to use them wisely. Take zinc, for example. Too much of it on an empty belly may cause an upset stomach. Another potential issue is inconsistent quality control with some cheaper brands. In general, it's best to choose supplements that are clinical grade and free of toxins. In addition, be aware that the cashier at your local drug store may not have adequate training to make the best recommendations for you.

In many cases, the benefits of nutraceuticals outweigh the downsides. Be sure to work with a knowledgeable health-care provider to determine the right options for your needs.

TODAY'S PRACTICE: *Check the ingredients on your vitamins and supplements, and use only those that have been verified by an independent third party. If they don't have that, find an alternative source.*

Supplement Basics for the Brain

Nutraceuticals are a low-cost option that should be considered.[96] *At Amen Clinics we are not opposed to medications, and we prescribe them when necessary.* We are opposed to medications being the first and only thing you do to help make your brain better. The pharmaceutical revolution has consumed psychiatry for the past 50 years, but unfortunately, outcomes have not improved along with the enthusiasm. One of the reasons outcomes lag behind is that many psychiatrists and physicians are working within the wrong paradigm—making diagnoses based on symptom clusters without any biological information and while ignoring overall brain health.

I first became interested in using nutraceuticals after looking at SPECT scans. I saw that some of the medications I was taught to prescribe, especially benzodiazepines for anxiety and opiates for pain, were associated with unhealthy-looking scans. In thinking of the principle all physicians are taught the first year of medical school, "primum non nocere," which is Latin for "first, do no harm," I started looking for less toxic options for our patients and was surprised to find a growing body of scientific literature to support the use of supplements for many of the issues I treated. I also consider short-term pain versus long-term gain and try not to fix one problem just to cause another one. I don't want my patients to start something they will have a hard time stopping (withdrawing from many antianxiety or antidepressant medications can be very hard), just to deal with the anxiety of the moment.

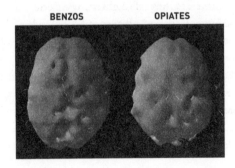

I recommend that everyone have a core nutraceutical program that includes a broad-spectrum multivitamin/mineral supplement and an omega-3 fatty acid supplement with EPA and DHA, from fish oil or a vegan algae source. These are all critical for your enzyme systems to work. Surveys by the Centers for Disease Control and Prevention (CDC) find many people are deficient in one or more of these vital nutraceuticals due to our poor-quality diet, or they are being depleted from our bodies due to stress or the effects of certain medications.[97]

TODAY'S PRACTICE: *Take a multivitamin/mineral supplement.*

Protecting Teenage Brains

From a neuroscience perspective, you are really not an adult until you are 25 or so. We assume that when kids turn 18 (or maybe 21) they become adults, but it's not true. They are still growing, specifically their brains. The prefrontal cortex (PFC), which controls planning, judgment, impulse control, decision-making, and empathy (required for maturity), is still developing up to 25 years old. Auto insurance companies knew this long ago—that's why insurance rates are higher for teen and young adult drivers. Rates drop after 25 because that's when we typically become more conscientious as drivers and are less likely to have accidents. Part of brain development is something known as myelinization, which is when brain cells are coated with a protective substance (myelin) so they work more efficiently. The process starts at the back of the brain and moves toward the PFC, which is the last part to gain this protective covering.

This matters because parents need to be vigilant about protecting their teenagers and young adults, especially while they still live at home. Parents often allow their kids to have more and more freedom as they grow up and stop overseeing meals, sleep, and stress. It's also easy to let them start making their own choices, even about sports with high risk of head injury, smoking, or vaping. In fact, we should do more to keep kids from going off to college too soon, where it's easy to start brain-destroying behaviors without the benefit of a strong PFC—things such as alcohol use, obsessive online games, betting, all-nighters, and porn.

Parents have good intentions and often spend thousands of dollars to set up their children for success with extracurricular activities, private tutors, and the latest technology. Too often the most important organ is left out. The brain is the one that tells the body how to shoot a basket, replay a piece of classical music, ace an exam, and balance en pointe in ballet. Investing in brain health is the best decision for any child's future.

TODAY'S PRACTICE: *Compare your own decision-making skills when you were age 18 versus age 25.*

Brain Warrior Alicia Dominates Her Husband in Table Tennis

The best way to improve sports performance is to improve your brain. Alicia, 53, was struggling with brain fog, memory problems, anxiety, and symptoms of ADHD/ADD (short attention span, distractibility, disorganization, impulsivity) when she first came to see us. Her SPECT scan showed low overall activity, especially in the prefrontal cortex (see images below). As we attacked each of her BRIGHT MINDS risk factors and used nutraceuticals, including omega-3 fatty acids, multivitamins, ginkgo, huperzine A, and phosphatidylserine, her brain fog cleared, and her memory and focus were better. And one more thing that was very important to her changed—her ping-pong game dramatically improved.

BEFORE   AFTER

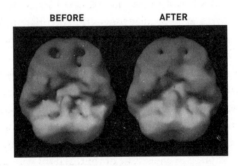

Alicia had been playing ping-pong for months in an effort to boost her brain, but initially she always lost to her husband because her mind would wander. Her husband even played left-handed in order to give her an advantage. After starting the nutraceuticals, she said, "I was beating my husband in ping-pong every game, and it happened overnight. . . . My husband was really angry that I was beating him." Alicia then hired a ping-pong coach because she wanted to keep beating her husband. She also said this about work: "I'm getting a lot more done, and I am happier." Her follow-up scan was much better. Not to be outdone, her husband started the nutraceuticals, lost 30 pounds, and became serious about his brain health. In addition, her adult children, who saw the benefit in their mother, started eating better, exercising, and taking nutraceuticals too.

TODAY'S PRACTICE: *Do one coordination exercise today—such as dancing, golf, or tai chi—for just a few minutes. I'm playing ping-pong.*

Discipline Your Mind

It's not the thoughts you have that make you suffer, it's the thoughts you attach to. How you feel is often related to the quality of your thoughts. If they are mostly negative, you will feel mostly negative; if they are mostly positive, you will feel mostly positive. Each thought you have triggers the release of certain chemicals, which makes you feel good or bad. It's true that negative thoughts release chemicals that affect you negatively and positive, uplifting, or sunny thoughts trigger chemicals that affect you in a positive way. Here's the thing: Thoughts occur automatically; they just happen. So it's important to recognize whether your thoughts are lying to you or telling the truth.

Undisciplined or negative thinking is like a bad habit. The more you engage in it, the more easily the ANTs will attack and take over your mind. These bad thinking habits form through a process called long-term potentiation. When neurons fire together, they wire together, and the negative thoughts become an ingrained part of your life. ANTs hook up with and build upon each other. One ANT often brings other ANTs to attack you. For example, the ANTs like to do this when you're tired, when there's been a drop in your blood sugar, on gray winter days, during PMS for women, when you're under stress, and when you lose someone you love. The coronavirus pandemic led to an ANT infestation unlike anything we've seen before.

Let me be very clear, I'm not a fan of positive thinking. Positive thinking says you can have the third piece of cheesecake or third glass of wine and it won't hurt you. I'm a fan of accurate thinking. I always want you to tell yourself the truth. Accurate thinking leads to better mental health, fewer bad habits, and a happier life, while unbridled positive thinking does not.

TODAY'S PRACTICE: *Whenever you feel sad, mad, nervous, or out of control, write down your automatic thoughts and ask yourself if they are true.*

Know the Nine Types of ANTs

There are many ways to distort the truth. Not all lies are the same. I've seen basically nine types of ANTs that steal your happiness. Here is a brief summary.

ANT Types

1. **All-or-Nothing ANTs:** Thinking that things are either all good or all bad
2. **Less-Than ANTs:** Where you compare and see yourself as less than others
3. **Just-the-Bad ANTs:** Seeing only the bad in a situation
4. **Guilt-Beating ANTs:** Thinking in words like *should, must, ought,* or *have to*
5. **Labeling ANTs:** Attaching a negative label to yourself or someone else
6. **Fortune-Telling ANTs:** Predicting the worst possible outcome for a situation with little or no evidence for it
7. **Mind-Reading ANTs:** Believing you know what other people are thinking even though they haven't told you
8. **If-Only and I'll-Be-Happy-When ANTs:** Where you argue with the past and long for the future
9. **Blaming ANTs:** Blaming someone else for your problems

TODAY'S PRACTICE: *Notice which ANT type is most common in your mind.*

How to Kill the ANTs

You do not have to believe every thought you have. If you want emotional freedom, you must become an expert at learning to kill the ANTs. Here's one of the most powerful exercises I do with my patients. Whenever you feel sad, mad, nervous, or out of control, write down your ANTs, identify which type they are, then ask yourself the five simple questions I learned from my friend Byron Katie.[98] There are no right or wrong answers; they are just questions. Meditate on each answer to see how it makes you feel.

ANT / ANT Type:[99]

> Question 1. Is it true? Sometimes this first question will stop the ANT because you already know the thought is not true. Sometimes your answer will be "I don't know."
>
> Question 2. Is it absolutely true? Do you know it with 100 percent certainty? This often cracks the thought.
>
> Question 3. How do I feel when I believe this thought? How do I act with this thought? What is the outcome of having this thought?
>
> Question 4. How would I feel and act, and what would be the outcome, if I couldn't have this thought?
>
> Question 5. Turn the thought around to its opposite. Then ask if the opposite of the thought is true or even truer than the original thought.

Here's an example: One of my patients called in a panic because she lost her job, and she told me, "I'll never be able to work again." I guided her through the five questions to work on that thought:

ANT: "I'll never be able to work again." ANT Type: Fortune-Telling

> Question 1. Is it true? Yes.
>
> Question 2. Is it absolutely true with 100 percent certainty? No, I already have part-time work lined up.
>
> Question 3. How do I feel and act, and what is the outcome, when I believe this thought? I feel trapped, victimized, and helpless. I then isolate. The outcome is a downward spiral.
>
> Question 4. How would I feel and act, and what would be the outcome, if I couldn't have the thought? I would feel relieved, happy, joyful, free. I would act by looking for a new job. The outcome would be personal progress.
>
> Question 5. Turn the thought around to its opposite: I can get work again. I already have part-time work.

TODAY'S PRACTICE: *Write down five of your worst thoughts and do the "Kill the ANTs" exercise on each one.*

Five Ways to Increase Willpower

Whether sticking to a diet, saving for retirement, or remaining faithful in your marriage, willpower can help you have a beautiful brain, or the lack of it can completely ruin your life. Here are five strategies to boost your willpower and self-control:

1. **Do not let your blood sugar get too low.** Low blood sugar levels are associated with poor impulse control. If you want better willpower, have frequent smaller meals that each have at least some protein and healthy fat.
2. **Get enough sleep.** Less than seven hours of sleep at night has been associated with lower overall brain activity and less willpower.
3. **On one piece of paper write down the specific goals you have for your life, relationships, work, money, and health.** Then every day ask yourself, *Is my behavior getting me what I want?* Focus and meditate on what you want. Your mind is powerful and it makes happen what it sees.
4. **You have to practice willpower.** Willpower is like a muscle. The more you use it, the stronger it gets. This is why good parenting is essential to helping children develop self-control. If I had given in to my kids every time they wanted something, I would have raised spoiled, demanding adults. By saying no, I taught them to be able to say no to themselves. To develop willpower, you need to do the same thing for yourself. Practice saying no to the things that are not good for you, and over time you will find it gets easier
5. **Balance your brain chemistry.** Issues such as ADD/ADHD, anxiety, depression, and past concussions decrease willpower. Getting help for these problems is essential to being in control of your life.

TODAY'S PRACTICE: *Where are you struggling with willpower in relation to your health? Practice strategy number three above in relation to it today.*

Be Curious, Not Furious

Realistically expect trouble and you won't be surprised by it. On a trip, I expect 10 things to go wrong, so I am not upset until the eleventh thing goes wrong. Be curious, not furious about relapses or setbacks. In order to change, you have to be prepared for the inevitable roadblocks and setbacks. It is critical to identify your most vulnerable moments and have a plan to overcome them. Change is a process! If you pay attention, the difficult times can be more instructive and helpful than the good times. Take bad days and turn them into great data.

I often go to the whiteboard in my offices and draw the following diagram.

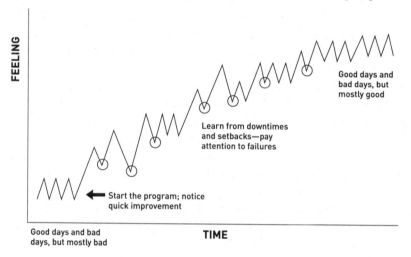

When people come to see me, they usually are not doing very well. Over time, if they cooperate, they get better. But no one gets better in a straight line. They get better, then there is a setback, then they get better still, then there may be another setback, then they continue to improve. Over time, they reach a new steady state where they are consistently better. The setbacks are important if you pay attention to them.

How do you respond when you fail? It all depends on your brain. For some people, failure lights up their *motivation* centers, which means they are often able to learn from failure and grow. Their brain motivates them to overcome challenges. For other people, failure lights up the *pain* centers in the brain—it literally hurts—meaning they will do everything in their power to forget and ignore what happened. The problem is that their brain has set them up for more failure because they miss the lessons. This explains why so many people repeat their mistakes. But when you choose to learn from your failures, they can become steps to success.

TODAY'S PRACTICE: *Think about the times you typically make mistakes, such as while traveling, on weekends, or after a hard day. Do you learn from your failures or ignore them?*

Feel Better Now and Later
vs. Now but Not Later

Some things help you feel good now and later, while other things help you feel good now but not later. Virtually all of us have felt anxious, depressed, traumatized, grief-stricken, or hopeless at some point in life. It's perfectly normal to go through hard times or experience periods when you feel panicked or out of sorts. How you respond to these challenges makes all the difference in how you feel—not just immediately, but in the long run.

All of us want to quickly stop the pain. Unfortunately, many people self-medicate with energy drinks, overeating, alcohol, drugs, risky sexual behavior, angry outbursts, or wasting time on mindless TV, video games, or shopping. Although these substances and behaviors may give you temporary relief from feeling bad, they usually only prolong and exacerbate the problems or cause other more serious ones, such as energy crashes, obesity, addictions, sexually transmitted diseases, unhappiness, relationship problems, or financial ruin.

I want you to think about what habits, foods, and relationships serve your health for the long run, not just the moment. There are plenty of things that may help in the short term but will make you feel worse—or cause more problems—in the long term.

TODAY'S PRACTICE: *Make a list of five things that help you feel good now and later. Then make a list of five things that help you feel good now, but not later.*

Be a Good Parent to Yourself

Firm and kind—these are two of the most important words to remember in your deal-ings with other people and yourself. Are you letting your inner spoiled brat run your life? If you have actual children, you would never let them get away with what your inner spoiled brat does. I've heard so many patients say, "I want what I want when I want it. I don't want to be deprived." Even though they want help for their health concerns, they often throw a tantrum when they hear the solution. They want something easy, a silver bullet, instead of an answer that will require discipline and hard work. If this is you, it's time to be a better parent to yourself.

When training parents, I often tell them that the best moms and dads are those who can be firm and kind. Why? Children require clear guidance and clear lines of authority within an environment of lovingkindness. Actually, we all need that. So don't ignore your inner spoiled brat, but acknowledge him or her with kindness—then make it clear you're the one in charge and don't give in to bad behavior even if he or she starts whining. The tantrum will pass if you respond to it with firm, kind authority.

I recall one patient who was having a hard time losing weight. He kept giving in to his cravings because he couldn't resist them. I knew one of his teenage sons had some behavior problems. So I asked my patient how helpful it would be if he always gave in to his son's angry outbursts. Immediately, he said, "He'd get worse!" All of a sudden, the light bulb went on.

If you are not firm and kind with your inner child's tantrums, cravings, and demands, then you'll only create more problems that ruin your health and kill you early. Start parenting yourself effectively, rather than letting your inner child rule the roost.

TODAY'S PRACTICE: *List one or two areas where you could be firmer with yourself.*

The One Thing

Getting well is about focusing on abundance and depriving yourself of illnesses. Many people fail because they focus on what they cannot have, rather than what they can have. This is a deprivation mindset. One of my favorite movies is *City Slickers*. Billy Crystal plays Mitch, a New Yorker in a full midlife crisis who is searching for his life's purpose by going on a cattle drive. Mitch is riding a horse next to Curly, a gruff cowboy played by Jack Palance. Curly reveals that the secret to life boils down to one thing. When Mitch digs deeper and asks what that secret is, Curly tells him he has to figure it out on his own. When Curly has a fatal heart attack soon after, Mitch is distraught that he didn't learn what the one thing was.

It reminded me of a patient who was having a hard time staying on track with his new healthy habits. Whenever he thought of something he wanted—unhealthy foods or alcohol—he didn't want to deprive himself. I asked him what he wanted most—the booze and sweets or a better brain and a better life? He assured me his top priority was a healthier brain.

That's when I told him about Curly and the "one thing." Except I actually filled him in on the secret. When you're treating your brain and body with respect, the sense of deprivation disappears. Deprivation is what happens when you go off track—drinking and eating sugary foods that deprive you of your main goal in life, which is to have physical vitality, a clear mind, and a purposeful life.

TODAY'S PRACTICE: *List four ways your life will be better when you stay on a brain health path. When you feel like cheating, remind yourself of the things you are giving up for what you really want.*

Where You Bring Your Attention Determines How You Feel

Be the designer of your mind, mood, and attitude. You can train your mind. Post this next sentence somewhere you can see it every day:

Where you bring your attention always determines how you feel.

If you focus on loss, you will feel grief.
If you focus on fear, you will feel afraid.
If you focus on being belittled, you will feel small.
If you focus on those who have hurt you, you will feel angry.
If you focus on sadness, negativity, and fear, you will feel depressed, negative, and afraid.

Yet the opposite is also true.

If you focus on gratitude, you will feel grateful.
If you focus on those who love you, you will feel loved.
If you focus on those you love, you will feel loving.
If you focus on the times you have felt joy, you will feel joyful.
If you focus on happy times, positivity, and what you are looking forward to, you will feel happy, more positive, and excited.

When you train your mind, you get to choose how you feel.

Train your mind to help you rather than hurt you. Unfortunately, many people focus on their worries and fears, which makes them feel awful. Negative thoughts raise cortisol, which makes you feel anxious and depressed. Positive thoughts release dopamine and serotonin, which help you feel so much better. Once you get your brain healthy, you then have to program your mind. For now, remember that where you bring your attention will determine how you feel.

TODAY'S PRACTICE: *Write down three positive things that happened today, no matter how big or small.*

Eliminate the Little Lies That Keep You Fat, Depressed, and Foggy-Minded

If you repeat a lie often enough, you believe it. Then you live as if it were true. The "little lies" you repeat to yourself are often the gateway thoughts to brain fog, dementia, obesity, and illness. Here are some of the common lies I hear in my office:

Little Lie #1: Everything in moderation. Just a little can't hurt. I call this one the gateway thought to illness, because it is an excuse to cheat.

Little Lie #2: My memory is no good; that is normal. Many people start struggling with their memory in their thirties and forties because of poor health habits. It is never normal to have a poor memory; it is a sign that your brain needs help.

Little Lie #3: Getting healthy is hard. Being sick is much harder.

Little Lie #4: Deprivation isn't for me. Eating good food is about abundance and fueling your brain and body so you can have a better life. Consuming bad food is what deprives you of your main health goals—physical energy, mental sharpness, and positive moods.

Little Lie #5: It's impossible to eat well while traveling. Yes, airports and hotels are filled with high-calorie, sugar-loaded, overly processed foods. But with some pre-planning, you can avoid these traps and eat healthy on the road.

Little Lie #6: All my relatives are fat (diabetic, addicted, depressed, anxious, etc.), so it's genetic. News flash: Genetics play a smaller role in your health—only an estimated 20 to 30 percent—than your everyday habits.[100] Bad decisions drive the vast majority of health problems.

Little Lie #7: Good food is too expensive. What is really costly is being ill—having heart disease, depression, or diabetes.

Little Lie #8: Holidays/birthdays/weekends are for celebrating. Why do you want to celebrate with something that hurts your brain and body?

Little Lie #9: My new habits begin tomorrow. Procrastinating this way can lead to a lifetime of tomorrows.

TODAY'S PRACTICE: *List one to three little lies you tell yourself, then tell one of your friends about one of them. This will help you be accountable to break it.*

Make Rules for Vulnerable Times

Everyone falls; failure only happens when you stop getting up. Many of my patients find it helpful to create simple rules for vulnerable times, such as:

1. Start your meal with healthy foods such as vegetables so there is less room for unhealthy ones.
2. Split entrees.
3. Don't go to a game or concert hungry; it leaves you vulnerable to the temptation of bad foods, such as cotton candy and hot dogs. Eat ahead of time.
4. Swap dinner plates for salad plates so it forces you to have smaller portions.
5. If you want to "cheat" on your nutrition, call a friend first. This will distract you, delay the craving, and enlist some support.
6. Have a plan when you experience cravings or feel out of control: take a walk, drink a glass of water (you may be thirsty but misperceive it as hunger), play Tetris for a few minutes (it actually decreases cravings) until the impulse goes away.[101]

If you are truly going to change, you must change what brings you pleasure. Find what you love about nutritious food. Learn to find what you love about exercise. One of my friends hates running but loves playing table tennis. Connect to who you are becoming; think like a healthy person. How would a healthy person order this meal? The simple act of identifying yourself as a "Brain Warrior," someone who is a healthy role model for others, can be enough to change the way you see yourself and the way you behave.

TODAY'S PRACTICE: *Which of these rules can you adopt for vulnerable times? Write it out and post it where you can see it.*

Brain Warrior Sherry and Investigating Setbacks

To prevent relapses, HALT—don't get too hungry, angry, lonely, or tired. Sherry visited our clinic for anxiety and binge eating and began improving quickly. Then she had a setback. She came into my office looking very sheepish and said, "I know you're going to be disappointed in me." She proceeded to tell me that she'd had a stressful day and was very anxious to learn she would have to give a presentation in front of the entire company. She was so nervous about it that she skipped lunch, and on the way home she stopped for a glass of wine—then a second one—to calm down. The alcohol lowered her brain activity and willpower, and on her drive home she was so hungry she couldn't resist whipping into the drive-through lane at her favorite fast-food joint. She ordered cheeseburgers, fries slathered in cheese, and two milkshakes, and she ate it all. Afterward, she felt miserable and defeated.

Rather than shaking my head or acting disappointed, I encouraged Sherry to be curious and investigate what went wrong. Here are four key things she learned:

1. If she is feeling anxious, she needs to eat a healthy snack because hunger can cause blood-sugar levels to drop, which increases anxiety.
2. She would benefit more from stress-reduction strategies like diaphragmatic breathing than from drinking alcohol.
3. If she is going to have a glass of wine, she needs to have a healthy meal beforehand, so it doesn't have such a powerful effect on her brain function.
4. If she is in a vulnerable state, she needs to be aware of environmental triggers (like that fast-food restaurant) and avoid them.

To help Sherry prevent future relapses, we went over the acronym HALT, which stands for:

- Hungry: Reduces blood sugar
- Angry/Anxious: Negativity decreases cerebral blood flow
- Lonely: More likely to use food or substances to soothe emotions
- Tired: Lowers blood flow to prefrontal cortex

By investigating this incident, Sherry learned important lessons that helped her manage her anxiety and curb her binge eating for the long haul.

TODAY'S PRACTICE: *When is the last time you felt hungry, angry, lonely, or tired? How did it impact your choices?*

Family and Friends—and You—Are Contagious

Every day, you are modeling health or illness. You get to choose which one. The people close to you can affect how long you live and how happy you are. It is important to be selective in your relationships because people affect your brain, mood, and physical health. A wealth of research indicates that being around individuals who have an unhealthy lifestyle increases the likelihood that you will pick up their bad habits. In one study, Harvard researchers followed 12,067 people for 32 years and found that the spread of obesity was largely linked to a person's friends and family. In this study, having a friend who became obese increased one's own chances of obesity by 57 percent. And if that person was the equivalent of a BFF, the odds jumped to 171 percent. Family matters too. If a sibling was obese, it increased the risk for the other siblings by 40 percent. And if a spouse joined the high BMI group, it raised the partner's risk by 37 percent.[102]

What can you learn from this study? Your social network can greatly influence your own health habits. By the same token, you can become a powerful role model for your friends and family. When you start modeling brain health in your thoughts and actions, you become "contagious" in a good way. You can start spreading beneficial habits not only to your family and friends but also to their extended social circles. Use your social connections to enhance health. People can connect to improve their lives through walking groups, healthy cooking groups, meditation groups, new learning groups, and so on. When you spend time with people who are focused on their health, you are much more likely to do the same.

TODAY'S PRACTICE: *Who are the five people closest to you? Are they a good or poor influence on your health? Are you modeling health or illness for them?*

Now Is the Only Time You Will Get Well

I have found that when you make the commitment NOW—rather than at some nebulous time in the future—to eliminate the behaviors that lead to illness, you can change your life in amazing ways. This simple choice empowers you to stop taking shortcuts and making up excuses that keep you stuck where you are. It is the first step to lasting health. From there, you must steadfastly weave the program into your daily life, bit by bit, in an intentional way for at least a year. Programs that promise big changes in a matter of days or weeks can be seductive, but they rarely result in lasting changes.

Here's one of my favorite examples of the negative effects of short-term thinking. While working on one of my public television programs, I noticed that one of the local hosts I knew looked fantastic compared to when I had last seen him. Curious, I inquired about how he had lost weight. He told me he was on the HCG (human chorionic gonadotropin) diet, which required him to be injected regularly with a pregnancy hormone (HCG), and eat only 500 calories a day, in 26-day cycles. His 30-pound weight loss was impressive. But then he told me that since he was just finishing the last cycle, he was celebrating by ordering two deep-dish pizzas from his favorite Italian restaurant in Chicago. Clearly, the horror on my face at what he had just said didn't go unnoticed. "What?" he asked.

I said, "It is like you are an alcoholic who just spent a month in a recovery center and are going out to have a few drinks to celebrate!"

Not surprisingly, when I saw him again, he had gained back the 30 pounds. Fortunately, many years after that, he had made a lifetime decision and has kept the weight off. He looks incredible now.

TODAY'S PRACTICE: *Look for examples of a short-term mindset or insanity in your behavior. What commitment can you make today to help eliminate a mindset or behavior that leads to illness?*

It's Not Me; It's What Happened to Me

One person can make a big difference in the world. Yuk-Lynn lived in Hong Kong. She was often fatigued and had marriage issues as well as a teenage son, Jonathan, who struggled in school and had some emotional problems. After reading my book *Change Your Brain, Change Your Life*, she knew our clinics could help them. Initially, Jonathan and Yuk-Lynn's husband, Roy, came for evaluations, which made an incredible difference in their lives. Jonathan had had a hard birth, and his brain scan showed evidence of physical trauma. The scan helped him see why he struggled so much and understand that it wasn't him—rather, it was what happened to him at birth that had caused challenges for him. This encouraged him to be compliant with the treatment plan, which helped him significantly. Roy also became more engaged, and this strengthened their marriage. Yuk-Lynn came for help too, as did her parents, siblings, and many other family members and friends. Following this, she had a positive impact on her community by introducing brain health concepts to the people she loved and cared about.

Given the difference in their lives, this family wanted to help me bring brain SPECT imaging to China and a wider level of acceptance throughout the world. Their foundation donated a significant amount of money to our Change Your Brain, Change Your Life Foundation so we could put all of our scans and anonymous patient information into a searchable database and publish large-scale research studies. Because of them, we have published the largest brain imaging studies ever done on posttraumatic stress disorder versus traumatic brain injuries (based on about 21,000 scans); weight and obesity (33,000 scans); and aging (62,000 scans).[103] I will be eternally grateful to Yuk-Lynn and Roy.

TODAY'S PRACTICE: *Identify one person you care about who needs to become healthier. What is one thing you can do to positively influence them?*

It's More Expensive Not to Get Help

What does it cost to have ineffectively treated psychiatric issues or a brain that is not working at its best? What is the cost of school failure, job failure, underachievement, divorce, bankruptcy, abuse, incarceration, addiction treatment programs, or failed medication trials? When Edward came to Amen Clinics, he was driving a truck for a living. He had just split from his second wife, felt sad, was extremely anxious, and was having suicidal thoughts. He frequently had the urge to drive his truck off a bridge or over a cliff. When I went to the waiting room to greet Edward for the first time, I saw him drawing in an artist's sketchbook. When I asked about it, he hesitantly showed me his picture. It was amazing. I thought that he must have been a trained professional artist, yet it was not mentioned in his background information. Edward's clinical evaluation and brain scans revealed he suffered from depression, anxiety, and ADD/ADHD. For all of his adult life, he had struggled to keep jobs and was a never-ending source of frustration to his romantic partners. He was sick of feeling bad and was now motivated to get help.

With treatment, which was a combination of dietary changes, exercise, nutritional supplements, medication, and strategies to manage his mind, he began to heal. It turned out that Edward had always wanted to be an artist. His teachers told him that he was gifted from the time he was in grade school. Yet he was never able to follow through and finish the projects he started. As his treatment began to take hold, he started completing art pieces. He was able to sell several paintings in a local gallery. Over the next year, the demand for his work increased and he was able to quit working for the trucking company to focus on his art full time. Three years after I first met Edward, he sold a painting for more than $100,000. Many people think they cannot afford to get help. Yet living with an untreated or ineffectively treated psychiatric illness is much more expensive than spending money to get the help you need.

TODAY'S PRACTICE: *List two or three costs in your life of a brain that is not working at its peak.*

Food Is Medicine or Poison

Getting your food right is not just for humans. To the left is a picture of Aslan, our white shepherd. He is the sweetest dog, but since the day we got him, he had chronic diarrhea, ear infections, and anxiety. One day we came home and found him bleeding and crying in the corner. He looked like he'd been attacked by another animal, his fur was macerated, and he wouldn't let me touch him. We were horrified and ended up spending thousands of dollars to find out he was having severe food allergies to the "high quality" premium dog food we were feeding him.

The vet suggested we put him on an elimination diet, which was funny because we do that all the time for our patients. His new dog food had just five ingredients: lamb or duck, sweet potatoes, cranberries, blueberries, and kale. Sound like a brain healthy diet? Within one week, his skin cleared up, his fur became shiny, and he was happier, calmer, and more playful.

Many people think good food is expensive, but being sick is way more expensive and painful.

Food is medicine . . . or it is poison.

TODAY'S PRACTICE: *If you have animals, are you feeding them in a brain-healthy way?*

It's Not about You, but Generations of You

Falling in love with your brain can transform the lives of those you love. Fatima worked with me to bring my work into corporations. At the time, she was encouraging her husband to get healthy, but Rob was not paying attention. He had back problems, arthritis in his knees, insomnia, and a sluggish memory. After knee surgery, his doctor told him that he would never run again. His father had his first heart attack at age 40 and died at 58. In addition, their boys, ages 10 and 13, were both struggling in school. As Fatima watched the videos of my program, Rob and the boys decided to join her. As they watched the shows, brain envy started to take over in their household and everything in their family changed—from their diet, to their activity level, to making smarter choices.

From Fatima:

> After watching your programs, we all fell in love with our brains, especially Rob. He began following a brain-healthy diet and lost 39 pounds! He also began taking fish oil, vitamin D, a high-quality multivitamin every day, and supplements for his brain. He says his memory, brain function, creativity, and mood have all been boosted. He now sees his choices as a "best value" for spending his calories. Rob's pain is gone, and he has just finished his second triathlon this year. At work, in a meeting recently he was able to come up with the name of a client they had seen 12 years earlier. The kids are both doing much better. Kaden, age 13, was struggling in school, but after a month on the program his teacher said he had made a "dramatic improvement," and "whatever you're doing different, please keep it up." Sage, 10, has also improved and is more amiable at home. Now that Rob has had such great improvement, his parents and siblings have also gotten on the program. Because of the changes in the household, I am less stressed and happier as well. Our family has really benefited from your programs!

TODAY'S PRACTICE: *Tell two or three people you love why you want to have a healthier brain and why you want them to join you in doing this.*

Give Your Mind a Name

Gain psychological distance from the noise in your head. Research shows that gaining psychological distance from the noise in your head can lead to more positive emotions, better self-control, and even wisdom.[104] One psychological distancing technique I love is to "give your mind a name."[105] Giving your mind a name allows you to choose whether to listen to it, just like you can choose whether to listen to your spouse or anyone else. When I first learned this technique from Dr. Steven Hayes, I knew almost instantly that I would name my mind Hermie, after the pet raccoon I had when I was 16. I loved Hermie, but like my mind, she was a troublemaker and got me into a lot of hot water. She once TPed my mother's bathroom, and when my father got home, Mom said, "Louie, it's either me or the raccoon!" No one ever told my dad what to do, and he told my mom not to let the door hit her in the rear. That was a bad day. A few months later, Hermie ate all of the fish in my sister's aquarium—another bad day—and Hermie would periodically leave raccoon poo in my shoes as a gift of love.

I often imagine Hermie holding up signs in my head, with random negative thoughts, such as *you're an idiot, you're a failure,* or *you're a fool.* Of course, none of that is true on most days. Knowing that I am not my thoughts, I can choose to ignore Hermie—metaphorically putting her in her cage. If you give your mind a name, you don't have to take yourself so seriously. You can gain psychological distance and be happier overall.

Michelle, who took our 30-Day Happiness Challenge (amenuniversity.com/happy), named her mind Mickey and said, "It's fun to yell at her when she is trying to make me think junk food is happy food." Troy, a police officer who suffered from PTSD, named his mind Andy after the parrot he had as a child who only had eight words. He realized his mind was just repeating the same negative nonsense that got stuck in his head.

TODAY'S PRACTICE: *What will you name your mind? Why?*

If You Knew a Train Was Going to Hit You, Would You at Least Try to Get Out of the Way?

Too many people do not seek help because they erroneously think there's nothing they can do. Several years ago, two women were in the news because they were trapped on an 80-foot-high railroad bridge in Indiana with a freight train barreling toward them and no way out! Ultimately, the women survived by lying down flat in the middle of the tracks while the train flew by above them. But what were they doing on an active railroad bridge with no way out?[106]

The story reminds me of how blind most people are to the health of their brains. If you knew brain problems were coming for you, would you at least want to start making better decisions today to get out of the way? Many people don't want to know about the health of their brain because they erroneously think there's nothing they can do to make it better. I've seen this mindset in many former NFL players. They don't seek help because they believe their situation is hopeless due to the thousands of hits to the head they've experienced. They worry they might have CTE (chronic traumatic encephalopathy) and their fate is a date with dementia and depression. This mindset is also common among people with memory problems or those who have family members with Alzheimer's disease or other forms of dementia. They have no hope anything can be done.

All of these groups are wrong. At Amen Clinics we have seen that you can improve your brain, even if you have been bad to it. In fact, when we did the big NFL study where we scanned and treated more than 300 active and former players, yes, there were high levels of damage, but 80 percent of our players showed improvement in as little as a few months.[107] We rehabilitated their brains, using techniques such as diet, natural supplements, and hyperbaric oxygen therapy. You are not stuck with the brain you have; you can make it better, and I can prove it.

TODAY'S PRACTICE: *If you have been putting off getting assessed for potential brain health or mental health issues because you fear you cannot improve, rethink that position and look into scheduling an appointment today.*

Brain Warrior Judy Changed Her Family

I'm going to be healthy long after you are dead. The Daniel Plan was a program Dr. Mark Hyman and I created along with Rick Warren, the pastor of Saddleback Church. Our goal was to use religious organizations as a vehicle for getting people healthy throughout the world.

About 12 months after the program began, a woman named Judy came up to Tana and me after church and shared how the Daniel Plan had helped not only her, but her entire family too. It taught Judy how harmful their sugar-laden, fast-food diet was. She also told us that when she learned about epigenetics, she realized that the unhealthy dietary decisions they were making not only affected the long-term health of their kids, but could adversely affect their grandchildren too!

Although Judy got right on board with the program, her 300-pound husband initially resisted, thinking the Daniel Plan was hogwash. Fortunately, she remembered that we had encouraged participants to lead by example rather than trying to force others to join them. Only once did she quip, "I'll be happy long after you are dead."

Judy chose to take her health and the program seriously and shed 45 pounds while gaining more energy. Ultimately, her successes inspired her husband, who wanted to feel good again too. When Tana and I chatted with her, he had already lost 75 pounds and significantly improved his fitness.

To top it off, all their children were following the program as well, and not only had they become more active, but they were also doing better academically. Together on this new journey, the whole family found support in one another.

What I love about Judy's story is that she and her husband came to realize that now they were going to leave a legacy of health to their descendants, rather than one of unnecessary sickness.

TODAY'S PRACTICE: *Identify the most important change you need to make right now to become healthier.*

Three Steps to Thrive in a Crisis

Develop a TLC mindset. How can you be happy while the world is falling apart? The people who are resilient versus those who are not have a TLC mindset. They see what is happening as temporary, local, and with some sense of control. People who crumble in hard times tend to see the situation as permanent (things will never change) and global (it's everywhere), and they feel as though they have no control over the situation (they feel like a victim). Here's how I used TLC to deal with the COVID-19 pandemic.

Temporary: The coronavirus pandemic will not last forever. Think about all the pandemics from the past—the Spanish influenza, bubonic plague, and cholera, for example. They all eventually resolved. This, too, will pass.

Local: Although COVID-19 was worldwide, it did not hit every street in every city in the world. While far too many died, the vast majority of those who contracted the virus survived. Even though my dad died not long after contracting the virus, my mom and others close to me survived it.

Control: What can I "control" during hard times and what can't I control? During the pandemic, I practiced good hygiene, wore a mask where appropriate, and shored up my immune system with vitamins D, C, zinc, and mushroom extracts. I also took one of the available vaccines, because my experience with my patients was that those who were vaccinated fared better than those who were not.

For managing the control aspect of TLC, I often say the Serenity Prayer. It is the essence of mental health: *God, grant me the serenity to accept the things I cannot change, the courage to change the things I can, and wisdom to know the difference.* This is the happy person's way of life. Practicing TLC will strengthen your resilience to get through any significant issue in your life.

TODAY'S PRACTICE: *Say the serenity prayer three times today.*

Disconnecting the Emotional Bridges from the Past

HEALTHY ACTIVE SCAN   EMOTIONAL TRAUMA

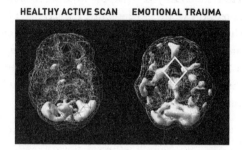

Don't let the past haunt the present. Sharon came to see me for being anxious and overweight. Her SPECT scan showed she had an emotional trauma pattern. We call it the "diamond pattern" because the overactive emotional part of the brain looks like a diamond. When I first asked her about trauma, she initially denied any. I then asked her why she overate. "I don't know," she said. "Sometimes I just feel so nervous, and food makes me feel better." So we used one of the effective tools I love called "Disconnecting the Bridges from the Past."

It involves four steps:

1. When was the last time you struggled with the behavior?
2. What were you thinking or feeling at the time?
3. Go back to a time when you first had that thought or feeling and ask if there may be a connection.
4. If you find the origin of the feelings, disconnect them by reprocessing them through an adult mindset. Consciously disconnect the emotional bridge to the past with the idea that what happened in the past belongs in the past, and what happens now is what matters. If it is too upsetting to process, a trauma therapist can help you disconnect from the past.

In Sharon's case, whenever she felt anxious, she had trouble breathing. When I asked her what she felt, she said she felt like she was suffocating. I asked her to go back in her mind to the first time in her life that she could remember having trouble breathing. Her mind immediately went back to a time when she was 4 years old and had a piece of steak stuck in her throat. She thought she was going to die. Someone did the Heimlich maneuver and dislodged the piece of meat. She was so upset that she couldn't stop crying. Her parents gave her cake and ice cream to calm her down. Once she understood the emotional bridge, she was able to disconnect her anxiety from the event and made significant progress on her weight over the next year.

TODAY'S PRACTICE: *Remember a recent time you were upset or triggered and use these four steps to disconnect from the past.*

Healthy Ways to Deal with Pain

Pain and depression go together. Pain is one of the most frightening symptoms that we can have. Chronic pain affects everything in a negative way, such as sleep, mood, memory, and concentration. SPECT scans have taught me that the use of chronic pain medications, such as Vicodin or Oxycontin, may be harmful to brain function. Long-term use of these medications makes the brain look as if the person drinks too much. I am not suggesting that you throw out your pain medications. I'm a baby when it comes to pain, and I know some people would rather die than live with pain. But because of what I've seen on scans, I developed an interest in alternative treatments for pain. Fish oil, acupuncture, music therapy, and hypnosis all have scientific evidence that they may be helpful.[108]

From a psychiatrist's standpoint, I have also learned that pain and depression tend to go hand in hand, and that for some people, using natural supplements such as SAMe or curcumins, or the antidepressant medicine Cymbalta, can help both problems. There are many natural ways to help the brain. Of course, you should talk to your doctor. If he or she does not know much about natural supplements, as many of us were never taught about them in school, sometimes a naturopath or integrative or functional medicine practitioner can be helpful.

One other thought on pain: Try getting rid of all the artificial sweeteners in your diet. When I was 37, I had arthritis. I had trouble getting up off the floor after playing with my children. As part of developing a brain-healthy life, I got rid of the diet sodas. Within a month, my pain went away. I don't think artificial sweeteners do that to everyone, but if you hurt, it is something to consider.

TODAY'S PRACTICE: *If you are struggling with pain, choose one or two natural strategies that can help you manage your symptoms.*

Can Red Dye 40 Get You into Trouble?

What do the following foods have in common: Froot Loops fruit snacks, Lucky Charms, Brisk Raspberry Iced Tea, Hershey's Lite Syrup (chocolate)? They all contain Red Dye 40. The food industry dumps 15 million pounds of artificial dyes into our food every year—over 40 percent of which is Red Dye 40, a petroleum-based substance.[109] Red Dye 40 is the number one food dye in the US, and it is found in most unnaturally red foods. Even though there are safe and natural color alternatives available, artificial food dyes are a cheap way for manufacturers to make processed foods brighter and more appealing when you see them on a shelf in the grocery store. Although Red Dye 40 has been approved by the FDA for use in food products and must be listed as an ingredient on labels, it has been banned at one time or another throughout Australia and most of Europe due to health concerns.

NO RED DYE 40   **RED DYE 40**

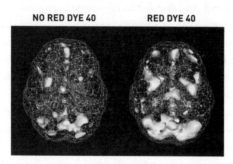

When Trey was 7 years old, his parents noticed that whenever he ate something bright red or drank a red Slurpee, he had various tics and strange neurological affectations, and his behavior became more aggressive and hostile. He would cry easily and storm off in a huff or throw things. His mother tried to minimize these foods in his diet, but he would often get them at school: Cheetos, Doritos, fruit punch, Red Vines, lollipops, and so on. What she didn't realize was that many of the "healthy" foods she was serving him at home—strawberry yogurt, whole-grain strawberry bars, and even the canned pasta sauce and ketchup—contained Red 40. When Trey was 14, we scanned him on and off the dye. His brain SPECT scan showed overall increased activity with exposure to Red Dye 40. By staying away from Red 40, Trey's mood stabilized and he was the kind, sweet, helpful teen he had always wanted to be.

TODAY'S PRACTICE: *Read the labels to see if anything you or your child ingests has Red Dye 40 (or any other artificial coloring or flavor) in it and start eliminating those from your diet.*

Can Brain Health Make You More Beautiful?

"Tell me the truth, Joni, did you get a mini face-lift?" Joni started attending one of the groups we have at the Amen Clinics to get healthier, both physically and emotionally. After about 10 weeks and 10 pounds down, she told me that she went out to breakfast with her twin sister, who asked, "Okay, Joni, tell me the truth. Did you have a mini face-lift?"

Joni said she was surprised and flattered. "No, I promise I haven't!"

"Seriously?" her twin replied. "Even my sons thought you'd had some 'work' done!"

All Joni had done was change her diet, exercise, add some high-quality supplements, and be more conscientious about her health.

In the process of getting her brain scanned, Joni found out she had ADD/ADHD, which shows up as low activity in the front part of the brain. The symptoms of ADD/ADHD include a short attention span, distractibility, disorganization, restlessness, and problems with impulse control. It explained so much to Joni, including her problem of impulsively running up her credit card bills. The only plastic surgery she had done, she told her sister, was cutting up all of her credit cards.

Joni's advice, and I agree, is if you are considering plastic surgery to look younger, wait six months, get your brain healthy, and see if you still want it. As it turns out, what keeps your brain young also keeps your skin young. And, even though there are no beauty contests for the brain, without a healthy brain you'll never look your best. Anger, depression, anxiety, and brain fog all show up on your face. Getting your brain healthy will also help your skin look younger and more beautiful.

TODAY'S PRACTICE: *Consider spending as much time and money on your brain as you do your skin care, cosmetics, and hair care.*

Never Let Grief Be Your Excuse to Hurt Yourself

Giving yourself the excuse to eat bad food, drink alcohol, or smoke pot to deal with the pain only prolongs it. There is an important finding in the longevity research: People who react to a loss or illness with depression, anxiety, or drinking die earlier than others, while those who stay healthy after a period of grief get a resiliency boost and live five years longer than average.[110]

I met Chris at one of my lectures, where she told me that two years before she lost her 12-year-old daughter, Sammie, to bone cancer. Chris had no idea how hard Sammie's loss would hit her. When she went to bed, Sammie's illness and death played over and over in her mind. Chris ate low-quality food and drank alcohol as a way to cope. Most mornings she woke up in a panic. She felt so useless and so depressed that she secretly planned to kill herself on the two-year anniversary of Sammie's death. Then Chris met a friend who told her about my work. It made sense to her, and she got rid of all the alcohol, ate no processed food, and began taking fish oil and vitamin D. The change was immediate. Within eight days she felt free of the depression and her cravings for bad food and alcohol went away. She slept through the night for the first time in years and didn't wake up with anxiety. After 10 weeks she had lost 24 pounds and was running four days a week. After five months she was down 35 pounds and lost eight inches off her waist.

Of course, she will never forget her daughter, but there is no way Sammie would have wanted her mother to be in such pain. The best time to start healing from a crisis is before it starts. Giving yourself the excuse to eat bad food, drink alcohol, or smoke pot to deal with the pain only prolongs it. Chris asked me to tell my patients, "Never let a crisis be your excuse to hurt yourself."

TODAY'S PRACTICE: *Reflect on how you typically deal with stress and grief. Does it serve your health or steal from it?*

Global Change Is Possible

Let's stop sending people to heaven early. Here's an example, as Tana and I told our readers in *The Brain Warrior's Way*:[111]

On a Sunday morning in August 2010 we went to a church near our home and Daniel told Tana that he would save them seats while Tana dropped Chloe off at children's church. As Daniel walked toward the sanctuary he passed hundreds of doughnuts for sale for charity, which really irritated him. . . . Then he walked by bacon and sausage cooking on the grill, and his irritation escalated. And then, just before he walked into the sanctuary, he passed hundreds of hot dogs being grilled for after-church fellowship. He felt the heat rising in his neck. Then as he sat down, he heard the minister talking about the ice cream festival they'd had the night before.

Daniel was so frustrated that when Tana found him in church he was typing on his phone, which Tana absolutely hates. . . . Then Daniel showed her what he was writing:

Go to church . . . get doughnuts . . . bacon . . .
sausage . . . hot dogs . . . ice cream.
They have no idea they are sending people to heaven EARLY!
Save them, then kill them. This is not the plan! . . .

During that service Daniel prayed that God would use us to help change the food at places of worship. . . . Two weeks later Pastor Rick Warren called Daniel. Rick is the senior pastor at Saddleback Church, one of the largest churches in America. . . . Rick told Daniel, "Last Sunday I baptized about 800 people. About halfway through I realized everyone was fat. Then I realized I was fat and a terrible example to my congregation. Will you help us?"

With his prayer fresh in his mind, Daniel said, "You had me from hello." Together with Rick and our friend Dr. Mark Hyman, we created the Daniel Plan, a five-step program [faith, food, fitness, focus, and friends] to get the world healthy through churches. The first week 15,000 people signed up for the program. Within the first year they lost *more than 250,000 pounds.*

The plan has been done in thousands of churches worldwide, using many of the same principles in *Change Your Brain Every Day*. Prayer and intention work.

TODAY'S PRACTICE: *What are you passionate about? How can you make an impact on the world? Put it into a fervent prayer or intention.*

Warning Sign Your Brain Is in Trouble: Poor Memory

If you had a million-dollar racehorse, would you ever feed it junk food? One of the most important questions in spotting brain troubles early is whether your memory is worse than it was 10 years ago. I once did an interview with Todd, Chief People Officer at Franklin Covey. He told me his memory was terrible at age 53. "I am sure it is just my age. I am just getting older," he said. "I often have no idea where I put my keys and sometimes find them in the refrigerator, next to the eggs."

"It is definitely not normal," I replied. "I'm 67, and my memory is as good as it has ever been. Tell me about your diet and exercise."

When Todd heard me mention exercise, he perked up. "I exercise five times a week. I run long distances and am in great shape." Something wasn't making sense to me. "And your diet?" I persisted. He looked down. "It's not so great. Every morning I have a Diet Coke and Pop-Tarts in the car on the way to work. The rest of the day doesn't get much better."

Putting toxic fuel in your body will definitely decrease its performance and hurt your brain, no matter how much exercise you do. "If you had a million-dollar racehorse," I asked, "would you ever give it junk food?"

"Of course not," he said. "You are so much more valuable than a racehorse. It is time to treat yourself with a little love and respect," I encouraged. Three months later, Todd told me his memory had significantly improved. He also said I haunt him at every meal. I am hoping to do the same for you. Don't ignore memory problems.

TODAY'S PRACTICE: *Write the answer to this question: "Do you treat yourself as well as an owner treats a million-dollar racehorse?" If not, why not?*

Nine Surprising Early Warning Signs of Dementia

Alzheimer's disease can start decades before you have any symptoms. Know the early warning signs. Here are nine to consider:

1. **Breaking the law.** Law-abiding citizens who suddenly begin stealing, trespassing, or driving recklessly may be exhibiting early signs of dementia. If this happens to someone you know, they need to get assessed.
2. **Eating weird stuff.** Changes in appetite and the foods you crave are an early warning sign of dementia, as dementia can attack areas of the brain that regulate appetite and taste buds.
3. **Falling more frequently.** Falls, as well as changes in gait, may precede any cognitive symptoms.
4. **Gum disease.** The mouth is host to an estimated 700 different species of bacteria. The bacteria that lead to gum disease are also linked to the development of dementia.[112] Floss daily.
5. **Inability to pick up on sarcasm.** If sarcastic remarks are going over your head, it may mean your frontal lobes are becoming less active.
6. **Engaging in compulsive behaviors.** New compulsive behaviors, such as hoarding, may be a signal of trouble.
7. **Your sense of smell is off.** Being unable to distinguish scents like cinnamon, baby powder, or gasoline could be an early warning sign of Alzheimer's, as the part of your brain that distinguishes smells is next to the memory centers.
8. **Depression.** Depression doubles the risk of cognitive impairment in women and quadruples it in men, especially new onset depression in the elderly.[113]
9. **Untreated ADD/ADHD.** It triples the risk of dementia.[114] Treating many psychiatric disorders can help save your memory.

TODAY'S PRACTICE: *How many issues on this list do you have? Take one step to decrease your risk.*

RELATING: *R* Is for Responsibility, Part 1

Responsibility means you have the ability to respond in a positive, helpful way. Over the next few days I'll talk about the brain and relationships. With my patients, I often use the mnemonic RELATING to help them remember the important points. Let's start with R is for Responsibility. The first step to creating great relationships is responsibility, which is not about blame, but rather your ability to respond, such as:

What can I do to make this relationship better?
How can I improve our communication?
Am I treating others as I would want them to treat me?

People who take responsibility for their own behavior do better in relationships. Those who blame others set themselves up for a lifetime of problems. Yet blame is fast, easy, and even seems hardwired in the brain. It may be self-protective against aggression, but it is also the first hallmark of self-defeating behavior. When you blame someone else, you become a victim and act powerless to change anything. Deflecting responsibility serves the purpose of temporarily making you feel better, but it also reinforces the idea that your life is out of your control, that others can determine your future.

Invariably, in classes when I teach responsibility, someone will tell me that they have problems blaming themselves, not others. The concepts of deflecting responsibility and putting too much on oneself are not mutually exclusive. A good "personal responsibility" statement goes something like this: "Bad things have happened in my life, some of which I had something to do with and some I did not. Either way, I need to learn how to effectively respond to whatever situation I am in."

TODAY'S PRACTICE: *What can you do today to make your relationships better?*

R is for Responsibility, Part 2

Do you want 50 percent responsibility for your life or 100 percent? Let me tell you why *responsibility* is one of my favorite words. It is the one word that changes everything for my patients and friends. When my wife, Tana, was in her twenties and recovering from cancer and depression, she went to a motivational seminar that her uncle Bob was teaching. He had been a heroin addict and terrified her as a child. He had been involved in a drug deal gone wrong where his older brother Ray had been murdered. Wracked with guilt after Ray's death, Bob tried to commit suicide with an intentional overdose of heroin, but fortunately he failed. After a lot of hard work, he later turned his life around.

At the seminar, when Bob saw Tana's self-pity, he asked her, "How much responsibility are you willing to take?"

Stunned, Tana said, "I can't take responsibility for cancer."

He replied, "I didn't ask you to take the blame. Responsibility is not blame. It is the ability to respond. Do you want 50 percent responsibility? Then you have a 50 percent chance to change the outcome. Or do you want 100 percent responsibility? Otherwise, someone or something other than you is in control."

Tana answered, "I want 100 percent ability to respond." That was a light switch moment for her. It caused her to immediately start taking responsibility for her behavior and changed her life forever.

You have the same choice before you now. Do you want 50 percent responsibility for your life or 100 percent? How much power and control over the outcome do you want?

TODAY'S PRACTICE: *Take an inventory to see if there are any areas of your life where you tend to blame others. Ask yourself what you can do in those situations to take more responsibility for how you respond and act.*

E Is for Empathy

The ability to see from the other person's point of view is a brain function. Empathy helps us navigate the social environment and answer questions such as: Is this person going to feed me? Love me? Attack me? Faint? Run away? Cry? The more accurately you can predict the actions and needs of others, the better off you are. The ability to "tune in" and empathize with others is a prerequisite for understanding, attachment, bonding, and love—all of which are important for our survival. In several studies about why executives fail, "insensitivity to others" or a lack of empathy was cited more than any other flaw as a reason for derailment.[115]

How is your empathy? Can you feel what others feel? Do you sabotage your relationships by being insensitive? Do you take the behavior of others too personally? Or when someone is rude to you, do you wonder what might be going on with him to act that way? Of course, you can carry that last question to an extreme and attribute any negative criticism directed your way to someone else's problem. Balance is the key.

When negative behavior comes your way, ask yourself two questions: (1) Did I do anything to cause it? (2) What is going on with the other person? Those two questions will help you to be more sensitive to other people and improve your relationships, which will help you feel better overall—now and for the long run.

Developing empathy involves a number of important skills, including being able to get outside of yourself and treating others in a way you would like to be treated.

TODAY'S PRACTICE: *The next couple of times you get into a disagreement with someone, try taking their side of the argument. At least verbally, begin to agree with their point of view. Argue for it, understand it, and see where they're coming from. This exercise will pay off royally if you use it to learn to understand others better.*

L Is for Listening, Part 1

Repeat back what you hear and then be quiet long enough for the person to really tell you what is on their mind. Too often in relationships we have expectations and hopes that we never clearly communicate to our friends, family, or colleagues. We assume they should know what we need and become disappointed when they don't accurately read our minds. Clear communication is essential if relationships are to be mutually satisfying. Here are six keys to effective communication in relationships:

1. **The first key is to have a good attitude and assume the other person wants the relationship to work as much as you do.** I call this having *positive basic assumptions* about the relationship.
2. **State what you need clearly and in a positive way.** Most people are too wrapped up in themselves to think about what's going on with you. In most situations, being direct is the best approach.
3. **Decrease distractions, and make sure you have the other person's attention.** Find a time when the person is not busy or in a hurry to go somewhere.
4. **Ask for feedback to ensure the other person correctly understands you.** Clear communication is a two-way street, and it's important to know if you got your message across. A simple "Tell me what you understood I said" is often all that is needed.
5. **Practice active listening.** Before you respond to what people say, repeat back what you think they've said to ensure that you've correctly heard them. Statements such as "I hear you saying . . ." or "You mean to say . . ." are the gold standard of good communication. This allows you to check out what you hear before you respond.
6. **Monitor and follow up on your communication.** Often it takes repeated efforts to get what you need. It's very important not to give up.

TODAY'S PRACTICE: *In your next conversation, practice active listening, where you allow the other person to finish their communication and then repeat back what they say before you give your input. This is the magic sauce in getting others to talk to you, including teenagers.*

L Is for Listening, Part 2

As humans, we all want to be liked. We want to be valued. We want to be respected. But so many of us are going about it in the wrong way. When meeting new people, interacting with colleagues or supervisors at work, or even looking for dates online, most people tend to focus on making themselves seem interesting. Are you one of them? Do you try hard to win people over by talking about yourself? Do you overload others with details about your accomplishments? Do you regale others with stories about what makes you so special? I have news for you. This strategy is not the way to win friends. In fact, you need to take the opposite approach.

Stop trying to be interesting; instead, be interested in them.

Find out what makes them tick. Be curious about their accomplishments. Ask questions about what makes them special. And be sure to listen to what they say. Brain imaging research from Harvard University found that brain regions involved in motivation and reward activated when the study participants were sharing information about themselves with others.[116]

Being interested in others and really listening to what they say is the quickest way to make them like you or even fall in love with you. To be a good listener, don't interrupt others while they're talking; repeat back what they said to let them know you understood them; and don't judge them. These simple tactics will make you more likable.

TODAY'S PRACTICE: *In one of your interactions with someone today, let them do the talking. Ask questions, and really listen to what they have to say.*

A Is for Assertiveness

We teach others how to treat us by what we allow in our lives. It's important to say what you mean. In that way, assertiveness and communication go hand in hand. Being assertive means you express your thoughts and feelings in a firm yet reasonable way, not allowing others to emotionally run over you and not saying yes when that's not what you mean. Assertiveness never equates with becoming mean or aggressive. Here are five simple rules to help you assert yourself in a healthy manner:

1. **Do not give in to the anger of others just because it makes you uncomfortable.** Anxious people do this a lot. They are so anxious that they agree with the other in order to avoid tension. Unfortunately, this teaches the other person to bully you to get their way.
2. **Say what you mean and stick up for what you believe is right.** People will respect you more. People like others who are real and who say exactly what's on their minds in a tactful way.
3. **Maintain self-control.** Being angry, mean, or aggressive is not being assertive. Be assertive in a calm and clear way.
4. **Be firm and kind, if possible.** But above all, be firm in your stance. We teach other people how to treat us. When we give in to their temper tantrums, we actually teach them the way to control us. When we assert ourselves in a firm yet kind way, others have more respect for us and they treat us accordingly. Ultimately, you also have more respect for yourself.
5. **Be assertive only when it is necessary.** If you assert yourself all the time for unimportant issues, you'll be perceived as controlling, which invites oppositional behavior. Assert yourself when it matters.

TODAY'S PRACTICE: *Be brave and stick up for yourself in a new way at least once this week.*

T Is for Time

Special time is magic for relationships. Early in my career, I found a way to help children adopt their parent's values: Bond with them. Children who are bonded to their parents tend to pick their values. Children who have a neutral or negative relationship with their parents tend to pick the opposite values, just to irritate them. Bonding requires two things: listening (days 148 and 149) and consistent time. In this era of commuting, two-parent working households, email, the internet, television, and video games, there are so many distractions that we have seriously diminished the time we have with the people in our lives. It doesn't have to be a lot of time, but it needs to be focused on the relationship.

There's an exercise in my parenting course I call "special time." It involves spending 20 minutes a day doing something with your child that he or she wants to do. It works for any important relationship. Twenty minutes is not much time, but this exercise makes a huge difference in the quality of your relationships. During this time period I have one rule: no commands, no questions, and no directions. It's not a time to try to resolve issues; it is just a time to be together and do something the other person wants to do, whether it's playing a game or taking a walk. The difference this activity made in parent-child relationships was much more dramatic than anything else I did for them, including medicine. Look for ways to spend time on the relationships that are important to you. Think of this time as an investment in the health of the relationship.

In a similar way, be present when you are spending time with others at work or at home. There are so many distractions that we are rarely present anywhere we are.

TODAY'S PRACTICE: *Pick one of your most important relationships and find a way to spend 20 minutes with that person, doing something he or she wants to do.*

I Is for Inquiring

When your ANTs mate with their ANTs, they create mutant ANTs that infest the relationship. We have already discussed eliminating the ANTs (automatic negative thoughts) that invade your mind. When you're suffering in a relationship, it's very important to inquire into the thoughts that make you suffer. If you are fighting with your husband, for example, and you hear yourself thinking, *He never listens to me*, write that down. Then ask yourself if it is true. The little lies we tell ourselves about other people often put unnecessary wedges between us and them. Relationships require accurate thinking in order to thrive. Whenever you feel sad, mad, or nervous in a relationship, check out your thoughts. If there are ANTs or lies, stomp them out. Here's how: The next time you have unhappy thoughts about your relationship or you are hurt or angered by something your significant other said, start inquiring.

1. Write down your negative thought.
2. Ask yourself if it is true.
3. Ask the other person what they meant by what they said. (Use active listening to help you avoid miscommunications.)
4. Let them know how you initially interpreted their comment.
5. Work together to find a solution to help avoid these miscues in the future.

TODAY'S PRACTICE: *Write down any negative thoughts you have about important relationships. Check the validity of your beliefs by also writing down the times when those same negative thoughts were not applicable.*

N Is for Noticing What You Like More Than What You Don't

Where you place your attention about others determines their behavior. What do you do when the important people in your life do not do what you want them to do? Do you criticize them and make them feel miserable? Or do you just pause and decide to notice what you like more than what you don't like? This is a critical point and important to changing behavior: Focus on the behaviors that you like more than the behaviors you don't. This is one of the secrets to having great relationships. Noticing what you like encourages more of the behaviors you like to happen. It turns out there is also a great deal of science behind this concept.

A marriage with five times more positive comments than negative ones is significantly less likely to result in divorce. A business team with five times more positive comments than negative ones is significantly more likely to make money. College students with three times more positive comments than negative ones are significantly more likely to have flourishing mental health.[117]

The amount of positivity in a system divided by the amount of negativity is called the *Gottman ratio*, after marital therapist John Gottman, who discovered that the number of positive comments to negative ones significantly predicted marital satisfaction and the chances of staying together versus getting divorced.[118] Keep in mind that balance is important. When comments are too positive they lose their impact.

TODAY'S PRACTICE: *With two different people today, notice what you like about them, and then tell them.*

G Is for Grace and Forgiveness

Holding a grudge is like drinking poison and expecting the other people to die. Scientists have found that a lack of forgiveness is associated with poorer relationships and increased stress.[119] By contrast, learning to give grace and forgiveness plays an instrumental role in helping a relationship flourish, and it can be powerfully healing. Research links forgiveness with decreases in depression and anxiety, fewer physical health problems, and reduced mortality rates.[120] Whenever I talk to my patients about this important topic, I tell them about the REACH forgiveness method, which psychologist Everett Worthington of Virginia Commonwealth University developed.[121] REACH stands for:

Recall the hurt. Try to think about the hurt without feeling like a victim and without holding a grudge.

Empathize. Try to put yourself in the shoes of the person who hurt you and see the situation from their viewpoint. Can you empathize with what they may have been feeling?

Altruistic gift. Offer your forgiveness as a gift to the person who caused you pain. If you're having trouble with this step, think of someone who forgave you for something you did and remember how good it made you feel.

Commit to the forgiveness. Rather than simply thinking about forgiving someone, make it more concrete by writing it down or making a public statement about it.

Hold on to the forgiveness. If you come in contact with the person who hurt you, you may feel a visceral reaction—anxiousness, anger, or fear, for instance—and think this signals a retraction of your forgiveness. Not so. This is simply your body's way of giving you a warning.

To help you work through the REACH method, keep this in mind: Forgiveness is a process. It does not mean you have to reconnect with the person who hurt you. It is an act of strength, not weakness. As my friend Byron Katie says, "Forgiveness is just another name for freedom."[122]

TODAY'S PRACTICE: *Think of one person who hurt you and use the REACH method to see if it helps.*

Tiny Habits for RELATING

It's the little things in relationships that help them soar or fall and break apart. Each of these habits takes just a few minutes. They are anchored to something you do (or think or feel) so that they are more likely to become automatic.

1. After I've had a fight with a loved one, I will take responsibility for my part and apologize. (Responsibility)
2. When someone acts negatively toward me, I will ask myself, *Did I do anything to cause it? What is going on with this person?* (Empathy)
3. When I am in a conversation with someone, before responding with my input, I will reflect back to them what I heard them saying. (Listening)
4. When I am challenged or bullied, I will state the case for what I believe, calmly and clearly. (Assertiveness)
5. When I set aside time to be with my child or spouse, I will spend 20 minutes doing whatever he/she wants to do with no agenda. (Time)
6. When I have a negative thought about my spouse, such as, *He never listens to me,* I will write it down and ask myself, *Is that true?* If it is not, I will squash the thought. (Inquiry)
7. When a friend does something annoying, I will turn my attention to the things I like about her rather than dwelling on the annoyance. (Noticing what I like)
8. When someone does something mean or hurtful to me, I will ask God for the grace to forgive them. (Grace and forgiveness)

Bonus: When my partner/spouse is in pain, I will hold his or her hand and focus on feeling empathy for his or her discomfort.

TODAY'S PRACTICE: *Pick one of the RELATING tiny habits and begin practicing it.*

Brutal Honesty Can Do More Harm Than Good

Many of my patients have said to me, "I am brutally honest." They wear this trait as if it is a badge of courage. I usually think to myself that this is not helpful. Relationships require tact. In lectures I often ask audiences, "How many of you are married?" Half the audience will raise their hands. Then I ask, "Is it helpful for you to say everything you think in your marriage?" The audience laughs and collectively says, "No!" Yet many people do it anyway.

I often say to my patients, "There are ways to say things, and there are ways to say things." Jenny came to see me feeling powerless in her relationship with her Air Force colonel husband. Even though she would scream at him, she had lost her voice in their relationship. I asked her to describe her concerns. "He never listens to me," she complained.

"What do you mean?" I said.

"He comes home and hides behind the newspaper. He doesn't talk to me."

"How do you try to communicate with him?" I asked.

"With emotion," she said. "I get in his face and yell at him that I want a divorce and wish I never married him."

Surprised by her comments, I chuckled.

She gave me a hostile look. "You think that is funny?"

"No," I said, "just not very effective. How would you feel if someone talked like that to you? I would be scared."

At first Jenny was defensive, telling me all the ways he had hurt her over the years, but over time she learned better communication skills. Several weeks after I started to see her, she went home determined to be more effective in communicating with her husband.

He was sitting in his chair reading the paper when she started. "I missed you today. When would you have time tonight to talk with me?"

Surprised, her husband looked up from his paper and said, "Any time you want, sweetheart. Am I in trouble?"

In that moment, Jenny realized how much her own behavior had contributed to the demise of their relationship, and because of that, she knew she could help make it better. She had more voice than she gave herself credit for. It is very hard for others to hear you when you yell.

TODAY'S PRACTICE: *When do you tend to be brutally honest? What may be a more effective way to communicate your thoughts?*

Effective Brain-Based Parenting Strategies

Everything from how you set goals and bond with your child to your thought life and lifestyle choices develops the neural pathways for lifelong success in your child. I've taught parenting courses for many years, especially to parents of challenging children. Here is a very short summary of some of the highlights:

1. **Set clear goals for yourself as a parent and for your child.** Then act in a way that is consistent with your goals.
2. **Relationship is key.** With a good parent-child relationship, almost any form of discipline will work. With a poor parent-child relationship, any form of discipline will probably fail. Relationships require two things: (1) Time—spend some special time with your child each day, even if it's only 15 to 20 minutes. (2) Listening—find out what your child thinks before you tell him or her what you think.
3. **Have clear expectations.** Post rules such as, "Tell the truth. We treat each other with respect."
4. **When a child lives up to the rules and expectations, notice it.** Notice and praise the behaviors you like, and you are likely to see more of them.
5. **Expect a child to comply the first time you say something!** Have clear, quick, unemotional consequences when they don't. Never discipline when you're out of control. Use discipline to teach rather than to punish. Nagging and yelling are destructive and ineffective and tend to be addictive for children with ADD/ADHD.
6. **Give choices to a child rather than dictating what they'll do, eat, or wear.** If you make all the decisions for your child, it will breed dependency and resentment.
7. **Parents need to stand together and support each other.** When children are allowed to split parental authority, they have far more power than is good for them. Children learn about relationships from watching how their parents relate to each other. Are you setting a good example?
8. **In parenting, always remember the words *firm* and *kind*.** Balance them at the same time.

TODAY'S PRACTICE: *Which of these tips can you put into practice today?*

10 Things Parents Should Never Do

It's common for parents to focus on what they need to do in order to raise healthy kids, but they often overlook what they should not do. Most parents want to help their children grow into stable, thoughtful, productive, and loving adults. So here are 10 things you should avoid doing:

1. **Ignore their brain.** If you want your child to be their best, you must teach them to take care of their brain.
2. **Rarely spend quality time with them.** Research has found that when parents are always distracted by their devices, children can act out and behave poorly in order to get their attention.[123]
3. **Be a poor listener.** When your kids are trying to talk to you, don't speak over them. Learn to be an active listener.
4. **Use name-calling.** They will internalize these negative names and begin to believe them, which can adversely affect their self-esteem.
5. **Be overly permissive.** Letting your kids do whatever they want may make them "happy" in the moment, but it can be detrimental in the long run. Children need clear boundaries to help them understand what is okay and not okay.
6. **Fail to supervise them.** You need to be your child's frontal lobes until theirs develop.
7. **Do as I say, not as I do.** If you're a poor role model, your kids will pick up on that and follow your lead.
8. **Only notice what they do wrong.** Catch kids doing what is right.
9. **Ignore their mental health issues.** On average, it takes 11 years from the time a child starts to develop symptoms of a mental health condition to when they are seen for their first psychiatric evaluation. Get them help when needed.
10. **Ignore your own mental health.** If you are suffering from any brain or mental health problems, it can devastate your children. You need to take care of yourself and be the best version of yourself so you can also be the best parent to them.

TODAY'S PRACTICE: *Which of these behaviors do you use when dealing with your children? Make a plan to stop these harmful behaviors by switching to a behavior from day 157.*

Male and Female Brains Are Wildly Different

Women have more active brains than men. In 2017 my team published one of the largest functional brain imaging studies ever, comparing 46,034 brain SPECT imaging studies across nine clinics. We discovered that the differences between the brains of men and women are significant.[124] This is a very important study to help understand gender-based brain differences. The quantifiable differences we identified between men and women are important for understanding gender differences in the risk for brain disorders such as depression, anxiety, and Alzheimer's disease.

The brains of women were significantly more active in many areas than men's, especially in the prefrontal cortex (PFC), involved with focus and impulse control, and the limbic or emotional areas of the brain, involved with mood and anxiety. The visual and coordination centers of the brain were more active in men. Subjects included 119 healthy volunteers and 26,683 patients with a variety of psychiatric conditions such as brain trauma, bipolar disorders, mood disorders, schizophrenia/psychotic disorders, and ADD/ADHD. We analyzed a total of 128 brain regions for subjects at baseline and while performing a concentration task.

Understanding these differences is important because brain disorders affect men and women differently. Women have significantly higher rates of Alzheimer's disease, depression (which is itself a risk factor for Alzheimer's disease), and anxiety disorders, while men have higher rates of ADD/ADHD, conduct-related problems, and a 14-fold increase in incarceration.

The study findings of increased PFC blood flow in women compared to men may explain why women tend to exhibit greater strengths in the areas of empathy, intuition, collaboration, and self-control. The study also found increased blood flow in limbic areas (emotional center) of the brains of women, which may also partially explain why women are more vulnerable to anxiety and depression.

TODAY'S PRACTICE: *Think of someone of the opposite sex whom you have known for a long time. Based on the information above, identify three ways you have seen their brain work differently than yours.*

Strengths and Vulnerabilities of the Female Brain

I've been surrounded by powerful women my whole life. From day one, women have been a remarkable part of my life's journey. My mother, a champion golfer at one time, was a very strong woman who raised my brothers and me in the company of our five successful sisters. In my own family, I have three daughters, two granddaughters, and two adopted nieces. All of them have helped me understand some of the key differences between female and male brains—but there was much more to discover.

A study we published a few years ago compared the brain scans of more than 25,000 men and women. The results revealed that female brains were considerably more active in 70 of the 80 areas we analyzed.[125] These variations are important for understanding the particular strengths and vulnerabilities of the female brain and provide critical information about how to improve function, when necessary.

As you learned yesterday, females have higher activity in their prefrontal cortex (PFC), which means they also tend to have greater self-control and an appropriate degree of worry. So, if you're a woman who is drawn to the "bad boy" type—you know, the ones who take a lot of physical risks and throw caution to the wind—a large research study found the "don't worry, be happy people" died earlier from accidents or preventable illnesses.[126]

The higher activity in the female brain also has a negative side. It can cause greater vulnerability to mental health issues and eating disorders, as well as difficulty sleeping and quieting the mind, and a greater sensitivity to pain.

If you're a woman, learn more about how your brain works, understand the best ways to take care of it, and support it with love and the right habits. Do these things and you will be unstoppable!

TODAY'S PRACTICE: *If you have any of these challenges, schedule an appointment for treatment to bring your brain into balance.*

Gray Matter vs. White Matter

Never let a girl hit a soccer ball with her head. In comparing female brains and male brains, there's another important difference—the amounts of gray and white matter. What is gray matter? It's primarily comprised of neuronal cell bodies. And how about white matter? It's the "wiring" that connects those cells so they can communicate effectively and increase processing speed. White matter gets its name thanks to high concentrations of a white-colored protective membrane called myelin that insulates the cells.

Overall, men tend to have more white matter in the brain, and women typically have more gray matter. However, this isn't true for all parts of the brain. In areas involved in general intelligence, it's the opposite—men have 6.5 times more gray matter than women, whereas females have 10 times as much white matter as their male counterparts.[127] This indicates that women likely harness several brain regions at once when problem-solving or tackling complex tasks, while men tend to rely on a more focused approach.

This doesn't mean that one is better than the other, as researchers have observed these differences in men and women with equal intelligence levels.[128] Think of the gray matter as the part of the brain that does the thinking, and the white matter as the stuff that connects various brain regions to enhance that thinking process.

In men, areas related to intelligence are spread throughout the brain. In women, however, 85 percent of those areas are housed in the frontal lobes, which is responsible for executive functions, such as focus, forethought, planning, empathy, judgment, worry, impulse control, and more. This is one reason why we should always protect the frontal lobes of females.

TODAY'S PRACTICE: *Do not let your kids—boys or girls—hit soccer balls with their head, and help them protect their brain by always wearing a helmet for activities that recommend it.*

More Male-Female Differences

While each person is unique, the differences between the brains of men and women are interesting to note because they help us understand each other better. As I mentioned on day 159, our large SPECT imaging study found that men generally have somewhat lower activity in the prefrontal cortex (PFC), the part of the brain that acts as your personal CEO. Among other functions, it is involved with forethought, planning, impulse control, judgment, insight, and empathy. Because of this, we have found that men can be more comfortable with risk-taking activities and spontaneity compared to women. Although there are many social and occupational advantages to this, the downside is that they are more likely to put themselves in situations that can lead to a head injury, which would further decrease their PFC activity.

Another interesting difference is that men tend to produce greater amounts of serotonin—as much as 52 percent more than women.[129] This neurotransmitter modulates many functions in our body and brain and plays a critical role in mood, pain, sleep, anger, and obsessiveness. The higher levels of serotonin in men help to explain why they tend to have less depression than women. In addition to mood problems, we know that lower levels of serotonin are seen in other problems, such as anxiety, chronic pain, and obsessive-compulsive spectrum disorders. The latter involves an area of the brain called the anterior cingulate gyrus (ACG). The ACG is the brain's "gear shifter." When it works normally, it helps us to shift from thought to thought, or from one activity to another. Our research found that compared to men, women are more likely to have an ACG that works too hard. This overactivity can make women more vulnerable to getting stuck on negative thoughts or behaviors as well as worries. And while men have worries too, they process them differently than women do.

Understanding the unique characteristics of male and female brains gives you the opportunity to discover new ways to navigate interpersonal challenges based on those differences.

TODAY'S PRACTICE: *Identify something about the way you think that is different from your spouse or a friend of the opposite gender.*

Stop Saying "I Love You with All My Heart"

Replace it with "I love you with all my brain." Our brain is the real organ of love, even though we express our feelings with heart-shaped symbols. What happens in the squishy organ inside our skull is everything we think, feel, and do. Every amorous expression we make—saying "I love you" or "My heart aches"—happens because of instantaneous communication going on in our brain. Granted, it is not very romantic to say "I love you with all my brain," but that is what you are actually doing. And because your brain is the organ of love and sex, it is imperative to take good care of it and not let it shrink due to bad habits. As far as the brain is concerned—unlike another organ—size really does matter.

I was a psychiatrist for nearly a decade before I started to look at the brain. I loved being a psychiatrist, but I was often frustrated because we had so little objectively useful information to help our patients. This was especially true of the difficult couples I saw. When I met with an angry couple, it was hard to know if she was overcontrolling or he was just being a jerk; if she talked too much or he couldn't pay attention; if she was too withholding or he was too demanding. The whole process seemed too soft, too arbitrary, and I had to rely on what the couples told me—as well as my own clinical intuition—rather than on any hard biological information.

So I decided to scan their brains. It helped me get to the root of some of their issues. They both needed to rehabilitate their brains if they wanted to improve their marriage. Get your brain healthy, and your relationships are likely to be much better.

TODAY'S PRACTICE: *What issues are most persistent in your most important relationships? How might your brain health be a factor in those problems?*

When Relationships Struggle, Think of the Brain

Is he a jerk, or is his brain troubled? I want to tell you about Dave and Bonnie, who failed marital therapy. After spending three years in therapy and over $25,000, the therapist told them to get divorced. When the couple protested, the therapist told them that she knew a doctor who takes care of complex cases and sent them to see me. The wife's brain scan was healthy, but the husband's looked awful, similar to a pattern we often see in drug abusers. But he said he didn't drink and had never used drugs. When I asked his wife if that was true, she said, "Yes, Dr. Amen, he doesn't drink or do drugs. He's just a jerk." I chuckled at her comment but wondered why his scan looked so bad. Potential causes included brain infections, near drowning, low thyroid, or environmental toxins. My next question to the husband was, "Where do you work?"

He said, "I work in a furniture factory finishing furniture." He *was* doing drugs! He was doing one of the worst drugs for the brain: inhaling organic solvents.[130] My next question was to the wife. "When did he become a jerk?" She said, "What do you mean?"

I said, "Did you marry him that way? Do you have father issues that you're trying to work out?"

"No," she said. "When we first got married, he was great. It wasn't until about five years ago that we started having trouble." Then she put her hand over her mouth and said, "Oh my, that was about the time he started this job. Do you think his personality change can be from his job?"

"Yes," I answered. "Something is damaging his brain."

BEFORE   **A YEAR LATER**

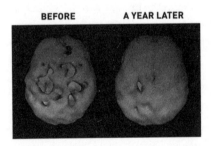

The first intervention was to stop the toxic fumes. I had him transfer to another place in the company where he was not exposed to solvents and put him on a brain-health program. With the right treatment, his behavior got better, as did their marriage. I wonder how many marriages are suffering because one partner has a brain problem that no one is aware of. How do you do marital therapy with a brain in trouble? It will never work until you change your brain.

TODAY'S PRACTICE: *If you know someone who has a relationship problem, tell them that toxins can damage the brain, leading to abnormal behavior. Suggest they get evaluated for it.*

Practical Neuroscience Can Bring More Love

When the other person gets stuck on no. When I speak at conferences, people often come up and tell me how my work has changed their lives. One of the most memorable things I ever heard came from a doctor who told me his marriage was better than ever. When I asked why, he explained that learning about the anterior cingulate gyrus (ACG) made all the difference. I call the ACG the brain's gear shifter, and when there's overactivity here people can get caught in a loop of negative thoughts and tend to be oppositional. "No" is often the first word out of their mouths. This doctor told me his wife had the "cingulate from hell." She seemed to say no to everything he suggested.

From my work, he'd learned that phrasing questions in the opposite way can help, so he started saying things like, "I doubt you want to go for a walk in the park with me, so I'll see you in an hour." Sure enough, she would retort that he was wrong and that she would love to go to the park with him. "It worked," the doctor said. "Our relationship is better."

I love these stories and thanked him for sharing it with me. But then he leaned in and whispered that he was still having problems implementing the strategy in one area—the bedroom. "It sounds weird to say, 'You probably aren't interested in having sex tonight.' What can I do instead?"

This is when I shared some practical neuroscience with him. I told him to start the evening with a small amount of spaghetti at dinner. Carbohydrate-rich foods like pasta increase serotonin in the brain, which boosts moods and increases flexible thinking. Then I suggested an after-dinner walk because physical activity also ramps up serotonin levels. For dessert, I recommended a morsel of dark chocolate because it contains phenylethylamine, a chemical that causes the brain stem to signal that something fun is about to happen. The next step in this neuroscience guide to romance, I said, involves sprinkling some baby powder on his neck. When he shot me a funny look, I explained that for women, this common scent is a powerful aphrodisiac. "What next?" he asked. Give her a neck or shoulder massage, I said, quickly adding that he should not mention a word about sex. "You'll have a much better chance of getting lucky," I said.

In my email inbox a few weeks after that encounter, I saw a message from the doctor. It was filled with hundreds of "thank you" phrases. Using neuroscience in a practical way can improve every aspect of your life, including your love life.

TODAY'S PRACTICE: *Do you know someone who tends to say no as their first response? Try saying the opposite to see if it helps.*

Better Relationships through Biochemistry

Holding grudges or being impulsive in relationships may be brain dysfunctions. Bob and Betsy came to see me for marital therapy. I was the fifth marital therapist they saw. My experience working with couples taught me that when they come into my office and sit as far apart as possible from each other, that is a really bad sign, and this is exactly what they did. Betsy was a pro at holding grudges. She was still harboring resentments about things that happened 15 years ago. Bob, on the other hand, was like a sharpshooter—he knew exactly what kinds of bad things to say to upset her again each time she calmed down. He seemed intent on provoking her.

They were such a difficult couple that after six months of trying to help them, I was getting stressed out working with them. After nine months, I felt like a failure and wanted to tell them to get divorced. But we had just started scanning brains, and rather than give up on them, I decided to scan them. Their brain SPECT scans revealed some of the underlying causes of their troubles. Betsy's scan revealed overactivity in her anterior cingulate gyrus, a finding that often causes people to get stuck on negative thoughts, be stubborn and argumentative, and hold grudges. The night before, I read an article that certain antidepressants calm down this part of the brain, so I put Betsy on one. Bob, on the other hand, had low activity in his prefrontal cortex—common among those with ADD/ADHD and conflict-seeking behavior—so I put Bob on a stimulant. I told them it would take time for the medicines to work, so I didn't want to see them again for at least 30 days.

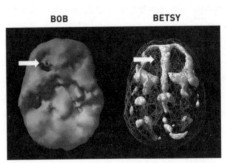

BOB　　　**BETSY**

When they returned to my office a month later, they sat close together. It was a first—and a positive sign in marriage counseling. It has been 32 years since I first saw them, and they are still together. They have a better marriage through biochemistry.

TODAY'S PRACTICE: *If you and your significant other struggle with conflict, identify one thing you do that contributes to the problem and something you can do to change that.*

New Love Is a Drug

New love is similar to an addiction in the brain. Did you know that love is one of the most powerful drugs on the planet? New love, especially, is like cocaine. Remember the last time you fell in love? How did you feel? If you're like most of us, you felt fabulous but also a little edgy. Your heart beat faster, and all you could think about was the new person. Researchers have performed brain scans on people who had just fallen in love and found that the same part of the brain that lights up when people do cocaine lights up with new love.[131] But just like with cocaine, the high rarely lasts.

Some people actually become addicted to the feeling of new love, and they tend to break up and fall in love a lot. Do you know anyone like this? Dating websites have encouraged this addiction now more than ever. You have to be very careful with these sites. If a relationship is in trouble, rather than working on it, many people just go online to try to find someone new.

For people who stay together in a healthy way, the brain chemistry of lasting love shifts from cocaine to our own natural endorphin- or morphine-like chemicals, and the relationship brings us a sense of warmth, peace, and pleasure. Lasting love is not about the high. Instead, boost the biggest brain chemical of love: oxytocin. It enhances bonding and trust in relationships. This powerful neurotransmitter has a reputation for playing Cupid because it's released when you snuggle up, have sex, or socially bond with friends. When you are with your mate, oxytocin stimulates a sense of contentment, lowers anxiety, and brings on feelings of calmness and security—key elements in happy relationships.

When we attach to others, they actually come to live in the nerve cell networks in our brains, which is why we hold them in our minds when they are not near us and why we miss them so much when they are gone.

TODAY'S PRACTICE: *Remember the last time you fell in love. How did your brain react in the beginning? Later in the relationship, how was your brain's reaction different?*

A Healthier Brain Equals a Sexier You

Make brain health central to your relationships. The first secret to making love last is brain health. If you do what you can to enhance your brain and your partner's brain, you are much more likely to get along better and obtain all the benefits of a close relationship. Like a lot of men who come in for marriage problems, Andy had little insight into the role he was playing in the disharmony with his wife. He believed she was too uptight and needed to be more accepting of him. However, his brain scan told me a different story. Although only 56 years old, Andy's brain looked like an 80-year-old's. When I inquired about what he might be doing to harm his brain, he said he wasn't doing anything bad. So I asked him how much alcohol he usually drank. He replied, "Not very much."

BEFORE	11 YEARS LATER

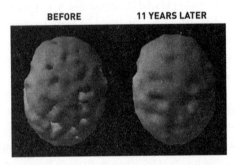

As a psychiatrist, I know that each patient's version of "not very much" is different, so I asked him to specify what it meant to him. He said, "I have about three to four drinks a day, but I don't get drunk—it's not a big problem."

His brain told me that that it was a huge problem. Frightened by his scan, he followed my instructions to stay away from alcohol. Plus, he developed brain envy and wanted a better brain, so he started on our brain health program. Eleven years later I did a follow-up scan, which had improved significantly, and he told me that he was getting along with his wife as well and felt like he was 30 years younger. You can have a better brain and a better love life starting now. Your choices every day affect the health of your brain. Taking care of your brain helps you take care of those you love.

TODAY'S PRACTICE: *List three ways your relationships will be better if you take brain health seriously.*

Embed Yourself in Your Partner's Brain

Make yourself unforgettable to your partner's brain. We love people because of the memories we have about them, and we hate people for exactly the same reason. If you want to make love last and really make it unforgettable, you need to embed yourself in your partner's brain in a loving way. Cards, flowers, foot rubs, physical affection, exciting experiences, and great chocolate all help this process, but the most efficient way to do this is to find ways to take your partner's breath away.

A close friend of mine was dating a new woman. On his birthday, his girlfriend gave him birthday cards signed by all four of his siblings and his ten cousins. He was stunned by her thoughtfulness. Not only was it unique, but it also showed that she had thought about him and planned something special weeks ahead of time. Her thoughtfulness was planted in his brain. I once gave my wife a gorgeous arrangement of white flowers. I knew it would be special, because five women who saw the arrangement at the store asked if I would be their boyfriend. Flowers are one of the best brain gifts. The scent helps to soothe and activate your emotional brain. My wife was a happy girl for weeks, which, of course, also meant that I was a happy boy.

Do small, memorable things on a regular basis and always be on the lookout for ways to take your partner's breath away. Plus, because women have a larger limbic or bonding brain, if you do something really special for someone she loves, you will be a hero in her brain for a long time to come.

TODAY'S PRACTICE: *Do something special for someone you love to embed yourself in his or her brain.*

Simple Answers Are Not Sufficient

The price we pay—and our loved ones pay—for undetected brain problems is very high. My best friend, Will, was raised in a home filled with trauma. His father had terrible anger problems that escalated whenever he got drunk. He was known to hit Will's mother when he was enraged. In addition to this, she held tightly to her own

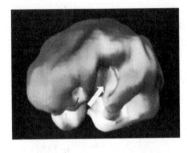

emotional wounds from the past. Naturally, everyone in the family was adversely affected by the dysfunction and domestic violence. Growing up, Will often stayed home from school because of terrible headaches. It is not surprising that as he got older, he had difficulty with trust and intimate relationships. Years later Will's father became psychotic after having open-heart surgery. Will contacted me to evaluate his dad, which I did. His brain SPECT images revealed a large area of low blood flow in his left temporal lobe. This type of finding is one we often see in people who are violent, which was consistent with his history.

I suspected that the defect in his temporal lobe was related to a brain injury, so I asked him if he had ever had one. He told me he had. He explained that when he was 20, he drove a milk truck that had lost its driver's-side rearview mirror. Whenever he needed to make a turn, he had to stick his head out of the window to see behind him. While doing this one day his head collided with a wooden pole and he lost consciousness. After this event, his temper got worse, as did his memory. When Will and his family saw the scan images, it helped them understand that the damage in his father's brain was the underlying cause of his terrible behavior. They began to see him differently, especially because his temperament and behavior got much better after treatment.

Before he had been scanned, Will's father was viewed in a negative light—the kind of person anyone might call "bad." But the imaging changed their perceptions and helped the family to become more understanding, which paved the way for them to forgive him for what he had done in the past. I will always remember when Will wept with relief as he finally released the hatred for his dad he had harbored for so long and filled his heart with love for him instead.

TODAY'S PRACTICE: *Is there anyone in your life whose behavior has been very troublesome, who has hurt you emotionally or physically? Is it possible that brain dysfunction may be present?*

The Strangest Things Can Hurt Your Brain and Ruin Relationships

The craziest people on the set are always the painters. From thousands of brain scans, I have learned that so many things hurt the brain and relationships. Although a brain scan isn't required to know that drug abuse and head injuries cause brain damage, I have seen less obvious things—red dye, MSG, and paint fumes—wreak havoc on some people's brains and their families. A Hollywood producer told me that he noticed that the painters on film sets were the craziest, often getting into fights no matter their gender. I've also scanned patients' brains before and after they ate food or drink containing red dye; it always shows negative changes in the brain.

One patient, Mark, came to see me because he had a bad temper, but he told me it only happened occasionally. Following my assessment, he asked me to scan his brain one more time after he had MSG. He told me he had been noticing a pattern in his behavior after he ate it: He became violent. So for the scan, Mark ate MSG-laced Chinese food. The scan images revealed problems in his left temporal lobe, which is often associated with violence.

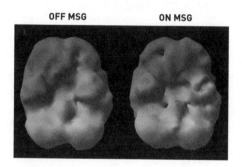

OFF MSG   ON MSG

When I gave Mark two options—taking a prescription medication to help his temporal lobe or cutting out MSG—he opted for the medication. I was a little surprised. But his explanation made sense. He knew MSG was hidden in many products and he was worried losing his temper again would lead to divorce. It's true. MSG is often a hidden ingredient listed with 20 other names on a label, such as textured protein, natural flavorings, and autolyzed yeast extract. If you have problems with your temper, get rid of foods that contain MSG and look for other environmental toxins that may also be ruining your love life.

TODAY'S PRACTICE: *Be a detective. When your behavior is off, think about potential triggers, such as artificial ingredients in food or a lack of sleep.*

Use Your Brain Before You Give Your Heart Away, Part 1

See the signs of trouble around the oasis of love. Love can make us do crazy things. Neuroscience provides insight into our love-fueled decisions. Love can lead to positive changes, including a longer life, as couples with strong marriages tend to outlive others. Love can also pave the way to ruinous decisions that leave people penniless, emotionally broken, or embroiled in violence. Love can have life-affirming or life-threatening consequences. But we don't always see it coming. That's due to something I refer to as "the oasis effect."

Think of singleness as a vast desert where you thirst for human connection. Finding love is like stumbling onto a desert oasis where you can drink to your heart's content. The delicious experience is thrilling, wondrous, and all-consuming. Falling in love unleashes a flood of oxytocin, a neurochemical that enhances bonding and trust to such an extent that it can blind us to trouble on the horizon. People become so laser-focused on their new love that they neglect to notice any signs of danger, such as the sick, dying, or deceased animals on the outskirts of the oasis. These are creatures that drank deeply of the oasis waters only to be stricken by disease or death—danger signs that you should be cautious before drinking freely. Similarly, the brain chemicals at play in the blissful days of new love can lead to blind spots that prevent you from seeing potential problems—those figurative animal corpses lining the oasis—and leading you to dive in too deep.

TODAY'S PRACTICE: *When you fell in love with the wrong person, how did your gut instinct alert you that something was not right about the relationship?*

Use Your Brain Before You Give Your Heart Away, Part 2

One piece of advice I gave my 16-year-old niece was, "Never fall in love with someone you would not hire at work." The chemistry you have with someone can be misleading at times, so it is very important to use your brain before you let someone have your heart. While no one is perfect, you should pay attention to any gut feelings that may forewarn you about trouble ahead. Some people are toxic, but their symptoms may be subtle. A person's past can significantly affect their ability to be in a healthy relationship. Here are some warning signs to be aware of as you embark on a new relationship:

- Something about the person makes you feel uneasy, even if you cannot put your finger on it.
- They often act like you have disappointed them.
- They are rushing the relationship.
- Your family and friends have concerns about your involvement with the person.
- The person does not stay in relationships for very long.
- Their behavior is erratic.
- They do not take responsibility for their own problems and mistakes.
- The person lies—a lot.
- The person never says, "I'm sorry."
- Their kids tell you bad things about them.
- Your children get bad vibes about the person.
- They use illicit drugs.
- They are dishonest with their taxes.
- The have anger issues and an explosive temper.
- They say condescending things to you.
- You are concerned about their alcohol use.
- When you are around them, you lose your sense of self.
- You try to change yourself to make the other person like you more.
- Their interest in you seems to wax and wane.

TODAY'S PRACTICE: *Share this list with anyone you know who is looking to start a new relationship.*

Have You Ever Been Mobbed? I Have

Mobbing tends to target people who are seen as "different" or a threat to the status quo.
Have you felt targeted by a group of people at work, at school, on social media, or
even in your church who spread lies about you, harassed you, or tried to oust you
from the community? That's "mobbing," a term that has emerged to define the way
individuals can develop a group mentality to relentlessly pick on one person. The
process of mobbing can include overt and/or covert psychological harassment, non-
violent hostility, gossiping, undermining, or making false accusations. It's a systematic effort by a group to diminish the value, contributions, or credibility of someone
with the primary objective of driving that person away.

Unfortunately, I have personal experience with mobbing. It's happened to me
consistently since the early 1990s, when I started talking about our brain imaging
work with colleagues. Instead of other psychiatrists being curious and open-minded
about it, they belittled, criticized, isolated, and diminished me. It has been disappointing and painful, but then I realized that almost anyone who challenges the
status quo better be ready for the fight of their life. Challenging a paradigm invites
cruel and bitter criticism. In the fifteenth century, the Italian politician Niccolò
Machiavelli explained, "It must be remembered there is nothing more difficult to
plan, more doubtful of success, nor more dangerous to manage than a new system.
For the initiator has the enmity of all who would profit by the preservation of the
old institution."[132] Our brain imaging work has helped tens of thousands of patients, and the stories of transformation made the criticism more tolerable.

Many people are adversely affected by the mental and physical health consequences of mobbing. I was anxious and angry for years about it. Research has found
that of those who had been subjected to workplace mobbing, 71 percent developed
symptoms of PTSD, 78 percent had major depression, and up to 57 percent
had an increased risk of cardiovascular disease![133] If you've ever been the target of
mobbing—or know someone who has—get help from your HR department, a
school counselor, or a mental health professional. You are not alone.

TODAY'S PRACTICE: *If you have ever been picked on or bullied, try to find a helpful
lesson you learned from the experience.*

Executive Function Time: Meet Your PFC

Your PFC is like the boss in your head. The prefrontal cortex (PFC), the front third of the brain, helps you decide between right and wrong and whether an action is helpful or not. It helps you direct your behavior toward your goals and stops unhealthy behaviors. Arguably the most important part of your brain in terms of making decisions that influence health and success, the PFC is called the executive region because it functions as the chief executive officer (CEO) of your life.

When it is healthy, this boss in your head is goal-oriented, focused, organized, thoughtful, and simultaneously present- and future-oriented; exhibits good judgment; learns from mistakes; and is able to control your impulses. When it is hurt, for whatever reason, it is as if the leader in your head has gone on vacation (*when the cat's away, the mice will play*), and you are more likely to act in impulsive, ineffective, irresponsible, or abusive ways. This not only hurts you; it can hurt others as well.

A helpful analogy to understand the PFC is to imagine yourself at the top of a mountain road in winter in a high-performance sports car. Your goal? Get to the bottom safely. To navigate the winding roads, effective brakes are a must. Damaged or worn brakes increase the risk of an accident. Brakes help the car adjust to any situation—rain, snow, ice, or others who are driving erratically. Similarly, a healthy PFC helps you safely navigate life in any situation. When the PFC is hurt or too low in activity, the brakes are weak and problems arise. You are more likely to figuratively skid off the road. When the PFC works too hard, as it often does in obsessive-compulsive disorder (OCD), the brakes are always on, stopping any progress down the mountain or in your life.

TODAY'S PRACTICE: *Ask yourself at what point in your life did you start making the best decisions for yourself? When do you have a hard time making decisions?*

Controlling Your Inner Child and Overly Harsh Inner Parent

You need healthy brakes in your head. Too little PFC activity goes with impulsivity; too much and you can't get anywhere. One of Sigmund Freud's concepts that has proved useful is his assertion that human personality is made up of the id, ego, and superego. These three aspects of personality also reflect developmental stages of the brain.

The id is our child mind that wants what it wants when it wants it. It is the most primitive component, involved with our basic needs and urges as well as the pleasure principle. The id is quite evident in the behaviors of infants and toddlers. At this age, their prefrontal cortex (PFC) is basically offline. The ego is our healthy adult mind and manages the incessant and selfish desires of the id and the harshness of the superego. It uses reason and is reality-based, reflecting the development and strength of the PFC. The superego is the parent inside our heads telling us what we should and should not do. It is very moralistic and involved with punishment, reward, and self-criticism.

Here is a good analogy of how the id, ego, and superego can manifest in adulthood. Effective CEOs have a healthy ego. Their PFC is fully engaged in decision-making processes, including the way they treat their employees. If a CEO has a superego that is too strong, he or she is likely to be a punitive micromanager. If their id is in control—meaning they have low PFC activity—they may try to engage in inappropriate behavior around the office.

TODAY'S PRACTICE: *Think back over your life and ask yourself when you tend to make bad decisions. Is there a pattern that might involve low or high function of your PFC?*

The Two Most Important Words for Brain Health: Then What?

Think forward. I first met Jose on a *Dr. Phil* show about compulsive cheaters. Jose had cheated on his wife eight times in the four years they were together. His wife had gotten a gun to take care of the situation, which is how they ended up on *Dr. Phil.* My role was to scan Jose to see if there were any problems contributing to his behavior. He had played football in high school, boxed, and used to break beer bottles with his skull. As you can imagine, he had a low-functioning prefrontal cortex (PFC).

I saw Jose for nearly a decade after that show; over time he got dramatically better and stayed away from his cheating behavior by optimizing his brain. The two words he and I repeated over and over were, "Then what? If I do this . . . *then what* will happen? If I say this . . . text this . . . look at this . . . eat this . . . *then what* will happen?" I had him post THEN WHAT? in his house and car. It made a big difference for Jose and his family. He even got me a carving of THEN WHAT that I still have on my desk, and he sent me the lyrics to Clay Walker's song "Then What?" about a friend who was thinking of cheating on his wife.

The PFC helps us stay on track toward our goals. Jose did not want his girls to grow up in a broken home like he did. Repairing and activating his PFC helped him be a better father.

TODAY'S PRACTICE: *Play Clay Walker's song "Then What?," and post the words THEN WHAT? where you can see them every day.*

Master Two Opposing Forces in the Brain: The Elephant and the Rider

Gain control over your emotional brain by strengthening your thoughtful brain. I like the metaphor of the elephant and the rider to help visualize two forces in the brain that are often in opposition. The prefrontal cortex (PFC) is the rider, the thoughtful part of your brain that attempts to direct your life. The limbic or emotional brain is the elephant. It is the powerful, emotional part of you that drives your impulses and desires. As long as the elephant wants to go where the rider directs him, things work fine. But when the elephant "truly, madly, deeply" wants to go somewhere that the rider prefers him not to go, who is going to win that tug-of-war? Most bets are on the elephant.

Cravings (elephant) are often controlled by the PFC (rider) when things are going well, but if the elephant is spooked or becomes nervous or afraid, it can stampede out of control. How do we integrate, then, the rider and the elephant so that our PFC and limbic brains, our goals and our desires, our thoughts and behaviors, are more in sync? We do it through continual training, in the same way animal trainers train powerful elephants. You tame the inner elephant with clear goals, ANT-free thinking, healthy sleep, blood sugar stabilization, and by always protecting your PFC, which is easily damaged by brain injuries.

Think of this scenario: Your inner elephant really wants a large pastry and nudges you toward the sugar high. But, as a consciously thoughtful person who loves your brain, you have trained your PFC to pause and think about the consequences of the pastry: fatigue, mental fog, diabetes, and excess weight. You want a more positive outcome, so you make a different choice, such as slicing an apple with some almond butter for a healthy snack, which satisfies your cravings and makes the elephant calm down. Notice what distracts you from your goals the most so you can learn to avoid it.

TODAY'S PRACTICE: *Write out two situations where your emotional brain tends to hijack your thoughtful brain. What strategies can you use to get back in control?*

The Neuroscience of Why You Lose in Vegas

Pretty women make men pretty stupid. Can the mere presence of an attractive woman make a man do dumb things? According to research out of Canada, the answer is a resounding yes! For this study, men played a dice game while viewing images of women—some very attractive and others not as appealing. The male study participants who gazed at pretty women exhibited increased impulsivity and ended up with bigger monetary losses. The study authors explained that the sight of a beautiful woman can make men discount the future by ignoring the lasting repercussions of their actions. Interestingly, when researchers asked female participants to view pictures of men while playing the same dice game, a man's looks had no impact on their actions.[134] Other research from the Netherlands found that after socializing with women, men's cognitive function declines.[135]

Casino owners in Las Vegas—and other parts of the world—are well aware of this concept. Gambling palaces are teeming with attractive female employees wearing skimpy uniforms. Combine that with the complimentary cocktails and late-night entertainment that robs customers of sleep, and it all adds up to a brain drain that zaps impulse control and impairs judgment. It's no surprise the house has the winning advantage. If you want to get your edge back, get good sleep ahead of time, focus on your cards (not the cute waitress), pass on the alcohol, and drink water when you're trying to win some of their money.

TODAY'S PRACTICE: *Identify the times you have made impulsive choices or decisions you regretted. Which of your lifestyle choices might have played a role?*

Crime, Treatment, and Punishment

No, it indicates bad planning. Peter, 62, had just lost a 12-year legal battle with his neighbors over trees on an easement. Over the course of those dozen years, he experienced two incidents of brain trauma—one from a fall and another from a stroke—and had begun acting more erratically. The morning after losing his court battle, he heard the unmistakable rumble of a chainsaw. He could picture his neighbors chopping down his trees, which enraged him. He dialed 911 and told the operator he was going to murder his neighbors and to send someone ASAP. Then he grabbed his gun and shot them. When I scanned Peter's brain at his lawyer's request, I saw highly abnormal activity in the prefrontal cortex (involved in planning, impulse control, and judgment) and the temporal lobes (involved with memory, temper control, and mood stability). Presenting scans like this at a trial allows a jury to see that a person's judgment was compromised; it isn't to let a defendant who murdered two people go free.

TOP DOWN   **BOTTOM UP**

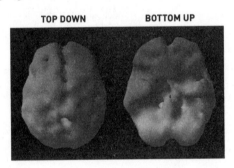

As I testified in the death-penalty trial, the prosecutor questioned my findings about Peter having poor planning and judgment linked to impairment in the PFC. He suggested Peter phoning 911 prior to the shooting was a sign of good forethought. I replied that it was an indicator of supremely poor planning and that it was nonsensical to call 911 before committing murder. Yes, many individuals think about harming others, but they refrain from following through with it. They practice healthy planning by thinking about the potential consequences of their actions and finding less violent ways to cope with their anger. Peter was found guilty of second-degree murder and avoided the death penalty but was sentenced to 80 years to life in prison.[136]

TODAY'S PRACTICE: *Read the news and see if you detect evil behavior in an event. Consider what kind of brain problem could have contributed to it.*

Six Lessons from the Scans of Murderers

Voted most likely to start World War III. On May 20, 1998, 15-year-old Kip Kinkel was caught with a stolen gun and suspended from school. After murdering his parents that night, the next morning, he went to Thurston High School, killed two students, and wounded two dozen others. Kip was sentenced to 112 years in prison. Kip had once been voted in school as "most likely to start World War III." Before the massacre, Kip wrote, "My head just doesn't work right. Damn these voices inside my head. . . . I have to kill people. I don't know why. . . . I have no other choice." At Amen Clinics we have scanned over 1,000 convicted felons and over 100 murderers. What do scans reveal about murderers? Here are six lessons:

1. **People who do bad things often have troubled brains.** Kip had one of the most damaged brain scans I've ever seen for someone his age.
2. **Murder does not always look the same in the brain.** Some of the scans show impulsivity, some show compulsivity, some show toxicity (like Kip's), some show damage from a traumatic brain injury (TBI).
3. **TBIs are a major cause of psychiatric illness and violence,** and few people know it because most psychiatrists and psychologists never look at the brain.
4. **Traditional mental health care is failing us.** Many of the mass shooters, including Kip, had seen psychiatrists or mental health professionals before committing their crimes.
5. **Murderous behavior based on brain problems can't be excused.** People who do bad things should not be excused and allowed to go home because they have a troubled brain. Many people who have troubled brains never do anything bad.
6. **Brains can be rehabilitated.** What if our society evaluated and treated troubled brains, rather than simply warehousing them in toxic, stressful environments? With better brain health, incarcerated people who get out of prison are more likely to be able to work, support themselves, and pay taxes. Russian author Dostoyevsky once wrote, "A society should be judged not by how it treats its outstanding citizens, but by how it treats its criminals."[137] Instead of just crime and punishment, we should also be thinking about crime, evaluation, and treatment.

TODAY'S PRACTICE: *If you or someone you love does bad things, consider that an unhealthy brain may be a source of the problem.*

Brain Warrior Michael Peterson: Good Habits Are the Keys to All Success

Did you say you broke bricks with your head? Country singer Michael Peterson is one of my favorite brain warriors, but he wasn't always that way. Michael rocketed to stardom in 1997 when his debut album produced the number one hit "From Here to Eternity" and other chart-makers like "Drink, Swear, Steal & Lie." He was high on life, but after more than a dozen years as a touring musician, he felt tired all the time, had constant pain, and had packed on too many pounds. After getting married, he and his wife decided to give themselves the gift of brain health and visited one of our clinics.

BEFORE   AFTER

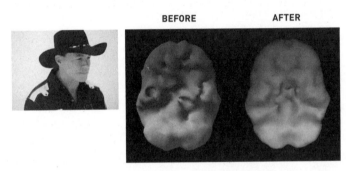

Michael's scans revealed a damaged brain, which prompted me to inquire about past head trauma. I wasn't surprised when he said he played college football, but my jaw dropped when he added that he once held a record for breaking a stack of bricks with his forehead. Seeing the horrified look on my face, he explained that postcollege he teamed up with an inspirational troupe that performed amazing athletic stunts for high school students. He would rip license plates in two with his bare hands, but his specialty was busting concrete blocks with his skull. Seeing his damaged brain on the scans gave Michael a healthy level of anxiety that led to major lifestyle changes—adopting a brain-healthy diet, taking nutraceuticals, and more. At his follow-up, his brain scan looked significantly better, his memory had improved, and he felt more energetic. He took what he learned and began sharing the benefits of brain health with teens nationwide. Seeing Michael improve his brain after years of brick smashing proves you can change your brain even if you've been bad to it. Gaining a healthy level of anxiety is the key.

Michael often quotes Og Mandino, who said, "The only difference between those who have failed and those who have succeeded lies in the difference of their habits. Good habits are the key to all success. Bad habits are the unlocked door to failure."[138]

TODAY'S PRACTICE: *What is the worst thing you ever did to your brain? Write it down and share it with someone who cares about you—if you dare.*

Dealing with Conflict-Seeking People

Many people who have lower-than-normal blood flow to their prefrontal cortex (PFC) use conflict-seeking behavior to give this part of their brain a boost. As irritating or upsetting as this might be, it is important for anyone who is typically the target of their actions to not "take the bait." In other words, try your best to respond calmly and keep your cool. Whether it is your spouse, one of your kids, or a coworker, there's no question that it can be tedious at times to be around people who regularly try to provoke you. Unfortunately, when you respond in kind by getting mad or screaming at them in frustration, it reinforces their conflict-seeking behavior. As hard as it may be, when you stay calm the person will likely try even harder to get a rise out of you. However, by holding your ground and keeping your cool, they will eventually stop.

People with conflict-seeking tendencies know exactly how to push your buttons—in fact, they are an expert at it. You have probably been navigating this dance with them for a long time. But you can change this pattern by denying them the response their brain craves—a rush of adrenaline—to activate their PFC. However, like any bad habit or behavior pattern, when you begin a new strategy of not responding with anger or being upset, they may go through a period of withdrawal and intensify their provoking behavior even more. Just hang in there, because with these tips, you can change the way the two of you interact with and respond to one another so it becomes a healthier way of relating.

These are some of the best ways to handle conflict-seekers:

- Keep your voice steady and calm. It should be inversely proportional to the tone and intensity of the other person's voice.
- Take a break if things feel uncomfortable or seem to be getting out of control.
- Try cracking a joke to lighten the mood.
- Listen to what the person is saying and notice the emotion behind the content.
- Let the other person know that when they can stay calm and focused, you will be happy to discuss the issue more.

TODAY'S PRACTICE: *Identify someone in your life who tends to be conflict-seeking and use these techniques next time he or she tries to trigger you.*

Your Brain Makes Happen What It Sees

Train your mind to visualize success. Jenny, 32, was a bus driver. She came to see me in her work uniform, looking sad and eight months pregnant. Her tears streamed down her face as she told me her family and boyfriend had just disowned her, and she felt alone and confused.

"How can this happen?" she started. "How can I look and feel pregnant, but not be? How can I make my own breasts larger? Have no periods? Have this belly?" Her voice raised as she put her hand on her distended abdomen. "How is this possible? Am I crazy?"

Jenny had a condition known as pseudocyesis, or false pregnancy. Believing she was pregnant, even though she wasn't, her brain sent the signals to the rest of her body to make it happen. Pseudocyesis has been known since antiquity. Hippocrates wrote of 12 women who "believed they were pregnant" in 300 BC. As I explained her condition, Jenny began to understand the power of her brain. After a family meeting and several sessions with her boyfriend, she reconnected with the people she loved.

Your brain is incredibly powerful. Seeing fear in your future, even where there is none, can make you feel so panicked you end up in the emergency room. Seeing your partner leave you in your mind can make you act insecure, clingy, and dependent. Negative thoughts can make negative things happen, while positive thoughts can help you reach your goals.

Tell your brain what you want and match your behavior to get it. Your mind takes what it sees and makes it happen, so it is critical to visualize what you want and then change your behavior to get it. Too many people are thrown around by the whims of the day, rather than using their prefrontal cortex to plan their lives and follow through on their goals.

TODAY'S PRACTICE: *What do you want? Visualize your success and write down three steps to achieve it.*

The One Page Miracle (OPM)

Clearly tell your brain what you want. One of the exercises I use with all of my patients is called the One Page Miracle (OPM).[139] If you want to be successful in any area of your life, you have to tell your brain what you want over and over again. Then ask yourself if your behavior is getting you what you want. Does it fit your goals? Do this now and post it where you can see it every day.

Instructions: On a single piece of paper or on your computer, write out what you want in the main areas of your life. Use the headings and subheadings below. Next to each subhead, briefly indicate your primary goals in each of these areas. Be sure to focus on what you want, not what you don't want. Once your OPM is completed, look at it every day and ask yourself if your behavior is helping you get what you want. To go further, write down five things you can do to obtain your goals and five things you do that might mess them up.

MY ONE PAGE MIRACLE

Relationships
Spouse/Partner
Children
Extended Family/Friends

Work

Money

Self
Physical Health
Emotional Health
Spiritual Health

TODAY'S PRACTICE: *Complete your One Page Miracle. Post it where you can see it daily. Ask yourself every day, "Does it fit?" Does your behavior fit what you want?*

Use Your Brain to Manifest Your Destiny

Manifesting—it's a concept that sounds like it belongs in the world of woo-woo, but it is actually rooted in neuroscience. If you visualize and focus on what you want out of life, you are much more likely to achieve it. Manifesting means thinking about and visualizing your desired future and the steps to make it happen. Manifesting sparks brain activity across your brain, especially in the prefrontal cortex (PFC), which is involved in goal-setting, planning, forethought, judgment, follow-through, and learning from the mistakes you make—the very skills you need to turn your dreams into reality. When you tell your PFC what you want, it will help you match your behavior over time to get it. Your brain makes happen what it sees. Many success coaches recommend their clients create a detailed vision board with the types of relationships, jobs, finances, health, and achievements they want. Since 30 percent of the brain is dedicated to vision, these boards can help you achieve your goals. Once you know your goals, always ask yourself if your behavior fits the goals you've set for your life.

Manifesting also involves changing your thinking patterns, mindset, and self-belief system—discarding negative thoughts and beliefs that hold you back and shifting to a more positive outlook that infuses you with the confidence to take action. The first step is giving your brain clear direction by writing down your goals with the One Page Miracle (see day 185). Adding an action plan with the steps you'll take to achieve those goals enhances the power of manifestation. Knowing what you want, planning how to reach your goals, and engaging in everyday actions activate your brain in ways that will help you realize your dreams. They are the keys to manifesting your destiny.

TODAY'S PRACTICE: *Create a visualization board along with the steps you are going to take to make your dreams a reality.*

Coordinate Your Mind and Body: Meet Your Cerebellum

The cerebellum is the Rodney Dangerfield part of the brain. It just gets no respect.
Located at the back bottom part of the brain, the cerebellum contains 50 percent of the brain's neurons but takes up just 10 percent of the brain's volume. Sometimes it is referred to as "the little brain." The cerebellum is involved with a wide range of functions, including motor coordination (when movements require two or more body parts), posture, gait, and the speed at which we process information. The cerebellum is critical for the coordination of thought, which reflects the quickness with which you can adjust cognitively or emotionally to existing or new stimuli or situations. The cerebellum also helps you make quick physical adjustments, such as those that are needed when you engage in sports or other physical activities. When the cerebellum does not work well, physical coordination can be more challenging, leading to clumsiness and being prone to accidents. Our brain SPECT scan data also shows that low cerebellar activity is associated with confusion, disorganization, and poor handwriting. We have found that individuals who have ADD/ADHD, learning problems, or autism spectrum disorder commonly have lower blood flow in this part of their brain.

Because of its role as the brain's primary center of coordination, physical and mental activities that involve coordination, such as playing sports and musical instruments, can help the brain function optimally.

TODAY'S PRACTICE: *Play a sport or dance to exercise your cerebellum.*

Flexibility Time: Meet Your ACG

Who survives a pandemic? Those who are flexible. There's an area deep in the frontal lobes called the anterior cingulate gyrus, or ACG, which allows us to be flexible, shift our attention, go from thought to thought, move from idea to idea, see options, go with the flow, and cooperate (getting outside of ourselves to help others). The ACG is also involved in error detection. If you come home and see the front door wide open, for example, even though you know you locked it, it triggers appropriate caution in your mind.

When the ACG is healthy, we tend to be flexible, adaptable, and cooperative, learn from our mistakes, and effectively notice when things are wrong. When it is underactive, often due to head trauma or exposure to damaging toxins, we tend to be quiet and withdrawn. Alternatively, when the ACG is overactive, often due to low levels of the calming neurotransmitter serotonin, people tend to get stuck on negative thoughts (obsessions) or negative behaviors (compulsions or addictions) and be uncooperative. Serotonin-enhancing strategies, such as supplements like 5-HTP or saffron and selective serotonin reuptake inhibitor (SSRI) medications, have been used for decades to treat anxiety, depression, and obsessive-compulsive disorder (OCD).[140]

Getting stuck can manifest itself in many ways, including worrying, holding grudges, and becoming upset if things don't go your way. On the surface, people with high ACG activity may appear selfish ("my way or the highway"), but from a neuroscience standpoint, they're not selfish but rigid. Inflexibility causes them to automatically say no even when saying yes may be their best option. They have trouble seeing options and tend to be argumentative and oppositional. Plus they tend to see too many errors—in themselves, their spouses, kids, coworkers, and organizations, such as schools, government, and churches.

In doing research on our extensive brain imaging/clinical database, we discovered that patients who have OCD or posttraumatic stress disorder (PTSD) show increased activity in the ACG. In both disorders, people get stuck on negative feelings, thoughts, and behaviors.

TODAY'S PRACTICE: *List two or three situations in which you tend to get stuck on negative thoughts or negative behaviors.*

What to Do When You Feel Stuck

God grant me the serenity. If you tend to get thoughts stuck in your head, one of the best things you can do is write them down. When you read what you have been obsessing about, it can shift your perspective to be more rational, which helps you address the thoughts more effectively. This is especially helpful when you climb into bed and close your eyes, only to find your mind won't shut down.

You can help manage this by keeping a pad of paper and a pen on your nightstand so you can write out the thoughts that are keeping you awake. For each one, write down what you have control over and what you cannot control. Here's an example: You have recently applied for a new job with a company you have been wanting to get into for some time. Yesterday, the recruiter scheduled you for an interview in a few days. Your mind has been racing with anxiety since the call.

1. Identify what your biggest concern is (e.g., "They won't think I am as good as the other candidates.")
2. Next, write down statements that can counteract this concern. For example, "I am hardworking and well-respected at my current job. I am a great team player. I am dependable and smart. I will practice talking about my experience and qualifications so I am prepared at the interview."
3. Then write down the things that are out of your control, such as, "I can do my best, but the decision is not up to me. I may not be the right fit for the job. They may need someone more qualified than I am."

Doing this quick and easy activity can help you sleep better at night.

TODAY'S PRACTICE: *Whenever you feel stuck, write down the thought, what you can do about the worry, and what you cannot do about it.*

Don't Try to Convince Someone Else Who Is Stuck

Take a break and come back later. When you're in an argument with someone who refuses to budge, taking a time-out can be helpful. Whether it's a matter of minutes, hours, or days, giving yourself a breather can be an effective way to gain clarity about what might otherwise be an unresolvable and exhausting situation. When someone gets stuck on a thought or their position, it is difficult to reason with them. I have found that using distraction is one of the most effective strategies for helping someone who tends to get "stuck." It can be a really simple distraction, like changing the subject. Diverting their attention in this way gives their subconscious mind time to process what I said without having to argue about it. When they get back to the issue, it's not unusual for the stubborn person to open their mind more about the issue.

My patient Jackie often held tightly to her own position. Not surprisingly, she and her husband were having problems. He said that she would dig her heels in and not be able to hear what he said. In turn, she criticized him for not paying attention to her. I couldn't help but point out that perhaps it was because she didn't listen to his opinion. She disagreed with me. Not wanting to activate her oppositionality, I dropped the subject and changed the direction of the conversation. The next time I met with them, Jackie told me she had been listening to her husband more. I was happy to learn that her subconscious heard what I said, even though she had dismissed it.

If you are in a relationship with someone who tends to go round and round, getting stuck on the same points during an argument, here is one of my favorite strategies: When things get tense, simply say you need to go to the bathroom, since no one will likely argue with that. This is an easy way to foster a little distraction and take a breather, which can help the situation.

TODAY'S PRACTICE: *The next time you get stuck in a disagreement or argument, take a bathroom break for as long as you need to get unstuck.*

Ask for the Opposite of What You Want

Reverse psychology doesn't work for everyone, but it does work for this group. Reverse psychology is often helpful for people who have frontal lobes, especially the anterior cingulate gyrus, that work too hard. Experts call it "strategic self-anticonformity," and here's how it works. If you want your oppositional 6-year-old to pitch in at dinnertime, try saying, "I bet you don't want to help me set the table." They will likely be eager to spring into action with the silverware.

Marriage counselors sometimes use this method with couples who refuse to comply with their recommendations. Let's say a couple is having trouble communicating or making time for physical intimacy. The counselor may recommend they refrain from talking to each other and avoid getting romantic. For couples who are resistant in therapy, this often becomes a gateway to increased communication and renewed interest in lovemaking.

In therapy settings, reverse psychology may also be referred to as paradoxical intention therapy, and it can help people who suffer from anxiety, fears, or phobias. Look at one study involving men who were so anxious about urinating in public bathrooms that they couldn't relieve themselves. The research team instructed the male participants to visit bathrooms and simulate the urination process without actually peeing. After multiple bathroom visits, the men managed to conquer their public restroom anxiety.[141]

You can make reverse psychology work for you in the workplace and at home. At work, if you need an employee to complete a project by the end of the week, try saying, "I doubt you can get this done by Friday." At home, if you have an argumentative child who tends to get upset when you ask them to do something, try saying, "I don't think you're able to do this without a tantrum, are you?"

TODAY'S PRACTICE: *Identify someone in your life who tends to be oppositional, and use subtle reverse psychology to see if it might help.*

Natural Ways to Boost Serotonin

Boost serotonin and your openness to change. When serotonin levels are low, the anterior cingulate gyrus (ACG) tends to be more active, which can inhibit change and contribute to inflexibility and getting stuck on negative thoughts or negative behaviors. Increasing serotonin can help calm these areas of the brain. This can be done with three simple strategies:

1. Physical exercise increases the ability of tryptophan, the amino acid that helps produce serotonin, to enter the brain. Walking, running, swimming, or playing table tennis will help you feel happier and more flexible. Exercise alone has been found to treat depression, with effectiveness similar to a serotonin reuptake inhibitor (SSRI) antidepressant.[142] Whenever you feel stuck in a rut, get moving.

2. Bright light exposure has been shown to increase serotonin and is a natural treatment for seasonal depression, premenstrual tension syndrome, and depression in pregnant women.[143] Depression and inflexibility are more common in winter and in places where sunlight is limited. To improve your mood and increase cognitive flexibility and learning, get more sun or use bright light LED therapy, which is a standard treatment for seasonal depression.

3. Combine tryptophan-containing foods, such as eggs, turkey, seafood, chickpeas, nuts, and seeds, with healthy carbohydrates, such as sweet potatoes and quinoa, to elicit a short-term insulin response that drives tryptophan into the brain whenever you feel stuck in a rut. Dark chocolate also increases serotonin.

TODAY'S PRACTICE: *Add fish to your weekly meal plan. See tanaamen.com/blog/category/recipes/seafood-recipes for recipe ideas.*

Notice When You're Stuck, Distract Yourself, and Come Back to the Problem Later

Be aware of when you start to loop. Having an overactive anterior cingulate gyrus (ACG) increases your chances of getting stuck on negative thoughts. One of the best ways to get unstuck is to become aware that you're caught in a loop of negativity and take action to intentionally distract yourself.

Here's how this worked for my patient Maurie.

A career-focused go-getter in his early thirties, Maurie visited Amen Clinics for help with constant worrying so severe it gave him pounding headaches, muscle tightness, and a quick temper. His primary worry concerned his work, where he was convinced his supervisor hated him even though his annual reviews were positive. The worrisome thoughts looped over and over in his mind, and he couldn't make them stop.

In my session with Maurie, I told him to keep a log of times when he started worrying about his job, which happened multiple times a day. Then I asked him to tell me what songs he liked. He gave me a quizzical look and said, "I'm here for help with my worrying. Why are you asking me about the music I like?" I smiled and explained that anytime Maurie noticed he was stuck in a negative loop of worry, he should sing one of those songs as a distraction strategy. He agreed to give it a try. He chose a few of his favorite tunes, and anytime he was overcome with worry, he would start singing one of them. It worked! Singing helped push the negative thoughts out of his head.

Distraction can be a powerful technique for people with a busy ACG. I generally recommend jotting down a list of activities that can be used for distraction, such as:

- Sing a happy tune.
- Turn on music you like.
- Go for a stroll.
- Do some housework.
- Play a game that requires brainpower.
- Recite a prayer or meditate.
- Repeat a single word in your mind. To block out competing thoughts, picture a broom sweeping them away.

By intentionally using distraction, you can escape the clutches of unwanted, looping thoughts and eventually gain better control over your mind.

TODAY'S PRACTICE: *Make a short list of activities you could do the next time your brain gets stuck on a loop.*

Argue with Reality, Welcome to Hell

One psychological trait that will ruin your life is rigid thinking. Everyone is struggling these days, but do you know who's got it the worst? People who are rigid thinkers— the creatures of habit who get bent out of shape when their routines are upended. Among neuroscientists, this trait is referred to as cognitive inflexibility, and it can ruin your life. It's the inability to roll with the ups and downs of everyday life, let alone with a pandemic. If you're one of these types, you may be finding it nearly impossible to cope with the uncertainty and constant changes we've had to endure, resulting in increased feelings of anxiety, moodiness, frustration, and irritability. Here's news for you: *When you argue with reality, welcome to hell.* I once heard my friend Byron Katie say this, and I share it with patients and think about it nearly every day.

Cognitive flexibility defines a person's ability to go with the flow, adapt to change, and deal successfully with new problems. During the pandemic, we've all had to make changes in our everyday routines at work, school, and home. For example, you may have had to pivot in several areas at work—finding a new customer base, devising innovative ways of providing your services, or using differ-ent technologies to collaborate. For people with too much activity in the anterior cingulate gyrus, it's common to get caught in a loop of negative thinking, such as *I can't work this way, Everything sucks,* or *Things shouldn't be like this.* Besides boosting serotonin (see day 192), seek the counsel of others when you feel stuck. Often just talking about feeling stuck will open new options.

TODAY'S PRACTICE: *In which situations do you tend to argue with reality? Write them down and write out what you can do about them and what you cannot do about them.*

Tiny Habits to Be More Flexible

Do small things to get unstuck. Each of these habits takes just a few minutes. They are anchored to something you do (or think or feel), which makes them more likely to become automatic.

1. After I answer the phone, I will stand up and walk while I talk.
2. After I start to argue, I will ask myself, *Is my behavior getting me what I want?*
3. When I get out of bed in the morning, I will open the curtains/shades to let the sunshine in.
4. When I feel anxious, I will eat a complex carbohydrate, such as a sweet potato or quinoa, to boost serotonin.
5. When I relapse or make a mistake with my health, I will ask myself, *What can I learn from my mistake?*
6. When I am tempted to eat unhealthy foods, I will eat the healthy ones on my plate first.
7. When I am dealing with someone who is stuck on a negative thought or arguing, I will ask them to go for a walk with me and will not bring up any charged topic for at least 10 minutes.
8. When I want to go out to eat, I will ask the healthiest person I know to go with me.
9. When thoughts run over and over in my head, I will write them down, which helps to get rid of them.

TODAY'S PRACTICE: *Pick one of the above tiny habits and put it into practice today.*

Relaxation Time: Meet Your Basal Ganglia

When your nervous system is revved too high, you can feel anxious, tense, and nervous.
The basal ganglia (BG), which surrounds the limbic system, has many functions,
including:

Coordinates emotions, thoughts, and physical actions: When there is balanced
activity level in the BG, it helps you think and react smoothly in any situation.
When there is increased activity in this area, it means you're more likely to
freeze in an emergency, shake when frightened, or get tongue-tied when you
get nervous.

Smooths motor control functions: The BG is involved in motor coordination
and is critical to handwriting. Heightened activity in this area is linked to better dexterity and a knack for detailed handiwork.

Eliminates involuntary motor movements: Deficiencies in the BG are associated with Parkinson's disease and Tourette's syndrome. These illnesses involve a
lack of control over movements.

Plays a role in calibrating inner anxiety settings: Whether you're one of those
people who feels relaxed and carefree or who feels tense and nervous depends
on activity levels in the BG. Heightened activity here makes you prone to
anxiety, fear, increased awareness, and tension.

Helps in forming repetitive behaviors: The BG is instrumental in the formation
of habits, healthy or unhealthy ones. People with excess activity here may be
prone to habits such as nail biting, teeth grinding, or skin picking.

Modulates ambition and initiative: In some cases, higher BG activity can act
as a motivator, which may help you strive for peak performance, increase your
productivity, and energize you to tackle a long to-do list.

Influences pleasure/euphoria: When there is low activity in the BG, people
tend to have difficulty feeling pleasure.

When the BG works too hard, people tend to struggle with anxiety, nervous-
ness, physical sensations of anxiety, a tendency to predict the worst, conflict avoid-
ance, social anxiety, risk aversion, muscle tension, and sensitivity to rejection.

TODAY'S PRACTICE: *On a scale of 1 to 10, rate your baseline anxiety level. When is it
worse? When is it better?*

You Need Some Anxiety

Low levels of anxiety kill people early. Here's something you won't read every day from health-care professionals: Positive thinking kills way too many people. Two of the most dangerous mindsets are mass denial and having anxiety that is too low.

Mass denial prevents people from doing anything significant about the health problems we face. There is no other way to talk about it when 50 percent of American adults are prediabetic or diabetic and 73 percent are overweight or obese.[144] I want you to know the truth about the health of your brain and body and then do something about it if you are headed for trouble or are in trouble already.

Along the same lines, some anxiety is absolutely critical to good health and success. Levels of anxiety that are too low are associated with underestimating risks, a lackadaisical attitude toward your health, and making bad decisions. Imagine soldiers who were not vigilant, even when the enemy was nearby. What might happen? Early defeat and death to them and their platoon is the likely result. The same principle applies to your health. According to one of the longest longevity studies ever published, the "don't worry, be happy people" die early from accidents and preventable illnesses.[145]

A lot of my patients are surprised when I tell them that having some anxiety is a good thing. So many people are under the false impression that eliminating anxiety is a great goal to shoot for. It isn't. Appropriate anxiety helps us make better decisions and keeps us from getting into trouble. It prevents us from running into the street as children, risking broken bodies, and running headlong into toxic relationships as adults, risking broken hearts.

TODAY'S PRACTICE: *Where could you use a little more anxiety in your life? Where could you use less of it?*

Protect Your Pleasure Centers

The evolution of technology in our society is wearing out our brain's pleasure centers. With the onslaught of video games, texting, Facebook, TikTok, online dating, pornography, and gambling, our pleasure centers, which have evolved over millions of years, are being worn out, and pretty soon we will not be able to feel anything at all. Our pleasure centers operate on dopamine, which is the same chemical that cocaine stimulates and one of the main chemicals of new love. Whenever a little bit of dopamine is released, we feel pleasure. If dopamine is released too often or too strongly, we become desensitized to it and it takes more and more excitement to get the same response, just like with cocaine. So work to keep your pleasure centers healthy.

Meet Christina and Harold. They had separated due to Harold's preoccupation with video gaming. Christina had tried to get him to put down the controller so they could enjoy some quality time together, but he was obsessed. Her attempts to get him to cut down on his gaming were met with snappy comments to stop being such a nag. Eventually, Christina left him. For Harold, that's when depression set in, and he realized he needed help. In talking with him, I could see that these two were locked in an unhealthy pattern that is common in couples where one person has an addiction. Christina loved Harold but could no longer live with the consequences of his addiction.

Our society has undergone a monumental transformation due to the introduction of new technology, but there has been an inadequate amount of research to understand how it is impacting the brain and human relationships. The research that does exist is troubling. Look at the results of a study showing that individuals who are distracted by their phones and inboxes while problem-solving temporarily lose 10 IQ points.[146] More caution is necessary. Do the people who are texting others while they are supposed to be talking to you make you crazy, or is it just me? Boost your brain and improve your relationships by cutting back on unnecessary screen time.

TODAY'S PRACTICE: *Take an inventory of your screen time. Dial it down by 25 percent this week.*

I Have No Idea Why I'm Anxious

Is your anxiety not yours, but from another generation? Ever feel fearful of something for no apparent reason? It could be an inherited trait. That's what happened to generations of mice in a fascinating animal experiment that appeared in *Nature Neuroscience*. The researchers employed a classic fear conditioning technique to make mice afraid of cherry blossoms. Basically, they gave the rodents a light shock whenever they were exposed to the scent of the small pink flowers.[147] This result was expected, but what is surprising is that the next two generations of offspring also feared the fragrance of cherry blossoms, despite a lack of exposure to any fear conditioning themselves. The shocks had changed gene expression—the way one's genes work—in the study mice and was subsequently passed down to the next two generations of offspring. This is known as epigenetics, the study of lifestyle effects on DNA.

This research is important for two reasons. First, it means your unexplainable fears, worries, anxiousness, and biases may be rooted in your family tree. Ancestral trauma has been linked to panic attacks, depression, insomnia, disruptive or aggressive behavior, memory problems, and more.[148] On the flip side, a family history of trauma may provide benefits. For example, other animal research points to increased resilience as a result of ancestral stress.[149] Experts suggest that epigenetics may be the body's way of preparing future generations to better handle the adversities experienced by ancestors.

Second, it indicates that your life experiences, environment, and behaviors can greatly influence your children and grandchildren in either a positive or negative way. This is another reason why you need to get serious about your brain health.

TODAY'S PRACTICE: *Look back into your family history to see if there are any anxieties or stresses you may have inherited.*

Diaphragmatic Breathing

This is one of the fastest techniques to decrease anxiety quickly. Breathing is essential to life. It delivers oxygen into your lungs, where your bloodstream picks it up and takes it to all the cells in your body so that they can function properly. Breathing also allows you to eliminate waste products, such as carbon dioxide. Slight changes in oxygen or carbon dioxide can alter the way you feel and behave.

When someone gets upset, angry, or anxious, their breathing becomes shallow and fast. This causes a change in oxygen and carbon dioxide in an anxious person's blood, making them more anxious. It becomes a vicious cycle, causing irritability, impulsiveness, confusion, and bad decision-making. Learning to direct and control your breathing has immediate benefits. It calms the amygdala (the alert center in your brain), counteracts the body's fight-or-flight response, relaxes muscles, warms hands, and regulates heart rhythms.

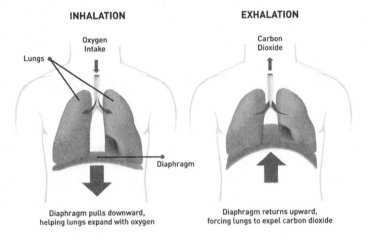

INHALATION

Oxygen Intake

Lungs

Diaphragm

Diaphragm pulls downward, helping lungs expand with oxygen

EXHALATION

Carbon Dioxide

Diaphragm returns upward, forcing lungs to expel carbon dioxide

I often teach patients to become experts at breathing slowly and deeply, mostly using their bellies. If you watch a baby or a puppy breathe, you will notice that they breathe almost solely with their bellies—the most efficient way to breathe. Expanding your belly when you inhale increases the amount of air available to your lungs and body. Pulling your belly in when you exhale causes the diaphragm to push the air out of your lungs, allowing for a more fully exhaled breath.

To calm yourself, breathe in a very specific pattern: Inhale for four seconds through your nose; hold for a second; exhale for eight seconds (twice as long as the inhale) through your mouth; hold for one second; repeat 10 times. This will take about two minutes and is deeply relaxing for most people.

TODAY'S PRACTICE: *Do diaphragmatic breathing in the rhythm above for four minutes today and record how you feel. If it relaxes you, do it each day for two to four minutes.*

Loving-Kindness Meditation

Kindness is a practice. Research has shown many positive benefits of a special form of meditation called Loving-Kindness Meditation (LKM), which focuses on developing feelings of goodwill, kindness, and warmth toward others. LKM boosts good feelings and brain cells while also improving how connected you feel. LKM reduces pain and symptoms from trauma.[150] Try a simple LKM by finding a quiet place where you can close your eyes for a few minutes. Breathe in deeply, then exhale slowly. Focus on your heart space in the middle of your chest as you take a few more deep breaths. To start, you'll meditate on loving and kind thoughts toward yourself, because only when you love yourself can you be loving to other people. Continue to breathe deeply as you say or think about these phrases:

"May I be safe; may I be well in body and mind; may I be content and peaceful."

Let these phrases become your intentions. Repeat them several times and let yourself begin to feel safe, well, content, and at peace. Next, change the focus from yourself to someone else. Bring to mind a person for whom you feel grateful and repeat the phrases with them in mind:

"May you be safe; may you be well in body and mind; may you be content and peaceful."

Next think of someone you have no strong feelings about either way, such as a neighbor you barely know or someone you passed on the street, and repeat the phrases with them in mind.

Finally, bring to mind a person who challenges you or causes negative feelings and direct your loving-kindness meditation toward them. Often it can feel empowering to send love toward those who make your life hard.

TODAY'S PRACTICE: *Practice LKM for five minutes.*

Heart Rate Variability Training

Your brain and health are completely connected. Heart rate variability (HRV) training is a simple way to lower stress and accelerate mindfulness. While you have an average number of beats per minute, each beat is not exactly the same distance apart; your heart rhythm has slight variations. This is a sign of a healthy heart. In fact, the more variability between beats, the better the health of your heart and brain, while less variation is an indication of illness.

HRV is one of the key markers used to monitor newborns. Doctors use scalp monitors to track a baby's HRV before birth. They are watching for noticeable variation between beats. If the rhythm is too consistent, they know something is wrong with the baby. Low HRV indicates distress at any age and can inform physicians of a patient's likelihood to survive after a heart attack or their risk of death even if there is no heart disease. Knowing what you do now about the relationship between your brain and physical health, it might not surprise you to learn that studies also show a relationship between high levels of anxiety and heart disease.[151] Research reveals a correlation between negative emotions and low HRV.[152]

The exciting news is that you can easily train your HRV. Positive feelings, gratitude, forgiveness, soothing music, lavender, exercise, and eating more plants help increase the beat-to-beat variation in your heart rate. I also often recommend HRV trainers, such as those found at heartmath.com. Many professional athletes are able to avoid injury and increase performance by using HRV training. Train smarter, not harder, and know when to rest.

TODAY'S PRACTICE: *Download an HRV app, such as Welltory, to measure your HRV.*

Hypnosis to Discipline Your Mind

Experienced doctors know hypnosis can help many medical and psychiatric conditions.
There are many myths and misconceptions about hypnosis, such as you will lose
control or open your mind to dark forces, but that is all Hollywood. Research
shows that using medical hypnosis, guided imagery, or progressive muscle relaxation
(PMR) can help a wide variety of conditions, including anxiety, depression, stress,
pain, and migraine and tension headaches.[153] There are many online audios that can
guide you. We have several on our app, which is available in the App Store. Hypnosis basically follows five simple steps.

1. **Focus:** Pick a spot on a wall that is a little bit above your eye level. Focus on it
   and slowly count to 20. Then close your eyes. You are focusing your attention
   externally and then bringing it internally.
2. **Breathe:** Take three slow, deep breaths, taking twice as long to breathe out as
   breathing in. Imagine breathing in relaxation and blowing out all your stresses.
3. **PMR:** Next, with your eyes closed, tightly squeeze the muscles around your
   eyes, hold for a second, then gently relax your eyes. Imagine that relaxation
   slowly spreading, like warm penetrating oil, from the tiny muscles around your
   eyes to the top of your head and all the way down to the bottom of your feet.
4. **Deepening:** When your whole body feels relaxed, imagine yourself at the top of
   an escalator and ride down, counting backward from 10. By the time you reach
   the bottom, you'll likely feel very relaxed.
5. **Safe Haven:** Then visualize a special place where you feel very relaxed. Imagine
   your special place with all five of your senses. Enjoy the tranquility for as long
   as you like. Then get back on the escalator riding up, counting to 10 as you go.
   When you get to 10, open your eyes, feeling relaxed, refreshed, and wide awake.

When you do this the first several times, allow yourself plenty of time. Some
people become so relaxed that they fall asleep for several minutes. If that happens,
don't worry. It's a good sign that you're really relaxed!

TODAY'S PRACTICE: *Try this exercise or watch my video "How to Learn Self-Hypnosis
to Calm Your Anxiety" at https://www.youtube.com/watch?v=4VpqDYHTp_w.*

Hypnosis Can Help Kids Too

The ability to be hypnotized peaks at age 11. You might think hypnosis is only for adults, but it can do wonders for children. I've used it with my own daughter. One year for a Fourth of July party, my wife, Tana, had made a new dessert out of nut butters. Our daughter Chloe decided to warm the dessert on the stove. When she thought it was ready, she tested it by dipping a finger into the sauce—ouch! That's when we heard her scream. Blazing hot and sticky, the sauce covered her finger. We tried cold water, aloe gel, and then ice cubes for her hand. But the pain was too much. "I'm so stupid. Why did I do that?" she cried, as ANTs flooded her mind. Tana tried to calm her down and prayed with her, but nothing was helping. The pain had overwhelmed Chloe. Tana said to me, "We need your help."

I sat with Chloe and analyzed what was going on. I knew this was an instance when hypnosis could work. I used a simple practice that I had used with many of my patients. First, I told her to focus on one spot on the wall, let her body loosen up, and breathe very slowly. Then I told her to close her eyes while imagining she was going down a flight of stairs. While she did that, I counted down from ten to one. Then I asked her to think of a beautiful park where she could see, smell, and hear wonderful things. She was safe there with family and friends. Next, I told her to think about stepping into a warm pool that had superpowers to heal and soothe her finger. Floating in the pool would also bring peace to her mind and body. She simply made a mistake; there was no reason to beat herself up. I could see her body relax, and she quietly fell asleep. When she woke up the next day, there was a tiny blister on her skin, but she wasn't in any more pain and felt fine. "Everyone makes mistakes," she said. "That was one of mine."

Hypnosis is a powerful way to soothe children (or adults).

TODAY'S PRACTICE: *If you have children, try this simple technique with them at bedtime. For small children, read my book* Time for Bed, Sleepyhead *(Zonderkidz, 2016) to them. It is a hypnotic bedtime story to help children sleep.*

Hand Warming

Warming your hands with your brain can have an immediate relaxation response.
Take a moment to focus on your hands. Feel their energy and temperature. When
you intentionally learn how to warm your hands by focusing on familiar warming
images, like holding a cup of hot tea, it causes your body to relax. Research studies
have found this strategy can lower anxiety and blood pressure, help with migraine
headaches in kids and adults, and even be useful in some cases of irritable bowel
syndrome.[154] Science has also demonstrated that holding on to something warm,
such as a puppy, can help you feel more trusting, generous, and connected to other
people.[155] Conversely, cold hands do the opposite. I've taught many patients how to
use their thoughts to warm their hands because it can reduce their stress and anxiety
often as well as medication can. put the paragraph break here

You can teach yourself this technique by doing some diaphragmatic breathing
along with picturing warming images. Here are 12 potential hand-warming images:

1. Holding someone's warm hand or touching their warm skin
2. Putting your hands in warm sand at the beach
3. Taking a hot bath or shower
4. Sitting in a sauna
5. Cuddling a baby
6. Cuddling a warm, furry puppy or kitten
7. Holding a warm cup of tea or sugar-free cocoa
8. Holding your hands in front of a fire
9. Wearing warm gloves
10. Being wrapped in a warm towel
11. Getting a massage with warm oil
12. Holding a hot potato with warm gloves

Find the hand-warming images that work for you and use them to reset your
nervous system to be more relaxed and counteract your stress response. You can buy
temperature sensors online (under brand names Biodots, Stress Cards, and Stress
Sheets) to get feedback on your progress. You can also run your hands under warm
water to calm yourself.

TODAY'S PRACTICE: *Try three of the images above for two minutes each to see which
one has the most relaxing effect on you.*

Remember the 18-40-60 Rule

Stop caring about what other people think of you, because they are mostly not thinking about you at all. I teach all of my patients the 18-40-60 rule: When you're 18 you worry about what everyone else is thinking of you; when you're 40 you don't care what anyone else is thinking about you; and when you're 60, you realize no one has been thinking about you at all. People spend their days worrying and thinking about themselves, not you.

"With age, you figure out that life is too short to waste time thinking about what other people think about you." That's what Grammy Award–winning superstar Christina Aguilera told *Health* magazine about turning 40.[156] She's not alone. A 2021 survey of 2,000 older adults found that 72 percent of them felt more content and more comfortable in their own skin when they hit their forties and stopped worrying about what other people think of them.[157] These people may not be aware of it, but they're prime examples of the most life-changing rule you never learned.

This single piece of insight into human nature is so powerful that it can literally change your life by reducing negativity, anxiety, and worry and increasing self-esteem, joy, and overall happiness. It's a shame it isn't taught in schools. Think how much happier and less stressed you might have been if you had known this earlier.

TODAY'S PRACTICE: *When you find yourself worrying about what others think of you, remind yourself that they are thinking about themselves, not you.*

Managing Road Rage

Be nice on the road, there are many people with troubled brains driving next to you.
Road rage can be deadly. In 2021, a young mother was driving her 6-year-old son
to kindergarten in Southern California, when a white sedan abruptly cut her off in
the carpool lane. The mother gave the other driver the middle finger as she merged
away from the carpool lane. Then she heard a loud noise and her son said, "Ow."
When she pulled the car over, the mother saw that her son had been shot. She
called 911 and the boy was rushed to the hospital, but sadly, he couldn't be saved.[158]
The young boy's mother will never be the same. Bad drivers, traffic jams, road construction, detours, and other delays can make anyone feel anxious, angry, frustrated,
or stressed. But what happens in the brain to make some drivers become so enraged
they snap?

Road rage is more common than you might imagine, causing nearly one in
three traffic accidents and leading to a shocking 30 murders every year.[159] About
half of all drivers who are the victim of road rage behavior respond aggressively by
making a rude gesture, shouting, or flashing their lights. In some cases, such as with
the tragic shooting of the 6-year-old, this leads to an escalation of rage and aggressive behavior.

The brain imaging work we do at Amen Clinics reveals three patterns in road
rage: low activity in the prefrontal cortex (impulsivity), high activity in the anterior
cingulate gyrus (they get stuck on negative thoughts or disrespect), and low activity
in the temporal lobes (more irritable and potentially aggressive). A bad combination.

Be careful when you notice yourself or another driver becoming furious with
road rage. It can quickly spiral downward. When a road rage incident begins,
remind yourself that you are responsible for your actions and take steps to defuse
the situation. If you're getting angry or find yourself thinking about engaging in
aggressive driving behaviors, don't. Take a deep breath and let the person pass by.
You may have just saved your life or the life of a loved one.

TODAY'S PRACTICE: *Next time you are in a car, start thinking about the brains of
other drivers and be even more cautious and kind.*

Four Steps to Break a Panic Attack

I was so anxious that I wanted to run out of the studio. Many years ago, I published an article in *Parade* magazine entitled "How to Get Out of Your Own Way." More than 10,000 people wrote to Amen Clinics for help with self-defeating behaviors. Clearly, I had written about a common problem. Someone from CNN learned about the popularity of the piece and invited me for an interview on a show. I had never been on television before. When I was backstage waiting to go on, anxiety crept over me. I felt like I couldn't breathe, my heart rate shot through the roof, and I felt so awful that I wanted to make a break for the exit door. Thankfully, I heard a small internal voice laughing at me: "You help people with anxiety and panic attacks. What would you say to them right now?"

Here are four simple steps I used to break my panic attack, and they can help you too. I often write these steps down on a prescription pad for my patients.

1. Don't leave. If you leave a situation that's really not dangerous because of your anxiety, the fear will control you and you may never go back. So I stayed put and did the interview.
2. Breathe slowly and deeply, especially when you exhale. Consciously taking slow, deep breaths, then taking twice as long to exhale, helps you regain control. I did that and started to feel calmer.
3. Record any automatic negative thoughts and ask yourself if they're true, and whether they are helping or hurting you. I talked back to my ANTs. ANT #1: "I'm going to forget my name." That was silly; had I ever forgotten my own name? ANT #2: "I'm going to stutter." I might stutter; I might not. Did it really matter? ANT #3: "Millions of viewers are going to think I'm an idiot." I knew the topic well and knew I could help people. If one person benefited from this show, it was worth it.
4. If the first three steps aren't strong enough for anxiety, then I suggest simple supplements like theanine, magnesium, or GABA to help yourself calm down.

TODAY'S PRACTICE: *When you feel anxious today or any day, put these four steps into practice.*

How to Make Your Child a Republican, Democrat, or Anything You Want

There's no influence without connection. If you are bonded to your children, they tend to pick up your values. If your bond is weak, neutral, or negative, children tend to pick the opposite values, just to rebel. So if you're a political conservative and want your kids to have the same views, make sure they get plenty of quality time with you, pay attention when they talk, use kind words, and love them unconditionally. If you want your children to become liberal politically—the opposite of you— ignore them, talk over them often, and dismiss their feelings. Be critical of or upset with them frequently and they will quickly find values that stand against yours. Teens who feel loved and have strong bonds to their parents are less likely to use drugs, engage in violence, or contemplate suicide.[160]

One study reported that the amount of quality time families spend together per day is just 37 minutes.[161] I find that scary when I think about all the hours children spend on screens. There is so much competition for their attention. Who wins out? Whoever or whatever gets the most of their time. The higher the exposure, the greater the number of messages your brain takes in. With enough time, those messages become hardwired into your brain. Consider it accidental conditioning. You become used to what you see, even violent images or unrealistic portrayals of beauty. So you may tell your children one thing, but what they see or hear onscreen says something else.

The other essential principle to help your children develop good character comes from firm parenting. The brain needs guidance, rules, rewards, and consequences in a loving, supportive environment. The brain, at any age, learns best that way. Studies on successful parenting come to the same conclusion: The parents who are firm and kind develop the healthiest kids. Permissiveness (being incapable of discipline and upholding rules) actually hurts children. Permissive parents wind up with kids who have relational and learning problems. The best thing you can do for your children is to set clear expectations about behavior and use positive reinforcement and consequences to uphold them. In the long run, your children will be better off.

TODAY'S PRACTICE: *If you have children, spend extra time with them today focusing on all their positive traits.*

Eight Tips to Master Performance Anxiety

Relabel anxiety as excitement.

1. **See it as a problem to solve rather than a character flaw.** You are a creative problem solver.
2. **Relabel anxiety as excitement.** The stress chemical adrenaline triggers a sympathetic nervous system response (heart racing, breathing funny, nausea, legs feeling like Jell-O) and fools your body into thinking something is wrong when you are actually excited. Research conducted at Harvard University showed that relabeling "anxiety" as "excitement" improved performance during anxiety-inducing activities, including public speaking, taking math tests, and singing karaoke. Before the activities, participants were asked to say, "I am excited," or "I am calm." Those who said they were excited gave speeches that were more persuasive, did 8 percent better on math tests, and sang better when they performed karaoke.[162]
3. **Diaphragmatic breathing** triggers a parasympathetic response that will calm you (see day 200).
4. **Make a list of what makes the anxiety better** before a performance and what makes it worse. Be curious about it, not furious when it happens.
5. **Limit or eliminate caffeine and sugar** on the day of a performance.
6. **An hour before the performance, eat a banana with some form of protein.**
7. **Shift the focus off of yourself and your fear to the blast of excitement you are providing to your audience.** Close your eyes and imagine the audience laughing, cheering, and having a party. Also encourage and thank those who helped you.
8. **Focus on what will go right** rather than what will go wrong.

TODAY'S PRACTICE: *The next time you have a presentation, talk, or performance, choose one of these strategies to turn anxiety into excitement.*

Feel Good Time: Meet Your Deep Limbic System

Set your emotional brain to happy. The limbic system is one of the most exciting and critical parts of being human and is power packed with functions—all of which are critical for human behavior and survival. The primary functions of the limbic system include:

Filtering your thoughts through an emotional lens. Think of it like putting a filter on a camera lens that makes everything seem a bit brighter or a shade darker. Lower activity in the limbic system is associated with a sense of positivity. When the limbic system is overactive, you're more likely to interpret events in a negative way.

Banking memories with great highs and lows, such as the best days of your life (college graduation, getting married, the birth of your first child) and the worst days (being in a horrific car accident or the death of a loved one).

Regulating appetite and circadian rhythm (sleep-wake cycles).

Cultivating relational bonds. When you have strong social connections, the limbic system boosts your mood and adds positivity to your life.

Processing aromas and scents. This helps explain why scents can have such a powerful influence on your moods and emotions.

Regulating your sex drive, which is why depression decreases sexual interest.

In general, lower activity in your limbic system means a more positive frame of mind. However, when the limbic system is working too hard, it is often associated with sadness, negative thinking, negative perception of events, a flood of negative emotions (hopelessness, helplessness, and guilt), appetite and sleep problems, decreased sexual responsiveness, social isolation, and pain.

TODAY'S PRACTICE: *On a scale of 1 to 10, rate your mood for the past five days. In the following days we will work to optimize it.*

Feel Great Anytime, Anywhere

Anchor happiness in your brain. Where you bring your attention determines how you feel. Unfortunately, many people focus on their worries and fears, which makes them feel awful. Negative thoughts trigger chemicals in your brain that make you feel anxious and depressed, while positive thoughts release ones that help you feel great.

Here's the exercise: Write down some of the best memories of your life and then anchor them to specific places in your home, using all of your senses. Then, whenever you feel upset, imagine walking through your home and reliving your happiest memories. With a little practice, you can train your brain to feel great, almost in an instant. Start by writing down five of your best memories. Let me show you how I do it.

In my mind, I start

1. At my front door, where I remember carrying Tana across the threshold. She's the best thing that's ever happened to me.
2. In the living room, I see one of my scientific collaborators giving me a framed copy of our research that was listed as one of the top 100 stories in science by *Discover* magazine.
3. In the kitchen, which smells amazing, I see my mom making dinner and she wants to hear all about my day. She's always been like that, and I know how blessed I am to still have her.
4. At the stove, I see myself as a child standing on a stool next to my grandfather, who is making fudge. He was a professional candy maker and my best friend when I was growing up. But now we're making a sugar-free version.
5. Upstairs, I see my daughter Chloe, when she was young, wearing her zebra hoodie, sitting on my shoulders, and telling me she loves me.

What happy memories do you want to anchor? With a little practice, this exercise can help you feel amazing anytime, anywhere.

TODAY'S PRACTICE: *Do this best memory exercise.*

Healing Scents

Flood your senses with happiness to feel better fast. Your olfactory system, which gives you your sense of smell, is directly connected to and processed in your limbic system or emotional brain. For this reason, we are drawn to pleasant scents such as fragrant flowers and find the smell of skunks to be offensive. A research article on aromatherapy published in the medical journal the *Lancet* studied the benefits of lavender oil. The results found that it can improve sleep, lift mood, and reduce feelings of stress.[163] Aromatherapy is very accessible and easy to use. A few drops can be added to a bath, the sheets on your bed, or put in a diffuser to fill a room with your favorite scent. The right scents can help calm your emotional brain and be like a natural anti-inflammatory. The scent of jasmine can be uplifting, ylang-ylang can help lower stress, and scents like peppermint can boost your energy. Filling your environment with any smells that are pleasing to you can have a positive impact on your brain.

My family is of Lebanese descent, a culture in which cinnamon is commonly used. My mother used it frequently in her cooking, and I still love the taste and smell of it. When I recently told her that the scent of cooked cinnamon is considered a natural aphrodisiac for men, she put her hand on her forehead and said, "That's why I have seven kids; your father would never leave me alone."

TODAY'S PRACTICE: *Try three different scents today to see which helps you feel calmer or more energized.*

Surround Yourself with People Who Provide Positive Bonding

People are contagious. Have you ever gone to a summer picnic that got ruined by an ant invasion? You may have been in the best mood until you found ants crawling on your food, making your bright mood turn sour. The same scenario can happen with negative people. You might be feeling great when you head into a room only to be attacked by their ANTs. Pretty soon, their ANTs will be infesting your mind and ruining your mood. The people who surround you influence the way you feel, so it's important to keep company with positive people.

Take a quick assessment of your social network—family, friends, coworkers, and so on. Are they positive types who support you and increase your confidence? Or do they focus on what's wrong and make you feel like you aren't good enough? Make an effort to spend more time with the folks who pump you up, and dedicate less time to those who bring you down.

As a college sophomore, I decided I wanted to go to medical school. I was on the speech team and told our coach my plan. She told me her brother hadn't made it into medical school, "and he was much smarter than you are."

Discouraged, I told my father what she had said. He shook his head and told me, "Listen, you can do whatever you put your mind to. And if I were you, I wouldn't spend much time with that coach."

TODAY'S PRACTICE: *Write down the five people with whom you spend the most time. On a scale of 1 to 10, rate how positive or negative they are (1 being very negative). Then add up the score and divide by 5. See if that number matches your mood if you rated it on a scale of 1 to 10.*

Recognize the Importance of Physical Contact

Physical touch is essential to life itself. In an inhumane experiment during the 1200s, German emperor Frederick II was curious where language came from and what language children would speak if they grew up without ever hearing anyone else speak. A monk during Frederick's reign wrote that Frederick took a group of babies away from their parents and assigned a few nurses to care for the infants but without interacting with them except what was necessary to feed and clean them. They received no physical touch or words of any kind. The newborns never learned to speak because they all died.[164] A more modern and humane study was done at the turn of this century with orphans in Romania who had been deprived of touch and relationship for years. They scanned the brains of these children and found overall decreased activity in their brains.[165]

The parent-baby connection created through physical touch such as holding, hugging, and cooing is necessary for bonding and brain development. All that physical interaction provides pleasure, love, trust, and safety for a baby to form healthy limbic (emotional) pathways. Those pathways then help grow the bond even more between parent and child. Without physical affection, an infant feels alone and unsafe and becomes irritable and unresponsive. Their emotional center cannot develop in a healthy way, which leads to an inability to trust or connect with others.

Adults also need affection. For close connection to build, couples must have regular eye contact and touch each other in loving ways (hugs, kisses, etc.). Both need to be engaged; the bond won't form if only one person gives affection. Physical expressions of love need to be reciprocal; if that doesn't happen, the affectionate person will feel hurt and rejected, which will chip away at the couple's connection to each other. Healthy touch is part of our humanity. Don't let our standoffish, lawsuit-mongering, pandemic-weary culture keep you from reaching out to touch those you love. Hug and hold your children, your spouse, and your loved ones often. Your emotional brain will thank you.

TODAY'S PRACTICE: *How often do you touch those around you? In a healthy way, increase your level of touch today. If it is hard for you, sign up for a massage.*

Create an Emotional Rescue Playlist

Music can soothe, inspire, improve mood, and help with focus. Music is important in every known culture on earth, with ancient roots extending back 250,000 years or more. After evaluating more than 800 people, researchers have found that people listen to music to regulate energy and mood, to achieve self-awareness, and to improve social bonds. It provides social cement—think of work and war songs, lullabies, and national anthems.[166] In his book *The Secret Language of the Heart*, Barry Goldstein wrote about how music affects the brain:

> Music stimulates emotions through specific brain circuits . . . [and] oxytocin, the "cuddle hormone" . . . can be released [which can enhance bonding, trust, and relationships]. . . . Listening to music can create peak emotions, which increase the amount of dopamine, a specific neurotransmitter that is produced in the brain and helps control the brain's reward and pleasure centers. . . . Music was used to assist patients with severe brain injuries in recalling personal memories. The music helped the patients to reconnect to memories they previously could not access.[167]

Based on the concept of entrainment, which means your brain picks up the rhythm in the environment, you can manipulate your mind with the music you choose. Create your own emotional rescue playlist to boost your mood quickly. Research shows it can be very effective to start with musical pieces you love. Here are 10 research-based suggestions:

"Sonata for Two Pianos in D Major (K. 448)," Mozart
"Clair de Lune," Debussy
"Adagio for Strings," Samuel Barber
"Piano Sonata No. 17 in D Minor (The Tempest)," Beethoven
"Weightless," Marconi Union
"Good Vibrations," The Beach Boys
"Don't Stop Me Now," Queen
"Uptown Girl," Billy Joel
"Dancing Queen," Abba
"Walking on Sunshine," Katrina and the Waves

TODAY'S PRACTICE: *Create your own emotional rescue playlist.*

Anchor Images

Thirty percent of the brain is dedicated to vision. The best way to perpetuate brain envy and stay the course with brain health is to keep images and reminders out where you can see them. I do this myself. I keep photos out of the people I love most (Tana, my kids, my grandkids) to remind me daily of my greatest motivation to have a great brain. Certain "anchor" images instantly evoke my big *why* for a better brain.

One of those images is of my granddaughter Emmy. She was born with a rare syndrome where parts of her chromosomes are missing. It results in severe seizures and heart disease, and it inhibits brain development. When she was still a baby, there was one day when she endured 160 seizures. Keeping my brain healthy allows me to be available to help Emmy and my daughter Breanne as much as possible. If I let my own health go, I can't be my best for those I love. My goal is to lead the way for my family for many more decades so they never have to take care of me. A good brain makes that possible. I see the visual reminders of my family all the time to make sure I don't forget how much I need to fiercely protect it. I advise everyone to do the same.

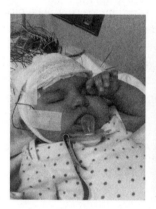 

TODAY'S PRACTICE: *What would be a motivating anchor image for you? Post it to remind you of why you need to be healthy.*

Positivity Bias Training Time

From mental illness to mental health. The "father of positivity psychology," Dr. Martin Seligman, has influenced me over the years. When he was elected president of the American Psychological Association in 1996, he gathered a dozen top psychologists and asked them to help him formulate a plan to move the entire discipline of psychology away from treating mental illness and toward human flourishing. For many years, psychology worked within the disease model—treating those with mental problems and psychopathological issues. In their rush to do something about repairing mental health damage, it had never occurred to psychologists to develop positive interventions that made people happier. That was the impetus for Dr. Seligman and other top psychologists on a strategy they called "positive psychology," which shifted the focus of interventions from problems to solutions.

They determined that positive psychology had five key aspects:

1. Positive psychology helps us look at life with optimism.
2. Positive psychology allows us to appreciate the present.
3. Positive psychology lets us accept and make peace with the past.
4. Positive psychology helps us be more grateful and forgiving.
5. Positive psychology helps us look beyond the momentary pleasures and pains of life.[168]

Research has shown many benefits of practicing positive psychology, including an increase in self-esteem, improved relationships, and a better outlook on life. Over the next few days, I'll discuss some of my favorite positive psychology techniques.

TODAY'S PRACTICE: *How would your life be different if you were more positive?*

Start Every Day with "Today Is Going to Be a Great Day"

Habits matter. They ultimately control your life. Develop the habit of starting each morning by saying, "Today is going to be a great day." Where you bring your attention determines how you feel. If you want to feel happier, start the day by directing your attention to what you are excited about, what you like, what you want, what you hope for, and what makes you happy, rather than the negative. I recommend families do it together as they are waking up their kids or eating at the breakfast table in the morning. I love this exercise so much that it's at the top of the to-do list that I look at every morning, just in case I miss saying it.

"Today is going to be a great day" may sound a bit, shall I say, Pollyannaish, especially during times like the pandemic when thousands were dying from COVID-19 or restaurant owners were forced to close their businesses. My heart grieved for those families personally hit with the coronavirus (mine included), yet being negative doesn't help anyone. We had a lot to do at Amen Clinics helping the thousands of people with mounting anxiety, depression, and suicidal thoughts.

By saying, "Today is going to be a great day," you will be protecting and directing your mind to see what is right, not just what is wrong, which is so easy to find. This helped me do hundreds of live chats on social media during the pandemic, encouraging our patients and followers.

Another reason I recommend this practice is because it plants seeds of optimism into the soil of everyday life. Healthy individuals look for the good that can come out of a situation, not just what can go wrong. One of my favorite sayings is one that is often erroneously credited to Winston Churchill, prime minister of Great Britain during World War II: "A pessimist sees the difficulty in every opportunity; an optimist sees the opportunity in every difficulty."

TODAY'S PRACTICE: *Start every day for the next year (and maybe your lifetime) with "Today is going to be a great day!" Post this affirmation in your bathroom to remind yourself.*

End Each Day with "What Went Well Today?"

Put yourself to sleep in a purposely positive way each night. At the end of the day, write down or meditate on the question, *What went well today?* Doing this will set up your dreams to be more positive, giving you a better night's sleep. Research showed that people who did this exercise were happier and less depressed at one-month and six-month follow-ups.[169] This simple exercise has been found to help people in stressful jobs develop more positive emotions.

I love doing this exercise every night because it helps me remember wonderful moments I might have forgotten in my busy life. I even did this on the night after my father died, and surprisingly, there were many things that had gone well that day. I received many loving text messages, my siblings and I all rallied to be there for my mom, and my wife, Tana, was with me every minute to support me. Ending my day by focusing on these things buoyed my spirits and helped me drift off to sleep.

Think of this nightly exercise as your personal highlight reel, similar to those daily sports recaps on television. Consider jotting down your daily highlights in a journal—like a gratitude journal—and read through it at the end of each month and again at the end of the year. Reflecting on all the amazing things that have occurred in your life can have a powerfully positive effect on your self-confidence, outlook, and sense of accomplishment.

TODAY'S PRACTICE: *When you go to bed tonight (and maybe for the rest of your life), ask yourself,* What went well today? *Post the question by your bed as a reminder.*

Look for Micro-Moments of Happiness

Big happiness often comes from small moments. Happiness doesn't have to be something "big" or "off the charts." Happiness stemming from small moments can actually be more valuable than significant milestones like your birthday, a graduation ceremony, or a party. Get in the habit of looking for and finding the teeny-tiny, itty-bitty, micro-moments of happiness throughout your day. It will train your brain to have a positivity bias. Keep a written journal or use the notes section of your phone to record them throughout your day. Then, refer to them at the end of your day to make sure you don't miss out on the little things that help you feel happy. When you really pay attention to these micro-moments, they can have a big impact on your chemicals of happiness and overall positivity. "Seek and you will find" (Matthew 7:7).

Here are some examples of micro-moments my patients have shared with me:

Seeing my baby smile
Noticing the leaves changing color
Hearing the first note of my favorite song come on the radio
The moment when I splash under the water at the pool
The smells when I start cooking
The sound of live music at the start of a concert
Walking down the Jetway at the start of a vacation
Holding an umbrella during a rainstorm
Finishing a puzzle
Tuning in to my favorite TV series
Listening to a worthwhile podcast
Hitting the "buy" button for airline tickets for my next vacation
Petting my dog; he looks at me with those eyes
Spotting the owl that visits my yard
Holding my spouse's hand
Hearing someone else laugh
Receiving a "good job" from my boss
Seeing my friends when I arrive at the tennis court
Driving to a scenic point and watching the sun go down

TODAY'S PRACTICE: *Record five micro-moments of happiness today.*

Interrupt Unnecessary Unhappy Moments

As you think, so you feel. As you feel, so you do. As you do, so you have. I learned this strategy from my friend Joseph McClendon III, a spellbinding orator who often teaches at Tony Robbins seminars. Joseph says that when unnecessary unhappy moments come up, he takes a simple, four-step process to get back on track:

1. **Feel bad on purpose.** Spend a few seconds feeling bad. Go to the dark place. Let the bad feeling wash over you. Sounds sort of crazy, doesn't it? But a few seconds can be empowering because if you know how to make yourself feel bad, you can also decide to interrupt it.

2. **Interrupt the pattern.** If the bad feelings are unnecessary or unhelpful, which they often are, interrupt them. After you practice feeling bad, say "Stop," stand up, and take three deep breaths. The physical act of standing up, creating a physical distraction, and intentionally focusing on breathing interrupts the pattern of feeling bad.

3. **Purposefully focus on happy memories.** Fill the void with happy memories so you can feel good on purpose. I ask all of my patients to write down 10 to 20 of their happiest life memories. Focus on one of those nice memories until you can truly feel happy or joyful. Imagine the memory with all of your senses: See what's there, hear any sounds, feel the sensations, and smell and taste what is in the air. Do this for several minutes until you can feel the memory in your soul.

4. **Celebrate.** Finally, wire the good feeling into your nervous system by celebrating your ability to interrupt the unnecessary unhappy moments. McClendon likes to clench his fist, smile, and say, "Yes!" I like to raise my arms like Kobe Bryant did at the end of a Lakers game when he made a three-point shot to win. Celebrating is essential to making new habits stick.

If you are feeling bad, go through this simple process and begin to gain mastery over your happiness.

TODAY'S PRACTICE: *Interrupt an unnecessary unhappy moment using these four steps.*

Gratitude and Appreciation

Direct your attention toward what you are grateful for and your brain will work better. I worked with psychologist Noelle Nelson to study the effects of gratitude and appreciation on the brain. As part of writing *The Power of Appreciation*, she had her brain scanned twice. Before the first SPECT scan, she spent a half hour contemplating everything in her life for which she was grateful, what she called an "appreciation meditation." This scan showed healthy, even activity across her brain. For the second SPECT scan, she spent time meditating on everything wrong that she was afraid would or could happen. She didn't hold back: "If my dog got sick, I couldn't go to work because I would have to stay home to care for him. If I didn't go to work, however, I would lose my job. If I lost my job, I wouldn't have enough money to take my dog to the vet and he would likely die. If the dog died, I would be so depressed I still wouldn't be able to go back to work. Then I would lose my home and become homeless."

GRATEFUL   FEARFUL

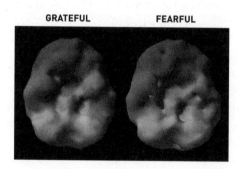

The scan after she focused on her biggest fears showed several areas of low activity: her cerebellum (which coordinates thoughts and motor skills), temporal lobes (which store memories and images), and her prefrontal cortex (which helps with decision-making and self-control).

Negative thoughts actually change the brain for the worse, yet concentrating on thankfulness literally makes you grateful for your brain. I've used this exercise of "appreciation meditation" with depressed patients to help them get better faster. A number of studies show that anyone who expresses thankfulness and appreciation frequently is healthier and more optimistic, succeeds with their goals, feels better, and becomes more helpful. Physicians who intentionally work at being grateful actually make the right diagnoses more often.[170]

TODAY'S PRACTICE: *List five things that you are thankful for. Then add five more. Writing it down helps embed them in your brain.*

Random Acts of Kindness

Kindness helps the brain work better. Can being kind to others make a meaningful difference in your level of happiness? Psychologist Sonja Lyubomirsky, from University of California–Riverside, decided to put this question to the test with a controlled study that asked students to carry out five weekly random acts of kindness of their choice, anything from buying food for a homeless person to helping a younger sibling with schoolwork. The students reported higher levels of happiness than the control group, with students who performed all five kind acts in one day feeling the best by the end of the six-week study period. Before this, other studies had found that altruistic people tend to be happy, but Dr. Lyubomirsky established that good deeds are actually a direct cause of an increase in well-being and can decrease depressive symptoms.[171]

In another study, researchers at the University of Wisconsin–Madison discovered that human kindness is teachable and can change how the brain works in the process. Helen Weng and colleagues trained young adults to engage in compassion meditation to increase feelings of empathy and compassion for people who are stressed and suffering. Participants focused on a time when someone else had suffered and then practiced praying that his or her suffering was relieved. They repeated phrases to help them focus on compassionate feelings, such as, "May you be free from suffering." The participants in the study first chose a person on whom it might be easiest to practice compassion, such as family members or a friend. Then they practiced expanding compassionate feelings to a stranger, and even to themselves. Finally, they were trained to extend these feelings to a "difficult person" in their lives.

Dr. Weng stated, "It's kind of like weight training. Using this systematic approach, we found that people can actually build up their compassion 'muscle' and respond to others' suffering with care and a desire to help." Brain imaging studies found that compassion training actually boosted the function in several areas of the brain, including the prefrontal cortex, which is involved with empathy.[172]

TODAY'S PRACTICE: *How many people can you show a small act of kindness to today?*

Thank You, Next

Gratitude for the past, looking forward. When I first heard Ariana Grande's song "thank u, next," I texted her. She and I had worked together on a special project.

"I have a fun story about 'thank u, next,' when you have time."

She responded, "I can't wait to hear it!"

I told her, "'thank u, next' is a great mental health concept. I explained it to my executive team today. It is mental health in three words. *Thank u*—looking at the past with gratitude, even if things didn't work out like you wanted." The song was about her past relationships that weren't quite right. "*Next*—looking forward to what you want for your future. It is about looking forward rather than being stuck in the past with regret. Be grateful for your experiences, then move on. They loved it."

She texted back, "I'm honored. It's the truth. You cannot be a prisoner to your past. It's hard work."

Ariana had done a lot of work on the concept. As the world knows, on May 22, 2017, a suicide bomber detonated a shrapnel-laden homemade bomb as people were leaving the Manchester, England, arena following one of her concerts. Twenty-three people died, including the attacker, and 1,017 were injured, some of them children. It broke her heart and caused significant emotional trauma. Within a few hours of the bombing, she posted, "broken. from the bottom of my heart, i am so so sorry. i don't have words."[173] On May 26, she announced a benefit concert for the victims of the attack and the British Red Cross that was aired live on BBC One with Miley Cyrus, Justin Bieber, Katy Perry, Chris Martin, and Pharrell Williams, among others, to benefit victims and the Red Cross on June 4, just 13 days after the bombing.

I have been her fan ever since.

TODAY'S PRACTICE: *Pick one thing in the past that was hard for you that you can now look back on with gratitude and one thing in the future you are looking forward to.*

Focus on Your Strengths and Accomplishments

An essential virtue of positive psychological interventions is focusing on what's right rather than what is wrong. I once saw a recording artist who had sold more than 400 million records. She was going through a period of depression and was focused on all the things that were wrong in her life, including an article 40 years prior in a rock-n-roll publication that was critical of her musical style. Despite all her money and fame, she had no ability to manage her mind. Her homework was to go home and write out a list of her accomplishments and strengths. The list made us both smile and was part of helping her heal.

Dr. Seligman participated in a 2005 study demonstrating that strength-based interventions effectively increased happiness and decreased depressive symptoms after just one month.[174] What are five things you're good at? If you aren't sure, what are five things your friends say you do well? When you have written something down, think of ways to use those attributes in your everyday life. For instance, you may have grown up in a bilingual home and have a proficiency in another language. Could you be putting that skill to better use in your career? The same goes for computer expertise, an ability to cook, or an ability to lead teams. Your personal skills can become your signature strengths.

Likewise, focus on your accomplishments. What have you achieved? When I asked one of my patients this question, he answered with, "I can't keep a relationship." He had been married 11 times. Using positivity bias training, we reframed the situation to show him that he was very good at starting relationships and getting women to fall in love with him. We were going to work on how the relationships could last. We noticed what was right and then focused on what could be improved.

TODAY'S PRACTICE: *What have you accomplished? Write it down. Look at it. I keep a file on my phone of "cool events" I've participated in or hosted, and I look at it whenever I feel down.*

A Simple 12-Minute Meditation to Change Your Brain

So simple, yet so powerful. Research shows that meditation and prayer lower stress and improve brain function. Amen Clinics did a SPECT study, sponsored by the Alzheimer's Research and Prevention Foundation, on meditation. We looked specifically at Kirtan Kriya, which is used in Kundalini yoga. We did scans on two

Saa   Taa   Naa   Maa

Adagio ♩ = 66

Saa Taa Naa Maa

different days: Day 1—participants were allowed to think about anything; Day 2—they participated in a meditation session.[175] During the meditation, the participants recited the following five primal sounds: "saa," "taa," "naa," "maa," (the "aa" at the end of each sound is considered the fifth one). They coordinated each sound with specific finger movements on both hands. It goes like this: Chant the sound "saa" as the thumbs touch the index fingers; chant the sound "taa" while touching thumbs to middle fingers; while chanting "naa," thumbs touch ring fingers; and thumbs to pinkies while chanting "maa." They repeated the chants and movements for two minutes whispering, four minutes silently, two minutes whispering, and two minutes out loud.

The SPECT scans taken after the meditation revealed lower activity in the left parietal lobes, which are in charge of the senses, perception, and direction. Some believe this result indicates less awareness of time and space. There was significantly higher blood flow in the prefrontal cortex compared to the baseline scans, indicating that the meditation activated this part of the brain. The results also showed high blood flow in an area associated with spirituality—the right temporal lobe.

Studies have shown that meditation also improves attention and planning, reduces depression and anxiety, decreases sleepiness, and protects the brain from cognitive decline associated with normal aging. In a study from UCLA, the hippocampus was found to be significantly larger in people who meditate regularly.[176] Research also points to increased thickness of the prefrontal cortex as well as other brain regions. Meditation has also been found to help with weight loss, decrease muscle tension, and tighten the skin.

TODAY'S PRACTICE: *Spend 10 to 15 minutes in meditation or prayer today.*

Tiny Habits for Trauma and Grief

Develop habits that help you feel better fast and last. Each of these habits takes just a few minutes. They are anchored to something you do, think, or feel so that they are more likely to become automatic.

1. Whenever I feel upset, I will cross my arms and stroke down from my shoulders to my lower forearms (this stimulates both sides of my brain and helps to have a calming effect on my mind) for one minute.
2. When I feel a wave of a traumatic memory or grief coming on, I will observe myself, write down any negative thoughts that come to my mind, and challenge them.
3. When painful memories from the past get stuck in my brain, I will write them out from an adult perspective, which can stop the thoughts from circling in my head.
4. When I feel anxious, I will take five diaphragmatic breaths to calm myself.
5. When memories of a traumatic event surface, I will ask myself what I am thinking or feeling. Then in my mind, I will go back to the very first time in my life that I can remember thinking those thoughts or feeling those feelings to see if my past is infecting the present. If it is, I will say to myself, "That was then, and this is now."
6. When a lost loved one's birthday (or other anniversary) arrives, I will spend time recalling happy memories and be grateful for the time we had together.
7. When I feel upset or lonely, I will call a friend and ask for their support.

TODAY'S PRACTICE: *Choose one or more tiny habits to place in your life when facing grief or trauma.*

Brain Warrior Tina:
Better Brain, Better Business

When your brain is better, your business gets better too. Intuitively, most people know that bad behaviors make us age more quickly. We see it in the skin of smokers or in the appearance of a methamphetamine addict or in the decreased cognitive functioning of people suffering from alcoholism. Unfortunately, in my experience most people do not have a clue about how their physical health affects their cognitive and mental health. For example, I did a fascinating project with a group of female businesswomen. One of the CEOs, Tina, was struggling with depression, obesity, and uncontrolled diabetes. Her brain SPECT scan looked awful.

Tina told me that she had been diagnosed with diabetes several years earlier but had not found the time to really get healthy. She thought she would eventually get around to it. Tina, like most people, had no idea that diabetes causes brain damage. It damages blood vessels, including those to the brain, and doubles the risk for Alzheimer's disease. Obesity, all by itself, is also a risk for 30 medical illnesses. Depression can be caused by uncontrolled diabetes and obesity.

BEFORE　　　　AFTER

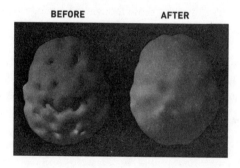

I looked at Tina and said, "Nothing in your life will work right, especially not your business, if your brain isn't right. Your physical health problems are a brain emergency. It is critical to get your weight and diabetes under control, plus when you do this, your mood will be better as well." Since we started working together, Tina has lost 40 pounds, her diabetes is under control, her mood is better, and she looks and feels much younger. Plus, her business has dramatically improved because she has better focus, energy, and judgment.

TODAY'S PRACTICE: *Find out if you have any health problems that are hurting your brain. If you do, take action to fix the problem(s) ASAP.*

Do You Spend Time with Friends or Accomplices?

The fastest way to get healthy is to find the healthiest people you can stand and then spend as much time around them as possible. Getting healthy is a team sport. You may feel like you're going it alone, but the people around you play an important role in your ability to reach your goals even if you don't realize it. I tell my patients to think about the people in their lives as either friends or accomplices.

Friends are the cheerleaders, coaches, and role models who encourage healthy habits and help keep you on track. Spend as much time as possible with these people. Adding those kind of friends improves your chances for success up to 40 percent, especially for weight loss and fitness.[177]

The nutritional gatekeeper in your life must become your friend and supporter for you to be successful. This is why you need to stop spending money on food that hurts your family or coworkers. It leaves them vulnerable to fail and hurts their chances for success. This is a matter of integrity.

Accomplices are the naysayers who discourage your efforts to get healthy, the reverse role models who exhibit bad habits, and the partners in crime who condone your negative behaviors. To make lasting changes in your life, you need fewer accomplices and more friends. Before you ditch the accomplices in your life, try having a heart-to-heart with them to see if you can turn them into friends. Spell out some of the ways they could help you and point out things they could stop doing. If they get on board, you're not only helping yourself, you're helping them too. That's what I call a win-win.

TODAY'S PRACTICE: *List the five people you spend the most time with. Are they friends or accomplices? Spend more time around the people who help you be healthy.*

DAY 231

Fork in the Road Exercise

Create a future of pleasure and pain. Guided imagery is a very powerful tool to help motivate you toward health. One exercise that is especially powerful I call "the fork in the road." In this exercise, you let your mind travel to a fork in the road. The path on the left is the path of bad decisions, and the path on the right is the path of good decisions.

First you go down the left road, where you eat everything you want, forget to exercise, use caffeine to wake up in the morning, and rely on alcohol to put yourself to sleep. You keep putting on more pounds and need to buy bigger and bigger clothes. Then, see what your life is like six months from now, five years from now, 20 years from now. How do you feel? How are your knees? How is your memory? How do you feel about yourself? One of my patients, who had been putting on a pound a year for the last 20 years, saw his energy, memory, and blood pressure continuing to get worse, and he wanted to go down a different path.

After you get a clear image where the road of bad decisions will take you, go back to the fork and travel down the right road, where your choices are much better, with great food, healthy sleep, exercise, new learning, and supplements. What will life be like in six months, in five years, in 20 years? You feel strong, vibrant, energetic, thinner, happier, and smarter. You feel younger next year, rather than older and more tired.

Which future do you want for yourself? Which road will you travel?

TODAY'S PRACTICE: *Visualize the two paths in the "Fork in the Road" exercise.*

Let's Stop Blaming Mothers

Within a few weeks of treatment, Kris was a dramatically different child. When Kris was 12, he attacked another child at school with a knife. But his problems had begun long before that. He had been impulsive, aggressive, and hyperactive since he was a young child. The stimulant medication prescribed for him at age 6 gave him hallucinations and made his aggression worse. At 8, antidepressant meds did nothing to help his behavior problems, nor did the many years of family therapy that followed. In fact, the therapist blamed Kris's mother for his problems.

Fortunately, after the knifing incident, Kris was brought to me for an evaluation. His SPECT scans revealed decreased activity in his prefrontal cortex, a finding that is often seen with impulsivity. There also was low blood flow in his left temporal lobe, which is often associated with violence. This pattern is consistent with a subtype of ADD/ADHD called temporal lobe ADD. By knowing what was really going on in his brain, I was able to put him on a targeted treatment plan that helped him significantly within just a few weeks. His aggression stopped, he was more focused in school, and overall he seemed like a happier kid. These changes made it clear to everyone that his mom wasn't the problem.

If Kris had never been properly treated for temporal lobe ADD, chances are good that he would have had numerous psychiatric hospitalizations (to no avail), been incarcerated, or perhaps even ended up dead before his eighteenth birthday. Instead, six years later when I saw him at his high school, where I was giving a lecture, he ran up and hugged me and introduced me to a bunch of his friends. To make matters even better, his mother had been able to release the burden of shame she once carried about being the cause of his problems. Let's stop blaming parents and look for the underlying biological causes of trouble.

TODAY'S PRACTICE: *If you know a teenager who engages in bad behavior, be an advocate for them to get their brain evaluated to see if there is an underlying problem.*

DAY 233

If You Don't Admit You Have a Problem, You Cannot Do Anything to Solve It

Brain-damaged NFL players were left without help or hope. In thousands of cases, we've seen that you can improve brain function even if you have been really bad to your brain. As mentioned, my colleagues and I did the world's first and largest brain imaging study on active and retired NFL players. We started our study in 2008, when the NFL seemed to be in denial that they had a problem. Despite forming their concussion committee in 1994, they had never sponsored a brain imaging study on players. Instead, they studied rats. But if you don't admit you have a problem, you can't do anything to solve it, and brain-damaged players were left without help or hope. On SPECT we saw high levels of damage but also the possibility of recovery in 80 percent of our players using a brain-smart program.

When I was in medical school, we were taught that the brain doesn't heal. But now we know that was wrong. If you put the brain in a healing environment, often it can get better—much better—but it requires forethought and a great plan. And it's not just true for football players. We have seen improvement in brain function for addicts, people with ADD/ADHD, and even people with dementia.

Amen Clinics is not the only one showing the brain's incredible power to heal. Dale Bredesen, MD at UCLA's Alzheimer's Research Center, put 10 patients who had either mild cognitive impairment—the precursor to dementia—or Alzheimer's disease on a brain rehabilitation program. The treatment strategy he gave them was similar to the one we have used at Amen Clinics. After following Dr. Bredesen's treatment protocol, all but one of the patients improved—with six of them functioning well enough to return to work.[178] When you do the right things, your brain and mind can show amazing progress, but you have to admit when there is a problem.[179]

TODAY'S PRACTICE: *What problems have you been putting off or ignoring? It's time to get help.*

SOUL Food for Your Brain

How your food was treated matters to the health of your body. Eating a healthy diet not only nourishes your body and brain, but it also supports your soul—the center point of your spiritual circle which fuels your sense of meaning, purpose, and passion in life. Your spirituality is fundamental to your connection to God, the health of our planet, the generations that have preceded you, and the generations that will follow you. Therefore, it is important to contemplate the meaning and purpose behind the food you choose for yourself and your family. Do you eat simply to get nourished, or is it because you like food? Do you eat to enjoy the company of others? Or is there something even more meaningful to you about food—such as its ability to sustain you so that you can fulfill your sense of purpose in life?

You can begin eating with a greater spiritual sense by following SOUL:

Sustainable: Find ways to grow food indefinitely without harming Mother Earth.

Organic: Choose food that is cleanly raised without harmful toxins, such as pesticides.

Unadulterated: Eat whole foods that are free of additives, artificial food dyes, and sweeteners.

Locally grown: Find local sources for your food. Not only does this support your local community, but it also increases the chance that the food is fresher than commercially raised foods are.

From a spiritual standpoint, think of how the food you ingest is raised. Also think of how the animals are treated and harvested. Is it humane? Would you feel sick if you found out? These are essential questions. Animals, like humans, release different chemicals in their bodies depending on whether they feel relaxed or stressed, happy or depressed, approachable or angry. If they live and are killed in a confined, toxic environment, eventually we will consume the chemicals the animals released when they were stressed, angry, and depressed. Think of eating as a spiritual discipline by giving thanks for the food you have and by taking a much more thoughtful approach to the way it is raised and consumed.

TODAY'S PRACTICE: *Spend a few minutes analyzing the food in your refrigerator. How much of it qualifies as SOUL food?*

High-Quality Calories and Not Too Many

Think of calories like money. Calories count, but not necessarily the way you think. The calories you consume are like investing money. Dump your cash into junk bonds, and you may not see any returns. Make wise investments, however, and you'll earn dividends. Be smart and budget your calorie expenditures for maximum physical, cognitive, and mental health benefits. Skip the junk food and invest in high-quality calories that brighten moods, reduce anxiousness, and enhance mental clarity.

A large popcorn at the movies can cost you over 800 calories and will zap your energy and dull your thinking. On the other hand, a delicious homemade stir-fry with brain-boosting salmon, immunity-enhancing mushrooms, antioxidant-rich asparagus, and high-fiber quinoa can cost less than 500 calories.

Do you know how many calories you eat on a daily basis? Most of us don't. I was shocked when I started taking note of the calories in the foods I ate and discovered that I was consuming far more than I thought. I see this in our patients, too. One of our NFL players said that counting his calories made him realize that his unhealthy eating habits were actually a form of self-harm. The same way you keep track of your spending, keep tabs on your calorie intake. Overeating is similar to overspending. When you overeat, you bankrupt your brain and your body.

Cutting back on calories can be beneficial in many ways. That's what a famous study involving two groups of rhesus monkeys found. The group of primates that ate 30 percent fewer calories than the other group were three times less likely to develop heart disease, cancer, or diabetes. On the flip side, the monkeys that ate more calories experienced significant shrinkage in the important decision-making areas of their brains.[180]

Eat This: The highest-quality foods you can find that are also calorie smart.

Skip or Limit That: Low-quality foods that increase your risk of brain health/mental health issues.

TODAY'S PRACTICE: *Count your calories today to get a realistic view of your calorie intake. You may need to make this a regular part of your life going forward if you are like me and have weight issues in your family.*

Mimic Calorie Restriction without the Side Effects

It comes down to five simple strategies. There is excellent research associating calorie restriction with health and longevity in many different animals. Calorie restriction boosts DNA repair, stabilizes blood sugar, slows aging, and decreases inflammation. But here's the secret: What isn't widely known is that you can mimic calorie restriction and get these benefits with five simple interventions. Most people can't eat 800 calories a day for long without feeling seriously crabby, and there are long-term side effects to calorie restriction. It lowers your testosterone, ruins your sex drive, and makes you irritable, which makes living longer less appealing than it could be.

Here are the five simple strategies to mimic calorie restriction: (1) exercise, (2) sleep seven hours at night, (3) manage stress with meditation, (4) eat a brain-healthy, anti-inflammatory diet of healthy oils, nuts, seeds, colorful fruits, and vegetables, and (5) take targeted supplements.

For most people, I recommend five supplements, including a high-quality multivitamin/mineral complex, omega-3 fatty acids, vitamin D, magnesium, and a probiotic. The omega-3s for your brain and heart are best obtained not through plant sources like flax seeds, but rather through fish or fish oil supplements, because plants lack the omega-3s EPA and DHA, which are essential to brain health. There are also vegan algae-based sources of EPA and DHA.

TODAY'S PRACTICE: *How many of the five strategies are you already incorporating in your life? If you are missing one or more, add another one today. Support your health instead of hurting it.*

Calorie Magic

Do the math. David, 70, was a high-level business executive who came to see me about being forgetful in meetings and feeling more depressed and hopeless than he could ever recall. He often felt tired, had trouble sleeping, and had a constant brain fog following him around. In addition, he was overweight, and his blood sugar was high. His brain scan looked awful, with marked decreases across the whole surface of his brain. When I asked him how much he drank, he said, "I have three shots of vodka at night to take the edge off." It was a ritual he had done for many years.

"Every night?" I asked.

He replied, "Yes."

During our first session I calculated the energy cost of what he drank at night:

- Typical shot of vodka 100 calories, three shots a night approximately 300 calories a night.
- 300 calories x 365 days = 109,500 calories a year of vodka.
- To gain a pound, most scientists say we need to consume an extra 3,500 calories over what we burn.
- Divide 109,500 calories by 3,500 = David was putting an extra 31.3 pounds of fat a year on his body just from the vodka.

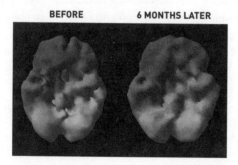

When David saw the calculations and his brain, he was shocked into reality. If he didn't start taking care of his brain, pretty soon he would not have a brain to take care of. Given that he also has Alzheimer's in his family, he became serious. He stopped drinking and took supportive supplements, including saffron for his mood and memory. Over the next six months, he lost 40 pounds and felt sharper than he had in decades. His brain looked better too.

TODAY'S PRACTICE: *Calculate the calories of a food or drink you consume regularly to see if it may be contributing to unhealthy weight gain.*

Drink Plenty of Water and Not Many Calories

Water your brain. Did you know your brain is 80 percent water, while the rest of your body is 70 percent water? Anything that even slightly dehydrates you, such as caffeine or alcohol, can mess with your mood and more, making you feel more depressed, anxious, tense, angry, or hostile, in addition to draining your energy, increasing pain, and lowering your ability to focus. Make sure you get plenty of water every day, such as 8 to 10 glasses a day.

You can also increase your healthy fluid intake with sparkling water, water flavored with slices of fruits (spa water), coconut water, herbal teas, and water-rich veggies and fruits such as cucumbers, lettuce, celery, radishes, zucchini, tomatoes, bell peppers, strawberries, melon, raspberries, and blueberries.

While on a business trip, I once saw a billboard that read, "Are You Pouring on the Pounds? . . . Don't Drink Yourself Fat." What an important message. Americans are drinking too many calories. One study found that an average of 22 percent of our daily calories come from beverages.[181] Other research shows that compared to 30 years ago, we're consuming twice as many calories per day from beverages.[182] It's easy to see why when you look at the popularity of those giant coffee drinks laden with syrup, whipped cream, and sugar; those fancy cocktails; and the 12-packs of sodas that line our store shelves. Keeping track of the calories you drink and replacing most beverages with water can be a powerful strategy in reaching and maintaining a healthy weight.

Drink This: Water, plain sparkling water, water flavored with cuts of fruits (spa water), water with flavored stevia from SweetLeaf, coconut water, green tea, black tea, and herbal tea.

Skip or Limit That: Calorie-laden drinks, cocktails, energy drinks, sodas, diet drinks—all of which increase your risk of brain health/mental health issues.

TODAY'S PRACTICE: *Drink 8 to 10 glasses of water today and don't consume any liquid calories.*

High-Quality Protein Keeps Cravings Away

Muscle is your protein reserve. Protein helps to balance blood sugar, keeps you full, and provides the building blocks for many neurotransmitters (your brain chemicals). Protein plays a major role in the healthy growth and functioning of your cells, tissues, and organs. After water, protein is the most abundant substance in your body. I think of protein as medicine that should be taken in small doses with every meal and snack, at least every four to five hours, to help balance your blood sugar levels and decrease cravings. Protein helps you feel fuller longer and burn more calories than you do after eating high-carb, sugar-filled foods. Your body can produce some of the amino acids it needs, but not all of them. Those that can't be manufactured in your body must come from food. These are called essential amino acids. They must be included in your diet on a regular basis because your body can't store them for future use. Plant foods, such as nuts, seeds, legumes, some grains, and vegetables, contain only *some* of the 20 amino acids you need. Fish, poultry, and most meats contain *all* of them.

Small amounts of high-quality protein are crucial to good health. But more is not better. Our bodies are simply not designed to effectively process large quantities of protein at a time. Eating too much causes increased stress and inflammation in the body. This contributes to accelerated aging and disease, and it can be hard on the kidneys and liver. Quality is more important than quantity. High-quality animal protein is free of hormones and antibiotics, free range, and grass fed. It is more expensive than industrial farm-raised animal protein but a good investment in your health. Compared with grass-fed meat, industrially raised meat is about 30 percent higher in unhealthy fat, which is associated with cardiovascular disease.[183]

Eat This: Healthy proteins include fish, lamb, turkey, chicken, beef, pork, beans and other legumes, raw nuts, and high-protein veggies such as broccoli and spinach.

Skip or Limit That: Low-quality proteins raised with pesticides, hormones, or antibiotics. Excessive protein, which strains your body systems.

***

TODAY'S PRACTICE: *Add high-quality proteins to at least two meals or snacks today.*

Be a Fat Head

A simple carbohydrate diet increases the risk of Alzheimer's disease by 400 percent.[184]
Although 80 percent of the brain is composed of water, 60 percent of the solid
weight of your brain is fat. For decades, the medical community demonized dietary
fat and touted low-fat diets as a primary strategy for good health. But they were
wrong. When it comes to brain health and emotional well-being, fat is not the
enemy. In fact, dietary fats are essential for optimal brain function and for positive
mood. For example, compelling research in the *Journal of Psychiatry & Clinical
Neurosciences* shows that low levels of cholesterol—possibly caused by shunning
fats in the diet—are associated with an increased risk of major depression and
suicidal thoughts and behaviors. In fact, people with the lowest levels of cholesterol
in this study had a 112 percent increased risk of suicide.[185] On a more positive
note, certain fats, such as omega-3 fatty acids, can help fight depression and reduce
symptoms associated with the mood disorder. These fats promote positive mood
and emotional balance.

A word of caution, though—not all dietary fats are created equal. I always
tell my patients to avoid trans fats—the fats that are sometimes used in foods like
store-bought baked goods, microwave popcorn, and frozen pizza—because they
have been linked to depressive symptoms. For any of my patients who struggle with
mood, I also recommend eliminating fats that are higher in omega-6 fatty acids
(e.g., refined vegetable oils)—as they have also been associated with inflammation
and depression.

Eat This: Focus on healthy fats, such as avocados, nuts (walnuts are associated with
less depression), seeds, sustainable clean fish and oils (avocado, coconut, flax, maca-
damia nut, olive, sesame, and walnut).

Skip or Limit That: Refined vegetable oils (canola, corn, safflower, soy), industrial
farm-raised animal fat and dairy, processed meats, and trans fats (any hydroge-
nated fats).

TODAY'S PRACTICE: *Keep a list of all the fats you eat today and label each one as
healthy or unhealthy to see what you need more or less of.*

Mood-Boosting Carbs That Last

Go for low-glycemic, high-fiber carbs from colorful vegetables and fruits. I think of "smart" carbohydrates as those that are loaded with nutrients, help to balance your blood sugar, and decrease cravings. Most vegetables, legumes, and fruits such as apples, pears, and berries that are low glycemic (unlikely to raise blood sugar) are smart carbs. High-glycemic, low-fiber carbohydrates (sugar, breads, pastas, potatoes, and rice) in significant amounts steal your health because they promote inflammation, diabetes, and depression.[186]

Fiber is a special type of carbohydrate, which enhances digestion, reduces the risk of colon cancer, and helps to balance blood pressure and blood sugar. The average American consumes far too little—less than 15 grams of fiber daily. Women should consume 25–30 grams of fiber every day; men, 30–38 grams. High-fiber foods such as broccoli, berries, onions, flax seeds, nuts, green beans, cauliflower, celery, and sweet potatoes (the skin of one sweet potato has more fiber than a bowl of oatmeal!) have the added benefit of making you feel full faster and longer.

Colorful vegetables and fruits have tremendous health benefits. They provide an enormous array of the plant nutrients, vitamins, minerals, and antioxidants that are necessary for good health. This boosts the level of antioxidants in your body, which reduces the risk of developing cognitive impairment and depression.[187]

A recent study found a linear correlation between the number of fruits and vegetables you eat and your level of happiness. The more colorful fruits and vegetables you eat—up to eight servings a day—the happier you become, and it happens almost immediately.[188] No antidepressant works this fast! Just stick with a two-to-one ratio of vegetables to fruits to limit sugar.

Eat This: Smart Carbs: Colorful low-glycemic, high-fiber vegetables, fruits, and legumes.

Skip or Limit That: High-glycemic, low-fiber foods, such as breads, pasta, potatoes, rice, and sugar that increase your risk of brain health issues.

TODAY'S PRACTICE: *Focus on low-glycemic, high-fiber carbs today. Track your carbs. How many of them are low-glycemic or high-glycemic? How much fiber did you get?*

Cook with Brain-Healthy Herbs and Spices

Herbs and spices are sometimes as powerful as medicine. Often thought of as the father of modern medicine, Hippocrates documented more than 500 medicinal purposes for spices and herbs, ranging from preventative treatments to improving longevity. One of the great benefits of herbs and spices is that most don't adversely affect us, whereas many pharmaceuticals have some terrible side effects. Unlike the Western world, 80 percent of developing countries still use herbal remedies and natural substances for medicine. Interestingly, most pharmaceuticals we use initially come from plants, even though by the time we see them they have been chemically processed.

Spices and herbs not only give us flavor that delights our taste buds, but they also provide us with nutrition that supports our health. In fact, you could almost store them in your medicine cabinet instead of on your spice rack. I find it interesting that so many of the seasonings we use for cooking come from the same plants our ancestors used to improve energy, relieve pain, and enhance healing. Fortunately, we don't have to risk our lives obtaining herbs and spices the way they did. Here is a short list of some of my favorite herbs and spices that help each of the BRIGHT MINDS risk factors:

- In multiple studies, a saffron extract was found to be as effective as antidepressant medication in treating people with depression.[189] It also enhances memory and sexual function.[190]
- Turmeric, found in curry, contains a chemical that has been shown to decrease the plaques thought to be responsible for Alzheimer's disease.[191]
- Scientific evidence shows rosemary, thyme, and sage help boost memory.[192]
- Cinnamon has been shown to help improve attention and blood sugar regulation. It is high in antioxidants and is a natural aphrodisiac.
- Garlic and oregano boost blood flow to the brain.
- The hot, spicy taste of ginger, cayenne, and black pepper comes from gingerols, capsaicin, and piperine, compounds that boost metabolism and have an aphrodisiac effect.

Eat This: Lots of herbs and spices tailored to your risk factors and needs.

Skip or Limit That: Artificial colors and flavors geared to hijack your brain.

TODAY'S PRACTICE: *Choose one new spice to cook with today.*

Make Sure Your Food Is as Clean as Possible

Eliminate artificial sweeteners, colors, and preservatives, and read food labels. Go organic, hormone-free, antibiotic-free, grass-fed, and free-range whenever possible. Pesticides used in commercial farming can accumulate in your brain and body, even though the levels in each food may be low. You are not only what you eat, but also what the animals you eat, ate. As much as possible, eliminate food additives, preservatives, and artificial dyes and sweeteners. To do so, you must start reading food labels. If you do not know what is in a food item or product, don't eat it. Would you ever spend money on something if you did not know the cost? Of course not. Now is the time to become thoughtful and serious about the food you put in your body. I understand that most people cannot afford to eat everything organic and sustainably raised. The Environmental Working Group produces a list every year of the foods that are a must to eat organic, and those which are not as important. You can stay updated at ewg.org. Here is a recent list:

- Foods with the lowest levels of pesticide residues: avocado, sweet corn, pineapple, cabbage, onion, sweet peas (frozen), papaya, asparagus, mango, honeydew melon, kiwi, cantaloupe, mushrooms, watermelon, sweet potato.[193]
- Twelve foods with the highest levels of pesticide residues (buy organic or don't eat them): strawberries, spinach, kale/collard/mustard greens, nectarines, apples, grapes, peaches, cherries, pears, tomatoes, celery, sweet bell and hot peppers.[194]
- Fish is a great source of healthy protein and fat, but it's important to consider the toxicity in some fish. Here are a couple of general rules to guide you in choosing more healthful fish: (1) The larger the fish, the more mercury it may contain, so go for the smaller varieties. (2) From the safe fish choices, eat a fairly wide variety of fish, preferably those highest in omega-3s, such as wild Alaskan salmon, sardines, anchovies, hake, and haddock. You can also learn more at seafoodwatch.org.

Eat This: Clean whole foods, sustainably raised, whenever possible.

Skip or Limit That: Food raised with pesticides, hormones, and antibiotics, or containing artificial sweeteners, dyes, and preservatives; fish high in mercury.

TODAY'S PRACTICE: *Eat as cleanly today as you possibly can.*

Consider Intermittent Fasting

Go 12–16 hours between your last meal of the day and the first one the next day. Intermittent fasting or time-restricted feeding has been shown to significantly improve memory,[195] mood,[196] fat loss,[197] weight, blood pressure, and inflammatory markers.[198] Memory loss is associated with the brain producing too much of certain toxic proteins that damage cells. One way your brain gets rid of these proteins is through a process called *autophagy* (from the Greek word for "self-devouring"). Think of autophagy as tiny trash collectors cleaning up the toxins and pieces of dead and diseased cells that gunk up your brain. This cleaning process lowers inflammation and helps to slow down the aging process.[199] Nightly 12-to-16-hour fasts turn on autophagy. This can help you think more clearly and feel more energetic, and it's simple—if you eat dinner at 6 p.m., don't eat again until 6–10 a.m. the next day. This will give your brain the time it needs to cleanse itself.

Not eating within two to three hours of bedtime also reduces your risk of heart attack and stroke.[200] In healthy people, blood pressure drops by at least 10 percent when they go to sleep, but blood pressure in late-night eaters stays high, increasing the risk of vascular problems. Also, recent research suggests that if you have more calories at lunch, and then eat a light dinner, you are more likely to lose weight than the other way around.[201]

TODAY'S PRACTICE: *Do an intermittent fast tonight and into tomorrow morning.*

Are You Hypoglycemic?

With a little food, he was once again the sweetest person. One of the young superstars I treated would have anger outbursts that made national news. When I checked his fasting blood sugar, it was dramatically low. Getting him to eat small meals regularly helped him stay in control of himself to be the wonderful, sweet person he always wanted to be.

Symptoms of low blood sugar—hypoglycemia—include:

- Sleepiness or feeling drugged
- Feeling mentally confused
- Difficulty concentrating
- Problems with memory
- Dizziness or light-headedness
- Feeling jittery or edgy
- Depression
- Being irritable or angry
- Feeling anxious or panicky
- A rapid heartbeat
- Trembling hands
- Having a nervous stomach
- Feeling sweaty or flushed
- Headache in the forehead area
- Difficulty sleeping
- Gastrointestinal issues

If you are concerned about these symptoms, ask your doctor to order a glucose tolerance test to see if you might be hypoglycemic.

If you have hypoglycemia, be sure to eat some healthy fat and protein at breakfast to minimize cravings and absorb your vitamins better. To help keep your blood sugar stable, it is vital to eat healthy food and have three to five small meals throughout the day. Don't ever let your blood sugar get too low, because aside from symptoms like the ones listed above, cravings for sugar can override your ability to make good decisions about what to eat.

TODAY'S PRACTICE: *How many of the above symptoms do you have?*

Is Gluten Good for Your Brain or Bad for It?

Gluten—a sticky subject. Over a decade ago, when I first started writing about gluten and how it affects physical, mental, and brain health, most people had never heard the word. That's changed dramatically, as the term *gluten-free* can now be found on thousands of food products, on restaurant menus, and in school cafeterias. Why has gluten earned a reputation as a substance to avoid?

A sticky protein found in some grains, including wheat and barley, gluten causes a variety of health problems. Autoimmune disorders, such as celiac disease; type 1 diabetes; and Hashimoto's thyroid disease have all been associated with gluten. Mental health issues such as anxiety and mood disorders, behavioral issues, brain fog, and memory problems have also been linked to the protein.

In terms of physical health, celiac disease (formerly known as celiac sprue) affects an estimated 1 percent of the US population. However, research suggests that number may be higher, as 83 percent of all people with celiac disease remain undiagnosed.[202] Celiac disease is a hereditary condition in which gluten consumption triggers an immune response that damages the small intestines where nutrients are absorbed. This results in decreased absorption of important vitamins and minerals, leading to deficiencies.

Far more common than celiac disease is *gluten sensitivity*, which affects up to 6 percent of Americans.[203] Gluten intolerance has been associated with dozens of symptoms, including digestive issues like constipation or diarrhea, as well as fatigue, joint pain, anxiety, depression, and brain fog. In addition, gluten is proinflammatory, high glycemic, and has negative impacts on the brain. In particular, it can decrease cerebral blood flow and has been associated with atrophy of the cerebellum and hippocampus.

Giving up gluten can have powerful effects. Gluten-free diets have been associated with improvements in ADD/ADHD, autism, and schizophrenia symptoms in some patients.[204] If you want to go gluten-free, be aware that gluten is pumped into thousands of everyday foods, such as baked goods, canned soups, salad dressings, spaghetti sauce, and more. Be sure to read the labels.

TODAY'S PRACTICE: *Go gluten-free today and see how you feel.*

Are You Addicted to Gluten and Dairy?

If you think about pizza constantly, you may be addicted. Have you ever tried to cut out foods like pizza or other gluten- and dairy-based meals, only to find you got a headache or felt nauseous, more depressed, or anxious? If so, you're not alone. Some people actually get a subtle opioid response in their brain from consuming dairy and gluten products. Who ever thought you could get a mild high from enjoying some pizza? There is a biological reason for this. During the digestion process, the casomorphins from dairy and gluteomorphins from gluten are released and bind to opioid receptors in your brain. This in turn can lead to feeling happier and more relaxed. Consequently, the consumption of these food can be addictive for some people, but like opiate drugs, giving them up can cause withdrawal symptoms.

There is real science behind the euphoric effects of dairy and gluten. This is well illustrated in a study done with binge eaters in a treatment center who were given the medication naltrexone, which decreases opioid-induced highs. The study found that by taking it, the binge eaters were able to reduce their consumption of wheat.[205]

The highly processed nature of many dairy and gluten products also enhances their addictive qualities. Manufacturers add sweeteners, unhealthy fats, and preservatives to make them even more tempting.

I know what it is like to have a weakness for pizza, because my mom used to make the most incredible pizza during the holidays. For years, I promised myself I would limit myself to one or two slices. But each time, my brain got hijacked by gluteomorphins and casomorphins, and I could barely stop myself from eating a whole pizza. Eventually, I learned the importance of having a healthy meal before going to my mother's house during the holidays, so now I am able to enjoy just a few bites of pizza without losing control.

TODAY'S PRACTICE: *How often do you consume gluten or dairy? What foods do you have a hard time resisting? How many of them contain gluten or dairy?*

Be Cautious with Corn

Why do farmers feed animals corn? To make them fat quickly! Corn is also inexpensive, which is why corn derivatives end up in nearly every packaged food. I once visited Mt. Vernon near Washington, DC, and as I wandered around the grounds I learned why hogs were a mainstay in George Washington's time. Pork, bacon, and lard were central to the diet of the Mt. Vernon community. Unlike modern-day swine, hogs back then usually roamed freely in the woods until the late fall, when they were rounded up and penned. They were then fed potatoes and corn to fatten them up before being slaughtered. Farm animals are still fed potatoes and corn. Do you know why? To quickly make them fat, which is what they can do to you, too!

In addition to being the most commonly genetically modified crop, the fatty acid profile of corn is more unhealthy than other grains. It is very low in omega-3 fatty acids but high in omega-6s, thus making it an inflammatory food. In addition, a type of mold known as Aspergillus and 22 different types of fungi breed on this crop. As with many other grains, corn can damage the intestinal lining, thereby promoting intestinal permeability. And because *lipid transfer protein* on the surface of corn cells cannot be digested by humans, it disrupts your blood sugar balance. This protein does not break down during the cooking process, either, and consequently is linked to allergic reactions to corn, with symptoms like gastrointestinal distress, asthma, skin rashes, and swelling of mucous membranes.

Another big concern I have is that glyphosate-based Roundup is commonly sprayed on corn. This notorious herbicide has been proven to be one of the most toxic substances to our cells.[206] In fact, it is even banned in some European countries. It is associated with a wide range of serious health problems, including cancer, multiple sclerosis, Parkinson's disease, hypothyroidism, liver disease, ADD/ADHD, and depression.[207] To minimize your consumption of corn, I recommend you avoid eating processed foods as well as any recipes or products that include corn kernels.

TODAY'S PRACTICE: *Go corn-free today and see how you feel.*

Milk Is for Baby Cows

News flash: For humans, drinking milk beyond infancy is not necessary. And consuming dairy products from other species such as cows is not only unnatural, it causes digestive problems for many people. After age 2, fewer than 35 percent of people produce lactase, the enzyme needed to digest lactose (milk sugar).[208] Without lactase, lactose remains undigested, fermenting in your intestines and leading to a number of gastrointestinal symptoms known as lactose intolerance. Even if your body can break down lactose, it is converted to galactose and glucose, which elevate blood sugar and can cause inflammation. Casein (a protein in milk) is an excitotoxin that can lead to brain inflammation and neurodegenerative diseases.

Research shows that casein also interferes with the powerful antioxidant properties found in coffee, tea, and other foods.[209] So that splash of cream in your morning beverage could be robbing you of the neuroprotective effects of those antioxidants.

The dairy industry has practically brainwashed our society into believing we must drink milk for calcium to protect our bones. In reality, calcium is plentiful in leafy greens, canned salmon, beans and lentils, seeds, and more. Research has found that rates of osteoporosis are higher in countries where milk consumption is greater.

Another reason to ditch cow's milk? Some milk may contain bovine growth hormones rBST and rBGH. These hormones cause the human liver to increase production of insulin growth factor 1 (IGF-1). Elevated levels of this substance have been associated with an increased risk of prostate cancer.

TODAY'S PRACTICE: *Go dairy free today and see how you feel.*

Make One Decision, Not Thirty

Protect yourself from future bad decisions now. Think ahead and always try to make one simple decision now that will prevent you from having to make thirty decisions later on. Decision fatigue will cause you to make many mistakes. For example, if you make the one decision at the store not to buy ice cream, you will not have to make the decision whether to eat it every time you walk by the refrigerator. Or, when you are at a restaurant, tell the waiter to immediately take the bread away from the table so that you don't have to make the same decision not to eat it every time you sneak a look at it, which wears down your self-control.

Here is a little-known secret why restaurants put bread on the table before a meal: You will eat more food if you start with bread. Since bread is a simple carbohydrate, it raises a chemical in the brain called serotonin, which relaxes your frontal lobes and tells your adult brain to take a break. Relaxed frontal lobes weaken your adult brain, and you are much more likely to order dessert, even when you promised yourself you wouldn't. A glass of alcohol before dinner does the same thing. Hold the beer or wine—at least until you have some food in your body.

TODAY'S PRACTICE: *In what situations can you think forward to make one good decision rather than several hard decisions to say no?*

Explaining a Brain-Healthy Diet to Teens

Just like a great car needs high-octane fuel, your brain and your body need great nutrition to function. Amen Clinics currently has a high school/early college course on creating brain-healthy lives called Brain Thrive by 25. Independent research in 16 schools showed that it decreased drug abuse, smoking, and depression, and increased self-esteem. In the course, we teach teenagers how to take care of their brains.[210] One of the lessons is about how to use food to enhance thinking skills. I start the lesson by asking kids to think about their favorite car. If you could have any car in the whole world, what would it be? A Porsche? A Ford Raptor truck? A red Ferrari? Then I ask the kids to imagine their favorite car in their garage. Imagine how happy it makes you feel. Do this with me. Now imagine that someone comes into your garage and pours a box of salt into the gas tank and ruins the engine. How would you feel? At this point I usually hear things like, "I would seriously hurt the person" or "I would kill him."

"Why?" I ask.

"Because the jerk is hurting something that is mine!"

Yet isn't that exactly what you do to yourself whenever you eat something that is bad for you, with lots of sugar, bad fat, or too much salt? Your body and brain are much more precious than any car could ever be! But by choosing bad foods, you treat yourself with such disrespect that soon your body and brain will break down. With a healthy brain, you are more likely to be able to buy the Ferrari or Raptor truck or anything else you want. Without a healthy brain, you are much more likely to be both sick and poor.

TODAY'S PRACTICE: *If you have a teen at home or know one, do this exercise with them. Find out which top-of-the-line vehicle they want, then ask if they would want to drive it without brakes or steering fluid and why.*

The Marshmallow Test

Delayed gratification, even at two years old, can supercharge success. It's important to talk about an idea critical to getting emotionally healthy called delayed gratification. Too often people live in the moment and forget about the consequences of their behavior over time. We act like impulsive children and not like thoughtful adults. There is a great series of experiments by Dr. Walter Mischel from Stanford that many of you might have seen called the Marshmallow Test.[211] This is where 4-year-old children were given the option of having one marshmallow immediately or two marshmallows if they waited for a few minutes. About 30 percent of the children could wait for 15 minutes and were rewarded with two marshmallows. But their rewards went much deeper. The children who were able to wait for something better down the road had more self-control and were more likely to achieve their goals later in life, including having better health and better relationships. Researchers found that children who had trouble delaying gratification had significantly higher BMIs as adults and were more likely to have had problems with drugs or alcohol.

The key to delaying gratification is bringing your attention not to what you want at the moment—such as the marshmallow or the cheeseburger and fries—but rather to what you really want. It's better to focus on longer-term goals, such as getting into that size 6 dress, or in my case the size 31 jeans, or, more importantly, long-term health and cognitive function.

TODAY'S PRACTICE: *Wait just 10 minutes longer to give in to an urge to do something unhealthy, and in those 10 minutes focus on a long-term health goal you want.*

Chloe's Game

Plant brain health early. Getting children involved in brain health early will serve them for the rest of their lives and help your grandchildren be healthier. I found the simplest way to start was by playing a game with my daughter Chloe that I have played since she was two. I call it Chloe's Game. You can call it by the name of the child or children you are working with. Whenever you do something, ask yourself, "Is this good for my brain or bad for it?" As mentioned before, this is the mother of all tiny habits, so let it do its work for your children.

Here's how I play the game with Chloe:

If I say red peppers, Chloe will reply, "Good for my brain" and give me a smile and a thumbs-up.

If I say fish, she'll ask me, "What kind of fish?" Some fish, like tuna, are high in mercury, which can be toxic at high levels. If I say salmon, she'll ask, "Wild salmon or farmed salmon?" because farmed salmon may have artificial coloring. If I say wild salmon, she'll give me two thumbs-up.

If I say riding a bike without a helmet, she'll roll her eyes at me, shake her head, and say, "Bad, bad, bad."

Sitting on the couch and bingeing on Netflix for hours and hours? She'll give me a thumbs-down.

Comparing yourself to others on Instagram? She'll reply, "So bad! That's a sure-fire way to feel depressed."

You can play this game anytime—while you're driving your kids to school, while making dinner, or when you're getting ready in the morning.

TODAY'S PRACTICE: *Start playing Chloe's Game with someone in your household or at work.*

Can Odd Behaviors Be Related to Your Diet?

Were the gorillas really crazy, or were they being poisoned? Unlike zoo gorillas, wild gorillas are not known to die from diabetes or heart disease, but sadly the latter is the primary cause of death for captive gorillas. Despite this, a hopeful story about two gorillas named Bebac and Mokolo emerged from the Cleveland Metroparks Zoo.[212] Their eating behavior was very abnormal and included vomiting their food and then eating the vomit and pulling out their hair and eating that too. Their health was very poor even though they were not even middle-aged. Their unusual behaviors had never been observed in wild gorillas. Fortunately, the zoologists who studied the animals' health figured out that Bebac's and Mokolo's diet was causing their deterioration. Like other zoo gorillas, they were fed grains, sugar, and starch in the form of so-called "nutritional cookies." Like the Standard American Diet does to humans, the food they were eating was slowly killing them.

Their diet was significantly modified to a more natural one with bamboo, vegetables, leafy greens, fruits, seeds, and nuts. And to encourage Bebac and Mokolo to move around more, the zookeepers scattered the food around their habitat so they would have to hunt for it. This encouraged the gorillas to spend much of their day looking for their food so they could eat. Both of them lost about 65 pounds within the first year. Bebac's heart function improved, and the progression of Mokolo's heart disease slowed. They also stopped pulling out their hair and eating their vomit. In 2017, at age 32, Bebac died from heart disease, but he lived two years longer than the average life expectancy of 30 for captive gorillas.[213]

TODAY'S PRACTICE: *Look at your diet and identify anything in it that is still bad for your brain.*

Eight Mood Foods to Treat Depression

Foods can either fire up overactivity in your brain's limbic system (emotional center), linked to depression, or they can calm activity to promote more positive moods. Many people with mental health disorders, such as depression, consume diets lacking in key nutrients for brain health. A growing body of evidence suggests that nutritional treatment—aka eating specific foods—may help prevent, treat, or improve depression, as well as other conditions, such as anxiety, bipolar disorder, or ADD/ADHD. In 2015, a group of scientists concluded that "the emerging and compelling evidence for nutrition as a crucial factor in the high prevalence and incidence of mental disorders suggests that diet is as important to psychiatry as it is to cardiology, endocrinology, and gastroenterology."[214] Here are eight foods you should include in your diet if you want to boost your mood and reduce symptoms of depression.

1. Berries: Blueberries, blackberries, raspberries, etc. are "smart" carbohydrates full of mood benefits, providing antioxidants, vitamins, and minerals.
2. Water: Staying adequately hydrated can help optimize mood, motivation, and energy level. Drinking H_2O is associated with a decrease in depression and anxiety.[215]
3. Lean Protein: Chicken, turkey, beef, fish, and lamb provide essential amino acids, which are necessary to create neurotransmitters (brain chemicals), including serotonin and dopamine, which play an important role in mood.
4. Salmon: Salmon is loaded with omega-3 fatty acids, and a wealth of research has shown that these fats can reduce symptoms of depression.[216]
5. Kimchi: Supports healthy gut bacteria, which is tightly linked to mood.
6. Saffron: In multiple studies, a saffron extract was found to be as effective as antidepressant medication in treating people with major depression.[217]
7. Avocados: Contain healthy fats that fuel brainpower and are high in oleic acid. A 2009 study that followed 4,856 adults for a decade found that women who consumed the most oleic acid were less than half as likely to suffer from severe depression.[218]
8. Dark Leafy Greens: Whether you prefer kale, spinach, or broccoli, these nutrient-dense vegetables fight inflammation, which has been linked to depression.[219]

TODAY'S PRACTICE: *Eat one or two of these foods today to boost your mood. Maybe you'd like to try guacamole and raw broccoli.*

Brain Warrior Angie and What Toxic Food Was Doing to Her

You've given me a new life. By the time Angie was 8, her mother had already sent her to Jenny Craig for being overweight. As a child, she used to hide in the kitchen closet bingeing on bags full of junk food, wondering what was wrong with her. Her shame was unbearable; she felt ridiculed and was socially isolated. Later, she tried every pill, diet, and quick-fix program—only to fail over and over. When she found our program, she was 5 feet tall, 225 pounds, and suffered from migraines, rosacea (which increases the risk for Alzheimer's disease), digestive issues, fertility problems, brain fog, and anxiety and depression.

Angie's breakthrough came when she said, "I realized it's not me, it's what the junk I'm eating is doing to me." She was a victim of the food companies who hire scientists to combine fat, sugar, salt, and chemicals to get the perfect meltiness, crunchiness, and aroma to trigger the bliss point in her brain and make her addicted to the junk she was eating. Once she learned to avoid low-quality food that is engineered to hijack her brain, she lost her cravings within days. When Angie learned how to read food labels, it was like learning a new language. "I felt hope for the first time!" she said.

BEFORE   AFTER

On our program, Angie lost 11 pounds in the first two weeks, and an incredible 103 pounds overall, and has kept it off for years. But weight loss was just the beginning. Her migraines are better, her skin is clearer, her digestion has improved, her focus and mood are better, and her confidence is soaring! She's even mentoring others. My favorite part of Angie's transformation was when she said, "I would thank you for giving me my life back, but this was never my life. You have given me a new life."

TODAY'S PRACTICE: *What foods do you crave? What are the ingredients? Which of those items hijack your pleasure centers?*

Consider Potential Food Allergies

Could it be what you are eating? Food allergies can be delayed, and reactions may not be seen for several days. Eating foods you are sensitive to can create metabolic disorders that lead to many "mental" symptoms, including fatigue, brain fog, slowed thinking, irritability, agitation, aggression, anxiety, depression, ADD/ADHD, learning disabilities, schizophrenia, and even dementia.[220]

To test the theory that food allergies may be involved in your issues, follow an elimination diet—remove dairy, gluten, corn, soy, sugar, and artificial dyes and sweeteners for one month to see how you feel. After a month, slowly reintroduce food items one at a time every four or five days. Eat the reintroduced food two to three times a day for three days to see if you notice a reaction. Look for symptoms, which can occur within a few minutes or up to 72 hours later. (If you notice a problem right away, stop consuming that food immediately.) Reactions to foods to which you have allergies can include brain fog, anxiety, depression, anger, congestion, headaches, sleep problems, pain, fatigue, skin changes, or changes in bowel function. If you have a reaction, note the food and eliminate it for 90 days. This will give your immune system a chance to cool off and your gut a chance to heal.

When our patients follow an elimination diet, it often makes a dramatic difference. Remember, you don't have to lose all of these foods forever, unless you are sensitive to them. A study from the Netherlands confirms how important this strategy can be on children with ADD/ADHD and oppositional defiant disorder (ODD).[221] The children ate only rice, turkey, lamb, vegetables, fruits, tea, pear juice, and water. No milk products, wheat, or sugar products. No food additives or artificial colors. In the study, about 70 percent of children who followed the diet showed an improvement of nearly 70 percent or more in ADD/ADHD symptoms, and a 45 percent reduction in ODD symptoms. They repeated this study and found similar results.

TODAY'S PRACTICE: *Eliminate gluten, corn, soy, dairy, sugar, and artificial dyes and sweeteners just for today.*

Tiny Habits for Nutrition and Nutraceuticals

Each of these habits takes just a few minutes. They are anchored to something you do (or think or feel) so that they are more likely to become automatic.

1. When I am tempted by french fries, sugary treats, or soda, I will resist and say to myself, "I only love foods that love me back."
2. After I pick up my purse or computer bag, I will put a full water bottle inside.
3. When I prepare my food shopping list, I will put fish and vegetables on it.
4. When I finish dinner, I will note the time and make plans to eat my next meal at least 12 hours later to give my brain time for the processes that help fight memory loss.
5. After I pick up a new item at the grocery store, I will read the food label.
6. When I'm in a low mood, I will eat a healthy carbohydrate like a sweet potato or black beans with some protein to boost my serotonin level.
7. When I eat a food I love that loves me back, I will note it in my "favorite healthy foods" list.
8. When a server comes for my order at a restaurant, I will say, "Please don't bring bread to the table" and make one good decision to avoid having to make many at one time.
9. When I go food shopping, I will look for organic fruits and vegetables first.
10. When I eat my first meal of the day, I will take a multivitamin/mineral and omega-3 fatty acid supplement, vitamin D (if needed), and any other supplements to support my brain type.
11. If I take medication, I will also take specific supplements to replenish any essential nutrients the prescription may be depleting from my body.
12. On Sunday mornings, I will refill my supplement organizer.

TODAY'S PRACTICE: *Pick one or more tiny habits about nutrition to place in your life today and every day going forward.*

Your Brain Is Always Listening to the Dragons from the Past

The stories we tell ourselves guide and direct our lives, driving happiness or depression, exhilaration or disappointment, rage or peace. My friend Dr. Sharon May, a renowned relationship psychologist, calls the stories that interfere with our lives Dragons from the Past that are still breathing fire on our amygdala (the almond-shaped structure on the inside of our temporal lobes involved in emotional reactions), driving anxiety, anger, irrational behavior, and automatic negative reactions. Unless you recognize and tame them, and consciously calm and protect your amygdala from overfiring, these dragons will haunt your unconscious mind and drive emotional pain for the rest of your life. What blows from an ember, or a small action of another, can turn into a destructive fire of anxiety and rage.

I started using this concept with my patients and over time identified 12 Dragons from the Past, including their origins, triggers that make them overpowering, and how they cause us to react. All of us have more than one Dragon from the Past driving our behavior, and they are always interacting with the Dragons from the Past of others, causing both internal and external battles—a modern-day *Game of Thrones*. Most people have an average of six Dragons from the Past.

1. **Abandoned, Invisible, or Insignificant Dragons:** feel alone, unseen, or unimportant
2. **Inferior or Flawed Dragons:** feel less than others
3. **Anxious Dragons:** feel fearful and overwhelmed
4. **Wounded Dragons:** bruised by past trauma
5. **Should and Shaming Dragons:** racked with guilt
6. **Responsible Dragons:** need to take care of others
7. **Angry Dragons:** harbor hurts and rage
8. **Judgmental Dragons:** hold harsh or critical opinions of others due to past injustices
9. **Grief and Loss Dragons:** feel loss and fear of loss
10. **Death Dragons:** fear the future and lack of a meaningful life
11. **Hopeless and Helpless Dragons:** have a pervasive sense of despair and discouragement
12. **Ancestral Dragons:** affected by issues from past generations

---

TODAY'S PRACTICE: *Go to KnowYourDragons.com to find out which dragons you have. How many are there?*

Brain Warrior Jimmy:
Taming the Dragons from the Past

His dragons were running wild. I met Jimmy, 39, the day he had been released from a psychiatric hospital because of suicidal thoughts. His Anxious Dragon, one of the Dragons from the Past, was running rampant in his brain. The latest "episode" began two weeks prior, when he found out he had to give a presentation at work. It filled him with dread. He told me, "If I had to describe the fear, it's like you're on death row and the clock's run out. The guard opens the door and you must take the first step—that kind of fear runs through my bones." Jimmy had struggled with the fear of public speaking since the age of 12 when his grandmother made him give an "impact statement" at Los Angeles County Superior Court about why his father, one of the leaders of a violent street gang, should not get the death penalty for a double homicide. He thought, *What if I cannot speak in court and end up killing my father?* Since then his ANTs (automatic negative thoughts) were out of control and the recent situation at work caused a new infestation: "I can't speak in public . . . so I'm going to lose my job . . . I'm a loser. . . . My wife will divorce me. . . . I'll end up on the streets. . . . I should kill myself."

Growing up, Jimmy experienced intense, persistent psychological trauma (Wounded Dragon). He saw his father dealing drugs and beating up other people. His father was incarcerated when Jimmy was a small child, and he went with his grandmother to visit his dad, where his dad made him go introduce himself to other gang leaders. He witnessed drive-by shootings and feared for his life on many occasions, including when a dozen SWAT officers crashed through his family's front door with weapons drawn while Jimmy was lying on the couch in his father's arms.

By diligently understanding and taming his hidden dragons and eliminating the ANTs, along with getting his diet, nutrients, and brain healthy, Jimmy thrived. Over the next six months, his mood stabilized, his anxiety lessened, and he was able to become an even more important part of his team at work, as well as a happier and more loving husband and father. In addition, he lost 37 pounds, felt stronger, and had more energy than he had in years.

TODAY'S PRACTICE: *Identify a dragon that often does battle in your mind. What one action will you take today to begin to tame it?*

Taming the Abandoned, Invisible, or Insignificant Dragons

Do you love underdog movies? That may be a clue that these are your dragons. Being a middle child and the second son in a Lebanese family meant I often felt insignificant. My father owned a chain of grocery stores, and in Middle Eastern families, the oldest son is expected to go into the family business. That meant my brother was "the chosen one," and I was not. Later I became very grateful to my brother as it gave me the freedom to do the work I love.

The origin of this dragon is a time you felt others did not see or recognize you, or you felt unimportant, abandoned, and lonely. This dragon is common in children whose parents were unable or unavailable to raise them. It is also common in middle children from large families (me) and those whose parents or siblings were dysfunctional, narcissistic (all about them), or sick. It is triggered when you perceive that others ignore or belittle you; when others are recognized and you are not; when you get laid off from work but your colleagues don't. This dragon fires up feelings of loneliness, worthlessness, or feeling small.

Tame this dragon by living a purposeful life, working to make a difference in the lives of others, and becoming part of a group (church, civic, environmental, etc.). Psychotherapy can also be very helpful, especially for abandonment issues. Be careful not to run away from therapy too soon. When you get close to the therapist and start to feel comfortable, it may make you nervous and want to run, which may also be a pattern in relationships. Daily affirmations to calm this dragon include: "I am loved." "I am unique." "I am significant." "I am seen by . . . (name the people who see you)." "I am making a difference in the lives of . . . (name them)."

TODAY'S PRACTICE: *List three ways your life influences others in a meaningful way.*

Taming the Inferior or Flawed Dragons

Do you like Marvel X-Men movies? That is a sign that these may be your dragons. Comparison is the enemy of joy. This dragon is born whenever you feel "less than" others in ability, looks, achievement, or relationships. Due to social media, these dragons are causing an epidemic rise of anxiety, depression, and suicide in young people. It is triggered whenever you are comparing yourself to others, competing against others, and even looking in the mirror. These dragons drive feelings of inferiority, depression, helplessness, and jealousy; being overly sensitive or a perfectionist; or having body dysmorphic disorder, where you only see your body's flaws.

Tame this dragon by recognizing when you are comparing yourself to others. Here are six ways to do it.

1. Be aware when you do it.
2. Know the triggers of when you compare yourself to others and avoid them (e.g., social media, magazine/TV ads).
3. Change your focus to something else.
4. Focus on your strengths and accomplishments.
5. Praise others because that makes it more likely you will praise yourself.
6. Avoid mindlessly scrolling through social media.

On one of *The Brain Warrior's Way* podcasts, my cohost and wife, Tana, relayed the story of doing Christmas shopping online, where she saw an image of another woman her age who looked perfect. She immediately started to feel inferior and thought of searching for plastic surgery sites. Thankfully, she recognized the dragon whispering to her brain and pulled herself away.

Realize that seeking perfection is a reason to fail and that when we constantly compare ourselves to others we are doomed to unhappiness. There will always be someone healthier, richer, prettier, bigger, or stronger than you. There will also always be someone poorer, uglier, smaller, and weaker than you. Where you bring your attention determines how you feel. Comparing yourself negatively to others, which society and social media promote, is a trap that damages many people. Don't be one of them. Daily affirmations to tame this dragon include, "I am unique." "I restrain comparing myself to others." "I will be my best, not someone else's best."

TODAY'S PRACTICE: *Notice the times you are comparing yourself to others today and work to stop it.*

Taming the Anxious Dragons

Do you prefer funny, uplifting movies? These may be indicators of your dragons. The Anxious Dragons are the most common of all dragons, as a third of the population will experience serious anxiety at some point in their lives.[222] They were born whenever we were first afraid or overwhelmed or when we thought the world was unpredictable or dangerous. A pandemic can certainly make these dragons roar to life, as can having an unpredictable upbringing or an alcoholic, angry, or erratic parent. The Anxious Dragons are triggered whenever we are reminded of situations from the past that originally caused our anxiety, such as someone getting angry, a disapproving look, a smell, or even a song. I love Cat Stevens. When I was a teenager in the late 1960s and early 1970s, his music made me happy. But I can't play it when Tana is nearby, because it reminds her of a dangerous time when she was young. She doesn't hear the words; she hears the memories of a difficult time in her life, which makes her feel bad. The Anxious Dragons drive panic attacks, fears, phobias, and predicting the worst. These dragons make some people avoid conflict and become sensitive to rejection. They can also lead to self-destructive behaviors to escape the anxious feelings, such as drug or alcohol abuse.

Here are four simple ways to tame the Anxious Dragons. Scientific evidence supports all of them.

1. Breathe in relaxing scents—the area of the brain that senses smell is overactive in anxiety, and calming it down with lavender, jasmine, or chamomile can quickly settle you down.[223]
2. Develop a playlist of relaxing music. The right music can lower anxiety. But you have to pick the right pieces of music. (See day 216.)
3. Natural supplements can help, such as magnesium,[224] theanine,[225] and GABA.[226]
4. Meditation and hypnosis are often incredibly helpful to reset your nervous system and can be done in only a few minutes each day.[227]

TODAY'S PRACTICE: *Get the essential oil lavender or one of the other scents mentioned above and diffuse it in the air nearby.*

Taming the Wounded Dragons

Do you like movies about healing? That may be a sign that these are your dragons. The Wounded Dragons are born whenever you experience emotional trauma. What triggers these dragons? Anything that reminds you of a past trauma, including the sights, smells, sounds, and dates, such as anniversaries. The brain works through association, and anything that in any way resembles the trauma can trigger it. When I was 5, we had a beautiful white goat named Sugar. She was a great pet but also loved eating my father's roses. One day my dad had had enough and sent Sugar away "to the farm," which devastated me. At dinner a few nights later, my dad laughed when he told us he was feeding us Sugar shish kebabs. Horrified, I ran to my room crying. Decades later, when I gave a lecture at a large arena in Monterey, Mexico, and saw goat meat for sale on the street, I had a panic attack when I flashed back to that dinner.

With Wounded Dragons, people relive the trauma, have nightmares, feel numb, or start to avoid situations that in any way remind them of the trauma. They startle easily, feel their future is shortened, and often expect bad things to happen. When trauma was severe or prolonged, as it was in the years-long pandemic, your limbic brain can get "stuck in overdrive," increasing the odds you will feel anxious, nervous, tense, sleepless, and have irritable bowel syndrome. For some people their emotional brain becomes overwhelmed and actually shuts down, leaving them feeling depressed, flat, tired, and confused. If your nervous system seems to be stuck in overdrive, calm it with meditation, prayer, hypnosis, calming scents like lavender, and supplements, such as GABA, magnesium, or theanine. If you feel shut down, activate it with physical exercise, upbeat music, scents such as peppermint or eucalyptus, or stimulating supplements such as rhodiola, green tea, or l-tyrosine.

TODAY'S PRACTICE: *Remember the last time you experienced a stressful event. Did it tend to activate or shut down your nervous system? Your answer could give you direction on how to help your stress.*

The Impact of Adverse Childhood Experiences (ACEs)

Our childhood experiences have a powerful influence on the rest of our lives. When the early years are marked by abuse, neglect, or trauma, it can have a lasting negative impact on health. The term "ACE" is an acronym for *adverse childhood experiences* that are very stressful and traumatic and can interfere with normal development. Researchers developed the ACE questionnaire with 10 questions, covering the most common causes of childhood trauma, including emotional abuse, physical or sexual abuse, neglect, household member substance abuse, mental illness, suicidal behavior, or incarceration. The questionnaire is scored on a scale of 1–10. They have found that 64 percent of the population has at least one ACE; 25 percent has three or more ACEs; having a score of four or more ACEs is associated with an increased risk of suicide by 1,200 percent; and six or more ACEs shortened lifespans by 20 years.[228] The higher the score, the higher the risk for long-term consequences, including diabetes, obesity, heart disease, substance abuse, and almost all psychiatric conditions.

The development of a child's brain is very sensitive to the environment. A loving, supportive, and predictable environment bodes well for the brain to organize and function in developmentally appropriate ways. For children who are repeatedly subjected to trauma, chaos, abuse, and/or neglect, healthy brain development is often obstructed. Enduring toxic levels of stress can lead to problems with self-regulation, learning, and social interactions, as well as controlling emotions, aggression, nightmares, and healthy attachments later in life. The negative effects of the adverse experiences can even alter a child's genes and be passed along to the next generation.

Not everyone with a high ACE score will develop health problems. Some children have natural strengths that can help them navigate the turmoil that surrounds them in a way that other children may not be able to. Also having a close relationship with a caring adult—or adults—can help buffer the adversity at home. A teacher who regularly provides extra help and support to the child or a loving aunt in whose home the child may occasionally find refuge can provide a sense of safety that helps the child build resilience against the consequences of their circumstances. If you have a high ACE score, get help. The strategies in this book will go a long way to extending your life in a healthy and happy way.

TODAY'S PRACTICE: *Take the ACE questionnaire here: acesaware.org.*

Healing Childhood Trauma:
Brain Warrior Rachel Hollis

It can be healed. Diamonds are a girl's best friend, as the saying goes. Not in the case of your brain. A diamond-shaped pattern of overactivity in the brain's emotional centers is often a sign of past emotional trauma. It was one of the findings I saw on the scans of mega-influencer Rachel Hollis, author of the bestselling books *Girl, Wash Your Face* and *Girl, Stop Apologizing*. She was on our Instagram Scan My Brain series when she revealed horrific experiences with her brother who had schizophrenia and depression. "When I was 14, my brother committed suicide," she said. "When I found his lifeless body in his room, I couldn't understand what I was looking at. My brain could not process what I was looking at."

Extreme emotional trauma like that can contribute to the diamond brain pattern. My colleagues and I published several studies about posttraumatic stress disorder that show increased activity in the anterior cingulate gyrus (the top of the diamond), which is often associated with thoughts that tend to loop in the brain; increased activity in the basal ganglia and amygdala (sides of the diamond), associated with issues with anxiety; and increased activity in the deep limbic areas (bottom of the diamond), associated with mood issues. In some people, the right lateral temporal lobe is also overactive. This area of the brain is involved in reading the intentions of other people. When activity here is excessive, people can misread cues from others.

Rachel's emotional brain was working too hard and the activity in her prefrontal cortex was low, making it harder for her to control her mind. "I have a really hard time controlling my emotions," she says. "It's affecting my ability to be productive and to do my work well and to be the kind of mom I want to be and the kind of human I want to be." With treatment, involving brain-healthy lifestyle choices, supplements, and specific psychological treatments for trauma, Rachel has done much better.

TODAY'S PRACTICE: *List two or three traumas from the past that you still think may be living in your brain and affecting you today.*

Taming the Should and Shaming Dragons

Do you like movies that poke fun at tradition? The origin of these dragons occurred when you felt humiliated, embarrassed, belittled, judged, or criticized. These dragons can cause you to feel foolish, distressed, exposed, overly sensitive, or submissive, and can make you want to hide, withdraw, or engage in self-harm in secret. Guilt and shame are not all bad. They can motivate learning, growth, and a desire to change and be better. They can help you lose weight and overcome an addiction. Guilt can motivate you to reconnect and reconcile with others. Shame can inform and protect you from acting on impulses to engage in unhealthy behavior.

Tame the Should and Shaming Dragons by knowing when "should" and "shame" are helpful and when they are not. Do these thoughts or emotions serve you by helping you change something harmful in your life, or do they hurt you, causing you to feel like you're bad, evil, or a failure? If they do not serve you, break up with them. During the later years of my father's life, I would think, *I should go see my dad.* But thinking *I should* just made me feel bad. Trying to motivate through guilt isn't helpful. I teach my patients to replace the word *should* with *It's my goal to* or *I want to.* So I started saying, "I want to see my dad," and it prompted me to visit him more often. Now that he's gone, I'm so grateful for that time we spent together. Daily affirmations to tame these dragons include, "I work to learn the lessons of my past." "Does it fit my overall goals to do this?" "That was then; this is now."

TODAY'S PRACTICE: *Whenever you think you "should" do something, replace it with the words, "I want to do it" or "it fits my goals to do it." If you don't want to or it doesn't fit your goals, seriously consider not doing it.*

How Shame Can Damage Your Brain

He called his medicine his stupid pills, stopped taking them, and it ruined his life.
Robert had been kicked out of 11 schools by the time he was in ninth grade. Robert
was hyperactive, aggressive, mean, and conflict-driven. At age 14, a neurologist
diagnosed him with ADD/ADHD and temporal lobe dysfunction, and he had an
incredibly positive response to Ritalin. He picked up three grade levels of learning
in a year, and his behavior settled down. He was happier and started to have healthy
friends for the first time. He stayed on Ritalin for two years, and although he was
doing better in almost every aspect of his life, he had one problem. Every time he
took the medicine, he felt "stupid" and called it his stupid pill, so he eventually
stopped taking it.

No one explained what the medication was doing for him—or what could
happen if he stopped taking it. And no one thought about the psychological aspects
of taking medication. A few months after he stopped Ritalin, his uncle came over
and said, "Let's go rob some women." Robert just went without thinking. They
followed a woman, grabbed her, and made her get in the car, go to the ATM, and
take money out. They robbed her. Then they both raped her. Two weeks later,
Robert was arrested and charged with kidnapping, robbery, and sexual assault. He
was convicted and sentenced to 25 years in prison. The judge seemed to understand
that Robert was working under a handicap, but, nevertheless, he was tried as an
adult because of the severity of the crime. I got involved at the request of Robert's
attorney and helped him get on the right medication, which really helped him in
prison. Even though he will spend decades in jail, the hope is that with a better
brain, he will be better in prison and when he gets out. The shame damaged his
brain and the brains of those he hurt.

TODAY'S PRACTICE: *Work to find self-compassion by being kind to yourself, practicing
forgiveness, and accepting your perceived flaws.*

Taming the Responsible Dragons

Do you like caretaker movies, like Patch Adams? *These may indicate your dragons.* Do you feel liable for the pain of others, often because you felt powerless to help someone you cared about, such as a parent or sibling? Did you feel insignificant, and fixing other people's issues helped you feel significant? Children believe they are at the center of the universe, so if something good happens, they think it's because of them; but if something bad happens to someone they love, they often think it is because of them and feel responsible, even though their thinking is irrational. The eldest child in a family often feels a natural sense of responsibility toward younger siblings, and neglectful parents sometimes task older children with taking care of the younger kids even though they are not emotionally equipped to handle the responsibility. These dragons are triggered when you perceive others in need and then react by being a fixer or caretaker. The Responsible Dragons can cause you to do too much for others, so they become dependent on you, which ultimately breeds entitlement and resentment and creates unbalanced relationships and long-term stress.

Tame these dragons by realizing that doing too much for others can create dependency and inhibit them from being independent and self-sufficient. It's a balancing act between being helpful and teaching others to be competent on their own. Self-care is not selfish. Prioritize taking care of yourself to the same degree that you care for others. This includes setting healthy boundaries. You're limited and need to accept your limitations; otherwise, you burn out, max out, and fizzle out. If you don't take care of yourself, it's easy to resent those you help, seeing them as needing and taking, taking, taking all the time.

Daily affirmations that can help include: "I have to take care of myself to effectively love others." "I love helping others, as long as I'm helping them become competent and independent." "It is better to give than to receive, as long as giving does not create unnecessary dependency."

TODAY'S PRACTICE: *Evaluate the things you do for others and ask if it's done to create healthy, independent people or because you feel obligated or responsible for them.*

Taming the Angry Dragons

Do you like horror movies? You may have these dragons. The Angry Dragons are often born out of hurt, shame, disappointment, being bullied or abused, or seeing others (e.g., parents) model anger. Sometimes they are born from a head injury or abnormal brain issues. These dragons can be triggered when anything reminds you of past hurts or when things don't go your way (for people who have high activity in the anterior cingulate gyrus). The Angry Dragons react with irrational rage, irritability, or being rude or inconsiderate. You may express your anger in actions, such as bullying, belittling, blaming, fighting, punishing, name-calling, or stonewalling. Common warning signs that these dragons are going to explode include heart rate increases, sweating, cold hands, muscle tension (especially in the neck), goosebumps, dizziness, or confusion.

Here are five strategies to tame the Angry Dragons:

1. Make a list of 10 things to do when you are angry to distract yourself, if only for a few minutes, to give your brain space to respond more appropriately.
2. Consciously focus on the goals you have for the outcome of the situation.
3. Be aware of your own danger signs before your anger is about to blow. When you feel these symptoms, take 10 deep breaths (four seconds in, hold for one second, eight seconds out, hold for one second), which takes less than two minutes, but I can guarantee it will help you express your feelings in a more effective way.
4. Take a time-out if you feel you cannot appropriately communicate or control yourself. This could mean leaving the house, hanging up the phone, or rescheduling a meeting.
5. Know when to seek help. Sometimes anger comes from brain systems that have been hurt or are dysfunctional.

If you've calmed yourself physically and assessed that your anger is not in relation to a current situation that is within your realm to address, then you may benefit from brain imaging to determine if undetected brain issues, such as a hidden traumatic brain injury, problems in the temporal lobes, or sleepy frontal lobes may be contributing to anger issues.

TODAY'S PRACTICE: *Notice what happens in your body when you start getting irritable or angry and write it down.*

Taming the Judgmental Dragons

Do you like vengeance movies? These may be indicators of your dragons. These dragons often have their origin in a childhood environment that was unsafe or where you were hurt or perceived life was unfair. These dragons are triggered whenever you feel injustice to yourself or others, or when you see others doing something you think is wrong. These dragons cause people to react by being condescending, critical, moralizing, or telling others what they should and should not think or do. My wife, Tana, has this dragon. When we first met, she had very strong opinions on criminal behavior, especially about drug addicts and child molesters, and she came across as the judge, jury, and executioner. Knowing that I had testified in death penalty murder trials for the defense made her wonder about my sanity. Her attitude was understandable when you learn that she grew up in an unsafe environment with an uncle who was a heroin addict. Her stepfather also molested her. Over time, as she understood our brain imaging work, her heart softened, and the Judgmental Dragon became more balanced.

Tame Judgmental Dragons by asking yourself a few questions:

1. Is the problem now, or are you trying to right a wrong from the past?
2. Do you have all the facts, or are you making assumptions about others that you do not know are true?
3. When you find yourself making a snap judgment about someone, ask what might be behind their bad behavior. Are they having a bad day? Did they just get laid off from work? Did they just find out a loved one has cancer? It's easy to say someone is bad; it's harder to ask why.

Daily affirmations to tame the Judgmental Dragons include, "I trade judgment for understanding." "I release judgment so I can feel free." "I treat people in pain with compassion, not more pain."

TODAY'S PRACTICE: *Notice when you are being judgmental and be curious if you are reacting to the current situation or something from the past.*

Taming the Grief and Loss Dragons

Do you like inspiring movies? These may point to your dragons. The Grief and Loss Dragons are easy to find because they're everywhere. These dragons show up when we lose someone important (such as from death, divorce, or empty nest syndrome), something important (such as your health or a job), or the attachment to an idea (such as your identity when you age or retire—professional athletes and models can experience this in their twenties or thirties). When I lost my father, it was very painful. After he died, Tana would find me in my office at home just playing his voicemails and crying. Tears are often very important in the grieving process. I wrote a poem for him called "Good Grief He's Everywhere in My Brain," which explains how grief is triggered. It can be triggered by anything—a sight, sound, routine, or anniversary that reminds you of what you lost. People react to grief in many ways: shock, sadness, denial, guilt, breathing trouble, chest pain, insomnia.

In healing grief, fix sleep first. If you aren't sleeping right, odds are that grief will be prolonged. I often recommend a combination of melatonin, magnesium, GABA, 5-HTP, and theanine. It's especially important to eat right, take your supplements, and exercise. This is often the missing piece in grief recovery. I believe in starting the healing process as soon as possible. People may tell you to wait to heal from grief, but if you broke your arm, when would you want to starting healing? Right away. Researchers write about the five stages of grief: denial, anger, bargaining, depression, and acceptance. Turn these five stages upside down. Rather than denial, admit your loss: *My father is gone.* Rather than anger, work to find peace: *He had a great life.* Stop bargaining for something that will not change: *Death is inevitable.* Reengage with others to avoid depression. And refuse to accept prolonged pain as a given.

TODAY'S PRACTICE: *Remember the last time you experienced grief. How did you react? What can you do better next time to start healing sooner?*

Taming the Death Dragons

Do you love afterlife movies? These may be a sign of your dragons. The Death Dragons are always with us and often rear their heads during midlife when you have a health scare or when your parents or the parents of your friends die and you start going to funerals. You wonder if this is all there is to life, hence a midlife crisis and the convertible Corvette. It can start earlier if you have to confront death for any reason, like living during a pandemic, being diagnosed with a life-threatening illness, or having a friend die from suicide. Fear of getting old or fearing others will not survive without you also feeds these dragons. How do you react to these dragons when they appear? You might have a sense of impending doom, death might preoccupy your thoughts, you may experience panic attacks, or you may have an intense fear of aging. In the young, these dragons can also lead to risky behaviors to test death.

Tame the Death Dragons by living with the end in mind. When I was in college, I took a death and dying class and wrote my own funeral. It was one of the most important assignments of my life, because when you live knowing there's an end, you can do a better job at making each day special. Accept death as a natural part of life—yet, we are not going to encourage the Death Dragons to come early. Focus on issues that have eternal value. Ask yourself, "Does this really matter in the grand scheme of things?" It helps me not sweat the small stuff, and over time the Death Dragons have taught me that most things are small stuff. I've found listing the good things about dying also helps to tame the Death Dragons. Here are three things on my list.

1. My faith leads me to believe in eternal life, and I may get to see my father and grandfather again.
2. No more Los Angeles traffic.
3. No more root canals or dentists poking around my mouth with drills and other sharp metal objects.

Knowing there is an end motivates us to make the most of life while we are here.

TODAY'S PRACTICE: *List three good things about dying.*

Taming the Hopeless and Helpless Dragons

Do you like movies that fit a negative mood? These may be indicators of your dragons. The Hopeless and Helpless Dragons are often born when stresses stack too high, such as during the pandemic when depression tripled in just a matter of months. These dragons can also originate from chronic frustration. It's a concept called *learned helplessness.* This is where you try to feel better, but it doesn't work, then you try again and it doesn't work, and you keep trying until you feel helpless and finally lose hope. It can also stem from a family history of depression, a pessimistic mindset, or a loss of control.

What triggers the Hopeless and Helpless Dragons? Anything that reminds you of when you felt overwhelmed or powerless. These dragons can make you react with sadness, negativity, and feelings of hopelessness, helplessness, or worthlessness. You begin to feel terrible about yourself and even wonder if life is worth living.

Many people reach for medicine as their first option to treat depression, but I believe the first thing to do is get your brain right. Your brain controls everything you think, do, and feel. If you're depressed, it likely means your brain is struggling. Talk to your doctor and get your important health numbers checked. Low thyroid can cause depression, as can having a past concussion. Then, make sure to nourish your brain. Eliminate processed foods that increase inflammation and depression, and add more colorful fruits and vegetables, such as blueberries, red bell peppers, broccoli, and pomegranate seeds. Research shows there's a linear correlation between the number of fruits and vegetables you eat and your level of happiness, up to eight servings a day.[229] If you're taking medicine, don't stop it without talking to your doctor. There are also many natural treatments that fight depression and tame this dragon, including exercise; supplements like fish oil, saffron, and curcumins; bright light therapy; saunas; the scent of lavender; and learning how to "kill the ANTs" (the automatic negative thoughts) that infest your brain and feed all the dragons.

TODAY'S PRACTICE: *Eat six to eight servings of fruits and vegetables today and see how you feel.*

Taming the Ancestral Dragons

Do you like movies from history? These may be related to your dragons. Ancestral Dragons are passed down to you by your ancestors. They're some of the sneakiest dragons of all because their origins are often shrouded in secrecy. Through a process called epigenetics, you can inherit your ancestors' fears, worries, or even prejudices without ever being aware of it. The anxiety or trauma is written in your genetic code. If you're afraid of something and have no idea why, look for clues in your family tree. Children and grandchildren of Holocaust survivors have a higher risk of anxiety disorders and PTSD, as do children of 9/11 survivors and those who had parents who served in Iraq or Afghanistan. Anyone who has lived in a war zone, experienced the early death of a parent, or lost a loved one to suicide may have their brains so deeply affected that it can change their genes for generations to come.

It's often unknown what triggers the Ancestral Dragons. It can be any reminders of stressful times stored in your genes. It could be when you were the same age as a parent or grandparent when they had the original trauma. How do the Ancestral Dragons cause you to react? You can have anxiety, panic, or fear for no apparent reason or have behaviors you just can't explain.

To tame the Ancestral Dragons, know your family history in as much detail as possible and talk to your parents, grandparents, or the family historian. It can help you understand some of your own automatic reactions. Ask questions about when they were children or what hard times they might have experienced. Let them say what they remember without interrupting them. Work to separate your issues from your ancestors' issues so that you can live in the present without being haunted by the past. This may require professional help. If you sense Ancestral Dragons breathing fire on your emotional brain, read *It Didn't Start with You* by Mark Wolynn. The great news about epigenetics is that your resilient behaviors also are stored in your genes, making the next generation better and stronger.

TODAY'S PRACTICE: *Reach out to one person in your family and schedule a time to speak with them about any past traumas they may have endured.*

They, Them, and Other Dragons

You're never just dealing with the moment; you're dealing with all the moments of all the voices in your head. Have you noticed people say, "They said this" or "They said that"? Have you ever wondered who "they" were? "They" are the collective voices in your head that are constantly judging or criticizing your thoughts and actions. In *Your Brain Is Always Listening,* I introduced people to a variety of They, Them, and Other Dragons that may be unconsciously impacting your happiness, relationships, and success, including:

1. **Parent Dragons:** The voices of your mother or father (or mother or father figures) criticizing you or pushing you to be better.
2. **Sibling and Birth Order Dragons:** Your birth order and the voices of your siblings, who were often competing with you for your parents' attention.
3. **Children Dragons:** Your children who often (although not always) adore you through their elementary school years then push away and criticize you during their adolescent and young adult years.
4. **Teacher and Coach Dragons:** Your teachers who graded your intelligence, effort, and potential, and your coaches who noticed your abilities and flaws.
5. **Friends, Popular Kids, Bullies, and Mean Girl Dragons:** Your past friends, as well as the popular kids, bullies, and mean girls when you were growing up. These relationships soothe your dragons (good friends) or cause them to breathe fire (bullies and mean girls).
6. **Former, Current, and Prospective Lover Dragons:** These are the most emotionally charged dragons of all, which is why they can make you more upset than any of the other ones, especially when the relationship goes sour.
7. **Internet Troll Dragons:** The people or bots on social media and the internet trolls who criticize you for sport. Unfortunately, this is happening with younger and younger ages.

In that same book, I share what triggers these dragons and provide helpful strategies to reduce their negative impacts so you can put an end to the battles in your head.

TODAY'S PRACTICE: *Which of the They, Them, or Other Dragons are most prominent in your internal dialogue?*

Finding Happiness in the Brain

The healthier your brain, the happier you are. In writing my book *You, Happier*, I decided to see if I could indeed find happiness in the brain. We gave 500 consecutive new patients at Amen Clinics the Oxford Happiness Questionnaire, which asks respondents how much they agree or disagree with 29 questions on a six-point scale. Our research team then compared the scans of the unhappiest people to the happiest. The results were fascinating. The SPECT scans of the high happiness group showed increased activity and blood flow overall, meaning the healthier your brain, the happier you are likely to be. We also saw increased activity and blood flow in the prefrontal cortex, basal ganglia, and nucleus accumbens (pleasure centers). In the low happiness group, the SPECT scans showed increased activity in the anterior cingulate gyrus, which I think of as the brain's gear shifter, meaning these people are more likely to get stuck on negative thoughts.

According to our statistician, Dr. David Keator from the University of California, Irvine, the most interesting result from our study was found in the reward or happiness circuits, composed of the ventral tegmental area, nucleus accumbens, and orbitofrontal cortex. These circuits have been associated with smiling, laughter, pleasurable feelings, and happiness. Higher activity in these areas correlated with higher total happiness scores. Get your brain right and your happiness will follow.

TODAY'S PRACTICE: *Take the Oxford Happiness Questionnaire: theguardian.com/lifeandstyle/2014/nov/03/take-the-oxford-happiness-questionnaire.*

Happiness Is a Moral Obligation

Happiness is about altruism, not selfishness, because of how we impact others. Why should we focus on being happy? As a psychiatrist, I've written about anxiety, depression, bipolar disorder, ADD/ADHD, aging, violence, obesity, memory loss, love, parenting, and other important topics. Yet underlying the reasons most people come to see us at Amen Clinics is the fact that they are unhappy. Helping people be happier day to day is at the core of getting and staying mentally and physically healthy. Extensive research has shown that happiness is associated with a lower heart rate, lower blood pressure, and overall heart health. Happier people get fewer infections, have lower cortisol levels (the hormone of stress), and fewer aches and pains. They tend to live longer, have better relationships, and be more successful in their careers. Plus, happiness is contagious because happier people tend to make others happier.[230]

One of my favorite short videos that I encourage all of my patients to watch is by Dennis Prager. In "Why Be Happy," he suggests that happiness is a moral obligation. He says, "Whether or not you're happy, and most importantly, whether or not you act happy, is about altruism, not selfishness—because it is about how we affect others' lives. . . . Ask anybody who was raised by an unhappy parent whether or not happiness is a moral issue, and I assure you the answer will be 'yes.' It is no fun being raised by an unhappy parent, or being married to an unhappy person, or being the parent of an unhappy child, or working with an unhappy coworker."[231]

TODAY'S PRACTICE: *List four people who are impacted by your mood and describe why you want to be a positive influence on their life.*

The Seven Lies of Happiness

More may not be better. For financial gain, marketers have been brainwashing populations for decades into believing happiness is based on things that actually damage our brains, ruin our minds, increase depression, and make us unhappy.

> *Lie #1: Having more and more of something (love, sex, fame, drugs, etc.) will make you happy.* Unfortunately, the more pleasure you get, the more you may need to make you happy. It's called hedonic adaptation.
>
> *Lie #2: A "Don't Worry, Be Happy" mindset, promoted by the popular 1988 Grammy Song of the Year of the same name by Bobby McFerrin, will make you happy.* In fact, this mindset will make you unhappy and kill you early. According to one of the longest longevity studies ever published, the "don't worry, be happy people" die early from accidents and preventable illnesses.[232]
>
> *Lie #3: Advertisers and fast-food restaurants know what will make you happy.* Take Happy Meals (and kids' meals on most restaurant menus), for example. They certainly will not make children happy. These meals should be called Unhappy Meals as the low-quality, nutrient-sparse, processed food-like substances increase inflammation and have been linked with depression, ADD/ADHD, obesity, cancer, and a lower IQ.[233]
>
> *Lie #4: You need a smartphone, watch, tablet, or the latest technology to make you happy.* Technology companies are constantly creating addictive gadgets that hook our attention and distract us from meaningful relationships.
>
> *Lie #5: Constantly being "in the know" by following your favorite news outlet will make you happy.* News outlets repeatedly and purposely pour toxic thoughts into our brains, making us see terror or disaster around every corner—all in an effort to boost their ratings and profits.
>
> *Lie #6: Alcohol or marijuana makes you happy.* Not so fast. The American Cancer Society links any alcohol consumption to seven types of cancer.[234] Alcohol can help you feel better quickly, but it can also damage your brain, decrease the quality of your decisions, and harm your relationships. Marijuana lowers overall blood flow, which is not associated with a happy brain.
>
> *Lie #7: Money makes you happy.* This is true, but only up to about $75,000 a year in the US, then the correlation with happiness completely falls off.[235]

TODAY'S PRACTICE: *Look around your environment today to see if you can recognize the marketing lies of happiness.*

Brain Warrior Steve Arterburn and Transformation

"I am supernaturally able to remember things, and they won't go away." Meet my friend Steve Arterburn, a multiple *New York Times* bestselling author, radio host, and entrepreneur. He came to see me for ADD/ADHD and memory problems, plus he had a family history of Alzheimer's disease, a condition he did not want to develop. About two months after our first appointment, he sent me this email late one night. He gave me permission to share it with you.

> My rental car confirmation number for Aruba was 63012078US2 and hotel was 55505510931. The reason I know this is that I'm supernaturally able to remember things that I would never even try to before. And they don't go away! My productivity and creativity is off the charts. I would say I am getting 4 X the work done 4 X better than ever and creativity has resulted in book ideas and proposals that I can't wait to publish. I have the ability to focus on tasks and connect with my wife in ways I have never experienced.[236]

Here is the strategy he used to boost his cognitive edge: He switched from running for a half hour to doing burst training instead. He completely gave up his four-sodas-a-day habit. He increased his protein intake, decreased his consumption of grains and processed carbs, and strictly limited sugar. He took the daily supplements I had recommended. He stopped making excuses for not using his CPAP machine to control his snoring. By doing brain training exercises, he elevated his problem solving to the ninety-ninth percentile and continued to work on his memory and other areas where he had been struggling.

Although I was not surprised, he was almost shocked at how so many areas of his life—including intimacy with his wife—had improved by making these lifestyle changes. Time and time again, I have witnessed how a better life always comes from having a better brain.

TODAY'S PRACTICE: *Read over Steve's six strategies and add one to your regimen that you're not already doing.*

Ultimate Brain-Based Therapy

Master your brain by controlling what goes into it. Your five senses bring the world into your brain, and they can make you feel happy or disgusted. Do an exercise right now. Remember the time you accidentally drank spoiled milk or smelled a skunk spray. Gross. Now, imagine tasting your favorite dessert or smelling your favorite flowers. Did you notice a difference in how you felt? Let me show you how to purposefully use your senses to feel amazing.

Vision: Did you know that 30 percent of your brain is dedicated to vision?[237] Create an album on your phone or at home of pictures that make you happy, such as your spouse, children, grandchildren, even your pets. Research also shows that images of nature can soothe stress and help you feel better fast.[238]

Hearing: Your brain picks up the rhythms in the environment, which means you can manipulate your mind with music. You can improve your mood and boost your happiness in just two weeks, simply by having the intention of being happier and by listening to mood-boosting music, such as the Beach Boys song "Good Vibrations," for just 12 minutes a day.[239]

Touch: Massage has been shown to decrease pain and anxiety; petting your dog or cat can immediately increase the cuddle hormone oxytocin; and holding the hand of a loved one in pain can actually help take away their pain.

Smell: Your sense of smell is directly connected to your emotional brain. Lemon, lavender, jasmine, rose, honeysuckle, and vanilla are some of the best-studied scents to immediately boost your mood and energy.

Taste: Chocolate (make it healthy), saffron, cinnamon, mint, or nutmeg has been shown to enhance mood.

Find fun ways to put this all together to immediately change how you feel: take a sauna while cranking up "Good Vibrations," or watch a video of ocean waves with the scent of lavender or vanilla in the air while sipping on a cinnamon, almond-milk cappuccino.

TODAY'S PRACTICE: *Choose one activity for each of the five senses and do it today.*

With Hope: A Veteran's Story

The brain scan images provide hope that there is a better way; there is hope for healing.
Security is a primary value for my wife, Tana. She grew up in an unsafe, chaotic
environment, and even though now we live in a very safe neighborhood, she
loves martial arts training (she has two black belts—Kenpo Karate and Tae Kwon
Do) and taking survival courses. She once took our daughter Chloe on a survival
weekend, and there she met Denny, one of the instructors. Her heart broke when
she heard his story. He is a former Marine who had three traumatic brain injuries,
including one in Fallujah, Iraq, in 2007, when his truck was hit by a roadside
bomb. He was knocked unconscious, and when he awoke, he was bleeding from
multiple places and two of his friends were dead. He was diagnosed with the chronic effects of multiple traumatic brain injuries and posttraumatic stress disorder. His
healing journey involved one medication after another, without much relief. He
became so hopeless that he tried to end his own life. No one had performed a functional brain imaging study on him, so Tana invited him to the clinic.

DENNY'S SPECT SCAN

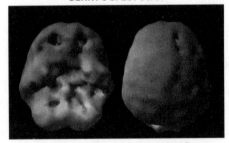

Holes indicate area of decreased blood flow

His SPECT scan showed severe damage, affecting his prefrontal cortex (focus,
forethought, judgment, and impulse control), left temporal lobe (memory, learning,
and dark thoughts), and occipital lobes in the back (visual processing). The good
news was that it was clear that his brain could be improved with the right treatments. After looking at his scan, Denny was actually grateful it didn't look worse
and that he had a physical reason why he felt as awful as he did. A week later he
wrote to Tana: "It's only been a week, and I can already feel a difference. Since the
scan, I have increased my activity level (fitness), modified my diet, and maintained
the supplement regimen. I'm doing great! My daughter and I have been outdoors
every day. Since I started adjusting my habits, I am happier and more positive." His
follow-up scan showed quite an improvement.

TODAY'S PRACTICE: *Write down three ways that having hope would motivate you to
make healthy changes in your life.*

Know Your Purpose in Five Minutes

Chinese saying: "If you want happiness for an hour, take a nap. If you want happiness for a day, go fishing. If you want happiness for a year, inherit a fortune. If you want happiness for a lifetime, help somebody." One of my favorite TEDx talks on how to find your life's purpose in five minutes is by Adam Leipzig.[240] He starts by telling a story about his twenty-fifth college reunion from Yale University. He said he made an astounding discovery: 80 percent of his privileged, well-off, powerful friends were unhappy. The difference between them and those who were happy was "knowing their purpose." To know your purpose, Leipzig said, you have to know the answers to five simple questions:

1. Who are you? What is your name?
2. What do you love to do? Examples include writing, cooking, design, creating, crunching numbers, etc. To get clarity of purpose, ask yourself, *What is the one thing I do that I feel qualified to teach others?*
3. Whom do you do it for? Or how does your work connect you to others?
4. What do those people want or need from you?
5. How do they change as a result of what you do?

When I answer these questions, it looks like this:

1. My name is Daniel.
2. I love optimizing people's brains and inspiring them to care about brain health.
3. I do it for my family, and those who come to our clinics, read my books, or watch my shows.
4. These people want to suffer less, feel better, be sharper, and have greater control over their lives.
5. As a result of what I do, people change by having better brains and better lives, and pass it on to others.

Notice that only two of the five questions are about you; three are about others. When you're at a gathering and someone asks you, "What do you do?" answer by telling them the answer to question number five. In my example, when people ask me what I do, I say, "I help people have better brains and better lives, and they pass it on to others."

TODAY'S PRACTICE: *Do this exercise.*

Can Purpose Help You Live Longer and Better?

When you know your why, you can survive almost any what. Having a clear purpose in life is linked to spirituality. Dr. Christina Puchalski, a world leader on integrating spirituality into health care, uses a definition I love: Spirituality is what gives meaning to one's life and draws one to transcend oneself.[241] When most people think of spirituality, they automatically think of organized religion. But the way I view it, spirituality encompasses so much more. It's all the ways you express your inner spirit, such as praying, meditating, communing with nature, volunteering, and connecting with God or a higher power. When you engage in these soulful activities each and every day, it makes you feel more purposeful. Having a strong sense of purpose has been linked with reductions in anxiety as well as greater longevity. The findings of a 2019 study involving nearly 7,000 adults over the age of 50 showed that people with the highest sense of "life purpose" were less likely to die from any cause during the four-year study period compared with people who had the lowest sense of purpose.[242] In particular, having a high sense of purpose reduced the likelihood of dying from heart, circulatory, or blood conditions.

Some people have trouble pinpointing their purpose in life. I have found that one single question can help you zero in on your why. Simply ask yourself, *Why is the world a better place because I breathe?* If you can't come up with a response right away, spend some time in contemplation. Think about any talents or skills you have that might be beneficial to others. Or think about what you can do to enhance your community or our society at large.

"I feel disconnected" is something we hear from many of our patients in our clinics. They have trouble finding meaning in their life and lack any sense of purpose. They don't have a relationship with a higher power and don't feel like they are connected to something "greater" than themselves. When there is an absence of meaning or life purpose, it can cause depressive symptoms as well as feelings of loneliness, unimportance, and insignificance. You can change this by spending some time focusing on your why.

TODAY'S PRACTICE: *Ask yourself,* Why is the world a better place because I breathe? *If you have a hard time answering that question, ask those closest to you.*

Decide What You Truly Want
and What You Don't Want

Know your positive and negative motivation. I find approaching motivation from both a positive and negative standpoint helps my patients. I ask them to decide what they truly want—to get healthy physically, cognitively, and emotionally. And to know their motivation—why are they working so hard to get healthy? Write six positive reasons to get and stay truly healthy, such as:

1. I will have more energy to accomplish my goals in life.
2. It will help me preserve my memory.
3. I will be a better example for my children.
4. I will feel more attractive.
5. It will help me stay physically healthy.
6. I will feel more confident.

Next, write six negative reasons why you must achieve and maintain your health.

1. I don't want to feel lazy or be an underachiever.
2. I don't want to lose my memory.
3. I don't want to teach my kids bad habits that will make their lives harder.
4. I don't want to look older and out of shape.
5. I don't want to increase my risk for cancer, heart disease, diabetes, and other health issues.
6. I don't want to feel bad about myself.

TODAY'S PRACTICE: *List six positive and six negative reasons to get healthy.*

I Used to See Ghosts

"Dr. Amen, I have a temporal lobe problem." I met Tommy, a 9-year-old boy who had read my book *Change Your Brain, Change Your Life* and had come to our clinic for a scan. When he first saw me, he said, "Hey, Dr. Amen, I have a left temporal lobe problem!"

"Really?" I asked, "How do you know that?"

He said, "I read your book."

"But how do you really know?"

He said, "I have a really bad temper, and you write that people who have bad tempers often have left temporal lobe problems." He was right. Then he added, "And I used to see ghosts."

"What?"

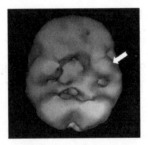

"I used to see these green things float in front of my eyes. I thought they were ghosts, and they would scare me until I read your book and realized those were just illusions that come from misfiring temporal lobes." Then he looked at me with his big, beautiful blue eyes and said, "And, last year, to get rid of the bad thoughts in my head, I tried to kill myself."

Tommy's scan showed a problem in his left temporal lobe, as he predicted.

People with temporal lobe issues, like Tommy, often respond to treatments such as anti-seizure medications, a very low carbohydrate diet, and a treatment called neurofeedback, where we train the brain to fire more normally.

DAILY PRACTICE: *Have you ever had weird sensations you couldn't explain? Write them down, and now that you know a bit about the brain, see if you can relate any brain areas to them. Refer back to days 175, 187, 188, 196, 211 for brain regions and functions.*

Get the Whole Family Involved

Don't let an ANT infestation take over your relationships with negativity. If you were raised by parents who've been traumatized and are depressed, anxious, or abusing drugs, the stress can reshape your brain to make you and future generations more vulnerable to depression and substance abuse.

Here are five simple ways to support everyone in the family.

1. Encourage communication. People cannot read your mind. They don't know what you're going through unless you tell them.
2. Use magic phrases to open communication: "I'm concerned about you . . . I'm here for you . . . Can we talk about how you're feeling? . . . Can I go with you to get help?"
3. Tell people that asking for help is a sign of strength, not weakness. Imagine if a business were in trouble and the owners ignored the problems. They'd go bankrupt. The same thing happens when you ignore brain health issues—your family will go bankrupt.
4. Tough love works for people whose brains work right, but for people with troubled brains, tough love is like doing software programming on people with hardware problems. It is not very effective.
5. When a person has a setback, it is hard on everyone, but it is better to be curious about what happened rather than furious and judgmental. Behavior is much more complicated than most people think.

TODAY'S PRACTICE: *Make it a point to share how you are feeling today with your family so they can support you if necessary.*

EMDR, Steven, and the Santa Monica Farmers Market

Trauma can be healed. Steven's father was an abusive alcoholic who once burned down their house. But Steven's trauma did not end there. He was a veteran of the first Gulf War, where he faced death like so many others who served in combat did. One day while working in Santa Monica as a bicycle repair mechanic, he walked to the three-block-long farmers market during his lunch break. As he was strolling along, an elderly man lost control of his car, plowing through the market. People were screaming and bodies flew everywhere. Steven saw the car heading straight for him but was able to jump out of the way. More than 50 people were injured, and 10 died from this horrible incident. Steven helped others using the medical skills he learned in the military. He held one woman as she passed away. For months after that day, his hands shook constantly and he could not sleep.

Not long after the farmers market tragedy, a CBS news anchor named Linda Alvarez brought her bike into the shop where Steven worked. After chatting together, she recruited him for a story she was doing on EMDR, which stands for eye movement desensitization and reprocessing. This is a very effective type of treatment for posttraumatic stress disorder (PTSD) and other traumatic experiences. EMDR incorporates alternating hemisphere stimulation, such as back and forth eye movements, to diffuse the power of traumatic memories.

Steven's evaluation at Amen Clinics included three scans. We first scanned his brain before he began EMDR treatment. His scans showed the classic pattern for PTSD, with very high activity in the emotional areas of the brain. We scanned him a second time during an EMDR session, and the scans showed some benefit. Steven continued with seven more EMDR sessions to reduce the impact of trauma in his brain. His final scans showed considerable improvement from the treatment. Afterward, not only did he feel much better, but his hands stopped shaking too. In time, Steven was also able to forgive his father for the pain he had caused him so many years ago.

TODAY'S PRACTICE: *Learn more about EMDR at emdria.org and consider getting treatment for any traumas you've endured.*

Use Humming and Toning to Tune Up Your Brain

Use your voice as a form of sound therapy. I am amazed by the therapeutic power of the human voice. When you open your mouth to sing, pray, chant, hum, or read aloud, you open yourself to enhanced mental health and well-being. A growing body of scientific evidence confirms it. For example, singing promotes positive emotions, boosts moods, lowers stress, decreases fatigue, and improves memory in people with dementia.[243] Chanting mantras has been found to reduce anxiety, promote relaxation, increase attention, and dampen stress.[244] Humming induces calmness, enhances sleep, and boosts happiness.[245] One of the most powerful forms of vocalization, however, is something you may not have heard of. It's called toning.

Toning involves a variety of vocalizations, such as grunts and cries, as well as simple vowel sounds, such as *A* (as in *say*), *E* (as in *be*), *Ah* (as in *saw*), *O* (as in *know*), and *OO* (as in *who*). In a 2018 study, toning frequently produced changes in awareness, consciousness, and attention.[246] Participants said it felt meditative and enhanced a sense of calm and relaxation. In his book *The Mozart Effect*, Don Campbell writes that toning also helps release fear, balance brain waves, and reduce physical pain, among other benefits. The author says that some toning vowel sounds are associated with specific benefits,[247] such as: *Ah*—promotes relaxation; *E* or *A*— enhances concentration while reducing physical pain and anger; and *O*—promotes muscle relaxation.

Consciously use your voice on a daily basis to enhance your psychological well-being. One of the best things about toning and some other forms of vocalization is that you don't need to be able to hold a tune to benefit from them.

TODAY'S PRACTICE: *Try toning for five minutes to see if it helps you.*

Learn to Love What You Hate, Do What You Can't, and Make Space Work for You

If you are having trouble changing your habits, try changing the way you think about them. One of the best ways to maintain change is to shift your focus from what you hate to what you love. For example, are you thinking about the high-calorie, sugary snacks you're missing? Flip that around and focus on something you like about the healthy foods you're trying to add to your diet. Maybe you like the crunch of raw carrots dipped in hummus or the smell of spices used in cooking. Similarly, learn to find what you love about exercise. My friend Pastor Steve hated running, but he loved playing Ping-Pong. Focus on what you love about something, and it will make you like it even more.

Next, learn to do what you can't. If you are relying too much on willpower to change, it is likely you do not have enough skill to change, and this can be fixed. Start with a skill scan: What do you need to learn? Maybe you need to learn more about great-tasting, nutrient-rich food and the best exercises for you.

Make your space work for you. It's surprising how many people are unaware of how their environment influences their daily habits. Your home, your workplace, restaurants, grocery stores, and other places you frequent have an impact on your thoughts, feelings, and actions. When you're trying to make lasting lifestyle changes, you may need to think about changing your environment too.

At home, you can easily minimize temptations by eliminating bad foods from your cupboards and refrigerator. Stock them with nutritious and delicious fare that makes you feel good. Take your home exercise equipment out of the back of the closet and put it where you can't miss it. You'll be much more likely to use it if you can see it. The same concept works at the office. Get rid of the candy bowl in the kitchen and replace it with healthy snacks. Bring your sneakers and leave them next to your desk so you are reminded to take a brisk walk on your lunch break.

Take advantage of these cues to jump-start healthy habits.

TODAY'S PRACTICE: *Take a skill inventory. What skills do you need to get healthy?*

Dopamine: The Molecule of More

Mick Jagger of the Rolling Stones has been romantically linked to thousands of women over the years, which adds new meaning to the lyrics, "I can't get no satisfaction." Dopamine is the neurotransmitter of wanting, especially wanting more. It is involved with anticipation, possibility, and love. It is released when you expect a reward (food, sex, money, shopping) or when you get an unexpected happy surprise. It is involved with motivation (going toward a reward), memory, mood, and focus. Dopamine is a salesman that drives you to pursue a better life. But like many salesmen, it can also lie to you and promise you pleasure when, in fact, pain will result (such as engaging in drug abuse or affairs). Too much dopamine has been associated with agitation, obsession, compulsions, and psychosis. Too little dopamine can cause depression, low motivation, apathy, fatigue, Parkinson's disease, and sugar cravings.

There are two main dopamine systems in the brain: the dopamine reward center involved with seeking pleasure and the dopamine control center that enhances the activity of the prefrontal cortex that helps you think before you act. I think of these two systems as the gas (dopamine reward center) and the brakes (dopamine control center); both are essential to get anywhere.

Fame also initially increases dopamine, as having mass numbers of people recognize you for your accomplishments meets so many basic human needs (achievement, being noticed, security, love, etc.). Throughout my career, I've been blessed to treat many famous people, from Olympic athletes and professional football, hockey, baseball, and basketball players to Oscar-winning actors, supermodels, and more. The dopamine highs of fame often lead to tolerance, where it takes more and more to get the same feeling, which is why many famous people often resort to drug abuse, affairs, fast cars, and gambling just to feel normal. Newly married celebrities are five times more likely to get divorced than ordinary people.[248] When you get too much of a good thing—pleasure—you will want more, and over time it wears out your pleasure centers, leaving you feeling flat and depressed. My prayer for my young stars is often, "Please God, do not let them be famous before their brains are developed." The dopamine control center is not finished developing until about age 25. Early fame and drug abuse can cause lasting damage to the brain. Protect your dopamine centers by loving your brain.

TODAY'S PRACTICE: *List three things that stimulate your dopamine centers that are good for you and three things that are bad for you. Today, choose the good ones.*

Seven Natural Ways to Boost Dopamine

Strategize to keep dopamine and happiness healthy. Here are seven simple strategies to boost dopamine in healthy amounts:

1. **Eat foods rich in tyrosine, the amino acid building block for dopamine.** In order to make dopamine, your body needs tyrosine, which can be found in almonds, bananas, avocados, eggs, beans, fish, chicken, and dark chocolate.

2. **Eat a high-protein, lower-carbohydrate diet. Ketogenic or paleo diets have been shown to increase dopamine availability in the brain.** Eating highly processed foods like cookies, potato chips, cakes, and pies leads to cravings and overeating, which leave a strong imprint on the pleasure centers in the prefrontal cortex and lead to weight gain. Being overweight can impair dopamine pathways.

3. **Exercise regularly.** In general, physical exercise is one of the best things you can do for your brain. It increases the production of new brain cells, slows down brain cell aging, and can increase your levels of dopamine.

4. **Listen to upbeat music.** It is no surprise that listening to upbeat music can increase pleasurable feelings, improve mood, reduce stress, and help with focus and concentration. Research has demonstrated that much of this occurs because of an increase in dopamine levels.[249]

5. **Get more sunshine.** Sunlight exposure has been found to increase dopamine in the brain.

6. **Supplements.** The herbals ashwagandha, rhodiola, and panax ginseng have been found to increase dopamine levels, promoting improved focus and increased energy while enhancing endurance and stamina.

7. **Set goals.** Always have new positive goals to strive for no matter your age or situation. Dopamine provides the energy for the journey, but not the destination.

TODAY'S PRACTICE: *Focus on increased protein at each meal to see how it affects your focus and energy.*

Serotonin: The Molecule of Respect

Serotonin and dopamine tend to counterbalance each other. Serotonin enhances and stabilizes mood, regulates stress, and helps us be more flexible and adapt to changes in our environment. It also helps us shift our attention away from unhelpful worries and be more open to cooperating with others. It is also involved in sleep. There is evidence that serotonin increases when we feel respected by others, which promotes self-esteem, and decreases when we feel disrespected or get our feelings hurt. Researchers in the 1990s were mapping serotonin receptors in the brain and found that the anterior cingulate gyrus contained many of them.[250]

Low serotonin is involved in depression, anxiety, worry, poor memory, pain, aggression, suicidal behavior, poor self-esteem, being oppositional or argumentative, and being rigid or cognitively inflexible. Low serotonin levels can lead to struggles with perseverative behaviors where brains get stuck in a specific state, such as obsessions or compulsions. Low levels also cause people to hate surprises.

Higher serotonin is associated with better moods, improved feelings of social status or respect, and flexibility. Higher levels can also decrease motivation. Serotonin and dopamine counterbalance each other. As one goes up, the other tends to go down. Balance between the two is important. Tryptophan, which your body uses to make serotonin, decreases quarrelsome behaviors, increases agreeable behaviors, and improves mood.[251]

Certain medications increase serotonin, especially selective serotonin reuptake inhibitors (SSRIs), which are the most commonly prescribed antidepressant medications (such as Prozac, Paxil, Zoloft, Celexa, Lexapro, and Luvox). While some advocate the use of psychedelic drugs such as LSD and psilocybin (the psychoactive component of magic mushrooms) because they also stimulate serotonin receptors and help people feel more open to change,[252] these can be addictive and have detrimental side effects.

TODAY'S PRACTICE: *List three situations in which you feel respected and three in which you feel disrespected. These can increase and decrease your serotonin levels.*

More Natural Ways to Boost Serotonin

Sugar boosts serotonin but also makes you sick. You feel good in the short term but bad in the long run. Here are more long-term, feel-good, serotonin-boosting strategies:

1. **Eat seafood.** Not only does seafood provide ample tryptophan, but the long-chain omega-3 fatty acids found in marine fat also increase serotonin production in the brain.[253] See day 192 for more foods containing tryptophan.

2. **Make an effort to compare yourself to others in a positive way.** Comparing yourself to others in a negative way is the most predictable way to lower your self-esteem.

3. **Take certain nutritional supplements.** The ones I recommend are saffron, 5-HTP, magnesium, vitamin D, vitamins B6 and B12, and curcumin.

4. **Indulge in regular massages.** People who received 20 minutes of massage therapy from a partner twice a week said they felt less anxious and depressed[254] and had higher serotonin levels after 16 weeks.[255]

5. **Focus on what you like more than what you don't like.** Brain scans revealed that people who focused on positive thoughts had more serotonin in the anterior cingulate gyrus.[256]

TODAY'S PRACTICE: *Select one of the strategies listed above and do it when you feel stuck on negative thoughts.*

Oxytocin: The Molecule of Trust

Oxytocin is the chemical of bonding and trust, but it can also bond us so tightly we become suspicious of those outside our group, which is why Red Sox fans hate the Yankees. Oxytocin has been called the cuddle or love hormone, but it is so much more. Studies have found that couples in the first stage of romantic love have higher levels of oxytocin, as well as higher dopamine (pleasure) and lower serotonin levels (obsessions) than their unattached friends. Oxytocin is increased during sexual activity and linked to the intensity of orgasms.[257] It has been associated with increased trust, well-being, bonding, generosity, stress reduction, and social interactions. Oxytocin has also been associated with behaviors that protect the social group. It causes people to gravitate toward those who are similar, even lying to protect others in their group. Oxytocin evokes feelings of contentment, reductions in anxiety, and feelings of calmness and security when in the company of your mate.

Low oxytocin levels have been associated with depression and a sense that your survival is threatened. Higher oxytocin levels can decrease cortisol and stress and increase the likelihood mates will be monogamous (it lowers testosterone). Like the other chemicals of happiness, there may be a downside to too much oxytocin. It may be related to people becoming too attached, trusting, or codependent. Higher levels may be associated with overlooking the flaws of others or staying with abusive partners or friends because the bond is too strong. Increased oxytocin levels have been associated with envy and "mama bear" aggression if anyone threatens your loved ones. It may also be involved in social contagion, groupthink, distrust of others who are not like you, and racial prejudice.

What lowers oxytocin? Testosterone, being apart from a loved one, isolation, betrayal, grief, and acute stress drain oxytocin. The pandemic was disastrous for many people's oxytocin levels and their levels of happiness. Oxytocin can be prescribed as a drug. Researchers have shown that those struggling with emotional trauma can benefit from oxytocin and that it can calm the fear circuits in the brain and decrease the symptoms of PTSD (posttraumatic stress disorder).[258]

TODAY'S PRACTICE: *Give someone you love a hug to increase your oxytocin levels.*

Eight Ways to Boost Oxytocin

Eat meals together. Here are eight ways to boost oxytocin:

1. **Develop social alliances.** When you're hanging out with your pals, you feel socially supported and less alone in the world. That's why the pandemic was so difficult for so many people—they lost the oxytocin from meeting their friends for a morning bike ride or after-church brunch.
2. **Touch.** When you need an oxytocin boost, reach out to touch someone you love. The simple act of holding hands can crank up oxytocin levels.
3. **Give (or get) a massage.** It works both ways—giving or getting a massage boosts oxytocin levels.[259]
4. **Give a gift.** If you want to encourage the release of oxytocin, surprise someone you care about with a gift. It doesn't have to be an extravagant present, just a little something that will make them smile.
5. **Make eye contact.** Gazing into the eyes of a loved one—even if it's just a furry four-legged friend—can trigger the release of oxytocin.[260]
6. **Pet your animals.** The simple act of stroking or caressing a dog's soft fur stokes the release of the molecule of trust. Research has found that cats—even with their sometimes persnickety and aloof temperament—make us feel happy too![261]
7. **Eat with someone you care about.** Too many people dine alone or on the go these days when the act of sharing food can do wonders for oxytocin production. Think about the stimulating conversations you've had over the years or how you felt when someone asked you, "How was your day?"
8. **Make love.** The intimacy that comes from having sex with your spouse is a powerful way to raise oxytocin levels.

TODAY'S PRACTICE: *Eat a meal with someone you care about.*

Endorphins: The Molecule of Pain Relief

Endorphins are triggered to manage pain and severe stress. In blocking pain, endorphins help us escape dangerous situations that are potentially life-threatening, such as escaping once we have been bitten by a wild animal, even if we have a broken leg. Endorphins are also released when we push ourselves to distress, such as a runner's high. They make us feel euphoric, which is why people can get addicted to intense exercise. These molecules are also involved in the pleasurable sensations of sex, listening to certain pieces of music, and eating delicious foods such as chocolate.

Low levels of endorphins have been associated with depression, anxiety, stress, mood swings, fibromyalgia, headaches, and trouble sleeping. As one would expect, this sets people up for addictions, especially to opiate drugs. These drugs, which are chemically similar to endorphins, help relieve pain, but unless prescribed with extreme caution, opiates can kill people. Drugs such as oxycodone, hydrocodone, codeine, morphine, fentanyl, and heroin are some of the most addictive substances and are ravaging our society.

Wanting and pain are closely connected because of endorphins. The way they are intertwined reminds me of the word *tantalized*, which comes from the story of Tantalus, a Greek mythological figure. He was punished for all eternity by being forced to stand in a pool of water under a fruit tree branch, but every time he reached out for food or drink, it receded beyond his grasp, leaving him wanting and achingly tantalized.[262] Roller coasters, horror movies, extreme sports, running with the bulls, or chronically conflicted relationships are all examples of this connection. When endorphin levels are too low, the temptation is to look for extremes that will boost them.

Have you ever wondered why people become cutters (intentionally cutting themselves repeatedly), spend hours in tattoo parlors, or engage in sadomasochistic sexual behaviors? They are causing pain to trigger endorphins and the associated euphoria. When you understand the endorphin system and response, the unusual behavior begins to make sense. They may be seeking an endorphin rush to block emotional pain. When I put them on the opiate blocker naltrexone, which blocks the euphoric effect, they often stop the behavior. Naltrexone has also been used with alcoholics to decrease the buzz and decrease alcohol intake.

TODAY'S PRACTICE: *Have a small piece of low-sugar dark chocolate that is at least 65 percent cocoa.*

Eight Ways to Increase Endorphins

Acupuncture can treat certain forms of depression.[263] *Here are eight healthy ways to balance endorphins:*

1. **Exercise.** Physical activity triggers the release of this pain-relieving neurochemical and can produce the "runner's high" that makes you feel great.
2. **Give to others.** When it comes to increasing the levels of endorphins, it is better to give than to receive, so find ways to be of service to others.
3. **Practice yoga.** The stress-reducing effects of yoga are well documented, but a lesser-known benefit is its ability to raise endorphin levels.[264]
4. **Meditate.** A regular meditation practice has been associated with increases in endorphins as well as positive mood.[265]
5. **Eat spicy foods.** The compound capsaicin—found in jalapeño, habanero, and other chili peppers that can make your head sweat—is associated with an endorphin rush and pain reduction.[266]
6. **Consume dark chocolate.** Why does eating chocolate reduce pain and enhance our mood? In part, it's because of anti-inflammatory ingredients in dark chocolate that also promote the release of endorphins.
7. **Laugh more.** You can thank endorphins for many of the benefits of laughter, including elevating the pain threshold. Simply watching a half hour of comedy with a few friends is enough to increase endorphin levels.[267]
8. **Try acupuncture.** The ancient therapy of acupuncture has been shown to help with depression, fibromyalgia, and insomnia.[268] In fact, I've treated many patients with treatment-resistant depression (meaning that traditional treatments have not worked) who told me that when they took an opiate, such as hydrocodone for a dental procedure, they felt instantly better. Of course, I would never give them an opiate prescription for depression (addiction vulnerability makes them way too dangerous), but that piece of history triggers me to send them to an acupuncturist, and they often find relief. Acupuncture doesn't work for all depressions, but it is effective for those with an endorphin deficiency.

TODAY'S PRACTICE: *Go for a walk or do some gentle yoga to ease pain.*

GABA: The Molecule of Calm

"You are so much smarter when I take GABA." Gamma aminobutyric acid (GABA) is the chief inhibitory neurotransmitter in the brain. GABA's primary role is to reduce brain cell excitability and slow down the firing of neurons. It helps balance more stimulating neurotransmitters, such as dopamine. Too much stimulation can cause anxiety, insomnia, and seizures; while too little nerve cell firing can cause lethargy, confusion, and sedation. It's always about balance. GABA has relaxing, antianxiety, and anticonvulsant effects, and increases a sense of calm in many of my patients. Low GABA levels have been found in patients with anxiety, panic attacks, alcoholism, bipolar disorder, tremors, and epilepsy.

GABA has been found to be helpful to reduce symptoms of anxiety, alcohol withdrawal, high blood pressure, overeating, premenstrual symptoms, and some cases of depression. I recently suggested a teenager take the supplement GABA. After a few weeks of trying it, his mother wrote, "GABA has helped my son! He had been struggling with racing thoughts. The pandemic seemed to have triggered something in him where his mind wouldn't calm down. I noticed a significant positive difference in his disposition. He makes sure to take it every day."

One of my favorite GABA pandemic stories happened at home. Tana and I work together. We have recorded over 1,000 episodes of *The Brain Warrior's Way* podcast and four national public television specials. For our public television specials, I write the scripts, and she edits her sections as we read through them. Sometimes that can bring up tension or disagreements. During the pandemic, the societal unrest caused a lot of anxiety for Tana, and I suggested she take our GABA Calming Support supplement. A few weeks later, we were preparing for one of our public television specials. During the script reading, she was thoughtful as usual, but much mellower. There was no tension at all between us. When we finished, she looked at me and said, "That was so easy. I didn't feel the need to continuously say no. You are so much smarter when I take GABA."

Certain classes of drugs, such as benzodiazepines (e.g., Xanax, Valium, Ativan), increase GABA, but they can be addictive so I generally avoid those drugs.

TODAY'S PRACTICE: *List three situations in which you could use more GABA.*

Eight Ways to Balance GABA

GABA could be a healthier alternative to alcohol. Here are eight healthy ways to balance this vital neurotransmitter:

1. **Eat the building blocks of GABA.** Foods do not contain GABA, but certain foods stimulate the body to produce it. GABA-promoting compounds include green, black, or oolong teas, lentils, berries, grass-fed beef, wild-caught fish, seaweed, noni fruits, and tomatoes. Your brain and body use those to create GABA.

2. **Get adequate amounts of B6.** Vitamin B6 is a required cofactor for GABA synthesis. Good sources of B6 include spinach, garlic, broccoli, brussels sprouts, and bananas.

3. **Consume fermented foods.** Beneficial bacteria in the gut can synthesize GABA. Fermented foods such as sauerkraut, kimchi, plain kefir, and coconut water kefir can increase GABA levels.

4. **Promote healthy GABA production with probiotics.** Probiotics, especially *Lactobacillus rhamnosus*, has been shown to boost GABA. Other strains to consider include *Lactobacillus paracasei*, *Lactobacillus brevis*, and *Lactococcus lactis*.

5. **Try nutraceuticals.** Supplements such as GABA, lemon balm, l-theanine, magnesium, taurine, passionflower, and valerian have been shown to enhance GABA.

6. **Meditate.** Research suggests that meditation is linked to GABA production and enhances emotional regulation.[269]

7. **Practice your downward dog.** One study found a 27 percent increase in GABA levels among yoga practitioners after a 60-minute yoga session when compared with participants who read a book for 60 minutes.[270]

8. **Eliminate GABA robbers.** Caffeine, nicotine, alcohol, and chronic stress all deplete GABA. If you have the Cautious Brain Type, do your best to limit or avoid these.

TODAY'S PRACTICE: *If you often feel anxious or stressed or have racing thoughts, try 500 mg of GABA daily to see how you feel.*

Cortisol: The Molecule of Danger

Cortisol from stress can shrink your hippocampus and put fat around your belly. Known primarily as the stress hormone, cortisol is so much more. Made in the adrenal glands that sit on top of your kidneys, its release is controlled by the brain, especially the hypothalamus and pituitary gland, when you feel danger. Because most cells in the body have cortisol receptors, it affects many functions. Cortisol is involved in the fight-or-flight response to threat, helps control blood sugar levels, regulates metabolism, decreases inflammation, and helps us form new memories, especially about possible threats. It also helps balance blood pressure and salt and water ratios. Cortisol is a crucial hormone to protect overall health and well-being. It is generally higher in the morning and gradually decreases throughout the day.

Cortisol is also released during periods of stress. If stress is too high or lasts too long (think the COVID-19 pandemic), cortisol can damage the body. High levels of cortisol are associated with anxiety, depression, irritability, grief, headaches, memory loss (shrinks the hippocampus), weight gain (especially around the belly and face), thin and fragile skin that's slow to heal, type 2 diabetes, easy bruising, a heightened vulnerability to infections, acne, and for women, facial hair and irregular menstrual periods. Chronically low levels of cortisol are associated with fatigue, dizziness, weight loss, muscle weakness, areas of the skin that turn darker, low blood pressure, and an inability to manage stress. Balance is important.

In a study of 216 middle-aged men and women whose cortisol levels were measured eight times during the day, researchers found that lower cortisol levels were associated with happiness.[271] Stress, caffeine, nicotine, intense prolonged exercise, long commutes, sleep apnea and poor sleep quality, unsettling noises, and low zinc all raise cortisol. Sugar releases cortisol, so it helps you feel good in the moment, but in the long term it increases inflammation and damages your immune system.

TODAY'S PRACTICE: *List three situations in which your stress (and subsequent cortisol levels) tend to be high.*

13 Ways to Balance Cortisol

Furry friends can decrease cortisol and stress. Here are 13 simple, healthy ways to balance cortisol:

1. **Get your zzz's.** Aim for at least seven hours of quality sleep each night.
2. **Get moving.** Physical activity keeps cortisol in check. Just don't overdo it.
3. **Meditation** lowers stress and cortisol levels.
4. **Hypnosis** can lower cortisol levels and help anxiety, pain, and sleep.
5. **Tapping.** Emotional Freedom Technique (EFT), referred to as EFT tapping, is a natural treatment for anxiety that can lower cortisol. Read more about it at https://www.medicalnewstoday.com/articles/326434 or check out The Tapping Solution app in the App store.
6. **Laugh more.** A good chuckle can decrease the molecule of danger.
7. **Deep breathing.** Just a few deep belly breaths can almost instantly lower cortisol, along with heart rate and blood pressure, to help you relax.
8. **Turn on some relaxing tunes.** Soothing music can curb cortisol.
9. **Practice tai chi.** This slow-moving form of martial arts reduces mental and emotional stress and causes a dip in cortisol levels.
10. **Massage.** Getting a rubdown can do wonders for your neurochemicals of happiness, lowering cortisol while increasing dopamine and serotonin.
11. **Get a furry friend.** Having a dog, cat, or other pet that you can cuddle has been shown to ramp up bliss and minimize the molecule of danger.
12. **Consume** dark chocolate, pears, fiber, green and black tea, and water.
13. **Try targeted nutraceuticals.** Supplements such as ashwagandha, rhodiola, phosphatidylserine, l-theanine, and fish oil can be beneficial in lowering the stress hormone.

TODAY'S PRACTICE: *Spend three minutes petting a dog or cat.*

Why a New 12-Step Program Is Needed

The current popular 12-step program was developed almost 90 years ago. It helps many, many people, but has no neuroscience in any of it. I'm a fan of Alcoholic Anonymous (AA) and other 12-step programs. I've seen them change people's lives, including the lives of my own family members. I've referred patients to them for decades. Yet when AA was started in 1935, the founders did not have access to sophisticated neuroimaging techniques, and they never considered brain health as an integral part of treatment. Anonymous programs are powerful, time-tested, and have worked for millions of people around the world. Yet they clearly do not work for everyone. A study conducted by the Department of Veterans Affairs showed 43 percent of attendees were sober at 18 months.[272] One of the reasons for the lower efficacy is that this program and many other recovery programs include no steps to address the physical functioning of the brain, which is the missing link to breaking any addiction. With this in mind, let me offer 12 new steps to breaking addiction. I'll use all four circles (see day 20): biological (B), psychological (P), social (S), and spiritual (Sp).

Step 1: Know your goals. (B, P, S, Sp)

Step 2: Know when you have been taken hostage. (P, S)

Step 3: Make a decision to care for, balance, and repair your brain. (B)

Step 4. Reach for forgiveness for yourself and others. (B, P, S, Sp)

Step 5: Know your addiction brain type. (B)

Step 6: Use the neuroscience of craving control. (B, P)

Step 7: Drip dopamine, stop dumping it, to keep your pleasure centers healthy. (B)

Step 8: Eliminate the pushers and users who make you vulnerable. (S)

Step 9: Tame your Dragons from the Past and kill the ANTs. (P)

Step 10: Get help from those who have tamed their own addictions. (S)

Step 11: List the people you have hurt and make amends when possible. (S, Sp)

Step 12: Carry the message of brain health to others. (S, Sp)

TODAY'S PRACTICE: *List the people you know who have been in a 12-step program. Consider sending them this section of the book.*

Step 1: Know Your Goals

Begin with the end in mind. Most addiction recovery programs start with trouble, by knowing when you are powerless over a substance or behavior. I think we should start one step earlier by knowing exactly what you want in life. If you tell your brain what you want, it can help make it happen. In the addiction world, therapists will often ask clients if they have a *high bottom* (you learn quickly) or a *low bottom* (you have to lose everything before you get help).

When I was 16, I got drunk on a six-pack of Michelob and half a bottle of champagne. I was sick for three days and have had very little alcohol since then. I often wonder why other people think it's fun. For me, it wasn't, plus I acted like a fool, which was embarrassing. So I have a high bottom. Actor Chris Browning, star of *Bosch, Westworld,* and *Sons of Anarchy,* joined us in 2020 on our podcast, *The Brain Warrior's Way.* He told my wife, Tana, and me that he used heroin for six years. He went from having a beachfront home in Malibu to being homeless under the 405 Freeway and was arrested multiple times before he finally got sober. He has a low bottom.

Some people are more motivated to avoid pain (me), while others are motivated by pleasure (Chris). Which are you? Do you learn from mistakes early or late? No one starts out wanting to have a low bottom. But addiction makes it easy to lose sight of what's most important to you. In order for you to break free from the chains of addiction, you must know what you want in life.

What do you want in regards to relationships, work, money, and physical, emotional, and spiritual health? Write it down in the One Page Miracle exercise on day 185. Then ask yourself every day, *Is my behavior getting me what I want?* Does your behavior serve your goals or hurt them? Does it fit? If not, it's time to work a program.

TODAY'S PRACTICE: *Review your One Page Miracle and ask yourself if your behavior is getting you what you want.*

Step 2: Know When You Have Been Taken Hostage

You are an addict if you got into trouble and then you did it again and again. This step is similar to AA Step 1: Admit you are powerless.[273] Know when your life is unmanageable. Many people are in denial about their behavior and very slow to admit when they have a problem. I often tell my patients the answer is simple: You're an addict when your behavior (drinking, drugs, eating, shopping, gambling, sex, etc.) gets you into trouble with your relationships, health, work, money, or the law—and you do it again. You either don't learn that the behavior gets you into trouble or you cannot stop it.

Addiction may affect all aspects of life. Check any of the following symptoms to see if an addiction is hijacking you or a loved one.

Biological symptoms may include increased cravings for the behavior, feeling sick or hung over, using increasing amounts of a substance or behavior to get the same feeling, withdrawal symptoms, or an inability to quit.

Psychological symptoms may include minimizing the consequences of behavior, annoyance or irritation when others question you, feelings of guilt about the behavior, and feeling anxious when unable to engage in the behavior.

Social symptoms include negative changes in work or school performance, withdrawing from family and friends, neglecting responsibilities, becoming new friends with people who share the addiction, spending more time engaging in the behavior, and avoiding situations where you can't engage in the behavior.

Spiritual symptoms may include a broken moral compass; breaking rules at home, at school, or in the community; cheating; lying to family, friends, or significant others; hiding things; or breaking promises and making excuses.

As you look at these lists of symptoms, be honest with yourself about the changes in your behavior and life. Take a pen and circle the symptoms that sound like you. The more symptoms you circle, the more likely there is a problem. Unless you recognize and admit that you have a problem, you'll never be able to fix it.

TODAY'S PRACTICE: *Look at the biological, psychological, social, and spiritual symptoms of addictions to see if any apply to you or a loved one.*

Step 3: Make a Decision to Care for, Balance, and Repair Your Brain

Think brain first. The missing link in nearly all addiction treatment programs worldwide is that very few of them look at and assess brain function on a routine basis. Your brain is involved in everything you do and everything you are. When your brain works right, you work right, but when it is troubled for any reason, you are much more likely to have trouble in your life, especially with addictions. You can diligently work any 12-step program with energy, enthusiasm, and commitment, but if your brain is not working at an optimal level (and most addicted brains aren't), you will have a much harder time getting and staying sober, despite your best efforts.

When I first started looking at the brain in 1991, it revolutionized my thinking and clinical practice. At the time, I was the director of an in-patient substance abuse treatment program, and the SPECT scans of my addicted patients were terrible compared to my other patients with psychiatric issues, such as anxiety, depression, or ADD/ADHD. It was clear that drugs and alcohol damaged brains; and if they damaged brains, they were damaging lives. Over time, it also became clear that pornography, gambling addictions, and video game addictions also damaged brains.

To beat any addiction, it is critical to understand and optimize the brain. You must fall in love with it and work to balance and repair it, so it can control your thoughts, feelings, and behaviors. Eating right, exercising, avoiding anything that hurts your brain, and engaging in regular brain-healthy habits is critical to beating any addiction. However, at addiction support groups, you're likely to see people smoking, drinking coffee, and offering each other unhealthy snacks. I once helped a well-known addiction treatment center in Florida add brain SPECT imaging to their evaluation services. I was excited about the expansion of my work until I saw what they were feeding their clients for breakfast on the morning of my first lecture: doughnuts, pastries, fruit juices, and sugar cereals. Sugar is another addictive substance. If you want your brain to beat addictions, it is critical to get your brain right, including getting your food right.

TODAY'S PRACTICE: *In all you do today, think brain first. Is whatever you are doing good for your brain or bad for it?*

Step 4: Reach for Forgiveness for Yourself and Others

Forgiveness is the gift that keeps on giving. The easy answer for addictions is that people should just stop the difficult behavior. But it's more complicated than that. Our brain imaging work taught me that tough love works for people whose brains work right; but for people with troubled brains, tough love is not very effective.

A critical step in beating any addiction is self-love, self-care, and forgiveness of yourself and others. If you do not love yourself, you won't take proper care of your brain and will likely continue to hurt it. Forgiveness is the gift that keeps on giving; it is powerful medicine. Research has linked forgiveness to reduced anxiety, depression, and major psychiatric disorders—and with having fewer physical health symptoms and lower mortality rates.[274]

Tana tells a story about the time we were asked to develop a program for the Salvation Army's largest chemical addiction recovery program. On her first visit, she was filled with highly judgmental thoughts about the addicts in the program. She wanted to participate, but how could she help people who brought up feelings of fear and loathing inside her?

Growing up, Tana directly experienced the consequences that drugs can have on people's lives. Her uncle was murdered in a drug deal gone wrong. She hated drugs and had no tolerance for anyone who did them. When she told me she didn't think she could follow through with helping at the Salvation Army, that God had picked the wrong person this time, I smiled and said, "God picked the perfect person." In fact, working with that population gave Tana new empathy for their backgrounds, which were not that much different from her own. And she realized that for every person she helped, there would be one less scared child in the world. Forgiveness helped her and helped her help others in need.

TODAY'S PRACTICE: *Think back on some of your biggest mistakes, and do the REACH for forgiveness exercise from day 154.*

Step 5: Know Your Addiction Brain Type

All brains, especially addicted ones, are not the same. Taking a one-size-fits-all approach invites failure and frustration, especially with addictions. SPECT scans helped us discover different addiction brain types, which helped us create unique strategies for patients' problems and treatments. Here is a summary of the best treatments for the five major brain types (refer back to days 105–110 for descriptions of each type).

Brain Type 1: Balanced: Although healthy overall, people with this type who do not care about their brain, are bad to their brain, or put their brain at risk can increase their vulnerability to addiction.

Brain Type 2: Spontaneous: Lower activity in the prefrontal cortex (PFC). Smokers and heavy coffee drinkers tend to fall in this category, as they use these substances to turn their brains "on." Natural strategies to boost activity in the PFC and raise dopamine help this type quit or avoid addictions.

Brain Type 3: Persistent: The anterior cingulate gyrus (ACG) is overactive, usually due to low levels of serotonin, which causes problems shifting attention. They tend to gravitate toward alcohol, ecstasy, and marijuana to soothe ACG overactivity. Taking natural supplements to boost serotonin combined with psychotherapy and attendance at a support group helps this type overcome addiction and compulsive behaviors like gambling.

Brain Type 4: Sensitive: Sensitive types have increased activity in the brain's emotional centers and struggle with moods, pessimism, and negative thoughts. Some addictive substances, such as opiates and alcohol, can be appealing because they stimulate positive feelings or calm the brain. Mood-boosting strategies are likely to be the most helpful, including saffron, omega-3 fatty acids, and SAMe,[275] which is crucial for the production of several neurotransmitters. Acupuncture can also help this type.

Brain Type 5: Cautious: Since this type has excessive activity in the brain's anxiety centers and struggles with physical stress symptoms, such as headaches, they often turn to addictive substances as a way to unwind. So calming strategies are the most helpful, including diaphragmatic breathing, meditation, hypnosis, or taking GABA and magnesium.

TODAY'S PRACTICE: *Take our Brain Health Assessment to know your type:* *brainhealthassessment.com.*

Step 6: Use the Neuroscience of Craving Control

Even after decades of sobriety or steering clear of gambling, bulimia, video games, or porn, your brain is still vulnerable to cravings and those old patterns of behaviors. All of us are vulnerable to cravings, but when you also have an addiction, just seeing a cigarette, smelling cookies, or seeing an ad for a new video game will spark the emotional memory centers in your brain and trigger cravings to indulge in your old behavior. Molly had to have a surgical procedure. She was 32 years clean from a heroin addiction. When her doctor prescribed an opiate for post-surgical pain relief, just taking one fired up the old addicted pathway in her brain. Fortunately, Molly had anticipated this and given the bottle to her husband, putting him in charge of them to dispense as directed. After a couple of days, her pain was more bearable, and she switched to an over-the-counter pain reliever and the cravings subsided.

It is critical to learn how to keep cravings at bay. The following five strategies will help you get control of your cravings to avoid relapse.

1. **Keep blood sugar balanced.** Low blood sugar levels are associated with lower overall brain activity, more cravings, and bad decisions. Eat healthy food often to stay in control.

2. **Decrease the artificial sweeteners.** They can trigger cravings. Scientists found alcohol floods the bloodstream faster when it's mixed with beverages containing artificial sweeteners rather than sugar.[276]

3. **Manage stress.** Anything stressful can trigger certain hormones that activate cravings.

4. **Outsmart sneaky addiction triggers.** Know the people, places, and things that fuel your cravings so you can plan ahead for vulnerable times. For example, I take a healthy snack with me when I go to the movies so I'm not tempted by the popcorn and licorice.

5. **HALT cravings.** Do not let yourself get too *h*ungry (low blood sugar is trouble), *a*ngry (anger lowers prefrontal cortex function), *l*onely (being disconnected from others increases bad decisions), or *t*ired (a lack of sleep is associated with low prefrontal cortex function). All of these factors impair your ability to control cravings.

TODAY'S PRACTICE: *When are you most vulnerable to cravings? Which strategy would help you most?*

Step 7: Drip Dopamine, Stop Dumping It, to Keep Your Pleasure Centers Healthy

Dopamine is a feel-good chemical that we all crave. As you've read, whenever we do something enjoyable, it's like pressing a button in the brain to release a little bit of dopamine to make us feel pleasure. If we push the pleasure button too often or too strongly, we reduce dopamine's effectiveness and wear out our pleasure centers. Eventually, it takes more and more excitement and stimulation to feel anything at all. When you take drugs, the amount of dopamine released can be two to ten times more than what your brain produces for natural rewards—you are dumping dopamine. Playing video games, gambling, and viewing pornography can produce the same effect. So can certain foods, especially sugar. When we eat a bowl of fresh berries or hold our spouse's hand, our brains release small amounts of dopamine, which makes us feel good. I call that dripping dopamine because it won't drain the dopamine stores in our brain.

Some simple actions will help you protect your pleasure centers and keep them healthy. They involve dripping dopamine—releasing it in a constant stream of small amounts—versus dumping dopamine, where you release a large amount all at once. Keep your pleasure centers healthy by limiting low-value dopamine activities, such as caffeine, nicotine, excessive television, video games, undisciplined digital behavior, and scary movies. Limit activities that dump dopamine, including drug and alcohol use, porn, and sugar. Engage in high-value dopamine activities that drip dopamine (see day 292). Make time to laugh—humor enhances the pleasure centers without wearing them out. Connect meaningful activities and pleasure, such as volunteering for activities you love. One example: I love table tennis and enjoy keeping score for others during tournaments.

TODAY'S PRACTICE: *List three of your behaviors that tend to dump dopamine and avoid them today, then list three that drip dopamine and be sure to engage in them today.*

Step 8: Eliminate the Pushers and Users Who Make You Vulnerable

The fastest way to get healthy is to find the healthiest people you can stand and then spend as much time around them as possible. Cultivating bad habits—and good ones—is a team sport. You become like the people you spend time with. Pushers and users are people who encourage or are complicit with your negative behaviors. Addictions need lots of accomplices to start and sustain them. Friends, mentors, or coaches are people who support your positive behaviors. Ask for their help. Adding friends improves your chances for success up to 40 percent,[277] and this is especially true for drug addictions, weight loss, and fitness.

If you want to change your behavior, you need to stop seeing your pushers and users or somehow turn them into friends. Some pushers and users can become friends if you have crucial conversations with them. Explain what they can start doing, stop doing, and continue doing to help you. Some people don't even realize that they are influencing you to make poor choices and will want to help once they understand your goals to kick addiction.

Riz had no problem sticking with his new eating regimen until he went to dinner parties with friends and family. Then his loved ones would offer him all kinds of foods and alcoholic drinks that he used to love but no longer fit into his new brain-healthy lifestyle. Riz's friends and family would try to pressure and coax him into eating or drinking things he had given up.

"What's wrong with you?" they would ask. "You're not obese. Why aren't you having any rice? You've always loved rice." They made Riz feel like he was being rude if he didn't give in and take a helping . . . or two. Then he told them about being a brain warrior and how good he felt when he ate healthy foods. He spent more time around those who understood and supported him, and much less time around the others.

You will face many types of pushers who will attempt to derail your health efforts. Do not let other people make you fat, stupid, and unhappy!

TODAY'S PRACTICE: *Identify your five most powerful friends who will support your good behaviors and five pushers/users who make it more likely you will not succeed in improving your brain health.*

Step 9: Tame Your Dragons from the Past and Kill the ANTs

Stop believing every harmful thought you have. To get and stay free of addictions, you have to tame your dragons from the past (see days 259–276) and kill the ANTs you tell yourself (see days 116–117). Corinne, 52, had smoked since she was a teenager. By the time she came to see me, she had been smoking for almost 40 years, and she had the wrinkled skin and breathing problems to prove it. Her loved ones desperately wanted her to stop smoking. Corinne wanted to quit but didn't believe she could do it. "I can't stop," she told me in one of our first sessions.

Corinne had started smoking after her mother abandoned her to run off with a new boyfriend, leaving Corinne with an aunt to raise her. She felt so much anxiety that her aunt would also abandon her that she started smoking as a way to soothe herself. This developed into Anxious Dragons that continued to haunt her throughout her lifetime. To help her quit smoking, Corinne had to tame her Anxious Dragons and kill the ANTs that kept her addicted to cigarettes. We worked together on her anxiety, and we tackled her "I can't stop smoking" ANT using the five questions you learned about on day 117.

> ANT: "I can't stop smoking."
> Question #1: Is it true? Yes.
> Question #2: Is it absolutely true? Initially, she said yes, she knew she couldn't do it. Then she thought about it and said, "Of course, I can't know for sure, especially if I got the right help."
> Question #3: How do you feel when you have the thought? "I feel powerless, sad, weak-willed, stupid, out of control, like a bad influence on my children."
> Question #4: Who would you be without the thought? "Hopeful, optimistic, more likely to give it my best effort."

Turnaround: What is the opposite thought? Is it truer than the original thought? "I can stop smoking." She thought about this for a while and said that if she got help and really tried, it could be true. Then she felt a sense of control and committed to a program.

Corinne eventually did stop smoking and felt better than ever. Controlling her ANTs and Dragons from the Past were critical steps in the process.

TODAY'S PRACTICE: *Try this tactic that comes from one of my patients—fill a spray bottle with water, and every time an ANT pops into your head, spritz your face with water.*

Step 10: Get Help from Those Who Have Tamed Their Own Addictions

Success leaves clues. Get help from people who have tamed their own addictions. Addiction mentors and support groups are often critical pieces to the healing process. The people you meet at support groups have walked your path and may have strategies that can help you. Other people who have struggled with your issue can help you feel less lonely and give you an outlet to express your thoughts. Often, just hearing what you are thinking out loud, with the input of others, can help eliminate many of your ANTs. Research shows that support groups can decrease anxiety and depression. They can help you stay motivated to stick to a new way of living. They can give you hope. They are also an affordable and often free way of getting help.

Choose your helpers wisely. You become like the people you spend time with. Choose people who represent how you want to live, not those who increase your risk of relapse. Here are some tips to choosing mentors or support groups:

1. Pick people who've been successful at taming their addictions.
2. Pick people who will tell you the truth with kindness. Sugarcoating is not helpful (and you know what I think of sugar), but neither is being condescending or mean.
3. Don't be afraid of those who are younger than you.
4. Choose people who will challenge you.
5. Choose people with similar values.
6. Choose people who listen.
7. Choose people you are not afraid to call or text.
8. Once you choose someone, be open to their input but also evaluate it. Don't be so open-minded that your brain falls out of your skull. That is how cults start.
9. Meet mentors at in-person or online support groups, through mutual friends, church, or other organizations. Be kind to everyone you meet because you never know when a mentor will appear.

TODAY'S PRACTICE: *If you already have a mentor, reach out to them to touch base. If you don't have one, go through the above list and write down the names of three people you could ask to be a mentor.*

Step 11: List the People You Have Hurt and Make Amends When Possible

Making amends helps to repair relationships and can restore trust. This is a combination of AA steps that is essential to improve your relationships and attain a better sense of yourself, but let's do this step with a healthier brain. Admitting your wrongs, asking for forgiveness, and making amends if possible can help free you from the Should and Shaming Dragons and make it less likely you'll continue the behavior that is hurtful to others.

Remember Jose, the compulsive cheater I met on the *Dr. Phil* show (day 177)? Jose's SPECT scan showed two major problems: (1) Increased activity in the anterior cingulate gyrus, which is the brain's gear shifter, often associated with compulsive behavior; and (2) decreased activity in the prefrontal cortex, so he had poor impulse control. Jose wanted help, and he wanted to stop hurting the people he loved. Going on the show was his way of making amends and proving to his wife that he was serious about changing his behavior. After the show, Jose agreed to continue to see me for help. It was another way Jose showed his wife, Angie, that he wanted to make amends. He was in enough pain that he was willing to follow my recommendations.

Over the next seven months, I regularly saw Jose and Angie to monitor their progress. In our sessions, we discussed his nutrition, supplements, and strategies to control his urges, which were becoming less and less powerful. He stopped drinking alcohol and caffeine, cleaned up his diet and ate multiple times a day to keep his blood sugar stable, and took supplements to help with his impulsivity and compulsions. On a brain-healthy program, he was able to stay faithful to his wife, and months later his scan was better. He eventually went back to school and became a nurse anesthetist. Jose could have apologized hundreds of times, but taking action showed he was serious about making amends. Because we first fixed his brain, he was able to change his brain and change his behavior.

TODAY'S PRACTICE: *Whether or not you have an addiction, reach out to someone you may have hurt to make amends.*

Step 12: Carry the Message of Brain Health to Others

Get it, give it away, keep it forever. This last step is similar to the twelfth step of AA and other anonymous programs: Carry the message to others. If you want to keep your sobriety, you need to share the principles with others. It works for brain health too. Your brain is always listening to what you do, but it is also listening to the actions of others. Make sure you are sharing brain health, not illness, with those you love.

Get it, give it away, and keep it forever. This a mantra I learned after creating The Daniel Plan with my friends Pastor Rick Warren and Dr. Mark Hyman, a program to get the world healthy through churches and religious organizations. If you want to keep your health, you have to learn how to be healthy yourself and then give it away to others. It is in the act of giving that you create your own support group, making it more likely you will stick with a brain-healthy lifestyle.

Many people ask me what they can do if their children, families, or coworkers are not receptive to a new way of eating or behaving. My answer is always, "You have to live the message." You cannot give something away that you do not live. Don't let others ever be your excuse to hurt yourself.

If these 12 steps don't give you freedom from the Addicted Dragons, get a professional assessment and consider having someone look at your brain.

TODAY'S PRACTICE: *Share what you have learned about these 12 steps with someone you know who needs help.*

Wanting vs. Liking

You can want something you do not like. Imagine people in a casino at the slot machines putting in coins and pulling the levers repeatedly for hours. Most look tired and bored and barely smile when they win. This is an example of compulsive persistence with little joy. Their brains want to do what they are doing, but there is little evidence they actually like it. Wanting and liking are both important to happiness, but they are separate in the brain. This is why we can want something we do not like, such as a mother craving (wanting) drugs even though it puts her at risk for losing her children, or a man compulsively gambling even though it causes him to lose his home and family.

Wanting is "anticipatory desire," which means looking forward to getting a reward in the future, such as craving a brownie, a cigarette, or a trip to a casino. Wanting relies on dopamine, the chemical of possibility.

Liking is "consummatory pleasure," which means it involves a much smaller brain system and is more fragile. It uses serotonin and endorphins to signal pleasure of what you are doing in the moment. Addictive substances create pleasure in the moment and appropriate the wanting circuitry, so if you are not careful, they can literally hijack your brain and life.

The major difference between wanting and liking has to do with how our brains operate: consciously or unconsciously. Nobel prize–winning psychologist Daniel Kahneman has divided the information processing into two systems: System 1, unconscious or automatic, and System 2, conscious.[278] Liking is conscious, meaning you are aware of it. Wanting is often unconscious, meaning your desires occur automatically and often without you noticing them. System 1 is where most of the work of our mind gets done: automatic skills, intuition, and dreaming are examples of unconscious processing. As much as 95 percent of cognitive activities happen in the unconscious mind.

TODAY'S PRACTICE: *List three things you want but do not like and try to avoid them today.*

Commit to a Lifetime of Brain Fitness

If you want a younger-looking brain, make lifelong learning a priority. At birth, the brain is only about 25 percent of its adult size, but it already has nearly all the neurons it will ever have. Doubling in volume in the first year, the brain will reach 90 percent of its adult size by age 5. After this, the primary way your brain "grows" is by establishing more connections between brain cells. As you learn new things, you increase and expand the connectivity within the brain. The more connections you develop over time, the more fortified your brain can become as you age. Research shows that this process can continue throughout your lifetime if your brain is healthy. Therefore, I cannot overstate how important it is to stay mentally active.

Think of your brain as a muscle—it needs to work out regularly to stay strong. Some strategies are as close as your local newspaper—word searches, crossword puzzles, and Sudoku—all of which activate your memory and other cognitive functions. Jigsaw puzzles and reading also work your brain, as do games like Scrabble, chess, backgammon, and trivia contests. Online brain training games are another fun way to build your brain power.

One of my favorite strategies to strengthen the brain is to learn new things. There are many rewarding ways you can do this. Take a class in something that interests you or get involved in a new hobby. Learn to speak another language or to read music and play a musical instrument. If you already play one, learn a new instrument.

Boost your memory by using mnemonics, which is a memory device that uses mental images, words, or sounds to help you retain or remember information. Memorize the alphabet backward or how to count to 10 in another language. Commit to learning the definitions of a few words each week and use them when you are conversing with other people.

Make the effort to step outside of your comfort zone and challenge your brain regularly so you can keep it strong.

TODAY'S PRACTICE: *Choose a new way to exercise your brain today.*

Eliminating the Bad Habits That Ruin Your Life, Part 1

Virtually everything you do is based on a series of habits developed over your lifetime. Your daily habits include hundreds of routines, such as saying no to bread, telling your spouse you love her at the end of phone calls, brushing your teeth, flossing, shaving, blow drying your hair (not mine), showering, putting away the dishes, doing the laundry a certain way. Habits are behaviors that have been automated, so you barely need to think about them. There is a constant dance between your prefrontal cortex (PFC), amygdala (the part of your emotional brain that responds to threats), and your basal ganglia (where habits are shaped and stored). When the PFC is healthy and strong, it can help direct and supervise the addition of healthy habits. When it is weak, your impulses can take over, causing many bad habits to form. Once formed, good or bad habits take the same amount of energy to maintain.

Some of your habits move your life forward in ways that make you proud; while other habits lead to trouble in relationships, work, and finances. Wasting time, allowing distractions, interrupting, arguing, and being disorganized or oblivious are habits that hurt you. Taking your words and actions off autopilot and using your PFC to direct them in a purposeful way will increase your happiness, improve your relationships, and lead to success. For example, whenever I go to a restaurant and the waiter asks if I want an alcoholic drink and leaves bread on the table, I am not oblivious to how my response will impact my health. I say no to the alcohol and ask him to take away the bread. My automatic responses are habits; they are stored in a part of the brain called the basal ganglia. Habits develop over time to either get and stay healthy or get and stay sick. I often say to my patients and myself, "Make one decision, not 30." If I make the one decision not to keep the bread on the table, I will not glance at it 30 times and have to make 30 decisions not to eat it.

TODAY'S PRACTICE: *What are two or three habits you would like to change?*

Eliminating the Bad Habits That Ruin Your Life, Part 2

Neurons that fire together, wire together. Habits and responses become an ingrained part of your life. Starting something new, whether it's good or bad for you, causes networks of brain cells to make new connections. Early in the learning process, the connections are weak (I had to really think about saying no to bread), but over time, as you repeat behaviors, the networks become stronger, making the behaviors more likely to become automatic, reflexive, or habitual. There are thousands of bad habits. Here are four steps to convert bad habits into good ones:

1. **Identify the bad habit and start tracking it.** Establish a baseline of how often it occurs. Work on only one bad habit at a time.
2. **Identify the cues or triggers.** When you notice an urge to do something, ask yourself questions such as, What is the time of day (Time)? Where are you (Location)? Who are you with (People)? How are you feeling (Mood)? What is happening (Action)? Answering these five questions will help you know the cues or triggers to the behavior.
3. **What are the rewards or benefits of the behavior?** Know what you are seeking. Is it pleasure, energy, excitement, happiness, relief, relaxation, acceptance, love, or something else?
4. **Build a new routine.** Now that you know the cues and rewards, build a new routine(s) to get what you want. Look back at your One Page Miracle. Focus on the rewards you will get without that bad habit.

For illustration, over the next several days, we will explore common bad habits that steal your happiness and brain health.

TODAY'S PRACTICE: *What are your most common triggers to your most irritating bad habit?*

The Bad Habit of Yes, Yes, Yes

Repeat, "I have to think about it." When someone asks you to do something, do you reflexively say yes, without thinking through all the consequences, and end up so busy you don't have time for family and other priorities? I once treated Carter, an attorney who told me he didn't have time to work out or eat healthy because he was so busy. When we went through his week, it was clear he had committed himself to many activities that served other people's needs but few of his own. I taught him the magic phrase "I have to think about it." I had him practice saying it in the mirror every morning. Then he was to filter every request through this question: Does this fit the goals I have for my life? He needed to decide if it fit his relational goals, work goals, financial goals, or goals for his physical, emotional, or spiritual health. If it didn't, he would politely decline. Over three months, this simple exercise changed his life. He had more time for his wife, children, sleep, and even pro bono work, which was one of his goals. The hallmark of a leader is someone who can say no to things that do not fit their goals.

ELIMINATE THE BAD HABIT OF YES, YES, YES

1. **Do you have this habit?** If you often feel overwhelmed, tired, or have no time for yourself, this bad habit is likely haunting you. Track it.
2. **What are the cues or triggers?** People-pleasing, impulsively responding, avoiding feelings of guilt.
3. **What are the rewards you get?** *Initial:* significance, being the good guy or gal, points in heaven. *Rewards without this behavior:* time for things that matter more.
4. **Build a new routine.** Whenever someone asks you to do something, start by saying, "I have to think about it." Then filter your response through the goals you have. If it doesn't fit, politely decline but be firm by saying something like, "I'm not going to be able to fit that into my schedule." Post "I have to think about it" in at least three places you see daily.

TODAY'S PRACTICE: *When someone asks you to do something today, say, "I have to think about it," to create a new habit. Then filter their request through your goals.*

The Bad Habit of No, No, No

The opposite of the last bad habit is being stuck in the terrible twos. It is normal for 2-year-old children to assert their independence and automatically say no. Children usually outgrow the automatic no between the ages of 3 to 4. It's cute when they're 2 but really irritating when they're 6, 16, 46, or 86. Many years ago, I noticed that people who tended to be argumentative or oppositional (automatically say no) had increased activity in the anterior cingulate gyrus (ACG). My dad had this bad habit and excessive activity in his ACG. Whenever I'd ask him for something, such as to borrow the car, the answer was automatically no. The No, No, No bad habit stresses relationships.

CONTROL THE NO, NO, NO BAD HABIT

1. **Do you have it?** If your first response is no or you start formulating an argument before a person has finished their thought, you likely have this bad habit. Notice it and start tracking it.
2. **What are the cues or triggers?** Whenever someone asks you for something or to do something.
3. **What are the rewards you get?** *Initial:* being right, staying in control, having sovereignty over your time and decisions. *Rewards without this behavior:* better relationships.
4. **Build a new routine.** Before answering questions or responding to requests in a negative way, catch yourself, take a breath, and think first if it's best to say no. Often it's helpful to take a deep breath just to get extra time before responding. For example, if your spouse asks you to do something, before you say no, take a deep breath and ask yourself if saying no is really in everyone's best interest, if it fits the goals you have for the relationship. In fact, you can use the same line that I gave for the last bad habit: "I have to think about it." The automatic no has ruined many relationships. Take enough time to ask yourself if saying no is really what you want to say.

TODAY'S PRACTICE: *With whom and for what do you have a tendency to say no without thinking? Next time, pause before you respond.*

The Bad Habit of Interrupting

Interrupting kills communication. Political pundits do it. Supervisors do it. Many parents do it. People with this bad habit tend to dominate conversations. Children and employees often shut down when their parents or supervisor suffers from this bad habit.

CONTROL THE BAD HABIT OF INTERRUPTING

1. **Do you have it?** Has anyone told you that you interrupt too much? Do people tend to shut down around you?
2. **What are the cues or triggers?** Conversations with people close to you, such as coworkers and friends; when you are intoxicated (stop drinking), hungry, tired, angry, in an argument, or overwhelmed by your partner's words.
3. **What are the rewards you get?** *Initial:* venting or blowing off steam, relieving stress, getting your point across, expressing the need to be right. *Rewards without this behavior:* more connection, more input, better relationships.
4. **Build a new routine.** The antidote to the bad habit of interrupting is active listening. It is simple and goes like this: (1) Listen and do not interrupt, no matter how much you get the urge. (2) Repeat back what you hear: "I hear you saying . . ." (3) Listen for the feelings behind what you're hearing: "Sounds like you are feeling frustrated." (4) Listen to their response carefully and reflect it back again. Active listening forces you to pay attention and stops you from thinking about what you're going to say next so you can hear the other person. The reward is increased communication, and it cools down conflicts. When people feel heard, they can often solve their own problems.

TODAY'S PRACTICE: *In your most stressful discussion today, use active listening and see how it goes.*

Trouble with the Truth Bad Habit

Lying leads to mistrust in your relationships, and if you can lie to others, you also lie to yourself. Lying is a common bad habit. In fact, according to one study most people lie once or twice a day.[279] People lie for many different reasons, including to avoid being punished, to protect oneself, to avoid disappointing others, to obtain a reward they did not earn, to promote oneself, or to get out of an uncomfortable social situation. Lying can even ruin your health. One study found that 81 percent of patients lie to their doctors.[280] It's nearly impossible for you to get the help you need if you're not honest with your caregivers.

There is a difference between "normal" liars—those of us who tell harmless little white lies—and pathological liars. Normal liars give compliments that are not 100 percent genuine; tell people they're doing well, when they really aren't; and say they are busy to avoid others. For pathological liars lying is habitual, even when there is no clear benefit. They lie to make themselves look like the hero or victim, and the stories they tell are dramatic, complicated, and detailed. I'd be lying if I said lying was an easy habit to break.

CONTROL THE BAD HABIT OF LYING

1. **Do you have it?** Track how many times you lied today and in a typical week.
2. **What are the cues or triggers?** When you feel trapped, when you don't want to hurt someone's feelings, or when you hate the truth.
3. **What are the rewards you get?** *Initial:* Avoiding embarrassment or disappointment, exercising power or control. *Rewards without this behavior:* Feeling better about yourself, remembering facts more clearly, less stress.
4. **Build a new routine.** See lying as a problem, not an indictment of your character. First, immediately stop lying to your health-care professionals. I often tell my patients their number one job in healing is to tell me the truth; otherwise, we are wasting everyone's time and their money. When you catch yourself starting to lie, take a breath, pause, and say, "I meant . . ." followed by the truth.

TODAY'S PRACTICE: *If you catch yourself telling any lies today, write them down, along with what triggered them.*

Truth Training: When Children Lie

Lying is a problem to solve rather than a character issue. As a child psychiatrist, I've been teaching parent training for many years. One of the first steps in the program is to have parents post a few rules. The number one rule is be honest. Telling the truth is one of the most important lessons you can teach a child. Honesty in relationships creates a sense of trust. Perhaps even more profound is that by speaking honestly, children are more likely to learn how to think honestly and rationally about themselves. So when they tell a lie to get out of trouble, they get one consequence for the wrong act and another one for lying. The rule is very clear: Be honest! This includes little lies and big ones. I've found that when you allow a child to get away with the little lies, the bigger ones are easier to say. Be aware that the "Be honest" rule applies to you, too. Kids learn by example, so you need to be a good role model in this regard. If someone comes to the door when you do not want to talk, do not ask your child to say you aren't home. That sends the message that lying is okay.

When lying is a problem, I teach parents an exercise called Truth Training. You identify that lying is a problem to be solved rather than an indictment on the child's character. When I told my mother a lie at age 6, she cried and told me she never thought she would have a child who would go to hell. Don't do that. Tell the child why lying is a problem—people will not trust them. Then tell them you are going to ask them questions you already know the answer to. If they answer honestly you will be very happy and give them a small reward, such as extra time together, and if they lie, there will be a consequence, such as extra chores. Do it in a matter-of-fact way, without emotion, and always root for them to tell the truth.

TODAY'S PRACTICE: *Practice truth training with any young ones who may have this bad habit.*

The Bad Habits of Being Distracted, Being Obsessive, or Multitasking

Smartphones, laptops, tablets, email, text messages, the internet, and streaming services are stealing our time and attention. Many people are not only watching TV, but they are also on other devices at the same time. Technology companies are constantly creating addictive gadgets that hook our attention and distract us from meaningful relationships. Many people are on their phones at mealtimes, rather than interacting with family members. Teens spend more time on social media (an average of nine hours) than they do asleep.[281] Technology has hijacked developing brains, with potentially serious consequences. They have been called "the cigarettes of this century" with equally addictive and potentially destructive side effects.

According to an article in the *Harvard Business Review*, "Beware the Busy Manager," our unhealthy lifestyles are diminishing our capacity at work.[282] In a ten-year study, only 10 percent of managers were high in both focus and energy, two of the main ingredients for success. The authors found that 20 percent were disengaged, 30 percent were high in procrastination, and 40 percent were easily distracted. This means that 90 percent of managers, and likely the rest of us, lack focus and/or energy.

CONTROL THE BAD HABITS OF BEING DISTRACTED, BEING OBSESSIVE, OR MULTITASKING

1. **Do you have it?** Track how many times an hour you are distracted.
2. **What are the cues or triggers?** Being bombarded by phone calls, emails, texts, etc.
3. **What are the rewards you get?** *Initial:* Satisfy an addiction of having to know what's next, escape so you don't have to face problems. *Rewards without this behavior:* More time, less stress, better focus.
4. **Build a new routine.** When you need to get things done, shut shown your email and put your phone on airplane mode. Your productivity will go way up. Try a digital detox app or use "do not disturb" functions to help stop your phone from distracting you.

TODAY'S PRACTICE: *Do a digital detox today for 20 focused minutes and see how you feel.*

The Bad Habit of Procrastination

Procrastination is the act of unnecessarily postponing decisions or actions. When you wait until the very last minute to get things done (schoolwork, paperwork, chores, bill paying, gift buying, etc.), it increases stress and often irritates those around you. If it isn't the last minute, this bad habit cannot kick its brain into gear to get work done. Many adults have told me that they never did term papers in school or they used amphetamines the night before a due date to get it done. Procrastination leads to poorly done or incomplete work. Procrastination is a hallmark of ADD/ADHD, where your prefrontal cortex is not as strong as it could be. Procrastination is also associated with abstract goals, depression, perfectionism, never feeling as though you can get something just right, fear of failure, and low energy.

CONTROL THE BAD HABIT OF PROCRASTINATION

1. **Do you have it?** Track how many times today you procrastinated or said, "I'll do it tomorrow."
2. **What are the cues or triggers?** You are faced with a task or a decision, but you would rather do something else or the timeline is not immediate.
3. **What are the rewards you get?** *Initial:* Don't have to expend the energy and effort, can stay in the present moment, value immediate rewards more highly than future rewards. *Rewards without this behavior:* Get more done with less stress and do a better job.
4. **Build a new routine.** Don't see procrastination as a character problem, but rather as a problem to solve. The secret to stop procrastinating is to have a method to get things done. I use one that is just a few simple steps:

   • Know what you want.
   • Have a one-minute huddle with yourself at the beginning of every day and write down three things you want to accomplish that day. Start with the most important one.
   • Bundle things you love to do with things you tend to procrastinate about— for example, listen to podcasts or audiobooks while exercising.
   • Give yourself a reward—tell yourself that after you finish a difficult task, you'll reward yourself with something special you want, such as a warm bath or cup of hot tea.

TODAY'S PRACTICE: *Do a daily huddle to plan your day.*

The Bad Habit of Disorganization

Nothing is more frustrating than to be waiting on someone who is poorly organized.
Many people struggle with organization, both of their time and space. They tend
to be late and have trouble completing tasks on time. They also tend to struggle
with keeping their spaces tidy, especially their rooms, book bags, drawers, closets,
and paperwork. Nothing is more frustrating to a boss, coworker, or family members than to be waiting on someone who is poorly organized, unprepared for their
daily tasks, or late. Being disorganized and chronically late is also a hallmark sign of
ADD/ADHD. When there is low prefrontal cortex activity, it is harder to be organized and on time.

CONTROL THE BAD HABIT OF DISORGANIZATION

1. **Do you have it?** How is your room, desk, purse, closets, drawers? How is your
   timeliness? What would your partner or parents say about your organization?
2. **What are the cues or triggers?** Being in a hurry; not devoting time to organize
   your day, tasks, or space; overloaded schedule; high stress; too many distractions.
3. **What are the rewards you get?** *Initial:* You believe it saves you time. *Rewards
   without this behavior:* You will save much more time in the long run by being
   more efficient.
4. **Build a new routine.** Schedule similar tasks together, such as errands, appointments, maintenance or phone calls. Spend your time doing things that are consistent with your goals. Keep a to-do list of the important tasks you need to get
   done today, this week, and in the near future. Update this list weekly. Relying
   on this list is more accurate than relying on your memory. If possible, schedule
   your most important activities for the hours when you are at your peak. Make
   a list of what not to spend your time doing and keep it in sight as a handy reminder. Cut unwanted calls or texts short. I often start conversations by saying
   something like, "I only have a minute . . ." End calls that are taking too much
   time by saying something like, "I need to go or I have an appointment" (even if
   the appointment is only with yourself).

TODAY'S PRACTICE: *Make a to-do list of your most important tasks today and do the
first thing.*

The Bad Habit of Creating Problems

Do you tend to create problems? Do you know people who are constantly stirring up trouble? I call this automatic tendency the "Let's Have a Problem" Bad Habit. I first noticed it in my ADD/ADHD patients and in my hyperactive daughter, who used to run up to her brother, kick him, and run away laughing. If he didn't chase her, she would kick him again. Without enough stimulation to the prefrontal cortex, which is common in my ADD/ADHD patients, the brain looks for ways to increase its own activity. Being mad, upset, angry, or negative acts as a stimulant that increases the fight-or-flight neurotransmitter adrenaline, which increases your heart rate, blood pressure, and muscle tension, like a cup of coffee or a hit of cocaine.

CONTROL THE BAD HABIT OF CREATING PROBLEMS

1. **Do you have it?** Do you tend to look for the negative or stir up trouble for no particular reason?
2. **What are the cues or triggers?** Waking up. Being around others. Feeling bored.
3. **What are the rewards you get?** *Initial:* Get a dopamine jolt. *Rewards without this behavior:* Less stress, better relationships.
4. **Build a new routine.** Before you say anything negative, ask yourself if the negativity serves your relationships or your own mental health. *Does it fit the goals I have for my life or this relationship?* The three powerful words *Does it fit?* will help break the pattern of negativity or conflict-seeking behavior.

TODAY'S PRACTICE: *If you feel the urge to stir things up today by saying something you know will cause a negative reaction, pause for a few seconds and ask yourself,* Does it fit?

The Bad Habit of Overeating

Don't be a victim of the Standard American Diet (SAD). Nearly everywhere you go (schools, work, shopping malls, movie theaters, airports, ballparks, etc.) someone is trying to sell you food that will kill you early. The SAD is filled with pro-inflammatory foods that increase your risk for diabetes, hypertension, heart disease, cancer, ADD/ADHD, depression, dementia, and obesity, which is now a serious national crisis, with 73 percent of Americans overweight and 42 percent obese.[283] Many published studies, including three of my own, report that as your weight goes up, the size and function of your brain goes down. Don't let this bad habit hijack your brain.

CONTROL THE BAD HABIT OF OVEREATING

1. **Do you have it?** If you are overweight, obese, or have little control over your eating behavior, admit it.
2. **What are the cues or triggers?** Notice what is happening around you—for some strange reason, whenever I pass a Jack-in-the-Box my brain wants an iced tea and a chicken fajita sandwich, which is not the worst thing in the world, but is certainly not the best.
3. **What are the rewards you get?** *Initial:* Satisfy cravings, enjoy the designer foods to get an explosion of flavor. *Rewards without this behavior:* You'll be leaner, smarter, happier, and healthier—and have a longer life.
4. **Build a new routine.** Your brain already has a food routine. Is it serving you or hurting you? If it is not serving you, create a new one. Here's mine: Breakfast—either eggs and organic blueberries or a healthy shake around 10 a.m. (I do 12–16 hours of intermittent fasting most days). Snack—fresh cut veggies with mashed avocados or an apple and almonds. Lunch—salad with grilled veggies and a protein, such as chicken or lamb. Afternoon snack—nuts and fruit. Dinner—protein and veggies. Dessert—brain-healthy hot chocolate, sugar-free dark chocolate, or fruit.

TODAY'S PRACTICE: *Write down any possible unhealthy food cues you will encounter today and how you will avoid overeating those trigger foods.*

The Bad Habit of Being Oblivious

Pay attention to your life if you want to love it. Being oblivious to your health (over-eating, never reading food labels, putting toxic products on your body, never thinking about the health of your brain and body) is likely the worst of all the bad habits. It is where you just don't think about the consequences of your behavior before you engage in it. This is what happens when you let your brain run on autopilot. This bad habit is killing us as a society—rates of hypertension, diabesity, depression, and obesity are skyrocketing. Seventy-five percent of health-care dollars in the United States are spent on chronic, preventable illnesses.[284]

CONTROL THE BAD HABIT OF BEING OBLIVIOUS

1. **Do you have it?** You have it if you do not have a sense of your calorie intake each day; if you do not read food labels; if you do not read personal or cleaning product labels; if you do not know the water quality in your neighborhood.
2. **What are the cues or triggers?** Almost any decision in your day.
3. **What are the rewards you get?** *Initial:* Being oblivious is easy and doesn't require any thinking. *Rewards without this behavior:* Health, energy, longevity.
4. **Build a new routine.** Before you buy anything, do anything, or say anything, ask yourself, *Is this good for my brain or bad for it?* Repeat it over and over until this question becomes a habit. Start getting serious about being well and learn what's good for you and your brain.

TODAY'S PRACTICE: *Write down the pros and cons of the decisions you make today.*

Outfox the Scheming Dragons

We live in a bizarre time. Nearly everywhere you go, you are being pounded by the wrong messages that will make you fat, depressed, and foggy-minded. For the next few days, we will look at 10 common Scheming Dragons that are attempting to hook you into habits and addictions that will make them rich while doing you harm. Scheming Dragons are everywhere, trying to make money off of your impulses, even if it makes you anxious, depressed, angry, forgetful, or at risk to die early. They use sophisticated neuroscience to hook you on whatever they're selling. They capitalize on the latest research on habits and addiction to make your brain crave their products and services and to automate their use so you don't even think about what you're doing. You mindlessly munch Hot Cheetos, don't notice you've spent hours scrolling through social media, and are shocked when you get your credit card bill.

I was once driving when I saw a billboard for a huge "Tower of Torta" sandwich, and then, no lie, as I turned my head to the other side of the freeway, I saw a billboard for Losing Weight with Lap Band. The message: Indulge yourself with high-calorie, low-quality food, then take care of your obesity with surgery. Pretty crazy.

Marketers use a four-step process to hook your brain: (1) A trigger kickstarts the process, such as a pop-up ad, email alert, or TV commercial. (2) You take action because you expect a reward—a tasty treat, a fun game, or a new outfit. (3) The reward isn't always the same; unpredictable rewards boost dopamine, the chemical of feeling good and addiction. (4) You engage with the product or service to make it easier to use, such as adding Hot Cheetos to auto-ship. But you can unhook your brain from these Scheming Dragons.

You can fight back against the Scheming Dragons with these five simple steps:

1. Recognize them.
2. Look past the marketing messages to see the motivation behind them.
3. Get the whole picture before you act.
4. Don't make it easier for the Scheming Dragons to hook you.
5. Limit your exposure to Scheming Dragons.

TODAY'S PRACTICE: *Pay attention to at least two ads today to see if they serve your health or they make money off of your early death.*

Food Pusher Dragons

Food Pusher Dragons are trying to sell you food that will kill you early. These dragons try to get you hooked on foods that are highly processed, pro-inflammatory, pesticide sprayed, artificially colored and sweetened, high glycemic, low in fiber, laden with hormones, and tainted with antibiotics. Food manufacturing corporations don't try to hide that they purposely make their junk foods addictive. Remember Lay's Potato Chips? "Bet you can't eat just one!" These junk food giants rely on food scientists to expertly engineer snack items with just the right amounts of fat, sugar, salt, and other ingredients to create the perfect combination of flavors, texture, crunchiness, meltiness, and aroma to overwhelm the brain and trigger the "bliss point." It's akin to taking a hit of cocaine, which activates the brain's reward system and makes you want more, more, more!

Huge corporations are also targeting your children and grandchildren. The toys fast-food companies use to entice children are highly effective in hooking their developing brains to want more of what will hurt their health. Plus, food companies purposefully connect gorgeous, scantily clad women to poor-quality food to hook your pleasure centers, somehow making the illogical connection that if you eat those foods, these women will want you or you will look like them. You also need to watch out for the do-gooders that are killing you, such as the receptionist who puts a bowl of candy on her desk, the school bake sales, and the doughnuts at church services. Additionally, well-meaning organizations, such as the Girl Scouts, enlist young girls to sell unhealthy cookies as a way to fund their activities.

OUTFOX THE FOOD PUSHER DRAGONS

1. Recognize them. Who is trying to get you to buy their products?
2. Look past the messenger to know their motivation. It's all about money.
3. Get the whole picture before acting; read food labels.
4. Don't sign up to receive notifications about deals and specials.
5. Limit exposure to marketing ploys. Avoid the aisles in the middle of the store and stick to the outside aisles.

TODAY'S PRACTICE: *List two or three food pushers in your life.*

Unhealthy "Health" Dragons

"I just kept hearing Dr. Amen in the back of my mind." The Unhealthy "Health" Dragons play on your desire to get well by offering easy, but harmful, ways to do it. They're the ones promising shortcuts—rapid weight loss from fad diets, quick-fix fitness solutions, and "health" foods that are actually just junk food in disguise. For example, certain fad diets might help you lose a few pounds in the short run, but they don't teach you how to eat for long-term brain and body health. Some hard-core fitness trends and gadgets actually put you at increased risk of injury.

And then there are all those so-called health foods. Walk down the aisles of the grocery store and you'll see products labeled with "gluten-free," "low-carb," "sugar-free," "vegan," "all natural," or some other trendy buzzword. If you're health-conscious, you may be trying to avoid gluten, refined carbs, and added sugars, so these products seem like good choices. But the Unhealthy "Health" Dragons hope you won't take the time to read the nutrition label and realize that their products are actually filled with ingredients that hurt you. Sugar-free? That may be schemer talk for "full of artificial sweeteners." Vegan? That can be the schemer's way of saying "highly processed, non-food substance." And gluten-free? That's the schemer's attempt to convince you that cake mix with artificial preservatives, food coloring, and pro-inflammatory ingredients is healthy. It isn't.

I remember a patient telling me, "I visited Costco for the first time ever this weekend. There was death everywhere, every corner. Samples of death covered in death. I just kept hearing Dr. Amen in the back of my mind. So I walked past it all! Got my organic goods and left, which is saying a lot because it was nearly lunch time and it all smelled so good! Thank you for giving me the tools to make good choices."

OUTFOX THE UNHEALTHY "HEALTH" DRAGONS

1. Watch for quick-fix solutions for complex problems. Examine claims such as "gluten-free," "low carb," "all natural," etc.
2. Don't fall for the idea that someone's product will make you look like the person in the ad.
3. Get the whole picture before acting. Read labels.
4. Don't sign up for ongoing emails.
5. Once you identify these schemers, avoid them.

TODAY'S PRACTICE: *At the grocery store, read the labels of three so-called health foods to see what's really in them.*

Substance Pusher Dragons

Quick fixes can cause long-term problems. Scheming Dragons also try to push prescription drugs. Think of all those TV commercials you see for medications to treat all sorts of conditions. The pharmaceutical industry is one of the biggest spenders when it comes to advertising. Their ads play on your emotions by depicting how their little pill can help someone with a debilitating condition quickly transform into a joyful person—dancing with a loved one or cuddling with a grandchild. They make it seem as if taking a pill is all you have to do. And while these heartwarming images roll, you hear a rapid-fire rundown of the nasty potential side effects—diarrhea, constipation, headache, blurry vision, suicidal thoughts. And, oh yeah, death. But these schemers know that almost a third of the human brain is dedicated to vision, so it's the images of the happy people in the commercial that stick in our brains, not the list of side effects we hear.

Substance Pusher Dragons also try to hook you into buying alcohol by spinning science to make it seem like it's a health food. In fact, a 2018 report found that one of the biggest ongoing studies on the effects of moderate drinking as part of a healthy diet was largely funded by—you guessed it—the alcohol industry.[285] When it comes to the brain, alcohol is not the health food the alcohol industry would like you to believe. All forms of liquor can impair your cognitive function. Some of the slickest Scheming Dragons of all time can be found in the nicotine and tobacco industry. Their advertising messages were so effective that Congress banned airing cigarette ads on TV and radio in 1970. Now, some 50 years later, the Scheming Dragons of the nicotine business are back at it by marketing vaping as a "healthy" alternative to smoking. It's not.

OUTFOX THE SUBSTANCE PUSHER DRAGONS

1. Recognize when they are making something seem healthy when you know it probably isn't.
2. Know who is really behind the information you're getting. Is it the pharmaceutical or alcohol industry?
3. Do your own research.
4. Don't start taking or using anything that may be hard to stop.
5. Turn off ads to limit your exposure.

TODAY'S PRACTICE: *Take note of any Substance Pusher Dragons you see today, whether it's online, in a commercial, or in the media.*

Toxin Pusher Dragons

The fear of COVID-19 caused many people to put toxic disinfectants on their skin over and over. If I told you a product could cause fatigue, depression, brain fog, ADD/ADHD, or psychotic behavior, would you use it? Of course not! But Toxin Pusher Dragons are constantly selling products filled with chemicals that poison the human brain and can cause those issues and many more. Toxin Pusher Dragons are in your grocery store where you least expect them: in the produce section. Mixed in with the good-for-you organic produce are bright shiny apples, big strawberries, and even dark green kale that have some of the highest pesticide levels. Head to the fish counter and you'll find the schemers selling fish pumped full of artificial dyes that have high levels of mercury. Toxin Pusher Dragons also rule the household cleaner space. Regular household cleaners are chock-full of potentially harmful chemicals. Some of the biggest Toxin Pusher Dragons are the ones who promise to make you look more attractive. It is estimated that the cosmetics, perfume, and beauty care industry spent over $3.7 billion on advertising in 2020 to entice us to spray, squirt, and smudge more of their products on our faces, hair, and bodies.[286] But the chemicals in many of these products that claim to make us more beautiful can do something very ugly to our bodies and brains.

OUTFOX THE TOXIN PUSHER DRAGONS

1. Understand that most regular household cleaners and personal care products contain some toxins.
2. Don't let the beautiful people in cosmetics ads fool you.
3. Read labels. Visit the Environmental Working Group for healthy cleaning products (ewg.org/guides/cleaners), clean foods (ewg.org/foodscores), the Dirty Dozen list of produce with the highest levels of pesticides (ewg.org/foodnews/dirty-dozen.php), and for safer personal care products (ewg.org/skindeep). Check seafoodwatch.org for good fish choices.
4. Don't sign up for coupons or free product offers for products that contain toxins.
5. Stick to safe, clean products.

TODAY'S PRACTICE: *Look around and list two or three toxic products in your own cabinets.*

Digital Dragons

As video game and technology usage goes up, so does tech addiction, "gaming disorders," anxiety and mood disorders, insomnia, impulsivity, forgetfulness, and relationship woes. The Digital Dragons are winning the war for your attention by using a laundry list of proven marketing strategies—scarcity (like Snapchat's disappearing posts), personalization (recommendations tailored to your interests), reciprocity (give something away to get something in return), and social proof ("likes" and comments)—to motivate you to become a compulsive user. They also tap into your desire to be part of a group and capitalize on the fear of missing out or "FOMO," the anxiety that comes from the feeling that you've been left out of a fun event or opportunity. The schemers in the video gaming industry hire professionals to help engineer games that encourage compulsive play. They also use many of the same tactics seen in Las Vegas casinos—variable and intermittent rewards, simplicity, and ease of reentry to the game (think of how easy it is to play a slot machine and to play again if you lose). The latest newcomers to the Digital Dragon brigade are streaming services that make binge watching way too easy. Just as one episode of a show is ending, the next one automatically cues up, and before you can decide to turn it off and do something meaningful with your life or go to bed to get the sleep you need, the new episode launches. The next thing you know, it's 2 a.m. and your alarm is set to go off at 6 a.m.

OUTFOX THE DIGITAL DRAGONS

1. Think of all your gadgets as Digital Dragons.
2. Remember that major corporations are behind the games, movies, and gadgets you love.
3. Ask yourself if it is good for your brain or bad for your brain.
4. Don't sign up for alerts and notifications.
5. Set time limits for your gadgets. Stick to the single-screen rule. Make your bedroom a technology-free zone.

TODAY'S PRACTICE: *Take a tech time-out today—unplugging from all your gadgets for just 15 minutes can help.*

Pornography Dragons

Pornography accounts for 20 percent of all mobile internet searches and 13 percent of all web searches.[287] *Pornography Dragons promise gratification for your most secret sexual desires, and they do it by offering easy accessibility, affordability, and anonymity.* These Scheming Dragons know that men's and women's brains are different when it comes to sexual imagery. They take advantage of brain imaging research showing that an area of the brain that controls emotions and motivation is much more activated in men than women when viewing sexual material. That's why they tempt men with a never-ending stream of graphic images of nude bodies. The Pornography Dragons also know that women tend to respond more to emotional intimacy, so they have developed female-friendly erotic material that focuses more on relationships.

The number of men and women watching pornography is rising, with a 2015 study reporting that "46 percent of men and 16 percent of women ages 18 to 39 intentionally viewed pornography in a given week."[288] Research has found that internet pornography addiction shares the same underlying neural mechanisms as substance abuse. Of our patients who meet the criteria for sexual addiction, two-thirds of them have low activity in the prefrontal cortex (associated with impulse control problems) and half have too much activity in the anterior cingulate gyrus (associated with a tendency to get stuck on thoughts or behaviors). The Pornography Dragons may lead to instant gratification, but they do not lead to lasting satisfaction. In fact, it can reduce interest in real sex and can come between you and your partner, leading to relationship troubles.

OUTFOX THE PORNOGRAPHY DRAGONS

1. Understand that all adult sites and streaming services are Scheming Dragons.
2. Remind yourself that the models enticing you to spend your time, attention, and money are only messengers. Corporations are cashing in on your use.
3. Ask yourself if your online activities are helping your real relationships or hurting them.
4. Don't subscribe to adult sites.
5. Set up blocks and filters on your devices.

TODAY'S PRACTICE: *If you routinely look at online pornography, you may be addicted. Take the first step today to seek support and set up filters so you can break this destructive habit.*

News Monger Dragons

Watching the news in the morning decreases happiness scores by 27 percent later in the day.[289] Do you reach for your phone first thing in the morning to check what awful things have happened in the world overnight? Do you check news websites throughout the day to stay on top of the latest scary developments? News flash: The News Monger Dragons have sucked you into their grasp. News outlets run 24-7 and repeatedly pour toxic thoughts into our brains, making us see impending terror or disaster around every corner to boost their ratings. The constant frightening images activate our brains' primitive fear (amygdala) circuits that once ensured our survival but are now obsolete.

News Monger Dragons tap into the neuroscience that shows the human brain is wired for negativity and pays attention to things that might harm us. That's why they highlight the most sensational crime stories, the latest possible health scares, and the natural disasters that might happen. They say it's to keep you informed and prepared, but it's actually to keep you hooked on their channels or websites. The News Monger Dragons increase anxiety, depression, and stress.

OUTFOX THE NEWS MONGER DRAGONS

1. Recognize them. All media—including newspapers, TV news, online news sites, and news in your social media feeds—can be News Monger Dragons.
2. TV anchors are usually attractive, friendly people who make you feel like you know them personally. You don't.
3. Are they reporting something that seems unbelievable or terribly frightening? Investigate. A few clicks can help you verify if a news story is factual.
4. Don't sign up for breaking news alerts.
5. Set limits and don't watch the news right before bedtime.

TODAY'S PRACTICE: *Download the Good News Network app and start your day with positivity.*

Social Media Dragons

Some of the sneakiest Scheming Dragons are the ones behind social media platforms. Some two billion people worldwide use social networks. As previously mentioned, the nine hours a day most teens spend on social media outnumber the hours they spend sleeping.[290] How do they get you hooked? To keep you scrolling, posting, and commenting, social media outlets have become masterful at using psychological warfare. These apps are free to join and available at your fingertips, so they're easy to access. And they have never-ending feeds that refresh constantly, keeping you in a perpetual state of FOMO (fear of missing out). They also play a numbers game. As the number of your followers or "likes" goes up, it triggers a release of feel-good dopamine and fires up the reward center in your brain. Research has shown that it's harder for people to resist checking social media than to say no to cigarettes or alcohol.[291]

What's really happening behind the scenes is this: Social Media Dragons need your eyeballs on their advertisers' ads. The more time you spend on your feed, the better for them, and the worse for you. Unfortunately, these networks and the social media influencers who have major followings create shame as teenagers and adults endlessly compare themselves to those online who appear to "have it all." The Social Media Dragons can make you feel worse about yourself and can increase feelings of loneliness. A growing number of studies have shown a connection between time spent on social media and feelings of anxiety and depression.[292]

OUTFOX THE SOCIAL MEDIA DRAGONS

1. Recognize every social media platform as a Scheming Dragon.
2. You may think you're connecting with your friends on social media, but you're really giving your time and attention to the major corporation behind it.
3. Ask yourself if you're spending time on social media because you're lonely and bored, and take stock of whether it makes you feel good or makes you feel bad.
4. Don't sign up for alerts and notifications.
5. Set specific times of day to use social media and limit the amount of time you spend on it.

TODAY'S PRACTICE: *Today, take a social media day off and see how you feel.*

Contact Sports Dragons

I played football in high school and used to love watching it until I realized I was watching the destruction of human lives and their families. The Scheming Dragons behind contact sports are expert spin doctors who make head injuries seem like exciting entertainment. And they make billions of dollars each year at the expense of the health of millions of children, teenagers, and young adults who participate in these sports and try to emulate the hard hits, knockout punches, and scuffles they see on the sports highlights. The Contact Sports Dragons try to justify the injuries by touting the benefits that sports provide, such as physical exercise, teamwork, strategy, and lessons in overcoming adversity. These are all good benefits, but you can easily get them in other sports that don't put you at risk of a head injury. Our brain imaging work has shown clear evidence of traumatic brain injuries in kids and teens who play Pop Warner and high school football, in college players, and in current and retired NFL players. The Contact Sports Dragons want you to believe that playing football and other contact sports is safe and that head injuries won't cause lasting problems. These are lies. Concussions, even ones that don't cause you to black out, can cause depression, anger, anxiety, memory loss, confusion, and more.[293]

OUTFOX THE CONTACT SPORTS DRAGONS
1. Understand that schools, coaches, community sports programs, and parents can try to rope you into playing or promoting contact sports.
2. The professional athletes you see who are making millions of dollars are the exception. Most people who play sports never make any money from it, but they may be harmed for life by a head injury.
3. Find out about the risk of concussions and head injuries before playing any sport.
4. If you want to send a message to these Scheming Dragons, don't watch their events on TV or pay for tickets to attend these sporting events.
5. Avoid playing any contact sport, and never let developing brains play them.

TODAY'S PRACTICE: *If you have a history of concussions or playing contact sports, consider brain SPECT imaging to see if you have damaged your brain.*

Holiday Dragons

Seems odd that we celebrate holidays with food that will kill us early. What could seem more festive and friendly than Holiday Dragons? These beasts promote holiday cheer and family togetherness, but they often end up causing stress, overspending, and suicidal thoughts. The Holiday Dragons put pressure on you to attend parties where you're encouraged to get in the spirit by overeating and drinking too much alcohol. There's nothing cheery about feeling bloated and hungover. And all those TV commercials and social media posts showing families celebrating together can make you feel like you have to spend time with relatives you don't like or who are unhealthy to be around. You may not have one of those Hallmark families, or you may not have any family at all, which makes you feel lonely and depressed.

Some of the most obnoxious Holiday Dragons are retailers who promote the spirit of giving, which translates into "buying" from them. More than six out of ten people say they feel pressured to overspend during the holidays—whether it's on gifts, social occasions, travel, or charitable donations.[294] Holiday Dragons pressure you to overeat, overspend, and overextend yourself. It can all lead to stress, loneliness, depression, anxiety, weight gain, and trouble in your relationships.

OUTFOX THE HOLIDAY DRAGONS
1. Know that retailers are behind much of the pressure that comes with the holidays.
2. Santa Claus, the Easter Bunny, and Uncle Sam are cute and likable characters, but the real message is coming from those retailers.
3. Ask yourself if holiday-related activities are good for your brain or bad for your brain.
4. Don't sign up for notifications about sales and specials.
5. Make a plan for your holiday activities and spending, and stick to it.

TODAY'S PRACTICE: *Plan a brain-healthy holiday party with good-for-you foods like veggies and hummus, chicken skewers, and sparkling "spa water" with sliced lemons and limes.*

Do You Have ADD/ADHD?

Many people who have clear ADD/ADHD have no idea they have it. So how do you know if you or a loved one has ADD/ADHD, attention deficit hyperactivity disorder, also called attention deficit disorder (ADD)? Answer these six questions:

1. Do you have a short attention span unless you're really interested in something?
2. Are you easily distracted?
3. Do you struggle with organization?
4. Do you tend to procrastinate?
5. Are you restless and have trouble waiting in line or sitting still?
6. Do you tend to get yourself into hot water by saying or doing things you wish you hadn't?

If you answered yes to three or more of these questions, and the symptoms interfere with your life, you may have ADD/ADHD. Let's talk briefly about each of these symptoms. Having trouble paying attention is considered one of the primary signs of ADD/ADHD. However, that lack of attention doesn't apply in all situations. In most cases, people with this common condition have difficulty maintaining focus when it comes to ho-hum everyday activities—think housework, paying bills, or school assignments. But what's confusing is that these same people may have no problem at all paying attention to things they really like, such as playing video games, drawing, or swimming.

Distractibility is another major symptom of ADD/ADHD. This is where people see too much, feel too much, and hear too much. The human brain typically filters out myriad distractions so we can focus on what's most important. In those with ADD/ADHD, however, that filter is looser, allowing more external information to pass through into their consciousness. This explains why these people tend to be acutely aware of so many things around them at once, such as their itchy mohair sweater, a bird that just flew overhead, or the whirring of a ceiling fan. Disorganization is another common trait, especially for their space and being on time, which can drive other people crazy. From early in life their personal spaces—bedrooms, backpacks, desks, lockers, and more—are usually cluttered and unkempt.

One of the biggest lessons we have learned from our brain imaging work is that ADD/ADHD is not a single or simple disorder. In fact, there are seven types of ADD/ADHD, and each has a unique set of symptoms that requires a customized treatment plan.[295]

TODAY'S PRACTICE: *How many of these symptoms do you have? Can you see any in your loved ones?*

Untreated ADD/ADHD Can Ruin Your Life

When ADD/ADHD is left untreated, the consequences are alarming. ADD/ADHD is one of the most controversial medical issues of our time. Everyone has an opinion about it. It's a myth, a fad, an excuse for bad behavior. You should take medicine for it, or you shouldn't take medicine for it. Yet, when it is left untreated, it can devastate a person's life and the lives of those they love.

Consider these sobering statistics about those with untreated ADD/ADHD: Unwanted pregnancies occur in 38 percent of young adults with it compared with just 4 percent of those without the condition; up to 58 percent of children fail a grade in school; and 46 percent of kids get suspended from school. Research shows that people with untreated ADD/ADHD are also more likely to smoke cigarettes and to abuse alcohol or drugs. Problems maintaining relationships, job instability, and parent-child conflicts have also been noted. And worst of all, untreated ADD/ADHD is associated with a marked increase in mortality rates.[296]

These are not just statistics; our clinics are filled with people who have struggled every day of their lives at school, in their relationships, and at work. The personal internal terror and shame of being out of control "year after year after year" tears at them and everyone around them.

Being treated ineffectively for ADD/ADHD is very expensive, since people end up going to doctor after doctor, trying multiple medications. And the shocking reality is that many doctors don't know whether their patients actually have ADD/ADHD. And even if they do know, most are unaware about what causes it and how easily it can be treated.

But the good news is it doesn't have to be that way. We've seen thousands of patients experience dramatic improvements that transformed their lives.

TODAY'S PRACTICE: *Do you or someone you know have ADD/ADHD? How has it impacted your life or theirs?*

ADD/ADHD Strengths

People with ADD/ADHD tend to think "outside the box." I start every presentation about ADD/ADHD by talking about its many strengths, including creativity, curiosity, and spontaneity. Many exceptionally bright and accomplished people have ADD/ADHD. For example, it was thought that Thomas Edison had ADD/ADHD and Olympian Michael Phelps was formally diagnosed with it. Hall of Fame quarterback Terry Bradshaw, Grammy winner Justin Timberlake, and JetBlue founder David Neeleman have talked openly about having ADD/ADHD in interviews. People with ADD/ADHD tend to "think outside the box" and are natural risk-takers, which explains why the condition is common among entrepreneurs. The positive traits associated with ADD/ADHD can also be a bonus for entertainers, salespeople, and creative types.

At Amen Clinics, we have studied the brains of emergency responders and found a high rate of ADD/ADHD among them. It makes sense that people with ADD/ADHD would be more likely to race toward a dangerous situation rather than run from it. People with ADD/ADHD also tend to choose highly stimulating jobs because they need the excitement or drama in order to pay attention.

In an interview with *ADDitude* magazine, Neeleman said ADD/ADHD is a double-edged sword. On the one hand, it can be difficult to focus, stay tidy, and see a task through to completion. On the other hand, it's made him more creative, energetic, and willing to take risks. "I knew I had strengths that other people didn't have. . . . I can distill complicated facts and come up with simple solutions. I can look out on an industry with all kinds of problems and say, 'How can I do this better?' My ADD/ADHD brain naturally searches for better ways of doing things."[297] Like the other successful ADD/ADHD entrepreneurs I've treated, Neeleman takes measures to counteract its negative effects, such as having an assistant to manage his schedule.

TODAY'S PRACTICE: *Think about someone you know with ADD/ADHD and send them a text letting them know you appreciate one of their unique strengths.*

The Harder You Try, the Worse It Gets

Having ADD/ADHD is like needing glasses. Sally was the first patient I ever scanned. She was admitted to the hospital for suicidal thoughts after a fight with her husband. As I got to know her, I noticed several signs of ADD/ADHD. Despite being highly intelligent, she was an underachiever at school and quit going to college. In addition, ADD/ADHD often runs in families, and she had a hyperactive child.

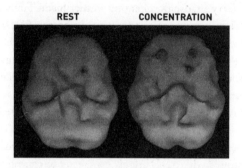

REST   CONCENTRATION

When I laid the pictures on the table in her hospital room and explained them to her, she started to cry. All these years, she'd thought her issues were a character flaw, not a medical issue. To illustrate the point, I reached into my pocket and pulled out a pair of eyeglasses. I told her that people who have ADD/ADHD are no different from those who need vision correction. Would anyone ever say that people who need contact lenses or glasses are lazy or just need to try harder to see? Of course not! It's similar for those with ADD/ADHD. Activity in the front part of their brain decreases during concentration when it's supposed to increase. In order to focus, they need treatment strategies to activate the brain.

In fact, as you can see, the harder you try, the worse it gets. This helped Sally make sense of her life. With the appropriate treatment, she was able to focus, which changed her life in so many ways. She finally earned her college degree, improved her relationships with her husband and son, and no longer thought of herself as a failure, but rather as someone who needed help for a medical problem. When you understand ADD/ADHD this way, you realize that not treating it amounts to withholding glasses from someone who cannot see. And that's not fair.

TODAY'S PRACTICE: *Every time you see someone wearing glasses today, think about how it's similar to someone with ADD/ADHD.*

ADD/ADHD in Females

Girls with ADD/ADHD often do not get diagnosed because they do not bring enough negative attention to themselves. It is much more common than most people know. Doctors typically talk about two types of ADD/ADHD: (1) combined type with both inattentive and hyperactive/impulsive symptoms; and (2) primarily inattentive type, without hyperactivity or much impulsivity. Males tend to have the first type, which can be really irritating, so they get diagnosed, while females tend to have the second type and suffer silently, struggling in school, at work, or in their relationships.

ADD/ADHD is most often associated with low activity in the prefrontal cortex. Women with ADD/ADHD are often sensitive to noise, so they may sleep with ear plugs or a fan on at night so they don't hear everything in the house. Because of the distractibility they may have sexual problems. What does an orgasm require, besides a reasonable lover? Attention! You have to pay attention to the feeling long enough to make it happen. Getting ADD/ADHD treated can make you and your spouse so much happier. Females with ADD/ADHD also sometimes seek conflict as a way to turn on their brains, so they tend to pick on the people they love. Do you know anyone like this?

When Mary grew up in the 1950s, no one knew about ADD/ADHD. She did poorly in school and was beaten by the school nuns for talking back, zoning out, and being unable to focus. As an adult she went through many relationships. Yet, despite her struggles, she started a very successful business manufacturing pet products, but was often in conflict with her ADD/ADHD brother, who worked with her. ADD/ADHD often runs in families. Getting them both treated made a big difference for themselves personally, plus they stopped complaining about each other and the business did much better. If you or a loved one has any of these symptoms, get checked out. Medicine can help, as can natural fixes such as a higher-protein diet, exercise, and certain supplements, including EPA fish oil.

TODAY'S PRACTICE: *If you suspect you have ADD/ADHD, take our ADD Type Test at addtypetest.com.*

Brain Warrior Jarrett and a Completely New View of ADD/ADHD

On someone's worst day, I want to make it better. Jarrett was diagnosed with ADD/ADHD in preschool. His mother said he was driven by a motor that was revved way too high. He was hyperactive, hyperverbal, restless, impulsive, and couldn't focus. He also didn't sleep and interrupted everyone all the time. He had no friends, as his classmates avoided him and their parents kept their children away from him. His third-grade teacher said he would never do well in school and cautioned his parents to lower their expectations. He had seen five doctors and was prescribed five stimulant medications for ADD/ADHD. All of them made Jarrett worse, triggering mood swings and terrible rages. He put holes in the walls of their home and scared his siblings. His behavior had gotten so bad that his last doctor wanted to put him on an antipsychotic medication. This is when his mother brought him to see us.

Jarrett's brain SPECT scan clearly showed dramatic overactivity in a pattern we call "the ring of fire." No wonder stimulants didn't work; it was like pouring gasoline on a fire. Our published research shows this pattern is made worse by stimulants 80 percent of the time.[298] It turned out Jarrett also had Lyme disease, which was likely triggering the hyperactivity in his brain. On a group of natural supplements to calm his brain, treating the Lyme disease, together with parent training and structured brain-healthy habits, Jarrett's behavior dramatically improved. His grades improved, the rages stopped, and he was able to make friends. He was on the honor roll or dean's list for 10 straight years. At the time of this writing, he is thriving in college and is on the water polo team. He is planning on being a firefighter, because as he told me, "On someone's worst day of their life, I want to make it better." After searching for so long, his parents are grateful to have found the correct treatment plan for him, which has completely altered the course of his life. There is no telling what the future would have held for Jarrett if he had stayed on his previous path.

TODAY'S PRACTICE: *If standard ADD/ADHD therapies are not working, investigate other potential causes of symptoms, such as Lyme disease.*

Is Medication for ADD/ADHD Always Wrong?

One of my own children went from being mediocre and hating herself to straight A's for 10 years on medication for ADD/ADHD. In the case of ADD/ADHD, which has been one of my primary areas of expertise, there is a great deal of negative bias against medication in our society. I've heard countless parents say, "I'm not going to drug my kid." "If you take this drug you won't be creative." "You won't be yourself." The problem is that most physicians assume ADD/ADHD is one thing, so they start everyone on the same class of medications—stimulants, such as Ritalin or Adderall. These medications help many people, but they also make many others much worse. Both "miracle" and "horror" stories about stimulants abound.

One of my own daughters was able to improve her grades while using a stimulant medication to optimize the low activity in her prefrontal cortex, and she was accepted to one of the world's best veterinarian schools. The medication stimulated her frontal lobes, giving her greater access to her own abilities, which also enhanced her self-esteem. On the other hand, I have another patient who was referred to me because he became suicidal on Ritalin. His brain was already overactive to start with, so stimulating it only made him more anxious and upset. The problem is, physicians assume everyone with the same symptoms has the same brain patterns, which is just not true and invites failure and frustration. You have to look at the brain to determine the precise type of ADD/ADHD and the best treatment.

TODAY'S PRACTICE: *If you're worried about having your child take ADD/ADHD medication, spend some time today educating yourself about the pros and cons.*

Thinking Ahead

Do you like attorneys? It is easy to cheat in the moment, whether it is cheating on your health, your taxes, your boss, or your spouse. But think about how your behavior fits with your goals over time. What kind of character do you desire? Matching your behavior to your goals is a prefrontal cortex function.

I once had lunch with a close friend who was having marital problems. I knew Chuck had ADD/ADHD and was struggling at home with his wife and children. As usual, Chuck was telling me about the turmoil. His wife was struggling with one of their daughters, who was being defiant. Then, all of a sudden, his affect changed, his eyes brightened, his tone became more excited and hushed, and he told me about a woman he had recently met on an airplane. She was pretty, smart, and interesting, and she seemed to really like him a lot. She had even come to his office for a visit. As he started to go on about her, I interrupted him. "Chuck, do you like attorneys?"

"What do you mean?" he asked, looking surprised.

"Play it out," I said. "You are having marital problems. You meet this attractive woman who seems interested in you. She has been to your office. The next step, if it has not happened already, is for you to have sex with her. Then your wife will probably find out. You have ADD/ADHD, so you are not good at hiding things. She has a hot cingulate (the brain's gear shifter), so she will never forgive you. She will file for divorce, you will spend a lot of money and time with attorneys, hate yourself for putting your family through all this stuff, then a year from now you will lose half of your net worth and you will be visiting your children on the weekends."

"Wow," Chuck said, looking deflated. "I never thought about it like that."

"That is what your prefrontal cortex does for you," I said. "It plays things out."

Fortunately, Chuck later told me that he never called the woman back. Make sure your decisions are breeding honesty and integrity. Think them through beyond the moment and make sure you keep your prefrontal cortex healthy.

TODAY'S PRACTICE: *Think of two decisions you made today and ask yourself if they are getting you what you want in your relationships, work, money, or health.*

Keeping Your Cool under Stress

Is that a tic or don't you like the lecture? The prefrontal cortex helps us think about and supervise our odd behaviors. People who have Tourette's syndrome (TS) have uncontrollable urges to move their muscles (tics) or say exactly what is on their mind. They can control the urges for a while, but like tension on a rubber band that needs to be released, the urges build until they must be set free. TS is classified as a tic disorder, where people have both motor (involuntary muscle movements) and vocal tics (involuntary vocalizations). Examples of motor tics include shoulder shrugging, leg movements, hip thrusts, excessive blinking, eyebrow raising, facial grimaces, head jerking, punching, and even sexual gestures. Examples of vocal tics include puffing, blowing, throat clearing, whistling, animal noises (barking, mooing, crowing), and swearing (termed *coprolalia*).

I have worked with many patients with TS, but I have never felt more disarmed by it than when I gave a speech to 400 people with tic disorders for the Tourette Syndrome Foundation of Canada (now known as Tourette Canada). Let me set the stage for you. Imagine speaking at a podium while hundreds of people in the audience are grunting, mooing, and grimacing. Believe me, it can throw you off your game. I'm usually very comfortable talking to large groups, but I was getting very distracted. Then someone hurled a curse word my way. *Zing!* That hurt. After hearing the same loud expletive for the third time, I finally had to stop midlecture and ask if the person was unhappy with my talk.

"Just a tic," the man shouted sheepishly. If a brain health expert can get rattled by someone's tics, just think how friends, relatives, and colleagues might misinterpret them. It's no wonder relationships can be difficult for those with TS. Fortunately, many people with this disorder respond well to treatments, such as behavioral therapy, lifestyle changes, nutraceuticals, and medication (when necessary).

TODAY'S PRACTICE: *Think of an upcoming stressful situation, such as a speech, and try to create that same pressure environment by practicing in front of others so you can become familiar with the feeling of discomfort.*

Can I Still Be Funny If I Get My Brain Treated?

Her scan was 10 years older than she was. I've been blessed to see many successful people—musicians, athletes, actors, and CEOs. Many of them worry that if they get their brains healthy it will take away their personality. Will it dull their creativity? Make them boring?

That's what stand-up comedian Jessimae Peluso wanted to know when she came to see me. She asked me, "What if my broken brain is the thing that makes me funny?"[299] Jessimae has spent a lifetime struggling with attention issues. In school, she was smart, but she caused problems. "I had a permanent desk in the hallway," she admitted, "because I drove the teacher so nuts because I was more focused on entertaining and just saying whatever came to my brain." As an adult, she wants to be able to follow through on projects without a million interruptions. In her everyday life, "I've done 1,000 things, but I never finished the thing that I set off to do."

The comedian had never really thought much about the health of her brain until her dad developed Alzheimer's disease. Pointing to her head, she said, "I would not like that house guest up here whatsoever." Her scan showed she had low activity in her prefrontal cortex, likely the cause of her ADD/ADHD symptoms. She also had scalloping or evidence of toxicity.

Jessimae said, "It looks like an aerial view of Arizona," then admitted that she was an avid pot smoker. Her scan was not a laughing matter. Her brain was 10 years older than she was, and she wanted to improve its health. But then she wondered, "How will this affect me as a comedian?"

I assured her that having a healthier brain would make her better—a more consistent performer and more adept with the business side of things. In closing I told her, "You'll still be able to look at things in an unusual way. Right? That's what makes you funny, but you'll be able to follow through. . . . Over time, with a healthier brain, you'll be happier overall."

TODAY'S PRACTICE: *If you're hesitant to balance your brain because you think it will make you boring, write down all the ways a healthy brain can help you be your best.*

How Learning Disorders Can Fuel Shame: Brain Warrior Lewis Howes

"I felt like I was dumb pretty much my whole life." Former professional football player Lewis Howes, who hosts the wildly popular podcast *The School of Greatness*, seems to have it all. But he shared with me that he didn't always feel like a success. In fact, the bestselling author and entrepreneur says, "I felt like I was dumb pretty much my whole life."[300] Lewis struggled in school, where he says he was always at the bottom of his class. He had a tutor and attended special needs classes during recess and after school, but no matter how hard he studied, he still got Cs and Ds. When he entered eighth grade, he tested at a second-grade reading level, and administrators wanted to hold him back a grade. It was a real blow to his self-esteem. "[Learning] was always stressful. It was always exhausting," Lewis said. Eventually, he thought, *What's the point of trying?* As a result of constantly trailing behind his peers academically, he struggled with confidence, insecurity, and anxiety that lasted into his twenties.

Learning disabilities encompass a range of issues that negatively impact academic performance. Common learning disorders include problems with reading, writing, spelling, speaking, or doing math. Close to 24 percent of youngsters with a specific learning disorder experience severe anxiety, 14 percent struggle with depression, and many others struggle with low self-esteem, which can spiral into suicidal thoughts.[301] According to one study, adults with learning disabilities were 46 percent more likely to attempt suicide.[302]

With the help of psychotherapy, workshops, and other therapeutic experiences, Lewis has managed to overcome his learning problems to run a big business and influence millions. The exciting news is that with appropriate diagnosis and treatment, learning disabilities are treatable, especially by improving brain function.

TODAY'S PRACTICE: *If you have a child with a learning disability, don't wait to seek help.*

Raven-Symoné and the Burrito Syndrome: What Depression Feels Like

When you wrap yourself up and hide from the world. Raven-Symoné gained a reputation as one of the greatest child stars of all time, and as an adult she has continued to make audiences laugh with *Raven's Home*. But she opened up to me about the depression, anxiety, and irritability in her life. There are times when she goes inside her brain and can't say a word or express herself. She calls it "burritoing."[303] It's a great term for something that so many people with depression experience. It's when you want to wrap yourself up and hide from the world. How can you tell if you're struggling with "burrito syndrome?" Look for these signs.

1. **You turn into a hermit.** You sink into a low mood and retreat from loved ones. When they try to offer support or ask you to talk about what you're feeling, you shut them out. But the more alone you feel, the more depressed you are likely to feel.
2. **You sleep too much (or too little).** Depression often comes with sleep issues. You may find yourself sleeping more than usual—cocooning in bed and taking numerous naps throughout the day.
3. **You have no energy.** You forget things like going out to dinner with friends. You may not be able to motivate yourself to go to the mailbox or to head to the kitchen to make meals.
4. **You have aches and pains.** Depression can manifest with physical symptoms such as back pain, joint pain, or headaches.
5. **You snap at others.** When you're all wrapped up in your own misery, it can lead to anger and irritability. If loved ones try to coax you out of your isolation, you're likely to lash out at them. This can lead to people avoiding you, which further contributes to your social isolation.

Depression is highly treatable. To overcome depression or "burritoing," get help. Push yourself to reconnect with others, work on fixing your sleep, and go for a walk, which has been shown to help with depression.

TODAY'S PRACTICE: *If you have been "burritoing," get out of your pajamas today.*

Overcoming the Lasting Pain of Bullying

Healing from the trauma of mean people. In some people's eyes, Nikki Leigh has it all. She is a beautiful actress, model, and host of "Positivity Time" on Instagram, with millions of followers on social media platforms. But she wasn't always so popular. In fact, she told me that in junior high school, she was bullied. "I had no friends; I felt super alone. . . . And people beat me up."[304] She tried desperately to get the people who didn't like her to change their opinion of her and become friends, but it didn't work. The bullying eventually got so intense that she told her mom one day that she just didn't want to live anymore. Nikki says, "She broke, and I didn't realize why [until later]. . . . Her dad had committed suicide."

Nikki's scan showed overactivity in the emotional centers, in a diamond-shaped pattern common in people with past emotional trauma. Being unpopular, which happened to many of us, can lead to significant problems, including higher levels of anxiety disorders, depression, suicide, and physical health challenges.

Nikki started "Positivity Time" during the pandemic to help others whom she knew were suffering. Knowing what it is like to struggle, she teaches others to express gratitude and shares random acts of kindness with her viewers. Nikki naturally focuses her energies now on being more upbeat.

Science explains why her strategies can be so helpful. Positivity bias training is a proven practice that can help you overcome negativity, low self-esteem, and other issues, even if they were embedded in your psyche during your formative years at school.[305] Positivity bias training basically means actively seeking out the positive in life—noticing what you like more than what you don't like, showing gratitude, and changing the way you think. With these techniques, you have the potential to emerge from decades of feeling bad about yourself. And when you feel happier and more self-confident, you are also more likely to adopt healthy habits that will further enhance your body and brain. It's a win-win situation.

TODAY'S PRACTICE: *List two things to be positive about today.*

Thoughts on Suicide

In my life, I've been surrounded by suicide. One of my aunts killed herself, as did my adopted son's biological father and my son-in-law's father. However, my first and most painful brush with suicide came in 1979, when as a second-year medical student, someone I loved tried to take her own life. Fortunately, she survived the attempt, and I took her to see a wonderful psychiatrist. Over time, I realized that if he helped her, which he did, it would not only help her, but it would also help her children, her loved ones, and even her grandchildren as they would be shaped by someone who was happier and more stable. I fell in love with psychiatry because I realized it had the potential to help generations of people.

The pain of suicide is unlike any other loss because people see it as a choice, rather than as the outcome of an illness. When someone dies from heart disease, it is sad, but people generally do not blame the person. It is different with suicide. I tell my patients who struggle with self-destructive thoughts that suicide is a "permanent solution to a temporary feeling or problem." The thought most often passes after the mood or crisis abates. Plus, I tell them to stop drinking or using drugs, because they may take the brake off of their behavior and they may end up doing something permanent that damages their whole family system. I also make it clear to my patients that if they have children and kill themselves, they've just taught their kids that suicide is a grown-up way of solving problems and their children will have a 300 percent increased chance of killing themselves.[306] These warnings help my patients get outside of themselves.

Having a troubled brain increases the risk of suicide. For example, research shows that experiencing a single concussion *triples the risk of suicide.*[307] Our brain imaging work shows decreased activity in the prefrontal cortex of those who have attempted suicide. Getting your brain healthy dramatically decreases the risk of suicidal thoughts and behaviors.

TODAY'S PRACTICE: *If someone you know has struggled with suicidal thoughts, encourage them to strengthen their PFC to reduce impulsivity and to stop drinking.*

Unwhack Yourself

Stacked stresses cause the majority of psychiatric issues. I was once on the *Dr. Phil* show to discuss Ridge, a 25-year-old man, who was exhibiting psychotic behavior. Before I went on, Dr. Phil had a rubber dummy, called Century Bob, wheeled onto the set. Dr. Phil had a baseball bat in his hands. Beforehand Phil and I had talked about the "stacked stresses" that were contributing to Ridge's erratic behaviors. Ridge had been diagnosed with a variety of psychiatric diagnoses, including schizophrenia, bipolar 1 disorder, depression, and substance-induced psychosis. To Ridge's mother and the audience, Dr. Phil said Ridge's issues were the result of many insults.

He explained that Ridge played linebacker in high school and had several concussions, including being knocked out. To illustrate, Dr. Phil hit the dummy in the head several times. *Whack, whack, whack.* Ridge went to school and started to experiment with drugs. Dr. Phil whacked the dummy again. He started taking a synthetic marijuana, called K2, which is 100 times more potent than marijuana and sprayed with toxic chemicals. *Whack, whack, whack.* Then Ridge drank alcohol. *Whack, whack, whack.* He joined a fraternity where he was hazed, choked, and likely had an anoxic (oxygen deprived) brain injury, causing both emotional and physical trauma. *Whack, whack, whack.* He developed tics, heard voices, and had several psychiatric hospitalizations and arrests. *Whack, whack, whack.*[308]

I thought the illustration was brilliant to help explain the concept of stacked stresses. Very few psychiatric issues have single or simple causes. They often involve two or more of the four circles of health and illness (biological, psychological, social, and spiritual). To get well, we have to address all of the stacked stresses.

Here's another example: My mother broke her hip in the fall of 2019, big *whack.* It caused her to stop playing golf, which she had played for 60 years, *whack.* In January 2020, she got shingles, *whack.* In March 2020, she and my father were both hospitalized with COVID, *whack, whack.* In May 2020, my father died, *whack, whack, whack.* After that blow her personality changed, and she was much more irritable and afraid. She was clearly not herself. I needed to intervene, but her distress wasn't caused by one factor. It was multiple whacks.

TODAY'S PRACTICE: *List two or three of the stacked stresses that impact your brain and body each day.*

Brain Warrior Trent Shelton:
Know Your Brain, Know Yourself

This helps me put two and two together. Trent Shelton is a former professional football player who now inspires millions with his books, motivational speaking, and podcast. He has been on a journey of self-exploration and personal development ever since his football career ended prematurely after suffering a concussion. In the years since then, he has looked inward to better his life and has encouraged others to look inside themselves to enhance their lives. But there was one thing Trent still hadn't seen—his brain. He told me, "How can you know yourself if you don't know your brain?" Trent was curious about his short-term memory problems, social anxiety, and lack of focus. "I'm a last-minute person," he admitted with a grin.[309]

Trent's scan provided clues to his concerns. It showed signs of brain trauma, likely due to the multiple big hits and blows to the head he took as a wide receiver in college and in the NFL. He also had decreased blood flow in his prefrontal cortex, which is commonly seen in people who tend to procrastinate, miss deadlines, or be late. Individuals with this brain pattern often need a little bit of stress to get motivated to get ready, such as a spouse telling them in no uncertain terms that they're going to be late. This helped Trent understand why he's a last-minute kind of person and how he could benefit from simple ways to boost focus. We also saw increased activity in his emotional brain, which increased his risk of anxiety and depression. In the past, Trent lost a friend to suicide, and he had recently grieved the death of his mother.

For Trent, seeing his brain was very helpful. "I'm connecting the dots," he said. "I don't feel like there's something wrong with me, with the thoughts that I think or how I felt in the past. I'm seeing my brain and understanding, okay, this is why. So, it just helps me put two and two together."

TODAY'S PRACTICE: *Write down one or two odd or quirky things about yourself and investigate how your brain may contribute to them.*

What about Cheat Days?

Would you give an alcoholic, smoker, or sex addict cheat days? When you're trying to follow a brain-healthy eating plan, you may wonder if you can get away with a weekly cheat day. The notion of cheat days as an acceptable part of a healthy diet is so common there are nearly four million posts on Instagram using the hashtag #cheatday along with photos of seriously decadent cheat foods—think cinnamon rolls, french fries, and homemade peanut butter cups with Oreo cookies stuffed inside. I'm not a fan of cheat days. I think they set you up for failure, and I'm going to explain why. I'll also share a better way to cheat that won't leave you wracked with guilt.

For many people, the idea of a cheat day centers on consuming unlimited quantities of sugary sweets, carb-filled foods like pizza, and alcohol. But these foods can mess with your brain in a number of ways that make you more vulnerable to falling back into unhealthy eating patterns. *They trigger cravings.* Sugar releases dopamine in the same area of the brain as cocaine and heroin. Desserts are full of it, and refined carbs like pizza crust and alcoholic beverages convert to sugar in the body. Overindulging in sweets reignites those areas and can cause the cravings to return, making it harder for you to get through the week in a healthy way.

It's best to aim for being really good with your diet 90 to 95 percent of the time. This means that rather than doing a weekly cheat day, it's better to do one cheat meal a week. That is far less likely to set you up to fail. And even in your cheat meal, follow the three-bite rule. If you really want the homemade baklava—*which I really love!*—only take three bites. It will satisfy the desire for something sweet without causing your brain to go into overdrive with cravings, losing impulse control, or making you feel moody. You can also say goodbye to feeling guilty or thinking you're a failure.

TODAY'S PRACTICE: *Assess your attitude toward cheat days and think about what is worth more—the momentary pleasure of cheating or lasting brain health?*

Seven Bad Excuses for
Not Getting the Help You Need

What does it cost you to have a brain that is not working at its best? Getting help can make a big difference in the lives of anyone struggling with brain health issues, but people use many excuses for not scheduling an appointment. Do any of the following excuses prevent you from reaching out for help?

1. **It's stigmatizing and embarrassing.** It is the strong person who gets help, not the weak one.
2. **You're too busy to seek help.** It's an investment in time, but with a better brain, you will be more efficient and ultimately have more time.
3. **You feel guilty because others have it worse.** Yet, if you are suffering, it is your job to take care of yourself.
4. **People go to therapy to complain about their lives.** That is bad therapy. Learning how to have a better brain and manage your mind should be central themes in therapy, not complaining.
5. **Been there once, and it didn't work.** Successful people are persistent, especially with a new way of thinking.
6. **It's too expensive to get treatment.** Being sick is way more expensive than getting help. It can interfere with school performance, work, relationships, and health, all of which can be devastating financially.
7. **You don't want to be judged.** In reality, you're the person who is likely judging yourself the most harshly.

Sometimes it can be hard to take that first step to get the help you need, but with the right information and persistence, you can feel, think, and act in ways that make you proud.

TODAY'S PRACTICE: *If you or a loved one is struggling with a brain health issue, go to amenclinics.com or the web to search for help.*

When You Change, Others Are Likely to Follow

Make healthy changes for yourself and those you love and your whole world will start to change—though maybe not right away. As I was growing up, my father was not always easy on me. A successful, driven man, he owned a chain of grocery stores. He was also the long-term chairman of the board of Unified Grocers, a 4-billion-dollar company. When I told him I wanted to be a psychiatrist, he asked, "Why don't you want to be a real doctor? Why do you want to be a nut doctor and hang out with nuts all day long?" When I encouraged him to get healthy, he belittled me and called me a health nut. He thought he was invincible and often said, "I give heart attacks. I don't get them."

Then when he was 85, mold was discovered in his home. He developed a cough and a heart arrhythmia that turned into heart failure. He was tired, short of breath, couldn't sleep, and had to stop driving. One day he looked at me and said, "Danny, what do you want me to do? I'm sick of being sick." I was afraid we'd lose him and told him to do the same strategies I've laid out for you in this book. This is where his stubbornness paid off. He did everything I asked. We assessed his brain. He texted me food labels; he ate perfectly 95 percent of the time; he took targeted supplements. And we worked out together, starting with very light weights but steadily increasing it over time. Within months his energy soared, he started driving again, returned to work full time, lost 40 pounds, and played golf again. He was even able to do a six-minute plank.

Then Dad started telling my six siblings: "Your brother wouldn't like you eating that. . . . What would your brother say about that decision?" (My siblings were tired of hearing "Daniel this . . . Daniel that.") It made up for all the years of belittlement. The only reason my dad asked me for help was that I lived the message. When you model health, many other people are likely to follow, although maybe not instantly.

TODAY'S PRACTICE: *Ask yourself, are you modeling health or modeling illness?*

What to Do When a Loved One Is in Denial about Getting Help

You have no influence without connection. Here are several suggestions to gently motivate people who are in denial to seek help:

1. **Use magic words to jump-start the conversation.** Phrases like "I'm here for you" and "I'm concerned about you" can open the lines of communication with someone who needs help.
2. **Listen, don't tell.** Avoid telling someone what they "should" do. Let them share their thoughts and feelings and be a good listener. Helping them become more aware of their own issues can be an important step in the healing process.
3. **Focus on behaviors, not the person.** When you keep the conversation focused on specific actions, it is less likely to come across as a judgment or indictment of the person's character or personality.
4. **Mention brain health.** Share the fact that many unwanted behaviors and feelings are not "mental" problems but rather brain health issues that can be addressed.
5. **Anticipate objections.** People may come up with a variety of excuses to avoid seeking help. Be prepared for these and offer any assistance you can—providing childcare, driving kids to school, scheduling appointments, and so on.
6. **Strengthen your relationship first.** People tend to listen to others when they feel connected to them. Make sure you have a trusting relationship before approaching them about getting help.
7. **Adopt brain-healthy habits now.** Don't wait for the person to get into treatment to start encouraging a brain-healthy lifestyle. And don't single them out. Encourage your whole family or your group of friends to eat nutritious foods, exercise, meditate, pray, and adopt other healthy habits. When you do it together, they may be more receptive to making changes.

TODAY'S PRACTICE: *Do you know someone who is struggling with a family member or friend who needs help? Make a plan to help them.*

Change the B Stuff

We are not controlled by events or people, but by our perceptions of them. In the early 1900s, a shoe salesman was sent to Africa by his company, but he returned home quickly after realizing the people there did not wear shoes. Another company then sent their rep to Africa to scope out the potential for shoe sales. This time, business went gangbusters because the salesman saw it as an opportunity—no one had ever heard of shoes. Although the people had not worn shoes before, they loved them, and this shoe salesman sold thousands of pairs. Even though both men entered the same situation, their perception of it varied dramatically, as did the outcome of their trips.

Your perspective of an event carries more weight in your mind than the event itself. Psychiatrist Richard Gardner noted that the world is similar to a Rorschach test, which asks clients to describe what they see in 10 meaningless ink blots. This test allows us to project our inner experience onto the ink blots. We cannot always change the circumstances that surround us, but we can shift our perception of them. I often teach my patients to use the A-B-C Model to help them become more aware of how their beliefs shape their perceptions:

A-B-C MODEL

A stands for the activating event—what happened

B is your belief about it—the way you interpret it

C stands for the consequences of your behavior—your reaction to the event

This is really important because events or things that other people do (A) can't "make" us behave or think a certain way. Rather, it is our belief or perception of whatever happened (B) that causes us to respond the way we do (C).

For example, take the time I yawned during a therapy session with a patient. He asked if I found him boring. I replied that it was important that he asked. I had been up most of the previous night with an emergency and was tired, but I found what he was saying interesting. My yawning was A; his interpretation that I was bored was B; and his asking me about it was C. I was glad he asked about my yawn because some patients would have inferred that I was bored, and their C would have been to leave the therapy session with a negative feeling. When we can allow ourselves to look at the alternatives and challenge our initial negative perceptions, we've traveled a long way toward emotional health.

TODAY'S PRACTICE: *What major situation in your life can you look at in a different way?*

Six Ways to Boost Spiritual Fitness

To be spiritually fit, you must work on it every day. Spiritual fitness is a new concept in medicine that centers on how you can reduce the risk of many physical and brain health issues by optimizing your deepest sense of meaning and purpose. Spirituality is a search for a higher power, for something sacred or divine, or for something larger than ourselves. Here are six ways to boost spiritual fitness:

1. **Harness the power of meditation.** Hundreds of studies have shown the physical, cognitive, and emotional benefits of meditation. Pick a simple meditation you like, such as Loving-Kindness Meditation (see day 201) or Kirtan Kriya (see day 227).
2. **Make prayer a daily practice.** A wealth of research shows that prayer has been found to calm stress; improve memory, focus, and mood; and enhance function in the prefrontal cortex.[310] Just as you schedule time to work out, make prayer or meditation a priority in your appointment book.
3. **Put your faith into action.** Regardless of your belief system, make it a central part of your everyday life. For example, if the tenets of your faith lie in forgiveness, find it in your heart to release the grudges you hold.
4. **Look for a spiritual trainer.** Just as you might hire a personal trainer to help you get the most out of your workouts, a mentor can be beneficial to your spiritual life. A mentor could be a pastor, rabbi, spiritual director, or any other person you trust who can guide you in your spiritual quest. The mentor-mentee relationship isn't about being told what to do or how to think. Rather, it's a way to explore and stretch your spirituality.
5. **Serve others.** Being of service to others is a key aspect of a healthy spiritual life. Research suggests that whenever you feel down, anxious, or angry, it is best to get outside of yourself to change your state of mind.[311] Connect meaningful activities and pleasure by volunteering for activities you love. For example, if you love basketball, you might enjoy volunteering to keep score at local tournaments.
6. **Find your purpose.** To strengthen your spiritual fitness, you need to know your purpose in life. See days 24, 28, 283, 284.

TODAY'S PRACTICE: *Of the six strategies listed above, pick one to do today.*

Tiny Habits for Your Sense of Purpose

Purposeful people live longer and are happier. Each of these habits takes just a few minutes. They are anchored to something you do (or think or feel) so that they are more likely to become automatic.

1. When I need to focus and get work done, I will put my smartphone on "do not disturb" as a discipline to be more focused and to stop the constant pings or drips of dopamine it tries to addict me to.
2. When I am on the train or bus on my way to work, I will read my One Page Miracle and ask myself, *Will my behavior today get me what I want?*
3. When I start getting upset about something happening in my day, I'll ask myself, *Does this have eternal value?*
4. When it is sunny outdoors, I will take a walk to soak up the sunshine and boost my vitamin D level.
5. Once a week, I will watch a comedy to boost my dopamine level (*Whose Line Is It Anyway?* is one example).
6. Before I go to bed at night, I will write down one purposeful thing I did that day.

TODAY'S PRACTICE: *Pick one or more tiny habits to place in your life today and every day forward.*

Brain Warrior Jill Lives the Message

I stopped going to funerals after the eleventh one. On September 11, 2001, Colonel Jill Chambers was at work inside the Pentagon. When the hijacked plane crashed into the building, she was just a few corridors away from where many of her friends and colleagues perished on that fateful day. She told me that after the eleventh funeral, she couldn't bring herself to attend anymore. It was too overwhelming and painful. For many years, she suffered silently with insomnia and nightmares of the burning aircraft. She accepted these problems as being normal in her field of work.

In 2007, the Chairman of the Joint Chiefs of Staff, Admiral Mike Mullen, asked Jill to become the first special assistant for Returning Warrior Issues to identify the transitional challenges that wounded service members face. This was at a time when suicides among this population had significantly escalated. By interviewing veterans with posttraumatic stress disorder (PTSD) around the country, Jill developed a dynamic program to reduce the stigma associated with mental health issues in the military culture.

Pleased with what she had accomplished throughout her career, Jill retired in April 2009. It was then that she recognized she had PTSD from the events of September 11. For the next three months, she became laser-focused on improving her mental and physical health. She began exploring integrative treatments and had life-changing results from using guided imagery and neurofeedback. Her nightmares stopped, and she was able to sleep much better. She also found my book *Change Your Brain, Change Your Body*, which inspired her to give up sugar and wheat and pay attention to her health numbers. She learned to care deeply about her brain.

After the success of her own posttraumatic growth, Jill turned her pain into passion. In 2010, she founded the nonprofit, This Able Vet (ThisAbleVet.com). Through her organization, she provides resources and brain-focused tools to veterans who are struggling with PTSD and traumatic brain injuries. Jill is a true brain warrior.

TODAY'S PRACTICE: *How can you turn your past pain into purpose? Write three sentences about it.*

Tiny Habits for Your Mind

You can discipline your mind. Each of these habits takes just a few minutes. They are anchored to something you do, think, or feel so that they are more likely to become automatic.

1. When my feet hit the floor first thing in the morning, I will say to myself, *Today is going to be a great day.*
2. After an ANT pops up, I will write down my negative thought and ask, *Is it true?*
3. After I put away my computer and keys, I will push play on a meditation audio.
4. Before I go to bed, I will ask myself, *What went well today?*
5. When I feel overwhelmed, I will take five deep breaths, taking twice as long to exhale to settle and center myself.
6. When I face a difficult situation, I will ask myself, *What is there to be glad about in this situation?*
7. After breakfast, I will think of one person I appreciate, then reach out and tell him or her in a quick text or note.
8. When I feel stressed, I will use stress relief techniques like meditation or prayer to calm these feelings.

TODAY'S PRACTICE: *Pick one or more tiny habits to place in your life today and every day from now on.*

Gratitude and Appreciation

So many people have been involved in creating *Change Your Brain Every Day: Simple Daily Practices to Strengthen Your Mind, Memory, Moods, Focus, Energy, Habits, and Relationships*. I am grateful to them all, especially the tens of thousands of patients and families who have come to Amen Clinics and allowed us to help them on their healing journey, with special thanks to the patients who allowed me to tell part of their stories in this book.

I am grateful to the amazing colleagues and friends at Amen Clinics who work hard every day serving our patients. Special appreciation to Frances Sharpe and Jenny Faherty, who helped me craft the book to make it accessible to our readers, and Natalie Buchoz, our amazing media director.

I am also grateful to Jan Long Harris and the team at Tyndale for their belief in the book and help in getting it out into the world, and my editor, Andrea Vinley Converse, who helped make this book the best it can be. I am grateful to my amazing wife, Tana, who is my partner in all I do, and to my family, who have tolerated my obsession with making brains better. I love you all.

About Daniel G. Amen, MD

Daniel G. Amen, MD, believes that brain health is central to all health and success. When your brain works right, he says, you work right, and when your brain is troubled, you are much more likely to have trouble in your life. His work is dedicated to helping people have better brains and better lives.

Sharecare named him the web's #1 most influential expert and advocate on mental health, and the *Washington Post* called him the most popular psychiatrist in America. His online videos have been viewed more than 300 million times.

Dr. Amen is a physician, board-certified child and adult psychiatrist, award-winning researcher, and 12-time *New York Times* bestselling author. He is the founder and CEO of Amen Clinics in Costa Mesa, Walnut Creek, and Encino, California; Bellevue, Washington; Washington, DC; Atlanta, GA; Chicago, IL; Dallas, TX; New York, NY; and Hollywood, FL.

Amen Clinics has the world's largest database of functional brain scans relating to behavior, with more than 200,000 SPECT scans and more than 10,000 qEEGs on patients from over 155 countries.

Dr. Amen is the lead researcher on the world's largest brain imaging and rehabilitation study on professional football players. His research has not only demonstrated high levels of brain damage in players, but also the possibility of significant recovery for many with the principles that underlie his work.

Together with Pastor Rick Warren and Dr. Mark Hyman, Dr. Amen is also one of the chief architects of The Daniel Plan, a program to get the world healthy through religious organizations, which has been done in thousands of churches, mosques, and synagogues.

Dr. Amen is the author or coauthor of more than 80 professional articles, 9 book chapters, and over 40 books, including 18 national bestsellers and 12 *New York Times* bestsellers, including the #1 *New York Times* bestsellers *The Daniel Plan* and the over-one-million-copies-sold, 40-week bestseller *Change Your Brain, Change Your Life*; as well as *The End of Mental Illness*; *Healing ADD*; *Change Your Brain, Change Your Body*; *The Brain Warrior's Way*; *Memory Rescue*; *Your Brain Is Always Listening*; and *You, Happier*.

Dr. Amen's published scientific articles have appeared in the prestigious journals of *Journal of Alzheimer's Disease*, Nature's *Molecular Psychiatry*, *PLOS ONE*, Nature's *Translational Psychiatry*, Nature's *Obesity*, *Journal of Neuropsychiatry and Clinical Neuroscience*, *Minerva Psichiatrica*, *Journal of Neurotrauma*, *American Journal of Psychiatry*, *Nuclear Medicine Communications*, *Neurological Research*, *Journal of the American Academy of Child and Adolescent Psychiatry*, *Primary Psychiatry*, *Military Medicine*, and *General Hospital Psychiatry*.

In January 2016, his team's research on distinguishing PTSD from TBI on over 21,000 SPECT scans was featured as one of the top 100 stories in science by *Discover* magazine. In 2017, his team published a study on over 46,000 scans, showing the difference between male and female brains; and in 2018, his team published a study on how the brain ages based on 62,454 SPECT scans.

Dr. Amen has written, produced, and hosted 17 national public television programs about brain health, which have aired more than 140,000 times across North America. As of March 2023, his latest show is *Change Your Brain Every Day*.

Together with his wife, Tana, he has hosted *The Brain Warrior's Way Podcast* since 2015, with over 1,000 episodes and 14 million downloads. It has been listed as one of the top 20 all-time podcasts in Mental Health on Apple.

Dr. Amen has appeared in movies, including *Quiet Explosions*, *After the Last Round*, and *The Crash Reel* and was a consultant for *Concussion*, starring Will Smith. He appeared in the docuseries *Justin Bieber: Seasons* and has appeared regularly on *The Dr. Oz Show*, *Dr. Phil*, and *The Doctors*.

He has also spoken for the National Security Agency (NSA), the National Science Foundation (NSF), Harvard's Learning and the Brain Conference, the Department of the Interior, the National Council of Juvenile and Family Court Judges, the Supreme Courts of Ohio, Delaware, and Wyoming, the Canadian and Brazilian Societies of Nuclear Medicine, and large corporations, such as Merrill Lynch, Hitachi, Bayer Pharmaceuticals, GNC, and many others. In 2016, Dr. Amen gave one of the prestigious Talks at Google.

Dr. Amen's work has been featured in *Newsweek*, *Time*, *Huffington Post*, *ABC World News*, *20/20*, the BBC, *London Telegraph*, *Parade* magazine, the *New York Times*, the *New York Times Magazine*, the *Washington Post*, *MIT Technology*, *World Economic Forum*, the *Los Angeles Times*, *Men's Health*, *Bottom Line*, *Vogue*, *Cosmopolitan*, and many others.

In 2010, Dr. Amen founded BrainMD, a fast-growing nutraceutical company dedicated to natural ways to support mental health and brain health.

Dr. Amen is married to Tana and is the father of four children and grandfather to Elias, Emmy, Liam, Louie, and Haven. He is also an avid table tennis player.

Resources

AMEN CLINICS, INC.

amenclinics.com

Amen Clinics, Inc. (ACI), was established in 1989 by Daniel G. Amen, MD. ACI specializes in innovative diagnosis and treatment planning for a wide variety of behavioral, learning, emotional, cognitive, and weight issues for children, teenagers, and adults. Brain SPECT imaging is one of the primary diagnostic tools used in our clinics. ACI has the world's largest database of brain scans for emotional, cognitive, and behavioral problems. It has an international reputation for evaluating brain-behavior problems, such as ADD/ADHD, depression, anxiety, school failure, traumatic brain injury and concussions, obsessive-compulsive disorders, aggressiveness, marital conflict, cognitive decline, brain toxicity from drugs or alcohol, and obesity, among others. In addition, we work with people to optimize brain function and decrease the risk for Alzheimer's disease and other age-related issues.

ACI welcomes referrals from physicians, psychologists, social workers, marriage and family therapists, drug and alcohol counselors, and individual patients and families.

Our toll-free number is (888) 288-9834.

Amen Clinics Orange County,
California
3150 Bristol St., Suite 400
Costa Mesa, CA 92626

Amen Clinics San Francisco
350 N. Wiget Ln., Suite 105
Walnut Creek, CA 94598

Amen Clinics Seattle
545 Andover Park West, Suite 101
Tukwila, WA 98188

Amen Clinics Los Angeles
5363 Balboa Blvd., Suite 100
Encino, CA 91316

Amen Clinics Washington, D.C.
10701 Parkridge Blvd., Suite 110
Reston, VA 20191

Amen Clinics New York
228 E. 45th Street, Suite 410
New York, NY 10017

Amen Clinics Atlanta
5901 Peachtree-Dunwoody Rd. NE,
Suite C65
Atlanta, GA 30328

Amen Clinics Chicago
2333 Waukegan, Suite 150
Bannockburn, IL 60015

Amen Clinics Dallas
7301 State Hwy 161, Suite 170
Irving, TX 75039

Amen Clinics Miami/Fort Lauderdale
200 South Park Rd., Suite 140
Hollywood, FL 33021

Amen Clinics Phoenix
Coming in 2023

BRAINMD

brainmd.com

For the highest-quality brain health supplements, courses, books, and information products

AMEN UNIVERSITY

amenuniversity.com

In 2014, Dr. Amen formed Amen University with courses on practical neuroscience, including:

- Amen Clinics Professional Brain Health Certification Course (with coaches in 56 countries)
- Brain Health Licensed Trainer Course
- Brain Thrive by 25, which has been shown to decrease drug, alcohol, and tobacco use, decrease depression, and improve self-esteem in teens and young adults
- Change Your Brain Master's Course
- Memory Rescue
- Concussion Rescue
- Healing ADD
- 6 Weeks to Overcome Anxiety, Depression, Trauma & Grief
- Autism: A New Way Forward
- The Brain Warrior's Way
- Brain Fit for Work and Life
- Overcoming Insomnia

Notes

1. B. J. Fogg, *Tiny Habits: The Small Changes That Change Everything* (Boston: Houghton Mifflin Harcourt, 2019), 4.

2. Justin Bieber, "The Dark Season—Justin Bieber: Seasons," February 3, 2020, in *Seasons*, video, 14:49, https://www.youtube.com/watch?v=Uz2-nYKCFlo; also see Amen Clinics, "How Justin Bieber Is Using Brain Science to Fight Depression," Resources, blog, February 3, 2020, https://www.amenclinics.com/blog/how-justin-bieber-is-using-brain-science-to-fight-depression/.

3. Ronald C. Kessler et al., "Lifetime Prevalence and Age-of-Onset Distributions of Mental Disorders in the World Health Organization's World Mental Health Survey Initiative," *World Psychiatry* 6 no. 3 (October 2007):168–76, https://www.ncbi.nlm .nih.gov/pmc /articles/PMC2174588/.

   See also Centers for Disease Control and Prevention, "About Mental Health," https:// www.cdc.gov/mentalhealth/learn/index.htm.

4. Rachel Tompa, "5 Unsolved Mysteries about the Brain," Neuroscience at the Allen Institute, March 14, 2019, https://alleninstitute.org/what-we-do/brain-science/news -press/articles/5-unsolved-mysteries-about-brain.

5. For more on this, see Daniel G. Amen, *Memory Rescue* (Carol Stream, IL: Tyndale Momentum, 2017).

6. Cision PR Newswire, October 14, 2016, https://www.prnewswire.com/news-releases /brain-thrive-by-25-improves-overall-brain-function-in-students-300345136.html.

7. Daniel G. Amen and Tana Amen, *The Brain Warrior's Way* (New York: New American Library, 2016), 36.

8. Jonathan Day et al., "Influence of Paternal Preconception Exposures on Their Offspring: Through Epigenetics to Phenotype," *American Journal of Stem Cells* 5, no. 1 (2016): 11–18.

9. Daniel G. Amen, *Magnificent Mind at Any Age* (New York: Three Rivers Press, 2008), 5–7.

10. Liesi E. Hebert et al., "Alzheimer Disease in the United States (2010–2050) Estimated Using the 2010 Census," *Neurology* 80, no. 19 (May 7, 2013): 1778–83, https://www.ncbi .nlm.nih.gov/pmc/articles/PMC3719424/.

    J. Wood, "Antidepressant Use Up 400 Percent in US," *PsychCentral*, October 25, 2011, https://ssristories.org/crimes-by-women-rising-in-u-s-chicago-tribune-antidepressant -use-up-400-percent-in-us-women-are-2-5-times-more-likely-to-take-antidepressant -medication-than-men-psychcentral/.

Andy Menke et al., "Prevalence of and Trends in Diabetes among Adults in the United States, 1988–2012," *JAMA* 314, no. 10 (September 8, 2015): 1021–29, https://pubmed.ncbi.nlm.nih.gov/26348752/.

Youfa Wang and Qiong Joanna Wang, "The Prevalence of Prehypertension and Hypertension among US Adults according to the New Joint National Committee Guidelines: New Challenges of the Old Problem," *Archives of Internal Medicine* 164, no. 19 (October 25, 2004): 2126–34, https://pubmed.ncbi.nlm.nih.gov/15505126/.

Cheryl D. Fryar, Margaret D. Carroll, and Joseph Afful, "Prevalence of Overweight, Obesity, and Severe Obesity among Adults Aged 20 and Over: United States, 1960–1962 through 2017–2018," National Center for Health Statistics, Health E-Stats (2020), updated January 29, 2021, https://www.cdc.gov/nchs/data/hestat/obesity-adult-17-18/obesity-adult.htm.

11. I learned this concept from Dave Grossman and Loren W. Christensen, *On Combat: The Psychology and Physiology of Deadly Conflict in War and in Peace*, 3rd ed. (Millstadt, IL: Warrior Science Publications, 2008).

12. Majid Fotuhi, "Can You Grow Your Hippocampus? Yes. Here's How, and Why It Matters," SharpBrains, November 4, 2015, http://sharpbrains.com/blog/2015/11/04/can-you-grow-your-hippocampus-yes-heres-how-and-why-it-matters/.

13. Daniel G. Amen, *Change Your Brain, Change Your Life* (New York: Harmony Books, 2015), 114.

14. Aliya Alimujiang et al., "Association between Life Purpose and Mortality among US Adults Older Than 50 Years," *JAMA Network Open* 2, no. 5 (May 3, 2019): e194270, https://pubmed.ncbi.nlm.nih.gov/31125099/.

15. Joana Araújo, Jianwen Cai, and June Stevens, "Prevalence of Optimal Metabolic Health in American Adults: National Health and Nutrition Examination Survey 2009–2016," *Metabolic Syndrome and Related Disorders* 17, no. 1 (February 2019): 46–52, https://pubmed.ncbi.nlm.nih.gov/30484738/.

16. Wendy M. Johnston and Graham C. L. Davey, "The Psychological Impact of Negative TV News Bulletins: The Catastrophizing of Personal Worries," *British Journal of Psychology* 88, no. 1 (February 1997): 85–91, https://pubmed.ncbi.nlm.nih.gov/9061893/.

17. Jenn Harris, "Girl Scout Sells Cookies outside Pot Dispensary: 117 Boxes in 2 Hours," *Los Angeles Times,* February 21, 2014, https://www.latimes.com/food/dailydish/la-dd-girl-scout-sells-cookies-pot-clinic-20140221-story.html.

18. Emily J. Jones et al., "Chronic Family Stress and Adolescent Health: The Moderating Role of Emotion Regulation," *Psychosomatic Medicine* 80, no. 8 (July 2018): 764–73, https://journals.lww.com/psychosomaticmedicine/Abstract/2018/10000/Chronic_Family_Stress_and_Adolescent_Health__The.10.aspx.

19. Max Planck, *Scientific Autobiography and Other Papers* (New York: Philosophical Library, 1949), 33–34.

20. Daniel G. Amen and Michael Easton, "A New Way Forward: How Brain SPECT Imaging Can Improve Outcomes and Transform Mental Health Care Into Brain Health Care," *Frontiers in Psychiatry* (December 10, 2021), https://www.frontiersin.org/articles/10.3389/fpsyt.2021.715315/full.

21. I first shared a version of this story in *Unleash the Power of the Female Brain* (New York: Harmony Books, 2013), 239.

22. Mitsutaka Takada, Mai Fujimoto, Kouichi Hosomi, "Association between Benzodiazepine Use and Dementia: Data Mining of Different Medical Databases," *International Journal of Medical Sciences* 13, no. 11 (October 18, 2016): 825–34, https://www.ncbi.nlm.nih.gov/pmc/articles/PMC5118753/.

23. Alzheimer's Association, *2022 Alzheimer's Disease Facts and Figures*, 2022, https://www.alz.org/media/Documents/alzheimers-facts-and-figures.pdf.

24. Stephanie Studenski et al., "Gait Speed and Survival in Older Adults," *JAMA* 305, no. 1 (January 5, 2011): 50–58.

25. Paul G. Harch et al., "A Phase I Study of Low-Pressure Hyperbaric Oxygen Therapy for Blast-Induced Post-concussion Syndrome and Post-traumatic Stress Disorder," *Journal of Neurotrauma* 29, no. 1 (January 1, 2012): 168–85, https://pubmed.ncbi.nlm.nih.gov/22026588/.

26. Justin Bieber, "The Dark Season—Justin Bieber: Seasons," February 3, 2020, in *Seasons*, video, 14:49, https://www.youtube.com/watch?v=Uz2-nYKCFlo.

27. Joshua J. Shaw et al., "Not Just Full of Hot Air: Hyperbaric Oxygen Therapy Increases Survival in Cases of Necrotizing Soft Tissue Infections," *Surgical Infections* 15, no. 3 (June 2014): 328–35, https://www.ncbi.nlm.nih.gov/pmc/articles/PMC4696431/.

28. Rahav Boussi-Gross et al., "Hyperbaric Oxygen Therapy Can Improve Post Concussion Syndrome Years after Mild Traumatic Brain Injury—Randomized Prospective Trial," *PLOS ONE* 8, no. 11 (November 15, 2013): e79995, https://pubmed.ncbi.nlm.nih.gov/24260334/.

Shai Efrati et al., "Hyperbaric Oxygen Induces Late Neuroplasticity in Post Stroke Patients—Randomized, Prospective Trial," *PLOS ONE* 8, no. 1 (2013): e53716, https://journals.plos.org/plosone/article?id=10.1371/journal.pone.0053716.

Shai Efrati et al., "Hyperbaric Oxygen Therapy Can Diminish Fibromyalgia Syndrome—Prospective Clinical Trial," *PLOS ONE* 10, no. 5 (May 26, 2015): e0127012, https://journals.plos.org/plosone/article?id=10.1371/journal.pone.0127012.

Chien-Yu Huang et al., "Hyperbaric Oxygen Therapy as an Effective Adjunctive Treatment for Chronic Lyme Disease," *Journal of the Chinese Medical Association* 77, no. 5 (May 2014): 269–71, https://pubmed.ncbi.nlm.nih.gov/24726678/.

I-Han Chiang et al., "Adjunctive Hyperbaric Oxygen Therapy in Severe Burns: Experience in Taiwan Formosa Water Park Dust Explosion Disaster," *Burns* (December 2016), https://pubmed.ncbi.nlm.nih.gov/28034667/.

Magnus Löndahl et al., "Relationship between Ulcer Healing after Hyperbaric Oxygen Therapy and Transcutaneous Oximetry, Toe Blood Pressure and Ankle-Brachial Index in Patients with Diabetes and Chronic Foot Ulcers," *Diabetologia* 54, no. 1 (January 2011): 65–68, https://link.springer.com/article/10.1007/s00125-010-1946-y.

Ann M. Eskes et al., "Hyperbaric Oxygen Therapy: Solution for Difficult to Heal Acute Wounds? Systematic Review," *World Journal of Surgery* 35, no. 3 (March 2011): 535–42, https://pubmed.ncbi.nlm.nih.gov/21184071/.

29. Paul G. Harch et al., "A Phase I Study of Low-Pressure Hyperbaric Oxygen Therapy for Blast-Induced Post-Concussion Syndrome and Post-Traumatic Stress Disorder," *Journal of Neurotrauma* 29, no. 1 (January 1, 2012): 168–85, https://pubmed.ncbi.nlm.nih.gov/22026588/.

30. Maureen Salamon, "Delaying Retirement May Help Stave Off Alzheimer's," WebMD, July 15, 2013, https://www.webmd.com/alzheimers/news/20130715/putting-off-retirement-may-help-stave-off-alzheimers.

31. Brandy Callahan et al., "Adult ADHD: Risk Factor for Dementia or Phenotypic Mimic?" *Frontiers in Aging Neuroscience* 3 (August 2017), https://www.frontiersin.org/articles/10.3389/fnagi.2017.00260/full.

32. José A. Gil-Montoya et al., "Is Periodontitis a Risk Factor for Cognitive Impairment and Dementia? A Case-Control Study," *Journal Periodontology* 86, no. 2 (February 2015): 244–53, https://pubmed.ncbi.nlm.nih.gov/25345338/.

Jianfeng Luo et al., "Association between Tooth Loss and Cognitive Function among 3063 Chinese Older Adults: A Community-Based Study," *PLOS ONE* 10, no. 3 March 24, 2015]: e0120986, https://journals.plos.org/plosone/article?id=10.1371/journal.pone.0120986.

33. Daniel G. Amen et al., "Quantitative Erythrocyte Omega-3 EPA Plus DHA Levels Are Related to Higher Regional Cerebral Blood Flow on Brain SPECT," *Journal of Alzheimer's Disease* 58, no. 4 (2017): 1189–99, https://pubmed.ncbi.nlm.nih.gov/28527220/.

34. Erik Messamore et al., "Polyunsaturated Fatty Acids and Recurrent Mood Disorders: Phenomenology, Mechanisms, and Clinical Application," *Progress in Lipid Research* 66 (April 2017): 1–13, https://www.ncbi.nlm.nih.gov/pmc/articles/PMC5422125/.

Jerome Sarris, David Mischoulon, and Isaac Schweitzer, "Omega-3 for Bipolar Disorder: Meta-analyses of Use in Mania and Bipolar Depression," *Journal of Clinical Psychiatry* 73, no. 1 (January 2012): 81–86, https://pubmed.ncbi.nlm.nih.gov/21903025/.

M. Elizabeth Sublette et al., "Omega-3 Polyunsaturated Essential Fatty Acid Status as a Predictor of Future Suicide Risk," *American Journal of Psychiatry* 163, no. 6 (June 2006): 1100–1102, https://ajp.psychiatryonline.org/doi/full/10.1176/ajp.2006.163.6.1100.

Trevor A. Mori and Lawrence J. Beilin, "Omega-3 Fatty Acids and Inflammation," *Current Atherosclerosis Reports* 6, no. 6 (November 2004): 461–67, https://pubmed.ncbi.nlm.nih.gov/15485592/.

Clemens von Schacky, "The Omega-3 Index as a Risk Factor for Cardiovascular Diseases," *Prostaglandins and Other Lipid Mediators* 96, nos. 1–4 (November 2011): 94–98, https://pubmed.ncbi.nlm.nih.gov/21726658/.

Michael H. Bloch and Ahmad Qawasmi, "Omega-3 Fatty Acid Supplementation for the Treatment of Children with Attention-Deficit/Hyperactivity Disorder Symptomatology: Systematic Review and Meta-Analysis," *Journal of the American Academy of Child and Adolescent Psychiatry* 50, no. 10 (October 2011): 991–1000, https://pubmed.ncbi.nlm.nih.gov/21961774/.

Yu Zhang et al., "Intakes of Fish and Polyunsaturated Fatty Acids and Mild-to-Severe Cognitive Impairment Risks: A Dose-Response Meta-analysis of 21 Cohort Studies," *American Journal of Clinical Nutrition* 103, no. 2 (February 2016): 330–40, https://pubmed.ncbi.nlm.nih.gov/26718417/.

J. D. Buckley and P. R. C. Howe, "Anti-Obesity Effects of Long-Chain Omega-3 Polyunsaturated Fatty Acids," *Obesity Reviews* 10, no. 6 (November 2009): 648–59, https://pubmed.ncbi.nlm.nih.gov/19460115/.

35. Lauren Manaker, "Getting Enough Omega-3s in Your Diet May Help You Live Longer," Verywell Health, May 7, 2021, https://www.verywellhealth.com/omega-3-risk-of-death-study-5183843#citation-2.

36. Joseph R. Hibbeln and Rachel V. Gow, "The Potential for Military Diets to Reduce Depression, Suicide, and Impulsive Aggression: A Review of Current Evidence for Omega-3 and Omega-6 Fatty Acids," *Military Medicine* 179, suppl. 11 (November 2014): 117–28, https://pubmed.ncbi.nlm.nih.gov/25373095/.

37. Hirohito Tsuboi et al., "Omega-3 Eicosapentaenoic Acid Is Related to Happiness and a Sense of Fulfillment—A Study among Female Nursing Workers," *Nutrients* 12, no. 11 (November 2020): 3462, https://www.ncbi.nlm.nih.gov/pmc/articles/PMC7696953/.

38. Roel J. T. Mocking et al., "Meta-analysis and Meta-regression of Omega-3 Polyunsaturated Fatty Acid Supplementation for Major Depressive Disorder," *Translational Psychiatry* 6, no. 3 (March 2016): e756, https://www.ncbi.nlm.nih.gov/pmc/articles/PMC4872453/.

39. Milan Fiala, "MGAT3 mRNA: A Biomarker for Prognosis and Therapy of Alzheimer's Disease by Vitamin D and Curcuminoids," *Journal of Alzheimer's Disease* 25, no. 1 (2011): 135–44, https://pubmed.ncbi.nlm.nih.gov/21368380/.

Esra Shishtar et al., "Long-Term Dietary Flavonoid Intake and Risk of Alzheimer Disease and Related Dementias in the Framingham Offspring Cohort," *American Journal of Clinical Nutrition* 112, no. 2 (August 2020): 343–53, https://academic.oup.com/ajcn/article/112/2/343/5823790.

40. Joshua Wolf Shenk, *Lincoln's Melancholy: How Depression Challenged a President and Fueled His Greatness* (New York: Houghton Mifflin, 2005), 12.

41. Joshua Wolf Shenk, "Lincoln's Great Depression," *Atlantic*, October 2005, https://www.theatlantic.com/magazine/archive/2005/10/lincolns-great-depression/304247/.

42. Gregory J. McHugo et al., "The Prevalence of Traumatic Brain Injury among People with Co-Occurring Mental Health and Substance Use Disorders," *Journal of Head Trauma Rehabilitation* 32, no. 3 (May/June 2017) : E65–E74, https://pubmed.ncbi.nlm.nih.gov/27455436/.

43. Nadia Kounang, "Former NFLers Call for End to Tackle Football for Kids," CNN, March 1, 2018, https://www.cnn.com/2018/01/18/health/nfl-no-tackle-football-kids/index.html.

44. Jason Duaine Hahn, "Brett Favre Warns Parents against Letting Kids Play Tackle Football Too Young: 'Not Worth the Risk,'" *People*, August 17, 2021, https://people.com/sports/brett-favre-asks-parents-not-to-let-children-under-14-play-football/.

45. Daniel G. Amen et al., "Reversing Brain Damage in Former NFL Players: Implications for Traumatic Brain Injury and Substance Abuse Rehabilitation," *Journal of Psychoactive Drugs* 43, no. 1 (Jan–Mar 2011): 1–5, https://pubmed.ncbi.nlm.nih.gov/21615001/.

46. Alec Rosenberg, "The Diagnosis That Rocked Football," University of California, October 21, 2015, https://www.universityofcalifornia.edu/news/diagnosis-rocked-football.

47. Vani Rao et al., "Aggression after Traumatic Brain Injury: Prevalence and Correlates," *Journal of Neuropsychiatry and Clinical Neurosciences* 21, no. 4 (Fall 2009): 420–29, https://www.ncbi.nlm.nih.gov/pmc/articles/PMC2918269/.

48. Daniel G. Amen et al., "Functional Neuroimaging Distinguishes Posttraumatic Stress Disorder from Traumatic Brain Injury in Focused and Large Community Datasets," *PLOS ONE*, July 1, 2015, https://journals.plos.org/plosone/article/metrics?id=10.1371/journal.pone.0129659.

49. Cyrus A. Raji et al., "Functional Neuroimaging with Default Mode Network Regions Distinguishes PTSD from TBI in a Military Veteran Population," *Brain Imaging and Behavior* 9, no. 3 (September 2015): 527–34, https://pubmed.ncbi.nlm.nih.gov/25917871/.

50. James S. Brown Jr., "Introduction: An Update on Psychiatric Effects of Toxic Exposures," *Psychiatric Times* 33, no. 9 (September 30, 2016), https://www.psychiatrictimes.com/view/introduction-update-psychiatric-effects-toxic-exposures.

Ki-Su Kim et al., "Associations between Organochlorine Pesticides and Cognition in U.S. Elders: National Health and Nutrition Examination Survey 1999–2002," *Environment International* 75 (February 2015): 87–92, https://pubmed.ncbi.nlm.nih.gov/25461417/.

51. "Don't Pucker Up," Campaign for Safe Cosmetics, October 12, 2007, http://www.safecosmetics.org/about-us/media/news-coverage/dont-pucker-up-lead-in-lipstick/.

52. Tanjaniina Laukkanen, "Sauna Bathing Is Inversely Associated with Dementia and Alzheimer's Disease in Middle-Aged Finnish Men," *Age and Ageing* 46, no. 2 (March 2017): 245–49, https://academic.oup.com/ageing/article/46/2/245/2654230.

53. "Alcohol Use and Cancer," American Cancer Society, last revised June 9, 2020, https://www.cancer.org/cancer/cancer-causes/diet-physical-activity/alcohol-use-and-cancer.html.

54. Remi Daviet et al., "Associations between Alcohol Consumption and Gray and White Matter Volumes in the UK Biobank," *Nature Communications* 13 (March 4, 2022): 1175, https://www.nature.com/articles/s41467-022-28735-5.

55. "Cannabis (Marijuana) DrugFacts," National Institute on Drug Abuse, December 2019, https://nida.nih.gov/publications/drugfacts/cannabis-marijuana.

56. Samuel T. Wilkinson, Elina Stefanovics, and Robert A. Rosenheck, "Marijuana Use Is Associated with Worse Outcomes in Symptom Severity and Violent Behavior in Patients with PTSD," *Journal of Clinical Psychiatry* 76, no. 9 (September 2015): 1174–80, https://www.ncbi.nlm.nih.gov/pmc/articles/PMC6258013/.

57. Gregory Rompala, Yoko Nomura, and Yasmin L. Hurd, "Maternal Cannabis Use is Associated with Suppression of Immune Gene Networks in Placenta and Increased Anxiety Phenotypes in Offspring," *PNAS* 118, no. 47 (November 15, 2021): e2106115118, https://www.pnas.org/doi/full/10.1073/pnas.2106115118.

58. Barynia Backeljauw et al., "Cognition and Brain Structure following Early Childhood Surgery with Anesthesia," *Pediatrics* 136, no. 1 (July 2015): e1–e12, https://www.ncbi.nlm.nih.gov/pmc/articles/PMC4485006/.

59. N. Efimova et al., "Changes in Cerebral Blood Flow and Cognitive Function in Patients Undergoing Coronary Bypass Surgery with Cardiopulmonary Bypass," *Kardiologiia* 55, no. 6 (June 2015): 40–46, https://pubmed.ncbi.nlm.nih.gov/28294781/.

60. "Personal Care Products Safety Act Would Improve Cosmetics Safety," Environmental Working Group, accessed April 14, 2022, https://www.ewg.org/personal-care-products -safety-act-would-improve-cosmetics-safety.

61. A. Guttmann, "Advertising Spending in the Perfumes, Cosmetics, and Other Toilet Preparations Industry in the United States from 2018 to 2020," Statista, July 19, 2021, https://www.statista.com/statistics/470467/perfumes-cosmetics-and-other-toilet -preparations-industry-ad-spend-usa/.

62. Stacy Malkan, "Johnson & Johnson Is Just the Tip of the Toxic Iceberg," *Time*, March 2, 2016, https://time.com/4239561/johnson-and-johnson-toxic-ingredients/.

63. Ian H. Stanley, Melanie A. Hom, and Thomas E. Joiner, "A Systematic Review of Suicidal Thoughts and Behaviors among Police Officers, Firefighters, EMTs, and Paramedics," *Clinical Psychology Review* 44 (March 2016): 25–44, https://pubmed.ncbi.nlm.nih.gov /26719976/.

64. Melanie A. Hom et al., "Mental Health Service Use among Firefighters with Suicidal Thoughts and Behaviors," *Psychiatric Services* 67, no. 6 (February 29, 2016): 688–91, https://ps.psychiatryonline.org/doi/10.1176/appi.ps.201500177.

65. Jon E. Grant et al., "E-cigarette Use (Vaping) Is Associated with Illicit Drug Use, Mental Health Problems, and Impulsivity in University Students," *Annals of Clinical Psychiatry* 31, no. 1 (February 2019): 27–35, https://pubmed.ncbi.nlm.nih.gov/30699215/.

66. "Surgeon General's Advisory on E-cigarette Use among Youth," Office of the Surgeon General, 2018, https://e-cigarettes.surgeongeneral.gov/documents/surgeon-generals -advisory-on-e-cigarette-use-among-youth-2018.pdf.

67. "Teens Using Vaping Devices in Record Numbers," National Institute on Drug Abuse, December 17, 2018, https://nida.nih.gov/news-events/news-releases/2018/12/teens -using-vaping-devices-in-record-numbers.

68. Gabriella Gobbi et al., "Association of Cannabis Use in Adolescence and Risk of Depression, Anxiety, and Suicidality in Young Adulthood: A Systematic Review and Meta-analysis," *JAMA Psychiatry* 76, no. 4 (April 2019), 426–34.

69. Megan Leonhardt, "44% of Older Millennials Already Have a Chronic Health Condition. Here's What That Means for Their Futures," CNBC Make It, May 4, 2021, https://www .cnbc.com/2021/05/04/older-millennials-chronic-health-conditions.html.

70. "The Health of Millennials," Blue Cross Blue Shield, April 24, 2019, https://www.bcbs .com/the-health-of-america/reports/the-health-of-millennials.

71. Nicole Racine et al., "Global Prevalence of Depressive and Anxiety Symptoms in Children and Adolescents during COVID-19," *JAMA Pediatrics* 175, no. 11 (August 9, 2021): 1142– 50, https://jamanetwork.com/journals/jamapediatrics/fullarticle/2782796.

72. Jordan Passman, "The World's Most Relaxing Song," *Forbes*, November 23, 2016, https:// www.forbes.com/sites/jordanpassman/2016/11/23/the-worlds-most-relaxing-song/.

73. "Exercise Is an All-Natural Treatment to Fight Depression," Harvard Health Publishing, Harvard Medical School, February 2, 2021, https://www.health.harvard.edu/mind-and -mood/exercise-is-an-all-natural-treatment-to-fight-depression.

74. Sean H Yutzy, "The Increasing Frequency of Mania and Bipolar Disorder: Causes and Potential Negative Impacts," *Journal of Nervous and Mental Disease* 200, no. 5 (May 2012):380-387, https://pubmed.ncbi.nlm.nih.gov/22551790/.

75. Mark Zimmerman, et al., "Psychiatric Diagnoses in Patients Previously Overdiagnosed with Bipolar Disorder," *Journal Clinical Psychiatry* 71, no. 1 (Jan. 2010): 26-31. https:// pubmed.ncbi.nlm.nih.gov/19646366/.

76. Jorge Correale, María Célica Ysrraelit, and María Inés Gaitán, "Immunomodulatory Effects of Vitamin D in Multiple Sclerosis," *Brain* 132, part 5 (May 2009): 1146–60, https:// pubmed.ncbi.nlm.nih.gov/19321461/.

77. See "Vitamin D, View the Evidence: 1377 Abstracts with Vitamin D Research," GreenMedInfo, accessed April 15, 2022, https://www.greenmedinfo.com/substance /vitamin-d.

78. Herbert W. Harris et al., "Vitamin D Deficiency and Psychiatric Illness," *Current Psychiatry* 12, no. 4 (April 2013): 18–27, https://www.mdedge.com/psychiatry/article/66349/depression/vitamin-d-deficiency-and-psychiatric-illness.

79. Paul Knekt et al., "Serum 25-hydroxyvitamin D Concentration and Risk of Dementia," *Epidemiology* (Cambridge, MA) 25, no. 6 (November 2014): 799–804, https://pubmed.ncbi.nlm.nih.gov/25215530/.

80. C. Annweiler et al., "Vitamin D Insufficiency and Mild Cognitive Impairment: Cross-Sectional Association," *European Journal of Neurology* 19, no. 7 (July 2012): 1023–29, https://pubmed.ncbi.nlm.nih.gov/22339714/.

81. Adit A. Ginde, Mark C. Liu, and Carlos A. Camargo Jr., "Demographic Differences and Trends of Vitamin D Insufficiency in the US Population, 1988–2004," *Archives of Internal Medicine* 169, no. 6 (March 23, 2009): 626–32, https://pubmed.ncbi.nlm.nih.gov/19307527/.

82. E. Sohl et al., "The Impact of Medication on Vitamin D Status in Older Individuals," *European Journal of Endocrinology* 166, no. 3 (March 2012): 477–85, https://eje.bioscientifica.com/view/journals/eje/166/3/477.xml.

83. Maxime Taquet et al., "Bidirectional Associations between COVID-19 and Psychiatric Disorder: Retrospective Cohort Studies of 62354 COVID-19 Cases in the USA," *Lancet Psychiatry* 8, no. 2 (November 9, 2020): 130–40, https://www.thelancet.com/journals/lanpsy/article/PIIS2215-0366(20)30462-4/fulltext.

84. Elizabeth M. Rhea et al., "The S1 Protein of SARS-CoV-2 Crosses the Blood–Barrier in Mice," *Nature Neuroscience* 24 (2021): 368–78, https://www.nature.com/articles/s41593-020-00771-8.

85. For example, see James S. Brown Jr., "Geographic Correlation of Schizophrenia to Ticks and Tick-Borne Encephalitis," *Schizophrenia Bulletin* 20, no. 4 (1994): 755–75, https://academic.oup.com/schizophreniabulletin/article/20/4/755/1933512.

Maxime Taquet et al., "Bidirectional Associations between COVID-19 and Psychiatric Disorder: Retrospective Cohort Studies of 62354 COVID-19 Cases in the USA," *Lancet Psychiatry* 8, no. 2 (November 9, 2020): 130–40, https://www.thelancet.com/journals/lanpsy/article/PIIS2215-0366(20)30462-4/fulltext.

86. Richard Shames and Karilee Shames, with Georjana Grace Shames, *Thyroid Mind Power: The Proven Cure for Hormone-Related Depression, Anxiety, and Memory Loss* (New York: Rodale, 2011), 3.

87. Gail B. Slap, "Oral Contraceptives and Depression: Impact, Prevalence, and Cause," *Journal of Adolescent Health Care* 2, no. 1 (September 1981): 53–64, https://pubmed.ncbi.nlm.nih.gov/7037718/.

88. Charlotte Wessel Skovlund et al., "Association of Hormonal Contraception with Depression," *JAMA Psychiatry* 73, no. 11 (2016): 1154–62, https://jamanetwork.com/journals/jamapsychiatry/fullarticle/2552796.

89. Andy Menke et al., "Prevalence of and Trends in Diabetes among Adults in the United States, 1988–2012," *JAMA* 314, no. 10 (September 8, 2015): 1021–29.

"Obesity and Overweight," National Center for Health Statistics, Centers for Disease Control and Prevention, last reviewed September 20, 2021, https://www.cdc.gov/nchs/fastats/obesity-overweight.htm.

90. Suzanne M. de la Monte and Jack R. Wands, "Alzheimer's Disease Is Type 3 Diabetes—Evidence Reviewed," *Journal of Diabetes Science and Technology* 2, no. 6 (November 2008): 1101–13, https://www.ncbi.nlm.nih.gov/pmc/articles/PMC2769828/.

91. Danielle Underferth, "Sugar, Insulin Resistance and Cancer: What's the Link?" MD Anderson, June 21, 2021, https://www.mdanderson.org/cancerwise/sugar--insulin-resistance-and-cancer--what-is-the-link.h00-159461634.html.

92. Rosebud O. Roberts et al., "Relative Intake of Macronutrients Impacts Risk of Mild Cognitive Impairment or Dementia," *Journal of Alzheimer's Disease* 32, no. 2 (January 1, 2012): 32939, https://www.ncbi.nlm.nih.gov/pmc/articles/PMC3494735/.

93. Robert Moritz, "Drew Carey: No More Mr. Fat Guy," *Parade*, September 26, 2010, https://parade.com/47683/robertmoritz/26-drew-carey/.

94. "Sleep and Sleep Disorder Statistics," American Sleep Association, accessed April 15, 2022, https://www.sleepassociation.org/about-sleep/sleep-statistics/.

95. Tammy Kennon, "5 New Brain Disorders That Were Born out of the Digital Age," *The Week*, February 28, 2017, https://theweek.com/articles/677922/5-new-brain-disorders-that-born-digital-age.

96. Jerome Sarris et al., "Adjunctive Nutraceuticals for Depression: A Systematic Review and Meta-Analyses," *American Journal of Psychiatry* 173, no. 6 (June 2016): 575–87, https://ajp.psychiatryonline.org/doi/10.1176/appi.ajp.2016.15091228.

97. "Micronutrient Facts," Centers for Disease Control and Prevention, last reviewed February 1, 2022, https://www.cdc.gov/nutrition/micronutrient-malnutrition/micronutrients/index.html.

98. Byron Katie, with Stephen Mitchell, *Loving What Is: Four Questions That Can Change Your Life* (New York: Harmony Books, 2002).

99. Daniel G. Amen, *Change Your Brain, Change Your Life* (New York: Harmony Books, 2015), 118–119.

100. Guiseppe Passarino, Francesco De Rango, and Alberto Montesanto, "Human Longevity: Genetics or Lifestyle? It Takes Two to Tango," *Immunity and Ageing* 13, no. 2 (April 2016), doi: 10.1186/s12979-016-0066-z.

"Genes Are Not Destiny: Obesity-Promoting Genes in an Obesity-Promoting World," Harvard T.H. Chan School of Public Health, https://www.hsph.harvard.edu/obesity-prevention-source/obesity-causes/genes-and-obesity/.

101. Jessica Skorka-Brown et al., "Playing Tetris Decreases Drug and Other Cravings in Real World Settings," *Addictive Behaviors* 51 (December 2015): 165–70, https://pubmed.ncbi.nlm.nih.gov/26275843/.

102. Nicholas A. Christakis and James H. Fowler, "The Spread of Obesity in a Large Social Network over 32 Years," *New England Journal of Medicine* 357, no. 4 (July 26, 2007): 370–79, https://www.nejm.org/doi/full/10.1056/nejmsa066082.

103. Daniel G. Amen et al., "Functional Neuroimaging Distinguishes Posttraumatic Stress Disorder from Traumatic Brain Injury in Focused and Large Community Datasets," *PLOS ONE* 10, no. 7 (July 1, 2015): e0129659, https://journals.plos.org/plosone/article?id=10.1371/journal.pone.0129659.

Daniel G. Amen et al., "Patterns of Regional Cerebral Blood Flow as a Function of Obesity in Adults," *Journal of Alzheimer's Disease* 77, no. 3 (2020):1331–37, https://content.iospress.com/articles/journal-of-alzheimers-disease/jad200655.

Daniel G. Amen et al., "Patterns of Regional Cerebral Blood Flow as a Function of Age throughout the Lifespan," *Journal of Alzheimer's Disease* 65, no. 4 (2018):1087–92, https://content.iospress.com/articles/journal-of-alzheimers-disease/jad180598.

104. Shayla Love, "Why You Should Talk to Yourself in the Third Person," *Vice*, December 28, 2020, https://www.vice.com/en/article/k7a3mm/why-you-should-talk-to-yourself-in-the-third-person-inner-monologue.

Igor Grossmann et al., "Training for Wisdom: The Distanced-Self-Reflection Diary Method," *Psychological Science* 32, no. 3 (March 2021): 381–94, https://pubmed.ncbi.nlm.nih.gov/33539229/.

105. Steven C. Hayes, "5 Effective Exercises to Help You Stop Believing Your Unwanted Automatic Thoughts," Ideas.Ted.Com, October 22, 2019, https://ideas.ted.com/5-effective-exercises-to-help-you-stop-believing-your-unwanted-automatic-thoughts/.

106. "2 Women Survive Ordeal along 80-Foot-High Indiana Rail Bridge," NBC 5 Chicago, July 30, 2014, https://www.nbcchicago.com/news/local/2-women-survive-ordeal-along-indiana-rail-bridge/65978/.

107. Daniel G. Amen et al., "Impact of Playing American Professional Football on Long-Term Brain Function," *Journal of Neuropsychiatry and Clinical Neurosciences* 23, no. 1 (Winter 2011): 98–106, https://pubmed.ncbi.nlm.nih.gov/21304145/.

Daniel G. Amen et al., "Reversing Brain Damage in Former NFL players: Implications for Traumatic Brain Injury and Substance Abuse Rehabilitation," *Journal of Psychoactive Drugs* 43, no. 1 (Jan–Mar 2011): 1–5. doi: 10.1080/02791072.2011.566489.

Daniel G. Amen, "Amen Clinics Position on Chronic Traumatic Encephalopathy (CTE)," blog, Amen Clinics, March 30, 2022, https://www.amenclinics.com/blog/amen-clinics -position-on-chronic-traumatic-encephalopathy-cte/.

108. Natalie Parletta et al., "A Mediterranean-Style Dietary Intervention Supplemented with Fish Oil Improves Diet Quality and Mental Health in People with Depression: A Randomized Controlled Trial (HELFIMED)," *Nutritional Neuroscience* (December 7, 2017): 1–14, https://pubmed.ncbi.nlm.nih.gov/29215971/.

Ji-Sheng Han, "Acupuncture and Endorphins," *Neuroscience Letters* 361, nos. 1–3 (May 6, 2004): 258–61, https://pubmed.ncbi.nlm.nih.gov/15135942/.

Barry Goldstein, *The Secret Language of the Heart: How to Use Music, Sound, and Vibration as Tools for Healing and Personal Transformation* (San Antonio, TX: Hierophant Publishing, 2016).

Gary Elkins, Mark P. Jensen, and David R. Patterson, "Hypnotherapy for the Management of Chronic Pain," *International Journal of Clinical and Experimental Hypnosis* 55, no. 3 (July 2007): 275–87, https://www.ncbi.nlm.nih.gov/pmc/articles/PMC2752362/.

109. Laurel Curran, "Food Dyes Linked to Cancer, ADHD, Allergies," Food Safety News, July 8, 2010, https://www.foodsafetynews.com/2010/07/popular-food-dyes-linked-to-cancer -adhd-and-allergies/.

110. Howard S. Friedman and Leslie R. Martin, *The Longevity Project: Surprising Discoveries for Health and Long Life from the Landmark Eight-Decade Study* (New York: Hudson Street Press, 2011).

111. Daniel and Tana Amen, *The Brain Warrior's Way* (New York: New American Library, 2016), 47–48.

112. José A. Gil-Montoya et al., "Is Periodontitis a Risk Factor for Cognitive Impairment and Dementia? A Case-Control Study," *Journal of Periodontology* 86, no. 2 (February 2015): 244–53, https://pubmed.ncbi.nlm.nih.gov/25345338/.

113. Kristine Yaffe et al., "Depressive Symptoms and Cognitive Decline in Nondemented Elderly Women: A Prospective Study," *Archives of General Psychiatry* 56, no. 5 (May 1999): 425–30, https://pubmed.ncbi.nlm.nih.gov/10232297/.

114. Nian-Sheng Tzeng et al., "Risk of Dementia in Adults with ADHD: A Nationwide, Population-Based Cohort Study in Taiwan," *Journal of Attention Disorders* 23, no. 9 (July 2019): 995–1006, https://pubmed.ncbi.nlm.nih.gov/28629260/.

115. Ellen Van Velsor and Jean Brittain Leslie, "Why Executives Derail: Perspectives across Time and Cultures," *Academy of Management Executive* 9, no. 4 (November 1995): 62–72, http://www.jstor.org/stable/4165289.

116. Diana I. Tamir and Jason P. Mitchell, "Disclosing Information about the Self Is Intrinsically Rewarding," *PNAS* 109, no. 21 (May 2012): 8038–43, https://www.pnas.org /doi/10.1073/pnas.1202129109.

117. "What's Your Positivity Ratio? Take the Positivity Quiz and Find Out!" *Happier Human* (blog), October 24, 2012, https://www.happierhuman.com/positivity-ratio/.

118. Kyle Benson, "The Magic Relationship Ratio, according to Science," Gottman Institute, accessed April 21, 2022, https://www.gottman.com/blog/the-magic-relationship-ratio -according-science/.

119. Loren Toussaint et al., "Effects of Lifetime Stress Exposure on Mental and Physical Health in Young Adulthood: How Stress Degrades and Forgiveness Protects Health," *Journal of Health Psychology* 21, no. 6 (June 2016): 1004–14, https://pubmed.ncbi.nlm.nih .gov/25139892/.

120. Kirsten Weir, "Forgiveness Can Improve Mental and Physical Health," *Monitor on Psychology* 48, no. 1 (January 2017): 30, https://www.apa.org/monitor/2017/01/ce-corner.

121. Everett Worthington, "REACH Forgiveness of Others," Everett Worthington (website), accessed April 21, 2022, http://www.evworthington-forgiveness.com/reach-forgiveness -of-others.

122. Byron Katie (@ByronKatie), Twitter, March 16, 2014, 10:45 a.m., https://twitter.com /byronkatie/status/445224290506801154.

123. Jenny Radesky et al., "Maternal Mobile Device Use during a Structured Parent-Child Interaction Task," *Academic Pediatrics* 15, no. 2 (Mar/Apr 2015): 238–44, https://www .ncbi.nlm.nih.gov/pmc/articles/PMC4355325/.

124. Daniel G. Amen et al., "Gender-Based Cerebral Perfusion Differences in 46,034 Functional Neuroimaging Scans," *Journal of Alzheimer's Disease* 60, no. 2 (2017): 605–14, https://pubmed.ncbi.nlm.nih.gov/28777753/.

125. Daniel G. Amen et al., "Gender-Based Cerebral Perfusion Differences in 46,034 Functional Neuroimaging Scans."

126. Howard S. Friedman and Leslie R. Martin, *The Longevity Project: Surprising Discoveries for Health and Long Life from the Landmark Eight-Decade Study* (New York: Plume, 2012).

127. Richard J. Haier et al., "The Neuroanatomy of General Intelligence: Sex Matters," *NeuroImage* 25, no. 1 (March 2005): 320–27, https://pubmed.ncbi.nlm.nih.gov/15734366/.

128. Haier et al., "Neuroanatomy."

129. S. Nishizawa et al., "Differences between Males and Females in Rates of Serotonin Synthesis in Human Brain," *PNAS* 94, no. 10 (May 13, 1997): 5308–13, https://www.pnas .org/doi/10.1073/pnas.94.10.5308.

130. Erika L. Sabbath et al., "Time May Not Fully Attenuate Solvent-Associated Cognitive Deficits in Highly Exposed Workers," *Neurology* 82, no. 19 (May 13, 2014): 1716–23, https://www.ncbi.nlm.nih.gov/pmc/articles/PMC4032208/.

131. Helen E. Fisher et al., "Intense, Passionate, Romantic Love: A Natural Addiction? How the Fields That Investigate Romance and Substance Abuse Can Inform Each Other," *Frontiers in Psychology* 7 (2016): 687, https://www.ncbi.nlm.nih.gov/pmc/articles/PMC4861725/.

132. Niccolò Machiavelli, *The Prince (Il Principe)*, 1513, translation.

133. Zeynep Baran Tatar and Şahika Yüksel, "Mobbing at Workplace—Psychological Trauma and Documentation of Psychiatric Symptoms," *Nöropsikiyatri Arşivi (Archives of Neuropsychiatry)* 56, no. 1 (March 2019):57-62. https://pubmed.ncbi.nlm.nih.gov/30911239/.

134. Margo Wilson and Martin Daly, "Do Pretty Women Inspire Men to Discount the Future?" *Proceedings of the Royal Society B* 271 (May 7, 2004): S177–S179, https:// royalsocietypublishing.org/doi/10.1098/rsbl.2003.0134.

135. Johan C. Karremans et al., "Interacting with Women Can Impair Men's Cognitive Functioning," *Journal of Experimental Social Psychology* 45, no. 4 (July 2009): 1041–44, https://www.sciencedirect.com/science/article/abs/pii/S0022103109001164.

136. Alex George, "Wallace Killer Chiesa Denied Prison Release," *Calaveras Enterprise*, February 24, 2012, http://www.calaverasenterprise.com/news/article_182d2f4a-5f13 -11e1-ac1d-001871e3ce6c.html.

137. Fyodor Dostoyevsky, *Crime and Punishment* (Russia: The Russian Messenger, 1866).

138. Og Mandino, *The Greatest Salesman in the World* (New York: Bantam Books, 1983), 54.

139. Daniel G. Amen, *Change Your Brain, Change Your Life* (New York: Harmony Books, 1998, 2015), 194–197.

140. Purushottam Jangid et al., "Comparative Study of Efficacy of L-5-Hydroxytryptophan and Fluoxetine in Patients Presenting with First Depressive Episode," *Asian Journal of Psychiatry* 6, no. 1 (February 2013): 29–34, https://pubmed.ncbi.nlm.nih.gov/23380314/.

A. Ghajar et al., "Crocus Sativus L. versus Citalopram in the Treatment of Major Depressive Disorder with Anxious Distress: A Double-Blind, Controlled Clinical Trial," *Pharmacopsychiatry* 50, no. 4 (July 2017): 152–60, https://pubmed.ncbi.nlm.nih.gov /27701683/.

141. L. M. Ascher, "Paradoxical Intention in the Treatment of Urinary Retention," *Behaviour Research and Therapy* 17, no. 3 (1979): 267–70, https://psycnet.apa.org/record/1980 -28336-001.

142. P. Salmon, "Effects of Physical Exercise on Anxiety, Depression, and Sensitivity to Stress: A Unifying Theory," *Clinical Psychology Review* 21, no. 1 (February 2001):33–61, https://pubmed.ncbi.nlm.nih.gov/11148895/.

143. Marije aan het Rot et al., "Bright Light Exposure during Acute Tryptophan Depletion Prevents a Lowering of Mood in Mildly Seasonal Women," *European Neuropsychopharmacology* 18, no. 1 (January 2008): 14–23, https://pubmed.ncbi.nlm.nih.gov/17582745/.

144. Andy Menke et al., "Prevalence of and Trends in Diabetes among Adults in the United States, 1988–2012," *JAMA* 314, no. 10 (September 8, 2015): 1021–29, https://pubmed.ncbi.nlm.nih.gov/26348752/.

   Cheryl D. Fryar, Margaret D. Carroll, and Joseph Afful, "Prevalence of Overweight, Obesity, and Severe Obesity among Adults Aged 20 and Over: United States, 1960–1962 through 2017–2018," National Center for Health Statistics, Health E-Stats (2020), updated January 29, 2021, https://www.cdc.gov/nchs/data/hestat/obesity-adult-17-18/obesity-adult.htm.

145. Howard S. Friedman and Leslie R. Martin, *The Longevity Project: Surprising Discoveries for Health and Long Life from the Landmark Eight-Decade Study* (New York: Plume, 2012).

146. "'Infomania' Worse Than Marijuana," BBC News, updated April 22, 2005, http://news.bbc.co.uk/2/hi/uk_news/4471607.stm.

   Mark Liberman, "An Apology," *Language Log* (blog), September 25, 2005, http://itre.cis.upenn.edu/~myl/languagelog/archives/002493.html.

147. Brian G. Dias and Kerry J. Ressler, "Parental Olfactory Experience Influences Behavior and Neural Structure in Subsequent Generations," *Nature Neuroscience* 17, no. 1 (January 2014): 89–96, https://www.ncbi.nlm.nih.gov/pmc/articles/PMC3923835/.

148. Olena Babenko, Igor Kovalchuk, and Gerlinde A. S. Metz, "Stress-Induced Perinatal and Transgenerational Epigenetic Programming of Brain Development and Mental Health," *Neuroscience and Biobehavioral Reviews* 48 (January 2015): 70–91, https://pubmed.ncbi.nlm.nih.gov/25464029/.

   Claire Gillespie, "What Is Generational Trauma? Here's How Experts Explain It," *Health*, October 27, 2020, https://www.health.com/condition/ptsd/generational-trauma.

149. Gang Wu et al., "Understanding Resilience," *Frontiers in Behavioral Neuroscience* 7 (February 15, 2013): 10, https://www.frontiersin.org/articles/10.3389/fnbeh.2013.00010/full.

150. James W. Carson et al., "Loving-Kindness Meditation for Chronic Low Back Pain: Results from a Pilot Trial," *Journal of Holistic Nursing* 23, no. 3 (September 2005): 287–304, https://pubmed.ncbi.nlm.nih.gov/16049118/.

   Xianglong Zeng et al., "The Effect of Loving-Kindness Meditation on Positive Emotions: A Meta-analytic Review," *Frontiers in Psychology* 6 (November 3, 2015): 1693, https://www.ncbi.nlm.nih.gov/pmc/articles/PMC4630307/.

   Barbara L. Fredrickson et al., "Open Hearts Build Lives: Positive Emotions, Induced through Loving-Kindness Meditation, Build Consequential Personal Resources," *Journal of Personality and Social Psychology* 95, no. 5 (November 2008): 1045–62, https://www.ncbi.nlm.nih.gov/pmc/articles/PMC3156028/.

151. Petra H. Wirtz and Roland von Känel, "Psychological Stress, Inflammation, and Coronary Heart Disease," *Current Cardiology Reports* 19 (September 2017): 111, https://link.springer.com/article/10.1007/s11886-017-0919-x.

   O. Olafiranye et al., "Anxiety and Cardiovascular Risk: Review of Epidemiological and Clinical Evidence," *Mind and Brain, the Journal of Psychiatry* (England) 2, no. 1 (2011): 32–37, https://www.ncbi.nlm.nih.gov/pmc/articles/PMC3150179/.

152. John A. Chalmers et al., "Anxiety Disorders Are Associated with Reduced Heart Rate Variability: A Meta-Analysis," *Frontiers in Psychiatry* 5 (July 11, 2014): 80, https://pubmed.ncbi.nlm.nih.gov/25071612/.

153. Lukas de Lorent et al., "Auricular Acupuncture versus Progressive Muscle Relaxation in Patients with Anxiety Disorders or Major Depressive Disorder: A Prospective Parallel Group Clinical Trial," *Journal of Acupuncture and Meridian Studies* 9, no. 4 (August 2016): 191–99, https://pubmed.ncbi.nlm.nih.gov/27555224/.

A. B. Wallbaum et al., "Progressive Muscle Relaxation and Restricted Environmental Stimulation Therapy for Chronic Tension Headache: A Pilot Study," *International Journal of Psychosomatics* 38, nos. 1–4 (February 1991): 33–39, https://pubmed.ncbi.nlm.nih.gov /1778683/.

Cecile A. Lengacher et al., "Immune Responses to Guided Imagery during Breast Cancer Treatment," *Biological Research for Nursing* 9, no. 3(January 2008): 205–14, https:// pubmed.ncbi.nlm.nih.gov/18077773/.

Yoon Bok Hahn et al., "The Effect of Thermal Biofeedback and Progressive Muscle Relaxation Training in Reducing Blood Pressure of Patients with Essential Hypertension," *Image: the Journal of Nursing Scholarship* 25, no. 3 (Fall 1993): 204–7, https://pubmed.ncbi .nlm.nih.gov/8225352/.

154. E. B. Blanchard et al., "Hand Temperature Norms for Headache, Hypertension, and Irritable Bowel Syndrome," *Biofeedback and Self-Regulation* 14, no. 4 (December 1989): 319–31, https://pubmed.ncbi.nlm.nih.gov/2631972/.

155. Lawrence E. Williams and John A. Bargh, "Experiencing Physical Warmth Promotes Interpersonal Warmth," *Science* 322, no. 5901 (October 24, 2008): 606–7, https://www.ncbi .nlm.nih.gov/pmc/articles/PMC2737341/.

156. Bethany Heitman, "Christina Aguilera Talks Confidence and Working Through Insecurities in the Public Eye," *Health*, April 13, 2021, https://www.health.com/celebrities/christina -aguilera.

157. Good News Network, "72% of Brits Feel More Confident When They Finally Stop Worrying about What People Think of Them in Their 40s," April 30, 2021, https://www .goodnewsnetwork.org/poll-onepoll-brits-become-confident-at-46/.

158. "6-Year-Old Aiden Leos' Killers Pleas Not Guilty in Road Rage Killing," NBC News, April 12, 2022, https://www.nbclosangeles.com/news/local/aiden-leos-road-rage -shooting-orange-county-plead-not-guilty/2868440./

159. Smiljanic Stasha, "20+ Mind-Numbing US Road Rage Statistics—2022 Edition," PolicyAdvice, 2022, https://policyadvice.net/insurance/insights/road-rage-statistics/.

160. Michael D. Resnick et al., "Protecting Adolescents from Harm: Findings from the National Longitudinal Study on Adolescent Health," *JAMA* 278, no. 10, (September 10, 1997): 823–32, https://pubmed.ncbi.nlm.nih.gov/9293990/.

161. Ben Renner, "American Families Spend Just 37 Minutes of Quality Time Together per Day, Study Finds," Study Finds, March 21, 2018, https://www.studyfinds.org/american -families-spend-37-minutes-quality-time/.

162. Alison Wood Brooks, "Get Excited: Reappraising Pre-performance Anxiety as Excitement," *Journal of Experimental Psychology: General* 143, no. 3 (June 2014): 1144–58, https://pubmed.ncbi.nlm.nih.gov/24364682/.

163. Mark Hardy, Michael D. Kirk-Smith, and David D. Stretch, "Replacement of Drug Treatment for Insomnia by Ambient Odour," *Lancet* 346, no. 8976 (1995): 701, https:// pubmed.ncbi.nlm.nih.gov/7658836/.

Namni Goel, Hyungsoo Kim, and Raymund P. Lao, "An Olfactory Stimulus Modifies Nighttime Sleep in Young Men and Women," *Chronobiology International* 22, no. 5 (2005): 889–904, https://pubmed.ncbi.nlm.nih.gov/16298774/.

164. Willow Winsham, "Emperor Frankenstein: The Truth behind Frederick II of Sicily's Sadistic Science Experiments," History Answers, August 19, 2017, https://www. historyanswers.co.uk/kings-queens/emperor-frankenstein-the-truth-behind-frederick -ii-of-sicilys-sadistic-science-experiments/.

165. Harry T. Chugani et al., "Local Brain Functional Activity following Early Deprivation: A Study of Postinstitutionalized Romanian Orphans," *NeuroImage* 14, no. 6 (December 2001): 1290–1301, https://pubmed.ncbi.nlm.nih.gov/11707085/.

166. Thomas Schäfer et al., "The Psychological Functions of Music Listening," *Frontiers in Psychology* 4 (2013): 511, https://www.ncbi.nlm.nih.gov/pmc/articles/PMC3741536/.

167. Barry Goldstein, *The Secret Language of the Heart: How to Use Music, Sound, and Vibration as Tools for Healing and Personal Transformation* (San Antonio, TX: Hierophant Publishing, 2016), 29, 31.

168. Madhuleena Roy Chowdhury, "19 Best Positive Psychology Interventions + How to Apply Them," blog, PositivePsychology.com, updated March 24, 2022, https://positivepsychology.com /positive-psychology-interventions/.

169. Martin E. P. Seligman et al., "Positive Psychology Progress: Empirical Validation of Interventions," *American Psychologist* 60, no. 5 (July/August 2005): 410–21, https://pubmed .ncbi.nlm.nih.gov/16045394/.

170. "31 Benefits of Gratitude: The Ultimate Science-Backed Guide," *Happier Human* (blog), August 1, 2020, https://www.happierhuman.com/benefits-of-gratitude/.

Courtney E. Ackerman, "28 Benefits of Gratitude and Most Significant Research Findings," blog, PositivePsychology.com, updated March 29, 2022, https://positivepsychology.com /benefits-gratitude-research-questions/.

171. Nancy L. Sin, Sonja Lyubomirsky, "Enhancing Well-Being and Alleviating Depressive Symptoms with Positive Psychology Interventions: A Practice-Friendly Meta-Analysis," *Journal of Clinical Psychology* 65, no. 5 (May 2009): 467–87, https://onlinelibrary.wiley.com /doi/abs/10.1002/jclp.20593.

172. Helen Y. Weng et al., "Compassion Training Alters Altruism and Neural Responses to Suffering," *Psychological Science* 24, no. 7 (May 21, 2013): 1171–80, http://europepmc.org /article/MED/23696200.

Jill Ladwig, "Brain Can Be Trained in Compassion, Study Shows," University of Wisconsin–Madison, May 22, 2013, https://news.wisc.edu/brain-can-be-trained-in-compassion-study -shows/.

173. Ariana Grande, Facebook, May 22, 2017, 10:35 p.m., https://m.facebook.com/arianagrande /posts/10154526340546027.

174. Martin E. P. Seligman et al., "Positive Psychology Progress: Empirical Validation of Interventions," *American Psychologist* 60, no. 5 (July/August 2005): 410–21, https:// pubmed.ncbi.nlm.nih.gov/16045394/.

Bryant M. Stone and Acacia C. Parks, "Cultivating Subjective Well-Being through Positive Psychological Interventions," in *Handbook of Well-Being*, ed. Ed Diener, Shigehiro Oishi, and Louis Tay (Salt Lake City: DEF Publishers, 2018), https://www.nobascholar.com /chapters/59.

175. Dharma Singh Khalsa et al., "Cerebral Blood Flow Changes during Chanting Meditation," *Nuclear Medicine Communications* 30, no. 12 (December 2009): 956–61, https://pubmed .ncbi.nlm.nih.gov/19773673/.

176. Sara W. Lazer et al. "Meditation Experience Is Associated with Increased Cortical Thickness," *Neuroreport* 16, no. 17 (November 29, 2005): 1893–7, https://pubmed.ncbi .nlm.nih.gov/16272874/.

177. Rena R. Wing and Robert W. Jeffery, "Benefits of Recruiting Participants with Friends and Increasing Social Support for Weight Loss and Maintenance," *Journal of Consulting and Clinical Psychology* 67, no. 1 (132–38), https://content.apa.org/record/1999-00242-015.

178. Dale E. Bredesen, "Reversal of Cognitive Decline: A Novel Therapeutic Program," *Aging* 6, no. 9 (September 2014): 707–17, https://www.ncbi.nlm.nih.gov/pmc/articles /PMC4221920/.

179. Daniel G. Amen, "Brain Warriors Tackle Football . . . and Discover an Incredible Truth," Amen Clinics NFL Study 2015, http://docplayer.net/15511811-Brain-warriors-tackle -football-and-discover-an-incredible-truth.html.

180. Julie A. Mattison et al., "Caloric Restriction Improves Health and Survival of Rhesus Monkeys," *Nature Communications* 8 (2017): 14063, https://www.nature.com/articles /ncomms14063.

181. Liz Parks, "Beverages Contribute One-Fifth of Calories Consumed," *Supermarket News*, January 29, 2007, https://www.supermarketnews.com/archive/beverages-contribute-one -fifth-calories-consumed.

182. Kiyah J. Duffey and Barry M. Popkin, "Shifts in Patterns and Consumption of Beverages between 1965 and 2002," *Obesity* 15, no. 11 (November 2007): 2739–47, https://pubmed.ncbi.nlm.nih.gov/18070765/.

183. Cynthia A. Daley et al., "A Review of Fatty Acid Profiles and Antioxidant Content in Grass-Fed and Grain-Fed Beef," *Nutrition Journal* 9 (2010): 10, https://www.ncbi.nlm.nih.gov/pmc/articles/PMC2846864/.

184. Rosebud O. Roberts et al., "Relative Intake of Macronutrients Impacts Risk of Mild Cognitive Impairment or Dementia," *Journal of Alzheimer's Disease* 32, no. 2 (2012): 329–39, https://www.ncbi.nlm.nih.gov/pmc/articles/PMC3494735/.

185. Soili M. Lehto et al., "Low Serum HDL-Cholesterol Levels Are Associated with Long Symptom Duration in Patients with Major Depressive Disorder," *Psychiatry and Clinical Neurosciences* 64, no. 3 (June 2010): 279–83, https://pubmed.ncbi.nlm.nih.gov/20374538/.

James M. Greenblatt, "The Implications of Low Cholesterol in Depression and Suicide," The Great Plains Laboratory, November 16, 2015, https://www.greatplainslaboratory.com/articles-1/2015/11/13/the-implications-of-low-cholesterol-in-depression-and-suicide.

186. James E. Gangwisch et al., "High Glycemic Index Diet as a Risk Factor for Depression: Analyses from the Women's Health Initiative," *American Journal of Clinical Nutrition* 102, no. 2 (August 2015): 454–63, https://www.ncbi.nlm.nih.gov/pmc/articles/PMC4515860/.

Kara L. Breymeyer et al., "Subjective Mood and Energy Levels of Healthy Weight and Overweight/Obese Healthy Adults on High- and Low-Glycemic Load Experimental Diets," *Appetite* 107 (December 1, 2016): 253–59, https://pubmed.ncbi.nlm.nih.gov/27507131/.

187. Medhavi Gautam et al., "Role of Antioxidants in Generalised Anxiety Disorder and Depression," *Indian Journal of Psychiatry* 54, no. 3 (July–September 2012): 244–47, https://www.ncbi.nlm.nih.gov/pmc/articles/PMC3512361/.

188. Redzo Mujcic and Andrew J. Oswald, "Evolution of Well-Being and Happiness after Increases in Consumption of Fruit and Vegetables," *American Journal of Public Health* 106, no. 8 (August 2016): 1504–10, https://pubmed.ncbi.nlm.nih.gov/27400354/.

189. Heather Ann Hausenblas et al., "Saffron (Crocus sativus L.) and Major Depressive Disorder: A Meta-Analysis of Randomized Clinical Trials," *Journal of Integrative Medicine* 11, no. 6 (November 2013): 377–83, https://pubmed.ncbi.nlm.nih.gov/24299602/.

190. Magda Tsolaki et al., "Efficacy and Safety of Crocus sativus L. in Patients with Mild Cognitive Impairment: One Year Single-Blind Randomized, with Parallel Groups, Clinical Trial," *Journal of Alzheimer's Disease* 54, no. 1 (July 2016): 129–33, https://pubmed.ncbi.nlm.nih.gov/27472878/.

Mehdi Farokhnia et al., "Comparing the Efficacy and Safety of Crocus sativus L. with Memantine in Patients with Moderate to Severe Alzheimer's Disease: A Double-Blind Randomized Clinical Trial," *Human Psychopharmacology* 29, no. 4 (July 2014): 351–59, https://pubmed.ncbi.nlm.nih.gov/25163440/.

Amirhossein Modabbernia et al., "Effect of Saffron on Fluoxetine-Induced Sexual Impairment in Men: Randomized Double-Blind Placebo-Controlled Trial," *Psychopharmacology* 223, no. 4 (October 2012): 381–88, https://pubmed.ncbi.nlm.nih.gov/22552758/.

Ladan Kashani et al., "Saffron for Treatment of Fluoxetine-Induced Sexual Dysfunction in Women: Randomized Double-Blind Placebo-Controlled Study," *Human Psychopharmacology* 28, no. 1 (January 2013): 54–60, https://pubmed.ncbi.nlm.nih.gov/23280545/.

191. Shrikant Mishra and Kalpana Palanivelu, "The Effect of Curcumin (Turmeric) on Alzheimer's Disease: An Overview," *Annals of Indian Academy of Neurology* 11, no. 1 (January–March 2008): 13–19, https://www.ncbi.nlm.nih.gov/pmc/articles/PMC2781139/.

192. Adrian L. Lopresti, "Salvia (Sage): A Review of Its Potential Cognitive-Enhancing and Protective Effects," *Drugs in R&D* 17, no. 1 (March 2017): 53–64, https://www.ncbi.nlm.nih.gov/pmc/articles/PMC5318325/.

193. EWG Science Team, "Clean Fifteen," *EWG's 2022 Shopper's Guide to Pesticides in Produce*, Environmental Working Group, April 7, 2022, https://www.ewg.org/foodnews/clean-fifteen.php.

194. EWG Science Team, "Dirty Dozen," *EWG's 2022 Shopper's Guide to Pesticides in Produce*, Environmental Working Group, April 7, 2022, https://www.ewg.org/foodnews/dirty -dozen.php.

195. Abdulaziz Farooq et al., "A Prospective Study of the Physiological and Neurobehavioral Effects of Ramadan Fasting in Preteen and Teenage Boys," *Journal of the Academy of Nutrition and Dietetics* 115, no. 6 (June 2015): 889–97, https://pubmed.ncbi.nlm.nih.gov /25840939/.

196. N. M. Hussin et al., "Efficacy of Fasting and Calorie Restriction (FCR) on Mood and Depression among Ageing Men," *Journal of Nutrition, Health and Aging* 17, no. 8 (2013): 674–80, https://pubmed.ncbi.nlm.nih.gov/24097021/.

197. Tatiana Moro et al., "Effects of Eight Weeks of Time-Restricted Feeding (16/8) on Basal Metabolism, Maximal Strength, Body Composition, Inflammation, and Cardiovascular Risk Factors in Resistance-Trained Males," *Journal of Translational Medicine* 14, no. 1 (October 13, 2016): 290, https://translational-medicine.biomedcentral.com/articles /10.1186/s12967-016-1044-0.

198. Mo'ez Al-Islam E. Faris et al., "Intermittent Fasting during Ramadan Attenuates Proinflammatory Cytokines and Immune Cells in Healthy Subjects," *Nutrition Research* 32, no. 12 (December 2012): 947–55, https://pubmed.ncbi.nlm.nih.gov/23244540/.

199. Andrea R. Vasconcelos et al., "Intermittent Fasting Attenuates Lipopolysaccharide-Induced Neuroinflammation and Memory Impairment," *Journal of Neuroinflammation* 11 (May 6, 2014): 85, https://jneuroinflammation.biomedcentral.com/articles/10.1186 /1742-2094-11-85.

200. Ben Spencer, "Why You Should NEVER Eat after 7 p.m.: Late Night Meals 'Increases the Risk of Heart Attack and Stroke,'" *Daily Mail*, August 31, 2016, http://www.dailymail.co.uk/ health/article-3767231/Why-NEVER-eat-7pm-Late-night -meals-increases-risk-heart -attack-stroke.html.

201. Ameneh Madjd et al., "Beneficial Effect of High Energy Intake at Lunch Rather Than Dinner on Weight Loss in Healthy Obese Women in a Weight-Loss Program: A Randomized Clinical Trial," *American Journal of Clinical Nutrition* 104, no. 4 (October 1, 2016): 982–89, https://pubmed.ncbi.nlm.nih.gov/27581472/.

202. "Celiac Disease: Fast Facts," Beyond Celiac, accessed April 23, 2022, https://www .beyondceliac.org/celiac-disease/facts-and-figures/.

203. "Celiac Disease."

204. Helmut Niederhofer, "Association of Attention-Deficit/Hyperactivity Disorder and Celiac Disease: A Brief Report," *Primary Care Companion for CNS Disorders* 13, no. 3 (2011): e1–e3, https://pubmed.ncbi.nlm.nih.gov/21977364/.

Paul Whiteley et al., "The ScanBrit Randomised, Controlled, Single-Blind Study of a Gluten- and Casein-Free Dietary Intervention for Children with Autism Spectrum Disorders," *Nutritional Neuroscience* 13, no. 2, (April 2010): 87–100, https://pubmed.ncbi .nlm.nih.gov/20406576/.

Antonio Di Sabatino et al., "Small Amounts of Gluten in Subjects with Suspected Nonceliac Gluten Sensitivity: A Randomized, Double-Blind, Placebo-Controlled, Cross-Over Trial," *Clinical Gastroenterology and Hepatology* 13, no. 9 (September 2015): 1604–12. e3, https://pubmed.ncbi.nlm.nih.gov/25701700/.

S. L. Peters et al., "Randomised Clinical Trial: Gluten May Cause Depression in Subjects with Non-Coeliac Glutensensitivity—an Exploratory Clinical Study," *Alimentary Pharmacology & Therapeutics* 39, no. 10 (May 2014): 1104–12, https://pubmed.ncbi.nlm.nih.gov/24689456/.

205. Stephani L. Stancil et al., "Naltrexone Reduces Binge Eating and Purging in Adolescents in an Eating Disorder Program," *Journal of Child and Adolescent Psychopharmacology* 29, no. 9 (November 2019): 72124, https://pubmed.ncbi.nlm.nih.gov/31313939/.

206. R. Mesnage et al., "Potential Toxic Effects of Glyphosate and Its Commercial Formulations below Regulatory Limits," *Food and Chemical Toxicology* 84 (October 2015): 133–53, https://pubmed.ncbi.nlm.nih.gov/26282372/.

207. Alexis Baden-Meyer, "15 Health Problems Linked to Monsanto's Roundup (EcoWatch)," Green America, July 30, 2015, originally published at EcoWatch, January 23, 2015, https://greenamerica.org/blog/15-health-problems-linked-monsantos-roundup-ecowatch.

208. Catherine J. E. Ingram et al., "Lactose Digestion and the Evolutionary Genetics of Lactase Persistence," *Human Genetics* 124, no. 6 (January 2009): 579–91, https://pubmed.ncbi.nlm.nih.gov/19034520/.

209. Giselle S. Duarte and Adriana Farah, "Effect of Simultaneous Consumption of Milk and Coffee on Chlorogenic Acids' Bioavailability in Humans," *Journal of Agricultural and Food Chemistry* 59, no. 14 (May 31, 2011): 7925–31, https://pubs.acs.org/doi/10.1021/jf201906p.

Philippe Bourassa et al., "The Effect of Milk Alpha-Casein on the Antioxidant Activity of Tea Polyphenols," *Journal of Photochemistry and Photobiology B* 128 (November 5, 2013): 43–49, https://pubmed.ncbi.nlm.nih.gov/24001682/.

210. "Brain Thrive by 25 Improves Overall Brain Function in Students," PRN Newswire, Oct. 14, 2016, https://www.prnewswire.com/news-releases/brain-thrive-by-25-improves-overall-brain-function-in-students-300345136.html.

211. Walter Mischel, *The Marshmallow Test: Why Self-Control Is the Engine of Success* (New York: Little, Brown, 2015).

212. James Ewinger, "New Diet for Gorillas at Cleveland Metroparks Zoo Helps Animals with Needed Weight Loss," cleveland.com, July 6, 2011, https://www.cleveland.com/metro/2011/07/new_diet_for_apes_at_cleveland.html.

213. Mary Papenfuss, "Cleveland Zoo Loses 32-Year-Old Gorilla Bebac to Heart Disease," *HuffPost*, January 8, 2017, https://www.huffpost.com/entry/cleveland-zoo-gorilla-bebac-dies_n_5871ab96e4b043ad97e3b76a.

214. Jerome Sarris et al., "Nutritional Medicine as Mainstream in Psychiatry," *Lancet* 2, no. 3 (March 2015): 271–74, https://www.thelancet.com/journals/lanpsy/article/PIIS2215-0366(14)00051-0/fulltext.

215. Matthew S. Ganio et al., "Mild Dehydration Impairs Cognitive Performance and Mood of Men," *British Journal of Nutrition* 106, no. 10 (November 2011): 1535–43, https://pubmed.ncbi.nlm.nih.gov/21736786/.

Lawrence E. Armstrong et al., "Mild Dehydration Affects Mood in Healthy Young Women," *Journal of Nutrition* 142, no. 2 (February 2012): 382–88, https://academic.oup.com/jn/article/142/2/382/4743487.

216. Erik Messamore et al., "Polyunsaturated Fatty Acids and Recurrent Mood Disorders: Phenomenology, Mechanisms, and Clinical Application," *Progress in Lipid Research* 66 (April 2017): 1–13, https://pubmed.ncbi.nlm.nih.gov/28069365/.

Roel J. T. Mocking et al., "Meta-Analysis and Meta-Regression of Omega-3 Polyunsaturated Fatty Acid Supplementation for Major Depressive Disorder," *Translational Psychiatry* 6, no. 3 (March 15, 2016), https://pubmed.ncbi.nlm.nih.gov/26978738/.

217. A. Ghajar et al., "*Crocus Sativus L.* versus Citalopram in the Treatment of Major Depressive Disorder with Anxious Distress: A Double-Blind, Controlled Clinical Trial," *Pharmacopsychiatry* 50, no. 4 (July 2017): 152–60, https://pubmed.ncbi.nlm.nih.gov/27701683/.

Xiangying Yang et al., "Comparative Efficacy and Safety of *Crocus Sativus L.* for Treating Mild to Moderate Major Depressive Disorder in Adults: A Meta-analysis of Randomized Controlled Trials," *Neuropsychiatric Disease and Treatment* 2018, no. 14 (May 21, 2018): 1297–305, https://pubmed.ncbi.nlm.nih.gov/29849461/.

218. G. C. Leng, "Impact of Antioxidant Therapy on Symptoms of Anxiety and Depression. A Randomized Controlled Trial in Patients with Peripheral Arterial Disease," *Journal of Nutritional and Environmental Medicine* 8 no. 4 (1998): 321–-28, https://www.tandfonline.com/doi/abs/10.1080/13590849861899.

219. G. Fond, "Inflammation in Psychiatric Disorders," *European Psychiatry* 29, no. S3 (2014): 551–52, https://www.cambridge.org/core/journals/european-psychiatry/article/abs/inflammation-in-psychiatric-disorders/87C75DB707FE32CAD5533C964FC1FD9B.

220. Lidy M. Pelsser et al., "Effects of Food on Physical and Sleep Complaints in Children with ADD/ADHD: A Randomised Controlled Pilot Study," *European Journal of Pediatrics* 169, no. 9 (September 2010): 1129–38, https://pubmed.ncbi.nlm.nih.gov/20401617/.

Paola Bressan and Peter Kramer, "Bread and Other Edible Agents of Mental Disease," *Frontiers in Human Neuroscience* 10 (March 29, 2016): 130, https://pubmed.ncbi.nlm.nih.gov/27065833/.

221. Lidy M. J. Pelsser et al., "A Randomised Controlled Trial into the Effects of Food on ADD/ADHD," *European Child and Adolescent Psychiatry* 18, no. 1, (January 2009): 12–19, https://pubmed.ncbi.nlm.nih.gov/18431534/.

222. "Any Anxiety Disorder," Mental Health Information, Statistics, National Institute of Mental Health, accessed April 28, 2022, https://www.nimh.nih.gov/health/statistics/any-anxiety-disorder.

223. Siegfried Kasper et al., "Lavender Oil Preparation Silexan Is Effective in Generalized Anxiety Disorder—a Randomized, Double-Blind Comparison to Placebo and Paroxetine," *International Journal of Neuropsychopharmacology* 17, no. 6 (June 2014): 859–69, https://pubmed.ncbi.nlm.nih.gov/24456909/.

Hossein Ebrahimi et al., "The Effects of Lavender and Chamomile Essential Oil Inhalation Aromatherapy on Depression, Anxiety and Stress in Older Community-Dwelling People: A Randomized Controlled Trial," *Explore* (New York) 18, no. 3 (May/June 2022), 272–78, published ahead of print S1550–8307, January 9, 2021, https://www.sciencedirect.com/science/article/abs/pii/S155083072100001.

Mohamad Yadegari et al., "Effects of Inhaling Jasmine Essential Oil on Anxiety and Blood Cortisol Levels in Candidates for Laparotomy: A Randomized Clinical Trial," *Journal of Nursing and Midwifery Sciences* 8, no. 2 (2021): 128–33, https://www.jnmsjournal.org/article.asp?issn=2345-5756;year=2021;volume=8;issue=2;spage=128;epage=133;aulast=Yadegari.

224. Neil Bernard Boyle, Clare Lawton, and Louise Dye, "The Effects of Magnesium Supplementation on Subjective Anxiety and Stress–A Systematic Review," *Nutrients* 9, no. 5 (April 26, 2017): e429, https://pubmed.ncbi.nlm.nih.gov/28445426/.

225. K. Kimura et al. "L-Theanine Reduces Psychological and Physiological Stress Responses," *Biological Psychology* 74, no. 1 (January 2007): 39–45, https://pubmed.ncbi.nlm.nih.gov/16930802/.

226. Adham M. Abdou et al., "Relaxation and Immunity Enhancement Effects of γ-Aminobutyric Acid (GABA) Administration in Humans," *BioFactors* 26, no. 3 (2006): 201–8, https://iubmb.onlinelibrary.wiley.com/doi/10.1002/biof.5520260305.

227. Andrew B. Newberg et al., "Cerebral Blood Flow Differences between Long-Term Meditators and Non-Meditators," *Consciousness and Cognition* 19, no. 4 (December 2010): 899–905, https://pubmed.ncbi.nlm.nih.gov/20570534/.

Heidi Jiang et al., "Brain Activity and Functional Connectivity Associated with Hypnosis," *Cerebral Cortex* 27, no. 8 (August 1, 2017): 4083–93, https://academic.oup.com/cercor/article/27/8/4083/3056452.

228. Robert F. Anda et al., "The Enduring Effects of Abuse and Related Adverse Experiences in Childhood. A Convergence of Evidence from Neurobiology and Epidemiology," *European Archives of Psychiatry and Clinical Neuroscience* 256, no. 3 (2006): 174–86, https://pubmed.ncbi.nlm.nih.gov/16311898/.

229. Redzo Mujcic and Andrew J. Oswald, "Evolution of Well-Being and Happiness After Increases in Consumption of Fruit and Vegetables," *American Journal of Public Health* 106, no. 8 (August 1, 2016): 1504–10, https://ajph.aphapublications.org/doi/10.2105/AJPH.2016.303260.

230. Nicole Celestine, "The Science of Happiness in Positive Psychology 101," *Happiness & SWB* (blog), PositivePsychology.com, last updated March 28, 2022, https://positivepsychology.com/happiness/.

231. Dennis Prager, "Why Be Happy?" PragerU, January 20, 2014, video, 5:05, https://www.youtube.com/watch?v=_Zxnw0l499g.

232. Howard S. Friedman and Leslie R. Martin, *The Longevity Project: Surprising Discoveries for Health and Long Life from the Landmark Eight-Decade Study* (New York: Plume, 2012).

233. Joel Fuhrman, "The Hidden Dangers of Fast and Processed Food," *American Journal of Lifestyle Medicine* 12, no. 5 (September/October 2018): 375–81, https://www.ncbi.nlm.nih .gov/pmc/articles/PMC6146358/.

Joel Fuhrman, "An Interview with Dr. Joel Fuhrman on the Importance of Diet," interview by Oliver M. Glass, *American Journal of Psychiatry Residents' Journal* 14, no. 3 (March 8, 2019): 6–7, https://psychiatryonline.org/doi/full/10.1176/appi.ajp-rj.2019.140303.

234. American Cancer Society, "Alcohol Use and Cancer," June 9, 2020, https://www.cancer .org/content/dam/CRC/PDF/Public/7770.00.pdf.

235. Daniel Kahneman and Angus Deaton, "High Income Improves Evaluation of Life but Not Emotional Well-Being," *PNAS* 107, no. 38 (September 7, 2010), https://www.pnas.org /doi/10.1073/pnas.1011492107.

236. Stephen Arterburn, email message to author. Daniel G. Amen, *Change Your Brain, Change Your Life*, rev. ed. (New York: Harmony Books, 2015), 343.

237. Salk Institute, "How the Brain Recognizes What the Eye Sees," ScienceDaily, June 8, 2017, https://www.sciencedaily.com/releases/2017/06/170608145602.htm.

238. Cecily Maller et al., "Healthy Nature Healthy People: 'Contact with Nature' as an Upstream Health Promotion Intervention for Populations," *Health Promotion International* 21, no. 1 (March 2006): 45–54, https://pubmed.ncbi.nlm.nih.gov/16373379/.

239. Yuna L. Ferguson and Kennon M. Sheldon, "Trying to Be Happier Really Can Work: Two Experimental Studies," *Journal of Positive Psychology* 8, no. 1 (January 2013): 23–33, https://psycnet.apa.org/record/2013-01626-003.

240. Adam Leipzig, "How to Know Your Life Purpose in 5 Minutes," TEDx Malibu, February 1, 2013, video, 10:33, https://www.youtube.com/watch?v=vVsXO9brK7M&list=PLiKtxxcS -pbQ9BPH68bS6yPK1L7T4GmLW&index=5.

241. Christina Puchalski and Anna L. Romer, "Taking a Spiritual History Allows Clinicians to Understand Patients More Fully," *Journal of Palliative Medicine* 3, no. 1 (Spring 2000): 129–37, https://pubmed.ncbi.nlm.nih.gov/15859737/.

242. Aliya Alimujiang et al., "Association between Life Purpose and Mortality among US Adults Older Than 50 Years," *JAMA Network Open* 2, no. 5 (2019): e194270, https://jamanetwork .com/journals/jamanetworkopen/fullarticle/2734064.

243. Daisy Fancourt et al., "Psychosocial Singing Interventions for the Mental Health and Well-Being of Family Carers of Patients with Cancer: Results from a Longitudinal Controlled Study," *BMJ Open* 9, no. 8 (August 10, 2019): e026995, https://pubmed.ncbi.nlm.nih.gov /31401592/.

Sara Eldirdiry Osman, Victoria Tischler, and Justine Schneider, "'Singing for the Brain': A Qualitative Study Exploring the Health and Well-Being Benefits of Singing for People with Dementia and Their Carers," *Dementia* (London) 15, no. 6 (November 2016): 1326–39, https://pubmed.ncbi.nlm.nih.gov/25425445/.

244. Felicity Maria Simpson, Gemma Perry, and William Forde Thompson, "Assessing Vocal Chanting as an Online Psychosocial Intervention," *Frontiers in Psychology* 12 (June 1, 2021): 647632, https://www.frontiersin.org/articles/10.3389/fpsyg.2021.647632/full.

"Mantra Chanting: How Do Mantras Affect Brain? What Are Its Benefits?" *Times of India*, July 9, 2020, https://timesofindia.indiatimes.com/religion/mantras-chants/mantra -chanting-how-do-mantras-affect-brain-what-are-its-benefits/articleshow/76867950 .cms.

245. Linda Wasmer Andrews, "Hum a Happy Tune for Wellness," *Psychology Today*, November 21, 2011, https://www.psychologytoday.com/us/blog/minding-the-body /201111/hum-happy-tune-wellness.

Jonathan Goldman and Andi Goldman, *The Humming Effect: Sound Healing for Health and Happiness* (Rochester, VT: Healing Arts Press, 2017).

246. Shelley Snow et al., "Exploring the Experience and Effects of Vocal Toning," *Journal of Music Therapy* 55, no. 2 (2018): 221–50, https://www.researchgate.net/publication/325355020_Exploring_the_Experience_and_Effects_of_Vocal_Toning.

247. Don Campbell, *The Mozart Effect: Tapping the Power of Music to Heal the Body, Strengthen the Mind, and Unlock the Creative Spirit* (New York: HarperCollins, 2001).

248. Harry Benson and Rehna Azim, "Celebrity Divorce Rates," Marriage Foundation, January 2016, https://marriagefoundation.org.uk/wp-content/uploads/2016/06/pdf-03.pdf.

249. Valorie N. Salimpoor et al., "Anatomically Distinct Dopamine Release during Anticipation and Experience of Peak Emotion to Music," *Nature Neuroscience* 14 (January 9, 2011): 257–62, https://www.nature.com/articles/nn.2726.

250. Ángel Pazos, Alphonse Probst, and J. M. Palacios, "Serotonin Receptors in the Human Brain—IV. Autoradiographic Mapping of Serotonin-2 Receptors," *Neuroscience* 21, no. 1 (April 1987): 123–39, https://pubmed.ncbi.nlm.nih.gov/3601071/.

251. Simon N. Young, "How to Increase Serotonin in the Human Brain without Drugs," *Journal of Psychiatry and Neuroscience* 32, no. 6 (November 2007): 394–99, https://www.ncbi.nlm.nih.gov/pmc/articles/PMC2077351/.

252. Imperial College London, "Rethinking Serotonin Could Lead to a Shift in Psychiatric Care," ScienceDaily, September 4, 2017, https://www.sciencedaily.com/releases/2017/09/170904093724.htm.

253. Rhonda P. Patrick and Bruce N. Ames, "Vitamin D and the Omega-3 Fatty Acids Control Serotonin Synthesis and Action, Part 2: Relevance for ADD/ADHD, Bipolar Disorder, Schizophrenia, and Impulsive Behavior," *FASEB Journal* 29, no. 6 (February 24, 2015): 2207–22, https://faseb.onlinelibrary.wiley.com/doi/full/10.1096/fj.14-268342.

254. Tiffany Field et al., "Massage Therapy Effects on Depressed Pregnant Women," *Journal of Psychosomatic Obstetrics and Gynaecology* 25, no. 2 (June 2004): 115–22, https://pubmed.ncbi.nlm.nih.gov/15715034/.

255. Tiffany Field et al., "Cortisol Decreases and Serotonin and Dopamine Increase following Massage Therapy," *International Journal of Neuroscience* 115, no. 10 (October 2005): 1397–413, https://pubmed.ncbi.nlm.nih.gov/16162447/.

256. Elisabeth Perreau-Linck et al., "In vivo Measurements of Brain Trapping of C-labelled Alpha-methyl-L- tryptophan during Acute Changes in Mood States," *Journal of Psychiatry and Neuroscience* 32, no. 6 (November 2007): 430–34, https://pubmed.ncbi.nlm.nih.gov/18043767/.

257. Melanie Greenberg, "The Science of Love and Attachment," *Psychology Today*, March 30, 2016, https://www.psychologytoday.com/us/blog/the-mindful-self-express/201603/the-science-love-and-attachment.

Scott Edwards, "Love and the Brain," Harvard Medical School, Spring 2015, https://hms.harvard.edu/news-events/publications-archive/brain/love-brain.

258. Martin Sack et al., "Intranasal Oxytocin Reduces Provoked Symptoms in Female Patients with Posttraumatic Stress Disorder Despite Exerting Sympathomimetic and Positive Chronotropic Effects in a Randomized Controlled Trial," *BMC Medicine* 15, no. 1 (February 2017): 40, https://www.ncbi.nlm.nih.gov/pmc/articles/PMC5314583/.

259. Lori Singer, "Why It Feels Good to Hug Our Babies and Get Massages," Be Her Village, September 24, 2020, https://behervillage.com/articles/oxytocin-more-than-a-love-hormone.

260. Miho Nagasawa et al., "Oxytocin-Gaze Positive Loop and the Coevolution of Human-Dog Bonds," *Science* 348, no. 6232 (April 17, 2015): 333–36, https://www.science.org/doi/10.1126/science.1261022.

261. Takumi Nagasawa, Mitsuaki Ohta, and Hidehiko Uchiyama, "Effects of the Characteristic Temperament of Cats on the Emotions and Hemodynamic Responses of Humans," *PLOS ONE* 15, no. 6 (June 25, 2020): e0235188, https://pubmed.ncbi.nlm.nih.gov/32584860/.

262. Kent C. Berridge and Morten L. Kringelbach, "Pleasure Systems in the Brain," *Neuron* 86, no. 3 (May 6, 2015): 646–64, https://www.cell.com/neuron/fulltext/S0896-6273(15)00133-6.

263. David P. Sniezek and Imran J. Siddiqui, "Acupuncture for Treating Anxiety and Depression in Women: A Clinical Systematic Review," *Medical Acupuncture* 25, no. 3 (June 2013): 164–72, https://pubmed.ncbi.nlm.nih.gov/24761171/.

264. Shiv Basant Kumar et al., "Telomerase Activity and Cellular Aging Might Be Positively Modified by a Yoga-Based Lifestyle Intervention," *Journal of Alternative and Complementary Medicine* 21, no. 6 (June 2015): 370–72, https://www.liebertpub.com/doi/10.1089/acm .2014.0298.

265. P. B. Rokade, "Release of Endomorphin Hormone and Its Effects on Our Body and Moods: A Review" (International Conference on Chemical, Biological and Environment Sciences, Bangkok, December 2011), https://www.semanticscholar.org/paper/Release-of-Endomorphin -Hormone-and-Its-Effects-on-A-Rokade/d9d6a77f113bb866ea1588edf646a60e25ca1755.

266. Sarah Moore, "Science of Spicy Foods," AZoLifeSciences, last updated December 14, 2021, https://www.azolifesciences.com/article/Science-of-Spicy-Foods.aspx.

267. Sandra Manninen et al., "Social Laughter Triggers Endogenous Opioid Release in Humans," *Journal of Neuroscience* 37, no. 25 (June 21, 2017): 6125–31, https://www.jneurosci .org/content/37/25/6125.

268. Ji-Sheng Han, "Acupuncture and Endorphins," *Neuroscience Letters* 361, nos. 1–3 (May 6, 2004): 258–61, https://pubmed.ncbi.nlm.nih.gov/15135942/.

269. Crissa L. Guglietti et al., "Meditation-Related Increases in GABAB Modulated Cortical Inhibition," *Brain Stimulation* 6, no. 3 (May 2013): 397–402, https://pubmed.ncbi.nlm.nih .gov/23022436/.

270. Chris C. Streeter et al., "Yoga Asana Sessions Increase Brain GABA Levels: A Pilot Study," *Journal of Alternative and Complementary Medicine* 13, no. 4 (May 2007): 419–26, https:// pubmed.ncbi.nlm.nih.gov/17532734/.

271. Andrew Steptoe, Jane Wardle, and Michael Marmot, "Positive Affect and Health-Related Neuroendocrine, Cardiovascular, and Inflammatory Processes," *Proceedings of the National Academy of Sciences of the United States of America* 102, no. 18 (May 3, 2005): 6508–12, https://www.ncbi.nlm.nih.gov/pmc/articles/PMC1088362/.

272. Lee Ann Kaskutas, "Alcoholics Anonymous Effectiveness: Faith Meets Science," *Journal of Addictive Diseases* 28, no. 2 (2009): 145–57, https://www.ncbi.nlm.nih.gov/pmc/articles /PMC2746426/.

273. The 12 steps are taken from *Alcoholics Anonymous: The Story of How Many Thousands of Men and Women Have Recovered from Alcoholism*, rev. ed. (New York City: Alcoholics Anonymous World Services: 2001).

274. Kirsten Weir, "Forgiveness Can Improve Mental and Physical Health: Research Shows How to Get There," *Monitor on Psychology* 48, no. 1 (January 2017): 30, https://www.apa.org /monitor/2017/01/ce-corner.aspx.

275. Teodoro Bottiglieri, "S-Adenosyl-L-Methionine (SAMe): From the Bench to the Bedside— Molecular Basis of a Pleiotrophic Molecule," *American Journal of Clinical Nutrition* 76, no. 5 (November 2002): 1151S–57S, https://academic.oup.com/ajcn/article/76/5/1151S /4824259. S-adenosyl-methionine, or SAMe, is important in producing neurotransmitters like serotonin, dopamine, and epinephrine.

276. Cecile A. Marczinski and Amy L. Stamates, "Artificial Sweeteners versus Regular Mixers Increase Breath Alcohol Concentrations in Male and Female Social Drinkers," *Alcoholism: Clinical and Experimental Research* 37, no. 4 (April 2013): 696–702, https://pubmed.ncbi .nlm.nih.gov/23216417/.

277. Rena R. Wing and Robert W. Jeffery, "Benefits of Recruiting Participants with Friends and Increasing Social Support for Weight Loss and Maintenance," *Journal of Consulting and Clinical Psychology* 67, no. 1 (132–38), https://content.apa.org/record/1999-00242-015.

278. Daniel Kahneman, *Thinking, Fast and Slow* (New York: Farrar, Straus and Giroux, 2011).

279. Bella M. DePaulo et al., "Lying in Everyday Life," *Journal of Personality and Social Psychology* 70, no. 5 (1996): 979–95, https://pubmed.ncbi.nlm.nih.gov/8656340/.

280. Andrea Gurmankin Levy et al., "Prevalence of and Factors Associated with Patient Nondisclosure of Medically Relevant Information to Clinicians," *JAMA Network Open* 1, no. 7 (November 2, 2018): e185293, https://pubmed.ncbi.nlm.nih.gov/30646397/.

281. Common Sense Media, "Landmark Report: U.S. Teens Use an Average of Nine Hours of Media per Day, Tweens Use Six Hours: New 'Media Use Census' from Common Sense Details Media Habits and Preferences of American 8- to 18-Year-Olds," Common Sense, November 3, 2015, https://www.commonsensemedia.org/press-releases/landmark-report -us-teens-use-an-average-of-nine-hours-of-media-per-day-tweens-use-six-hours.

282. Heike Bruch and Sumantra Ghoshal, "Beware the Busy Manager," *Harvard Business Review*, February 2002, https://hbr.org/2002/02/beware-the-busy-manager.

283. "Obesity and Overweight," National Center for Health Statistics, Centers for Disease Control and Prevention, last reviewed September 20, 2021, https://www.cdc.gov/nchs /fastats/obesity-overweight.htm.

284. National Center for Chronic Disease Prevention and Health Promotion, *The Power of Prevention: Chronic Disease . . . the Public Health Challenge of the 21st Century* (CDC, 2009), https://www.cdc.gov/chronicdisease/pdf/2009-Power-of-Prevention.pdf.

285. Roni Caryn Rabin, "Federal Agency Courted Alcohol Industry to Fund Study on Benefits of Moderate Drinking," *New York Times*, March 17, 2018, https://www.nytimes.com/2018/03 /17/health/nih-alcohol-study-liquor-industry.html.

286. A. Guttmann, "Advertising Spending in the Perfumes, Cosmetics, and Other Toilet Preparations Industry in the United States from 2018 to 2020 (in Million U.S. Dollars)," Statista, July 19, 2021, https://www.statista.com/statistics/470467/perfumes-cosmetics -and-other-toilet-preparations-industry-ad-spend-usa/.

287. "Pornography: Is it Addictive?" *Prairie View Blog*, December 20, 2019, https://prairieview .org/resources/blog/pornography-is-it-addictive.

288. Mark Regnerus, David Gordon, and Joseph Price, "Documenting Pornography Use in America: A Comparative Analysis of Methodological Approaches," *Journal of Sex Research* 53, no. 7 (2016): 873–81, https://www.tandfonline.com/doi/abs/10.1080/00224499.2015 .1096886.

289. Shawn Achor and Michelle Gielan, "Consuming Negative News Can Make You Less Effective at Work," *Harvard Business Review*, September 14, 2015, https://hbr.org/2015/09 /consuming-negative-news-can-make-you-less-effective-at-work.

290. Common Sense Media, "Landmark Report: U.S. Teens Use an Average of Nine Hours of Media per Day, Tweens Use Six Hours: New 'Media Use Census' from Common Sense Details Media Habits and Preferences of American 8- to 18-Year-Olds," Common Sense, November 3, 2015, https://www.commonsensemedia.org/press-releases/landmark-report -us-teens-use-an-average-of-nine-hours-of-media-per-day-tweens-use-six-hours.

291. Wilhelm Hofmann et al., "Desire and Desire Regulation," in *The Psychology of Desire*, ed. Wilhelm Hofmann and Loran F. Nordgren (New York: Guildford Press, 2015), 61–81.

292. Ethan Kross et al., "Facebook Use Predicts Declines in Subjective Well-Being in Young Adults," *PLOS ONE* 8, no. 8 (August 14, 2013): e69841, https://journals.plos.org/plosone /article?id=10.1371/journal.pone.0069841.

Ariel Shensa et al., "Social Media Use and Depression and Anxiety Symptoms: A Cluster Analysis," *American Journal of Health Behavior* 42, no. 2 (March 1, 2018): 116–28, https:// www.ncbi.nlm.nih.gov/pmc/articles/PMC5904786/.

293. Russell James Schachar, Laura Seohyun Park, and Maureen Dennis, "Mental Health Implications of Traumatic Brain Injury (TBI) in Children and Youth," *Journal of Canadian Academy of Child and Adolescent Psychiatry* 24, no. 2 (Fall 2015): 100–108, https://www .ncbi.nlm.nih.gov/pmc/articles/PMC4558980/.

Gregory J. McHugo et al., "The Prevalence of Traumatic Brain Injury among People with Co-occurring Mental Health and Substance Use Disorders," *Journal of Head Trauma*

Rehabilitation 32, no. 3 (May/June 2017): E65–74, https://pubmed.ncbi.nlm.nih.gov /27455436/.

294. Adrian D. Garcia, "Survey: Holidays Bring Spending Stress for Most Americans," Bankrate, November 13, 2019, https://www.bankrate.com/surveys/holiday-gifting-november-2019/.

295. Daniel G. Amen, *Healing ADD: The Breakthrough Program That Allows You to See and Heal the 7 Types of ADD*, rev. ed. (New York: Berkley Books, 2013).

296. Monica Shaw et al., "A Systematic Review and Analysis of Long-Term Outcomes in Attention Deficit Hyperactivity Disorder: Effects of Treatment and Non-treatment," *BMC Medicine* 10 (2012): 99, https://www.ncbi.nlm.nih.gov/pmc/articles/PMC3520745/.

Eve Kessler based on a presentation by Alan Wachtel, "Untreated ADHD: Lifelong Risks," Smart Kids with Learning Disabilities, accessed May 1, 2022, https://www.smartkidswithld .org/getting-help/adhd/untreated-adhd-lifelong-risks/.

Chanelle T. Gordon and Gregory A. Fabiano, "The Transition of Youth with ADD/ADHD into the Workforce: Review and Future Directions," *Clinical Child and Family Psychology Review* 22, no. 3 (September 2019): 316–47, https://pubmed.ncbi.nlm.nih.gov/30725305/.

Alaa M. Hamed, Aaron J. Kauer, and Hanna E. Stevens, "Why the Diagnosis of Attention Deficit Hyperactivity Disorder Matters," *Frontiers in Psychiatry* 6 (2015): 168, https://www .ncbi.nlm.nih.gov/pmc/articles/PMC4659921/.

Søren Dalsgaard et al., "Mortality in Children, Adolescents, and Adults with Attention Deficit Hyperactivity Disorder: A Nationwide Cohort Study," *Lancet* 385, no. 9983 (May 30, 2015): 2190–96, https://pubmed.ncbi.nlm.nih.gov/25726514/.

297. David Neeleman, interview by Lois Gilman, "How to Succeed in Business with ADD/ ADHD," *ADDitude*, updated February 18, 2021, https://www.additudemag.com/ADD/ADHD -entrepreneur-stories-jetblue-kinkos-jupitermedia/.

298. Daniel G. Amen, Chris Hanks, and Jill Prunella, "Predicting Positive and Negative Treatment Responses to Stimulants with Brain SPECT Imaging," *Journal of Psychoactive Drugs* 40, no. 2 (June 2008): 131–38, https://pubmed.ncbi.nlm.nih.gov/18720661/.

299. Amen Clinics, "Does Treating Mental Health Issues Make You Lose Your Sense of Humor?" Resources, blog, May 27, 2021, https://www.amenclinics.com/blog/does-treating-mental -health-issues-make-you-lose-your-sense-of-humor/. See Amen Clinics and Dr. Daniel Amen, "'Will I Still Be Funny if My Brain Is Fixed? With Comedian Jessimae Peluso," *Scan My Brain*, May 27, 2021, video, 15:08, https://www.youtube.com/watch?v=iYtqiJKmPLU&t=43s.

300. Amen Clinics, "How Learning Disorders Fuel Anxiety, Depression, and More," Resources, blog, September 16, 2021, https://www.amenclinics.com/blog/how-learning-disorders -fuel-anxiety-depression-and-more/.

301. Anuja S. Panicker and Anujothi Chelliah, "Resilience and Stress in Children and Adolescents with Specific Learning Disability," *Journal of the Canadian Academy of Child and Adolescent Psychiatry* 25, no. 1 (Winter 2016): 17–23, https://www.ncbi.nlm.nih.gov /pmc/articles/PMC4791102/.

302. Esme Fuller-Thomson Samara Z. Carroll, and Wook Yang, "Suicide Attempts among Individuals with Specific Learning Disorders: An Underrecognized Issue," *Journal of Learning Disabilities* 51, no. 3 (May/June 2018): 283–92, https://pubmed.ncbi.nlm.nih .gov/28635417/.

303. Amen Clinics, "Actress Reveals What Depression Feels Like," Resource, blog, October 5, 2021, https://www.amenclinics.com/blog/actress-reveals-what-depression-feels-like/.

304. Amen Clinics, "The Heartbreaking Psychological Impacts of Being Unpopular," Resources, blog, October 19, 2021, https://www.amenclinics.com/blog/the-heartbreaking-psychological -impacts-of-being-unpopular/. See Amen Clinics and Dr. Daniel Amen, "How Bullying Affects the Brain, with Nikki Leigh," *Scan My Brain*, October 19, 2021, video, 14:42, https:// www.youtube.com/watch?v=xqcJ6sIn23M.

305. Madhuleena Roy Chowdhury, "19 Best Positive Psychology Interventions + How to Apply

Them," blog, PositivePsychology.com, updated March 24, 2022, https://positivepsychology.com /positive-psychology-interventions/.

306. "Children Who Lose a Parent to Suicide More Likely to Die the Same Way," Johns Hopkins Medicine, April 21, 2010, https://www.hopkinsmedicine.org/news/media/releases/children _who_lose_a_parent_to_suicide_more_likely_to_die_the_same_way.

307. Michael Fralick et al., "Risk of Suicide after a Concussion," *Canadian Medical Association Journal* 188, no. 7 (April 19, 2016): 497–504, https://pubmed.ncbi.nlm.nih.gov/26858348/.

308. *Dr. Phil*, "From Football Star to Manic Episodes: Can My Son Be Helped?" aired April 1, 2022. See clip at Dr. Phil.com, https://www.drphil.com/shows/from-football-star-to -manic-episodes-can-my-son-be-helped/.

309. Amen Clinics, "How Can You Know Yourself if You Don't Know Your Brain?" Resources, blog, August 25, 2021, https://www.amenclinics.com/blog/how-can-you-know-yourself -if-you-dont-know-your-brain/. See Amen Clinics and Dr. Daniel Amen, "'What Exactly Did Football Do to My Brain?' Trent Shelton's Brain Scan Results," *Scan My Brain*, August 25, 2021, video, 14:53, https://www.youtube.com/watch?v=riSynxVulak&t=4s.

310. Jennifer N. Belding et al., "Social Buffering by God: Prayer and Measures of Stress," *Journal of Religion and Health* 49, no. 2 (June 2010): 179-87, https://pubmed.ncbi.nlm.nih .gov/19462239/.

311. Timothy D. Windsor, Kaarin J. Anstey, and Bryan Rodgers, "Volunteering and Psychological Well-Being among Young-Old Adults: How Much Is Too Much?" *Gerontologist* 48, no. 1 (February 2008): 59–70, https://pubmed.ncbi.nlm.nih.gov/18381833/.

A SAMPLE OF OTHER BOOKS BY DANIEL AMEN

You, Happier, Tyndale, 2022

Your Brain Is Always Listening, Tyndale, 2021

The End of Mental Illness, Tyndale, 2020

Conquer Worry and Anxiety, Tyndale, 2020

Feel Better Fast and Make It Last, Tyndale, 2018

Memory Rescue, Tyndale, 2017

Stones of Remembrance, Tyndale, 2017

Captain Snout and the Superpower Questions, Zonderkidz, 2017

The Brain Warrior's Way, with Tana Amen, New American Library, 2016

Time for Bed, Sleepyhead, Zonderkidz, 2016

Change Your Brain, Change Your Life (revised), Harmony Books, 2015, *New York Times* Bestseller

Healing ADD (revised), Berkley, 2013, *New York Times* Bestseller

The Daniel Plan, with Rick Warren, DMin, and Mark Hyman, MD, Zondervan, 2013, #1 *New York Times* Bestseller

Unleash the Power of the Female Brain, Harmony Books, 2013, *New York Times* Bestseller

Use Your Brain to Change Your Age, Crown Archetype, 2012, *New York Times* Bestseller

Unchain Your Brain, with David E. Smith, MD, MindWorks, 2010

Change Your Brain, Change Your Body, Harmony Books, 2010, *New York Times* Bestseller

Magnificent Mind at Any Age, Harmony Books, 2008, *New York Times* Bestseller

The Brain in Love, Three Rivers Press, 2007

Making a Good Brain Great, Harmony Books, 2005, Amazon Book of the Year

ADD in Intimate Relationships, MindWorks, 2005

New Skills for Frazzled Parents, MindWorks, 2000